Praise for *Writing ~~Interactive~~ Music for Video Games*

"Behind every great game experience is an interactive score that defines the emotional through-line of a game. *Writing Interactive Music for Video Games* will show you how to create such a score, from basic concepts to sophisticated techniques. It is filled with advice from some of the greatest video game composers working today, and written with the clarity and insight that comes from experience."

—Tracy Fullerton, Director, USC Game Innovation Lab

"Michael Sweet's book provides a much-needed text that walks a composer through all of the critical considerations when first starting to work in the video game industry. Not simply a 'how-to' but a 'why-to' that dives deep into the aesthetics and best practices of writing an interactive score. Through his years of work in the industry and years of teaching, he is able to bring together a comprehensive discussion on composing interactive scores. Professor Sweet brings together the nuts and bolts, the business, and pertinent historical moments—all while setting composers' expectations for working in the industry. There is no better book to be found if you are a composer looking to understand writing for games."

—Jeanine Cowen, Vice President for Curriculum and Program Innovation, Academic Affairs, Berklee College of Music

"Michael Sweet demonstrates a formidable depth and breadth of knowledge related to adaptive music. He adroitly covers both the creative and technical components critical to being successful in this field. This book is a must-read for newcomers and experienced composers wanting to learn more about the art of video game composition."

—Chuck Doud, Director of Music, Sony Computer Entertainment Worldwide Studios

"Clear, complete, concise, and filled with vital information. This is a must-read for any composer serious about scoring for games. If you want to know what makes game music unique, look no further; this book will take you to the next level!"

—Steve Horowitz, Composer

"The processes and techniques for composing for games has typically been a black art of strange terms and byzantine processes. *Writing Interactive Music for Video Games* uncovers the issues you have to deal with when composing music for games and presents them in an easy-to-understand way, from the creative and technical issues to making bids and dealing with contracts. An excellent resource for both the professional and aspiring composer, this book should be on the shelf of anyone interested in writing music for games."

—Brian Schmidt, Executive Director, GameSoundCon, and President, Game Audio Network Guild

"Michael Sweet has written a thorough and comprehensive guide for any composer or audio professional wishing to understand the technical and creative aspects of scoring video games. Students and professionals at all levels will find this book valuable and well worth reading."

—Garry Schyman, Composer, *Bioshock* series, *Middle-earth: Shadow of Mordor, Dante's Inferno,* and *Xcom: The Bureau Declassified*; and Adjunct Professor, USC's SMPTV Program

Writing Interactive
Music for Video Games

The Addison-Wesley
Game Design and Development Series

FROM CONCEPT TO PLAYABLE GAME WITH UNITY™ AND C#

Introduction to GAME DESIGN, PROTOTYPING, and DEVELOPMENT

Jeremy GIBSON

A PLATFORM-AGNOSTIC APPROACH

Game Programming ALGORITHMS and TECHNIQUES

Sanjay MADHAV

EXPLORING THE FOUNDATIONAL PRINCIPLES BEHIND GOOD GAME DESIGN

A GAME DESIGN VOCABULARY

Anna ANTHROPY
Naomi CLARK

A PRACTICAL GUIDE TO GRAPHICS PROGRAMMING

REAL-TIME
3D RENDERING
with
DIRECTX and HLSL

Paul VARCHOLIK

✦ Addison-Wesley

Visit **informit.com/series/gamedesign** for a complete list of available publications.

Essential References for Game Designers and Developers

These practical guides, written by distinguished professors and industry gurus, cover basic tenets of game design and development using a straightforward, common-sense approach. The books encourage readers to try things on their own and think for themselves, making it easier for anyone to learn how to design and develop digital games for both computers and mobile devices.

Make sure to connect with us!
informit.com/socialconnect

the trusted technology learning source

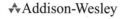
✦ Addison-Wesley

ALWAYS LEARNING

PEARSON

Writing Interactive
Music for Video Games

A Composer's Guide

Michael Sweet

♦♦Addison-Wesley

Upper Saddle River, NJ · Boston · Indianapolis · San Francisco
New York · Toronto · Montreal · London · Munich · Paris · Madrid
Capetown · Sydney · Tokyo · Singapore · Mexico City

Credits and permissions appear on page 477, which is a continuation of this copyright page.

Many of the designations used by manufacturers and sellers to distinguish their products are claimed as trademarks. Where those designations appear in this book, and the publisher was aware of a trademark claim, the designations have been printed with initial capital letters or in all capitals.

The author and publisher have taken care in the preparation of this book, but make no expressed or implied warranty of any kind and assume no responsibility for errors or omissions. No liability is assumed for incidental or consequential damages in connection with or arising out of the use of the information or programs contained herein.

For information about buying this title in bulk quantities, or for special sales opportunities (which may include electronic versions; custom cover designs; and content particular to your business, training goals, marketing focus, or branding interests), please contact our corporate sales department at corpsales@pearsoned.com or (800) 382-3419.

For government sales inquiries, please contact governmentsales@pearsoned.com.

For questions about sales outside the U.S., please contact international@pearsoned.com.

Visit us on the Web: informit.com/aw

Library of Congress Cataloging-in-Publication Data
Sweet, Michael, author.
 Writing interactive music for video games : a composer's guide / Michael Sweet.
    pages   cm
 Includes bibliographical references and index.
 ISBN 978-0-321-96158-7 (pbk. : alk. paper)
 1. Video game music—Instruction and study. I. Title.
 MT64.V53S84 2014
 781.5′4—dc2   2014025804

Copyright © 2015 Pearson Education, Inc.

All rights reserved. Printed in the United States of America. This publication is protected by copyright, and permission must be obtained from the publisher prior to any prohibited reproduction, storage in a retrieval system, or transmission in any form or by any means, electronic, mechanical, photocopying, recording, or likewise. To obtain permission to use material from this work, please submit a written request to Pearson Education, Inc., Permissions Department, One Lake Street, Upper Saddle River, New Jersey 07458, or you may fax your request to (201) 236-3290.

ISBN-13: 978-0-321-96158-7
ISBN-10: 0-321-96158-7
Text printed in the United States on recycled paper at RR Donnelley in Crawfordsville, Indiana.
First printing, September 2014

Editor-in-Chief
Mark L. Taub

Executive Editor
Laura Lewin

Development Editor
Michael Thurston

Managing Editor
John Fuller

Project Editor
Elizabeth Ryan

Packager
Anna Popick

Copy Editor
Jill Hobbs

Indexer
Jack Lewis

Proofreader
Anna Popick

Technical Reviewers
Chuck Doud
Paul Lipson
Brian Schmidt

Editorial Assistant
Olivia Basegio

Cover Designer
Chuti Prasertsith

Compositor
Shepherd, Inc.

I dedicate this book to all my former, current, and future students, who continue to surprise me every semester with their talent and ability to teach me equally about life, music, and supporting one another.

Contents

About This Book

When I first meet new students every semester, I tell them how difficult the music industry can be. Many of the friends with whom I went to music college many years ago are no longer in the music industry. To me, the most important aspect of being a teacher is to pass on all the knowledge that I have gained about the music industry to enable my students to be successful. I want to improve their odds of being in music decades after they graduate. This book is an extension of those ideas. I've tried to assemble much of the experience and knowledge that I have learned as a professional video game composer in hopes that I can help others become successful composers. I believe that our collective wisdom will help shape future generations of composers, allowing music to get even better.

Acknowledgments

I have many people to thank for helping me develop and write this book. Without my editor at Addison-Wesley, Laura Lewin, there would be no book at all. Her encouragement, support, and commitment helped me believe that I should write this book. At many points during the writing process, I suggested to her that it would be much easier for me to just write a piece of music. Luckily for you and me, she didn't accept this offer, and now you hold this book in your hands. Many additional people at Addison-Wesley contributed their talents to this book by helping to connect my ideas together, politely keeping me organized and on task, and correcting a crazy amount of grammatical errors. Special thanks to Olivia Basegio, Stephane Nakib, Elizabeth Ryan, Michael Thurston, and everyone else at Addison-Wesley, and to freelancers Anna Popick and Jill Hobbs.

My enormously talented and experienced technical editors, Brian Schmidt, Paul Lipson, and Chuck Doud, were the first to read the book. They offered sage wisdom and advice to make this book much better than I ever imagined.

I'd also like to thank all the incredible composers who contributed sidebars to this book, including Yoshino Aoki, Vincent Diamante, Ben Houge, Noriyuki Iwadare, Akari Kaida, Laura Karpman, Yuzo Koshiro, Bear McCreary, George "The Fat Man" Sanger, Tetsuya Shibata, Yoko Shimomura, Rich Vreeland, Duncan Watt, and Guy Whitmore. Special thanks to Shota Nakama, founder of the Video Game Orchestra, and Maho Azuma for coordinating and translating the contributions from Japanese composers.

Additional thanks go out to Peter Bufano and his expert knowledge in the craft of scoring music for circuses. Thanks also to my friends Eric Zimmerman and Tracy Fullerton for continuing to believe in, support, and evangelize my music over the last 20 years.

Berklee College of Music gave me the opportunity to come to Boston in 2008 to create its video game scoring curriculum. This adventure helped me build on my professional experience by allowing me to spend time analyzing many video game scores, giving me the opportunity to talk with myriad talented composers, and enabling me to develop curriculum and resources for students. Thanks to the many talented and supportive individuals at Berklee, including Jeanine Cowen, Dan Carlin, Alison Plante, George Clinton, and Kari Juusela, for helping to guide and support the game scoring programs.

Last, I'd like to thank my family, Robin and Lucas, for believing in me and loving me every day. You inspire me to become a better person and help me laugh at myself. Thanks to my mom and dad for continuing to support everything that I've ever done, without an ounce of criticism, only with love.

About the Author

Michael Sweet leads the development of the video game scoring curriculum at Berklee College of Music. For the past two decades, Michael has been an accomplished video game audio composer and has been the audio director for more than 100 award-winning video games. His work can be heard on the Xbox 360 logo and on award-winning games from Cartoon Network, Sesame Workshop, PlayFirst, iWin, Gamelab, Shockwave, RealArcade, Pogo, Microsoft, Lego, AOL, and MTV, among others. He has won the Best Audio Award at the Independent Games Festival and the BDA Promax Gold Award for Best Sound Design, and he has been nominated for four Game Audio Network Guild (GANG) awards.

INTRODUCTION

Have you ever wondered what goes into creating
a music score for a video game? Scoring music for
games is very different than composing music for
other linear media like film and television. This book
aims to teach you how composers work with game
development teams to create interactive music
scores in an effort to make better games.

Welcome

Many of today's video games use numerous interactive music techniques to adapt to how the player drives the action in real time. Video game music changes dynamically based on decisions that a player makes. The composer must score multiple outcomes and be able to transform the music from one emotional state to another seamlessly.

This book will teach you the fundamental music approaches and skills that professional composers use to create these interactive scores for games. This book focuses on these game scoring techniques from conceptualization, to creation, to implementation, through to the game's release. Using numerous examples, we'll examine each technique in depth, and then compare and contrast the various techniques.

This book illustrates these techniques as used in video game scores and assesses their effectiveness. Readers will also gain insight into fundamental concepts by evaluating historical perspectives on interactive composition. This book serves as a gateway for discovering innovative interactive music throughout the twentieth century, exploring numerous scores with applications for modern video games. These scores can be a jumping-off point for inspiring and developing your own compositional strategies.

In addition, readers will learn about the business aspects associated with being a music composer for games. This coverage includes marketing and sales advice, explanation of typical contract language, ways to price music services, the challenges of pursuing this career, and strategies to break into the industry.

When I first began composing music for video games more than 20 years ago, it was difficult to imagine a time when students entering college would want to learn the craft of composing video game scores because it was such a small field. Now, some of the world's leading contemporary music institutions are teaching video game scoring to their students.

How did we get here? In this introduction, we take a quick look at the game industry and see how it relates to music scoring for games.

Games and Popular Culture

Video games have been evolving for many decades. As we approach the fiftieth anniversary of the first video game with sound (*Pong*, 1972), contemporary video game scores are now being played by many of today's elite orchestras. Live showcases of orchestral video game music like *Video Games Live* and *Final Fantasy: Distant Worlds* sell out concert venues around the world to young audiences who have grown up playing video games.

Fundamentally, video games are another medium through which we express ideas and tell stories to one another. As with the best storytelling, we are able to share similar experiences in the same way that film, television, and the arts have brought us new perspectives by allowing us to relate to one another.

From colossal AAA (pronounced "triple-A") games played on consoles like the Xbox, Play-Station, and Wii, to casual games played on handhelds and social networks, the diversity of audiences that play games is enormous. Video games no longer exist only on the fringe of society, but rather have become an integral part of mainstream and popular culture. In 2014, according to the Entertainment Software Association (ESA), there were some remarkable statistics on the diversity of gaming:

- Approximately 58 percent of Americans play video games.
- The average game player is 30 years old and has been playing games for more than 13 years.
- Approximately 25 percent of people older than the age of 50 play video games.
- Nearly 45 percent of all game players are female.

For people involved in game development, this diversity allows teams to create games in many different genres that appeal to a wide range of audiences. Composers and music teams have the opportunity to specialize in myriad musical styles, ranging from kids' music (*Lego Universe*, 2010; *Minecraft*, 2009), to jazz (*Grim Fandango*, 1998; *L.A. Noire*, 2011) and orchestral scores (*Bioshock*, 2007; *Dead Space*, 2008), to world music (*Prince of Persia*, 2008; *Uncharted: Drake's Fortune*, 2007) and historically inspired music (*Assassin's Creed III*, 2012).

At the time this book was written, games were producing global revenues of approximately $60 billion each year. The size of these revenue streams, along with the explosion of popularity of video games in modern society, creates many opportunities for composers and musicians to create music for games. A typical game budget for a console game might run from a few million dollars to $50 million or more. Budgets for music and sound typically represent 5 to 10 percent of the overall production budget for the game. As a consequence, a sizable amount of money may be spent to create music for games.

Contemporary video games have an enormous reach in culture and society. They can provoke broader discussions about life and culture, including relationships (*Papa Y Yo*, 2013; *Braid*, 2009), life (*The Sims*, 2008; *Passage*, 2007), discovery (*Mass Effect*, 2007; *Journey*, 2012), and music (*Chime*, 2010; *Rez*, 2001).

Over the past several years, games have also evolved into an art form. Shows featuring video games have popped up at some of the nation's leading art museums, including "The Art of Video Games" at the Smithsonian (*Myst*, 1993; *Flower*, 2009) and "Applied Design" at the Museum of Modern Art (*Katamari Damacy*, 2004; *Portal*, 2007).

Many of today's games also turn players into content creators by giving them the tools needed to create their own game content (examples include *The Sims*, 2000, and *Little Big Planet*, 2008). Players are able to express their own creativity, stories, and ideas through games. In the same way that narrative forms like film and television are being remixed and recombined on YouTube, so games are becoming a means of expression—a trend that has wide cultural implications. Musicians and composers can also take advantage of our mash-up and mod-ing culture by placing their own music into games to tell their own stories.

Scoring for Games

Writing music for games relies on many techniques inherited from dramatic film scoring, including harmonic development, cadences, non-song-form–based music development, and themes. But, as you'll learn in this book, video game music differs significantly from the music found in linear media such as film and television.

Many contemporary video games use numerous interactive music techniques to adapt to the player in real time. Video game music changes dynamically based on the decisions that a player makes. For example, the game player might have the choice to sneak around an enemy using camouflage or enter into a fight with guns blazing. The music that accompanies this scene should adapt to the choices made by the player. In turn, the composer must score these multiple paths with several music cues that are able to transform from one cue to another in a seamless fashion.

Music teams working on a game can range in size from a single individual who composes all the music to a huge team of people that may include a composer, an audio director, editors, an orchestrator, programmers, and implementers. Whether you're working on a small iPhone or Facebook game, or a large AAA PlayStation title, this book teaches you about the different kinds of interactive scoring methods that will be available to you. We'll explore the creative, methodology, technology, and business issues associated with the creation of the score for all these types of games.

Although many games use the techniques outlined in this book, choosing to use interactive music in a game is a complicated decision that takes into account many different factors, including the overall music budget, programming resources, and investment of the time it takes to create and implement an interactive score. Also, there may sometimes be a lack of understanding of how interactive scores work within games.

This book informs readers about their choices regarding the creation and implementation of music interactivity in their games. It shows how interactive music can enhance storytelling in games as well as improve the overall game experience.

You'll learn the fundamental music approaches and skills that professional composers and game development teams use to create interactive music for games from the initial stage of conceptualization and creative direction of the music, through to the composition and creation process, until the final implementation of the music into the game. Important concepts you'll learn about in this text include the following:

- Music conceptualization and creative direction
- Music critique and analysis

- Interactive music
- The composition process
- Music production
- Audio implementation
- The business of creating music for games

Intended Audience

This book is intended for a variety of audiences, from novices to experienced professionals, who are interested in how they can improve the music in their games. Whether you're a game designer looking to understand how music works in your game or a composer looking to understand interactive techniques for video games, this book will help you discover the innovative processes involved in the creation and integration of music into games.

All readers will gain insight into what makes a great music score through examples. This book also teaches you how to listen to current games so as to better understand how the music is implemented; such greater appreciation will allow you to broaden your game music knowledge and listen more critically. This will, in turn, help add depth and innovation to the design and implementation of your own scores.

Readers will walk through every step that goes into the creation of a score, from the score conceptualization phase all the way through implementation and release of the video game.

One of the goals in writing this text was to help the individual teams working on a game collaborate to create the best score and music implementation for their game. Once an entire team understands how interactive music works, it becomes easier to use music to its full potential.

Game Development Teams

From a design perspective, game development teams will acquire a broader understanding of how music can shape and enhance the overall mood and feel of their game. In turn, they'll learn about how music systems work within games to augment the player's experience. They'll also take away ideas about how game mechanics can be used to control the music score within their game.

In game production, producers need to know what the music costs and which best practices can ensure efficient music design in a game. This book discusses the assets and costs associated with the production and implementation of various interactive music techniques. The coverage provided here gives producers a better understanding of music production processes for a game.

Programmers will discover the best ways to collaborate with composers by learning how to implement interactive music and how such techniques affect the audio physics of the game world. This book covers a variety of implementation options, ranging from basic techniques all the way through advanced implementation including middleware solutions.

Audio Teams

Musicians and composers will learn about fundamental and advanced interactive music techniques that will enable them to create their own interactive scores for games. In addition, they'll gain an understanding of the business acumen that is required to break into the world of game audio. Professional composers who are already working in video games or looking to enter into the video game industry will find this book a valuable resource, as it shows techniques and examples of methods that are currently being used in video game scores.

Sound designers and audio directors will also be interested in this text, as it will teach them about music techniques and explain how those techniques relate directly to their own fields. By better understanding how music engines work, they'll gain a broader perspective on the entire sonic landscape that makes up the game. In addition, some of the interactive music techniques can be applied directly to sound design.

Game Players

Fans of game music will gain a greater insight into the creation process that many composers use to score video games. Once you've read through the techniques described here, you'll be able to hear music in games differently—that is, you'll be able to identify different musical structures and listen to the "music mechanics" of games. In addition, you'll be able to hear links between your actions in the game and appreciate how these decisions are reflected in the music of the game.

Structure of the Book

This book is structured in such a way as to allow readers of different backgrounds to quickly grasp the basic concepts of designing music in games, then continue on to explore fundamental and advanced scoring techniques. As you read through this book, you'll find that each chapter builds on the concepts discussed in the previous chapter.

Each chapter begins with an overview of the chapter. It then expands on the topics covered by explaining techniques through specific examples used in video game scores and offering tips to assess their effectiveness.

Throughout the book, you'll find suggested exercises that put the techniques described in the book into practice. After each chapter discussing a specific game scoring technique, there is an

"Exercises" section in which game audio scenarios challenge readers to write or edit their own music to see how it works.

At the end of each chapter, concepts and techniques are reinforced with a review, followed by sample exercises.

This book is augmented with a series of software tools specifically created to accompany this text. The fundamental interactive techniques described in this book are reinforced by this software, which seeks to help composers simulate how their music might work in a game. These indispensable tools help readers learn each technique in turn, so they can better understand the pros and cons of each compositional method.

The companion course website (see page 426) also includes suggested lesson plans to help use this book as a teaching tool in higher learning institutions.

The chapters in this book are organized into five parts. What follows is a detailed overview of each section of the book and its learning outcomes.

Part I: Scoring for Games

In the first part of this book, you'll explore the language of storytelling through music in games, and break down the basic ways to approach game scoring. We begin with an overview of how music for games is conceptualized, including interactive music methodology and creative decisions regarding how a score is created for a game. This material doesn't require you to have a music composition degree, but rather is a top-down overview of the terminology and the thinking that goes into building a score.

Topics include how to analyze a game for musical opportunities, develop thematic ideas, apply basic integration and synchronization of music to game events, think about control inputs and triggers, and perform game score analysis. In addition, Part I explores how game genres affect music choices.

Last, you'll learn about historical perspectives on interactive music in video game composition and about composers in the age of post-modernism. You'll explore the history of interactive music and the different techniques that helped composers implement their scores.

Part II: Fundamental Video Game Scoring Techniques

As the book progresses, you'll dig deeper into how these scores are actually written and learn interactive scoring best practices and various implementation techniques. Composers and students will receive practical advice on composing multiple types of interactive scores for video games, including coverage of video game music analysis, historical perspectives, methodologies, and future trends in music for video games.

In Part II, we break down the fundamental interactive scoring techniques found in games. We show you how to write effectively in each of the different interactive music models and how to manage game considerations that influence which model to use. Among the techniques we'll focus on are horizontal resequencing, vertical remixing, transitions and stingers, and use of music as a gameplay element.

Every fundamental technique is explained and reinforced with case studies from real games. Readers will be able to enhance their composition skills with an understanding of how to create interactive-based music and best practices for each technique.

Part III: Advanced Video Game Scoring Techniques

Part III delves into advanced video game scoring methods, including the use of virtual instruments within games, real-time tempo and harmonic variation, aleatoric methods, and algorithmic techniques. This section is primarily intended for advanced composers and implementers looking to augment basic music techniques in their games.

In addition, Part III looks at the current generation of audio middleware tools that composers often use to implement advanced scores and that offer fewer of the programming challenges associated with building your own music engine. Figure 0.1 shows an example of the audio middleware tool Fmod with some interactive music that was written for a game level.

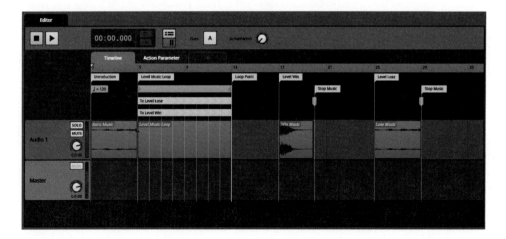

Figure 0.1   Fmod is an example of audio middleware software implemented to play interactive music.

Part IV: Bringing Music into the Game

Continuing into Part IV, we focus on the actual technology associated with both the writing and the implementation of music in the game. We explore the digital audio workstation (DAW), notation and recording for games, file formats, creation of virtual instruments for games, collaborative tools, and audio middleware for games.

This section is meant to complement Parts II and III by going beyond the conceptual language and getting into the practical side of creating an interactive score using your DAW. It also explains the entire process, from setting up for recording live musicians to implementing the music within the game.

Part V: The Business of Scoring Music for Video Games

In Part V, readers will find chapters detailing the business of being a composer for video games. Topics covered include pricing, contracts, negotiation, sales and marketing, the challenges of working as a composer, and strategies to break into the industry. You'll learn about the noncreative skills that are required to be a successful composer and see how to develop those skills.

The business chapters of the book do not rely on the same foundational material in earlier parts of the book. Consequently, they can be read at any time.

Part VI: Conclusion and Appendixes

In the conclusion, you'll find closing thoughts as well as an analysis of future trends in video game music. The appendixes contain useful information including a glossary and additional reference material, along with recommended organizations and groups.

Digital Tools

Included with this book is a set of software tools that demonstrate fundamental interactive scoring techniques. These tools can be found at the book's companion website (see page 426). With these tools you'll be able to take music that you create in a DAW and simulate how it might operate in a game. Throughout the book, we'll point out how to use these tools to better reinforce the concepts you're reading about.

These digital tools will help you compose and test your own interactive compositions. In addition, they allow composers and producers to play interactive music for game developers before that music has even been implemented in the game, thereby demonstrating how the music might work in tandem with the game's action.

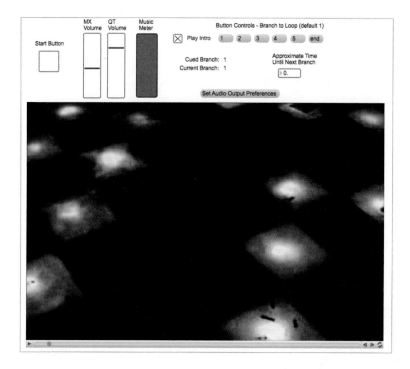

Figure 0.2   The Branching Engine Music Tool, which is one of the tools included with this book to help compose interactive music.

When a composer is writing interactive music, it's very difficult for the composer to show a game design team what the music will sound like in the final game because it may take weeks for the programmers to implement the score. The included software tools allow game designers to hear the interactive music a composer has written before it is programmed into the game (Figure 0.2); they can use this information to make creative decisions about the music faster and get a more complete picture of what the final product will sound like. Many hours have been spent putting these tools together so that composers can concentrate on creating great music instead of getting hopelessly bogged down in figuring out a way to play their music for the game designers.

Companion Website

This book's companion website contains a variety of useful information, including web links to many gameplay examples from the text as well as updates and errata for the book. Throughout the text we'll show interactive techniques in action through examples used in actual games. The companion website provides links to gameplay videos showing these examples. Also available on the course website are example projects using the fundamental interactive music techniques found in audio middleware engines such as Fmod and Wwise. See page 426 for information about accessing the site.

Conventions Used in This Book

Several different elements are used to enhance your learning in this book. This section provides examples of what they indicate.

> **note**
>
> A note provides additional clarification or information about a concept.

> **warning**
>
> **WARNINGS LOOK LIKE THIS**   A warning gives you a heads-up about ways to avoid problems.

> **tip**
>
> A tip gives you specific hints or advice about putting techniques into practice.

SCORING FOR GAMES

CHAPTER 1

THE LANGUAGE OF MUSIC STORYTELLING IN GAMES

In this chapter you'll learn about the language of music storytelling in games and basic approaches to game scoring. Beginning with an overview of how game music is conceptualized, you'll understand the methodology to make the best creative music choices for your game. This material doesn't require you to have a music composition degree, but rather is a top-down overview of the fundamental processes and terminology that drives the creation of a game score. You'll learn about game music types, music functions within a game, and the building blocks for critical analysis of interactive scores.

What Makes a Video Game Unique?

To build a language to use when describing video game music, it's important to understand some of the unique characteristics of the medium of video games. This chapter begins by breaking down the anatomy of a video game, comparing and contrasting elements to linear media. These differences affect how the music is conceptualized, composed, and synchronized to work within a game.

There are several key differences between scoring for linear media like film and scoring for video games. If we look at a direct comparison between films and games, as you'll see in Table 1.1, you'll begin to discover and identify some of these key differences.

Passive versus Active Interaction

Video games require the player to be actively involved so as to make decisions based on the action that is occurring on screen. This active interaction is the most important element that distinguishes the medium. Players are actively involved in determining the outcome of a game, whereas in linear media like film there is no interaction; instead, viewers watch passively.

This interaction between player and story in video games creates a reactive feedback loop, with each one affecting the other. The level of interaction is determined by the rules and mechanics of the game and is usually controlled by the player through a game controller or a keyboard/mouse combination.

This active interaction between the game and the player also affects how the music must change and react to player decisions. The music must be written in such a way that it is adaptable based on the player interaction. Throughout this book you'll learn about different ways to compose adaptive and interactive music compositions for video games.

Table 1.1   Key Differences between Films and Games

Attribute	Film	Console Game
Type of experience	Passive watching	Active interaction
Average length	2 hours	10+ hours
Number of plays	Usually once	Many times
Structure	Linear: one beginning, one middle, one end	Nonlinear: multiple outcomes and evolving storylines
Average amount of music	1 hour	2–3 hours

Table 1.2 Length of Music in Games

Game Type	Play Experience	Average Amount of Music
Casual game	2–3 hours	15+ minutes
Console game	10+ hours	2–3 hours
MMORPG	50+ hours	15+ hours

Variable Length of Experience

Length of the gameplay experience is one of the most important aspects in determining the amount of music that must be conceived and written for a game. Video games vary greatly in the length of experience compared to film. Furthermore, each game genre has a length that is most suitable for the style of play, whether it's puzzle solving in a game like *Myst* (1993) or defeating an alien invasion in a game like *Halo* (2001).

Casual games (*Tetris*, 1984; *Bejeweled*, 2001; *Diner Dash,* 2004) that are played from beginning to end might be only 2 to 3 hours in length, whereas a massively multiplayer online roleplaying game (MMORPG) like *World of Warcraft* (2004) might have a play experience totaling more than 50 hours. Typically AAA (pronounced "triple-A") console titles for Xbox or PlayStation have a play experience that lasts 10 or more hours.

Table 1.2 summarizes the differences in the length of play between different game types.

The time it takes to play a game depends on many different factors, including length of the story, game variability, and the experience of the player. These additional factors are discussed throughout the chapter. In some very large games, players sometimes play for as much as 20 to 30 hours per week!

Many games today also have expansion packs that allow the game to grow by extending the player experience with new storylines and additional content. These expansion packs may also increase the amount of music in a game. Popular games that include expansion packs include *Angry Birds* (2009) and *Bioshock: Infinite* (2013).

note

Game players from around the world play MMORPGs together on computer servers where they interact with one another in real time, helping each other with quests and battles. These games are massive in scope and take hundreds of hours to complete. Consider the scale of a game like *World of Warcraft* (2004):

- The average *World of Warcraft* player plays approximately 20 hours per week.

- There is more than 23 hours of composed music within *World of Warcraft*.

- At the game's peak success, there were approximately 14 million subscribers, each paying a monthly fee of $15 to play the game.

- The game development team that works exclusively on *World of Warcraft* consists of several hundred members, along with a team of audio professionals working on the music and sound.

Number of Plays

The play experience in games is significantly longer than the experience with most linear media. Consequently, players often don't finish games in one session. Instead, it typically takes many sessions for a game player to finish a game.

This has direct implications for the music. How do we approach the interruptions caused by players stopping and starting in our music? Is there a way to bring the player back into the story more seamlessly, reminding the player where he or she left off?

A composer can use several different approaches to enhance the storytelling in the game between interruptions. For example, composers often use thematic material to tie the story together by representing characters or places in their music. The "Music Conceptualization" section of this chapter discusses this in more detail.

warning

THE REPETITION PROBLEM   George "The Fat Man" Sanger—a pioneer video game composer primarily known for his work on *Wing Commander*—is generally credited with the quote "Repetition is the problem" with regard to video game music.

You may have noticed in Table 1.2 that the play experience is typically far longer than the music can support. Video games in the past have been known for their repetition, and it's a problem to look out for when developing music for video games.

Composers are challenged by many constraints when working on video games, including memory, voices, and games growing in scope and size. Sometimes the music must be repeated within games because of one factor or another.

Composers must take this issue into account when creating their scores. To minimize music repetition in games, composers frequently look to interactive composition techniques. Modern composers have many more options for getting more mileage out of the score by using various interactive techniques that you'll learn about in this book.

Game Mechanics

In addition to a storyline, video games have specific game mechanics that make them different from film. These mechanics or rules define the play experience and dictate how the player interacts with the game system. For instance, in the early arcade game *Space Invaders* (1978), the basic gameplay mechanic is to shoot the impending alien march while avoiding getting hit by the enemy's lasers or having the aliens reach your home world. Put even more simply, the mechanic is about winning or losing a specific game level. The player's skill level determines whether the game continues or ends. Other examples of game mechanics include solving puzzles, taking turns, racing against a clock, beat-matching, and many more.

Game mechanics are a system of rewards and challenges that a player faces when entering the game. Game music systems need to be aware of game mechanics and, in turn, enhance the play experience by supporting these mechanics.

Pacing, Synchronization, and Flow

Video game players typically drive the storyline at their own pace. Players can move quickly or more slowly through a level, depending on their skill level. Since a composer cannot write a customized score for every individual player, he or she may instead write an adaptive score that takes the player's skill level and pacing into account. This way the composer supports the same emotional pacing for each player. For example, in an open-world game like *World of Warcraft* (2004), the player at any given moment may decide to go to places within the world like Elwynn Forest or Ironforge. These decisions affect which music will play and determine the transitions that happen to get us from one piece of music to the next.

Unlike in linear media, where a composer can synchronize the music to a specific frame number, the game storyline is driven by the player. Synchronization in music is achieved by following changes in emotional context. These changes then direct how the music might play, in the same way that a conductor cues the woodwinds in a symphony.

The interactive music system in a game can take into account many different factors besides location, including the player's health, proximity to enemies, various artificial intelligence (AI) state(s), the length of time the music has been playing, and so on. These variables can help change and adapt the music so it is synchronized to the events that unfold for the player.

Multiple Story Paths and Repeatability

When you watch a film, the experience is static—it doesn't change from viewing to viewing. In games, however, the narrative and dramatic arcs are based on real-time choices made by the player. This may mean that there are multiple story outcomes.

Because of this possibility, the music must follow the player's decisions throughout the game to support the emotional context for the scene or level at any given time. The music must change dynamically based on these decisions and conditions, which requires composers, music editors, and game designers to think differently when approaching the composition of the score. For instance, in the game *Mass Effect* (2007), the player makes decisions about which characters to support throughout the story. Characters that aren't supported may actually die during the game. Since these characters have musical themes attached to them, we need to be aware of how these themes are shaped and evolve over time based on the player's decisions.

When games have multiple outcomes, they can be played through multiple times. This increases the chance that a player might hear music multiple times. Many composers use the interactive music techniques outlined in this book to minimize the repetition. For example, one technique is to play back a music cue in a different order. A composer might also write multiple introductions to the same piece of music so the player will hear it begin differently each time it plays. More of these techniques will be reviewed in later chapters of this book.

Technology

Composing for video games is ostensibly reliant on the underlying technology used to play back music within the game. Hence interactive music systems are tied to advances in this technology. Composers who are interested in creating music for games need to be fearless when it comes to learning about new technology because they are often asked to learn a new music format while they are writing in it.

Mobile and web games typically have greater memory and voice constraints than console games, making composing for these platforms very challenging. Conversely, a game like *Batman: Arkham City* (2011) uses the audio middleware engine Wwise by AudioKinetic. Wwise is a very advanced interactive audio and music engine. Even so, when composing for this system, the audio team needs to understand its strengths and limitations to use the system effectively.

Recent technology advances such as cloud storage and remote rendering for games are rapidly changing how games are delivered to consumers. In the future, therefore, game developers may have fewer limitations in terms of technology.

Although it can be a huge benefit to composers to understand the technology and score design that will ultimately be integrating their music into the game, it isn't essential knowledge. On large games, an entire team of people may work on creating the music for a game. In these circumstances, getting the right creative fit may be more important than having a composer who knows about the technical and adaptive techniques that will be implemented in the final game. The team would include interactive music specialists who take the raw materials from the composer to create the adaptive music components. In this scenario, composers may never have to deal with formats other than handing off their Pro Tools sessions (or similar digital audio workstation [DAW] files).

> ## note
>
> There are many unique challenges to composing music for games:
>
> - Repetition is caused by play repeatability, size of game, and budgetary constraints.
>
> - There are often technology constraints like limited memory, limited voices, and new formats depending on the platform.
>
> - Games require music to be programmed and implemented based on a rule set.
>
> - Games are interactive and require variable synchronization.

Types of Music within Games

Composers can use music in many different ways within games to achieve the desired emotional effect. In this section we begin by defining the categories of music used within video games. In the next section you'll learn about the function of music in games.

Sometimes as composers we're adding music to support the game on an emotional level (extra-diegetic). At other times we're adding to what the avatar of the player might be hearing as part of the game universe. It's useful to define these different types of music in terms of function.

Extra-Diegetic Music (Underscore)

Extra-diegetic music, or non-diegetic music, refers to music that is added to a scene purely to enhance the emotions that the player should be feeling. This is commonly known as underscore. The musical ensemble or device that plays this music is not established to the player in the game. Its existence is not even inferred in the game world. Underscore works on a sub-conscious level to bring story elements together in its use of themes and motifs, as well as to intensify the emotional context of a scene. It also may inform the player or viewer of something that might be off-screen. Extra-diegetic music also helps with setting the stage by implying a specific time in history or a place within the world. With extra-diegetic music, the viewer does not expect to see the instruments on the screen playing the music.

It is commonly said that the best film scores are not noticed by the audience or viewer. More obvious (and clumsier) scores take the viewer out of the experience of watching a movie by bringing what should be an unconscious element to the forefront for the listener.

A classic film example is John Williams's two-note motif from *Jaws* (1975). Whenever there is impending danger of the shark, the audience hears this motif. Later in the film, even though the shark is not on screen, this motif builds tension for the viewers because they expect to see the shark soon. Williams is a master film composer, as he actually uses this motif to teach the audience that this music equals an impending shark attack. Later in the film he breaks this mechanic by not playing the two-note motif before the shark's entrance; when the shark appears, it's one of the most terrifying moments in the film. Williams uses music to trick the audience into believing something based solely on his use of music, increasing the horror of the film.

In almost any modern video game, we hear extra-diegetic music enhancing the emotional underpinning of the story. In the game *Red Dead Redemption* (2010), for example, we hear an Ennio Morricone–inspired score as we follow the adventures of a former outlaw in the American frontier. The interactive score changes dynamically as the player goes from scene to scene, and from plot point to plot point. In the game *Bioshock* (2007), Garry Schyman composes music for an underwater city engulfed in chaos using aleatoric music techniques, along with solo violin passages creating a terrifying but beautiful collage of themes.

COMPOSER PERSPECTIVE: REPETITION KILLS SUSPENSE

Bear McCreary

The more often the audience is exposed to a sonic idea, the less impact it has. For film and television, you can bend (or even take advantage of) this rule, because you know exactly how often the audience will hear a musical idea. In video games, however, repetition is often at the mercy of the gamer's decisions. Composers must be extra careful to maximize the impact of their music.

The primary function of music in video games is to create tension. The resolution of that tension amplifies the gamer's euphoria when finishing a goal, feeding his or her desire to keep playing. Historically speaking, this tension has been created using music that repeats.

Why does repetition kill suspense? Have you ever heard an annoying car alarm blaring for so long that you notice it again only when it finally shuts off? Have you ever been in a loud, crowded restaurant, but noticed that after a few minutes you are chatting with your friends without interference?

Our brains have evolved to filter out information that has no meaning. Our early ancestors developed the ability to register changes in their surroundings to survive. A creature constantly focused on the sound of a babbling brook may not notice the new sound of rustling reeds that hail the arrival of a deadly lion preparing to pounce. Without our ability to subconsciously filter out repetitive sounds, our entire perception of the world would be a chaotic cacophony.

Let's apply this logic to video games in a hypothetical scenario. You've composed a scary cue to underscore the player engaging a new enemy. During the first encounter, the gamer is tense and on edge, because his or her subconscious mind momentarily struggles to categorize this new, dissonant sound. If the music and the situation are both the same the second time around, the impact is diminished. Before long, the subconscious makes a connection between that music and that event and filters out the music, because the information no longer carries meaning. Music you wrote to be as ominous as a lion in the reeds is now no more effective than a babbling brook!

It may never be practical or even desirable for a video game score to provide completely new music for every single moment in the game. Composers should remember this rule and work with developers to push the boundaries of technology to allow for music that feels less repetitive. We are very near the moment when a video game score will finally rival the narrative satisfaction of a score for scripted narrative in film and television.

Long live suspense!

Diegetic Music (Source Music)

Diegetic music is music that a character would hear if he or she were actually in the game world itself. In films, we usually refer to this as "source music." If we see someone on screen playing a violin, we expect to hear the violin. The function of diegetic music function is to enhance the player's experience. Typically it's used to increase the realism of the simulated world.

In *Bioshock Infinite* (2013), there are moments when we see various musical ensembles, including a barbershop quartet. When we see the barbershop quartet on screen and hear them singing, it's an example of diegetic music.

Another example is from *Mass Effect 2* (2010). When the player is standing outside of a nightclub, he hears the music from inside. This is music that the player would be hearing as part of the world itself.

Games like *Grand Theft Auto V* (2013) and *L.A. Noire* (2011) are 3D simulations of another world. Both games revolve around a driving mechanic where players drive different vehicles through this simulated world. These vehicles have radios, and players can change the radio station, so the music changes as they're driving through this world. This is another example of diegetic music.

One last example of diegetic music within games occurs at the beginning of *Assassin's Creed III* (2012), when the player is sneaking around a theater while an opera is being performed. We see the actors and musicians, and the music is coming from the universe itself.

In all of the previous examples, the music placement in the speakers is also very important to simulate where the music is coming from. We use real-time panning, equalization, and reverb techniques to simulate the position within the 3D space. As the player moves around this 3D space, the instruments or devices must pan dynamically to simulate the fact that this is a real place.

In many instances, diegetic music is *licensed music*. Licensed music has been created previously by an artist, and the game publisher must obtain the rights to use this music within a video game. On large games, a music supervisor may coordinate the licensing process by obtaining (and paying for) the relevant rights to the piece of music.

While playing a game, if we see a jukebox or some other music-making device or musician on screen, then we'll want to hear the music that it creates. The realism of that world or simulation would be broken if we didn't hear the sound. As composers, it's critical to be wary of destroying the illusion of a world for the player.

Occasionally the distinction between diegetic music and extra-diegetic music becomes blurred. For example, we might start off listening to diegetic music, but then as the story progresses the same theme can be heard holding emotional elements of the storyline together.

Music as Gameplay

The third classification of music in games is music as gameplay—that is, when the player generates the music in real time as he or she plays the game.

One might consider all interactive music in games to be "music as gameplay," but the difference here is that the game system is reacting *directly* to the actions of the player. Most interactive music systems have an indirect relationship to the underlying music system. For instance, when a player makes choices in a game that then affect the state of the character (e.g., explore or combat), the music would change based on those indirect choices. This is *not* an example of music as gameplay.

Games that use the music-as-gameplay paradigm typically operate on a lower level of detail than state changes in the music. If the game player makes an action that triggers a sound in rhythm or creates a sequence of notes, that would fall into this classification.

Game developers work with composers to devise an overall music system that complements the gameplay, defining the rules of how the music will play on a note-to-note or phrase-to-phrase level.

There are several different gameplay scenarios in this classification, including simulated performance, player-generated music, and rhythm action.

Simulated Performance

Games like *Rock Band* (2007) and *Guitar Hero* (2005) use musical controllers to simulate the effect of being in an actual band performing the music. These games typically use licensed music from popular bands and artists. The music in these games is played back depending on how well the player performs in the game. The better the player performs, the closer to the original licensed song the result will be.

Player-Generated Music

In some games, the player creates music dynamically while playing the game. In *PaRappa the Rapper* (1996), for example, the player is able to direct the lead character to rap. In what is essentially a rhythm action game, the player presses the control in rhythm in a specified order to get the lead character to rap in real time.

Another example of player-generated music is found in the first-person shooter/rhythm action game *Rez* (2001) from game designer Tetsuya Mizaguchi. In this game, the player creates music dynamically by shooting down geometric shapes in rhythm with the music, triggering musical notes and patterns.

Last, the game *Bit.Trip Runner* (2010) is a 2D platformer where the avatar runs from left to right at a constant pace. As the player jumps or collects coins in the world, a musical phrase or set of notes begins to play.

Just as we sometimes blur the lines between diegetic and extra-diegetic music, so you could make a case that games like *Portal 2* (2011), which allow you to manipulate physical objects in a 3D world that make noise, feature player-generated music.

Rhythm Action

The last category of music as gameplay is rhythm action games. *Dance Dance Revolution* (1998), *Amplitude* (2003), and *Space Channel 5* (1999) are all examples of rhythm action games. In these games, players listen to the rhythm of the music and then synchronize their actions by either dancing or hitting buttons on a controller in time with the music to gain rewards.

Player Customized Music

Players may also choose to import their own music into a game. The original Xbox 360 release mandated that every game must be made in such a way that you could turn off the musical underscore and replace it with user-chosen content. If the player wanted to hear John Williams's *Superman* (1978) theme while he played *Halo*, for example, the system would allow for that.

To enable users to bring their own music into a game, systems would allow the players to encode music from a CD or flash drive directly to the memory of the console. Then, while playing a game, users could select to hear their personalized music within the game.

Entire games have been built around customized music, including *Audiosurf* (2008) and *Vib Ribbon* (1999). These rhythm action games create dynamic game levels built around the music that the player chooses.

Player-customized music is also popular in racing games. The 2012 release of *SSX*, which is a snowboarding game, allows players to import any music that they want into the game. The game then uses various digital signal processing (DSP)—filters, beat-matching delays, reverbs—remixing on the fly during gameplay to augment and enhance the custom music.

Exploring Music Function within Games

Music can be a compelling and useful device to bring players into the game or to enhance the storytelling aspects of character-driven games. Breaking it down even further, music within video games has various functions, ranging from ephemeral state changes to longer-lasting thematic devices. Following are the various music functions that we find in games:

- **Set the scene.** Players need clues about where they are when they enter a virtual game environment. Music can help define the time and place by using instrumentation and/or harmonic relationships. The *Final Fantasy* series (1987–2010) is known for its extensive use of musical themes to establish locations within the game. In *Super Mario Bros.* (1985), different parts of the level have their own themes (e.g., aboveground versus underground).

- **Introduce characters.** Throughout many games, a tapestry of characters may be introduced to the player. Character themes can help the player develop perceptions of certain characters (allies or villains) or enhance the emotional connection between characters. In addition, themes may help organize a large cast of characters in a very sizable game. The *Mass Effect* trilogy (2007–2012) uses many character themes and is a great example of how to weave these themes throughout an enormous game.

- **Signal a change in game state.** Music is often used to signal when a player has gone from one state to another. Typically this is an ephemeral change that quickly goes back to its original state. This technique is frequently used in vertical resequencing (layering of tracks), which we'll focus on in the next part of the book. *Red Dead Redemption* (2010) uses this technique to distinguish between the exploring, riding, and combat states.

- **Increase or decrease dramatic tension.** Tempo and the addition of music layers are frequently used in games to increase the tension. In both the early games *Asteroids* (1979) and *Space Invaders* (1978), the tempo increases to raise the dramatic tension toward the end of each level.

- **Communicate an event to the player.** Frequently in games, composers use musical stingers to signal something to a player. In many games a musical stinger is played when a character dies in a particular level. A musical stinger is a short musical phrase (3–12 seconds) that acts like a musical exclamation point and is played to enhance a particular event in a game or film. In the game *Metro: Last Light* (2013), a musical stinger plays once the combat sequence has been completed.

- **Emotionally connect a player to a game.** Developing an iconic theme for your game, like the themes in the *Legend of Zelda* (1986–2013) and *Halo* (2001–2013) series, can go a long way toward establishing the overall tone and feel of your game and instilling anticipation and excitement when players hear it.

- **Enhance narrative and dramatic story arcs.** Similar to films, games generally have an overarching narrative and dramatic arc that plays out across the story. The music can enhance the emotional high and low points in your game.

BREAKING DOWN THE STRUCTURE OF A VIDEO GAME

Games can be broken down into a number of elements. Following is a description of each of the elements commonly found in games:

- **Introduction Movie:** An introduction that plays generally when the game begins.

- **Attract Sequence:** A movie that plays after the game is left alone for a period of time; it is used to advertise the video game in game shops.

- **Main Menu and Title Screen:** Generally a mostly static screen that waits for the user to start the game; it appears after the introduction movie.

- **Loading and Transition Screen:** After the player has chosen to start the game from the main menu, this screen appears while the game is loaded from the media or Internet. In general, it is difficult to put music on this screen because it consumes too many hardware resources.

- **Cinematics (Cut-Scenes or Full-Motion Video [FMV]):** A full-screen movie that plays to introduce the story or exposition elements during the game. Cinematics are typically linear video with very limited or no player interactivity.

- **Gameplay:** When the player is actually playing the game by either solving puzzles or controlling an avatar.

- **In-Game User Interface (UI) Screens/Level Select Screens/Pause/Settings:** User interface screens that typically interrupt gameplay. Special care must be taken to figure out how to handle the music in these sections.

Synchronization and Integration of Music

Inside film and linear media, we can usually rely on time codes or streamers and punches to synchronize our music. In contrast, in a game, the player is essentially directing the next shot in real time.

The game engine that is built makes requests to the music engine to change from one state to another, or to play a musical stinger. These requests are called "hooks" because the game is hooking into the music engine.

In many cases a programmer from the development team needs to program these hooks into the game for the music system to run properly. The game development team and the composer strategize about which actions in the game would trigger a music hook. This allows the music to stay appropriately in sync with the gameplay. After all, it's unlikely that you would want to hear the intense boss-battle music when you killed the boss minutes ago. The best video game scores are connected to the game engine so that the music is aware of what's happening in the game.

Although you'll explore this topic more in depth in the next chapter, here's a list of triggers you might see in a game that affect the music:

- Changing the emotional state (e.g., going from explore to combat)
- Moving to a different location within the game
- Number of enemies that are attacking
- Amount of health the player has remaining
- Time of day or the weather
- Proximity of an enemy
- Solving a puzzle or finding a treasure
- Killing a boss or finishing a stage

Serendipitous Sync

What happens when there is no synchronization of music in a video game? This is typically called serendipitous sync. It's similar to turning on the radio while watching a movie. Sometimes the music lines up wonderfully, but mostly it doesn't. There are ways to write music that suits the game without using external synchronization, but it might not be as reliable. Probably the most famous example of serendipitous sync is Pink Floyd's album *Dark Side of the Moon* (1973) played in tandem with the film *The Wizard of Oz* (1939).

Some games rely on serendipitous synchronization, including the original *Bioshock* (2007). In that game, music cues begin when you enter a new area, but the music is static after that point—meaning that it doesn't change based on player control. It may end serendipitously when you finish a battle, but it also may end earlier.

Music Conceptualization

To create successful music for a game, the game development team works with the composer to conceptualize the music. Conceptualization helps define the stylistic, creative, and functional goals of the music before the actual composing begins.

In this section we discuss how to conceptualize the score. You'll find some guidelines for how to establish the overall creative direction, but you should feel free to revise these ideas based on whatever process works best for your team. Music conceptualization is often jointly developed between the composer and the game developer, although very large games may be an exception (see the note on this topic on page 32).

When setting out to write music for a game, it's best to come up with an overall strategy first. The following steps will help you keep focused as you determine which direction is the most effective for your game.

1. Gather and Assess Materials

When beginning to generate the overall creative framework for a music score, the first step is to gather all the materials related to the game: game design documents, scripts, art assets, prototypes, and notes. Some or all of these assets might be missing when you begin the project, and in many cases composers start with very little on a project. Don't be too concerned if there isn't a lot to go on. You can revise the creative direction as more material is defined.

2. Prioritize Primary Music Objectives

The materials gathered in the first step will help you start to prioritize the most important ideas that you want to convey in your music. If you had to distill all the information down to a few key ideas, what would they be? For instance, are the puzzle elements the most important aspect of the game, or is the overall story more important, or a particular character? Making these decisions will better inform the music you create for your game.

Once you've narrowed down your primary objectives, then it'll be easier to determine how the music will function in the game. Compare your objectives with the music functions listed earlier in the chapter.

Are there secondary objectives that you might want to include in the overall creative strategy? Many games use multiple objectives in defining the overall music direction.

COMPOSER PERSPECTIVE

Tetsuya Shibata

When I'm composing music for a video game, the first step involves a meeting with the director where we closely examine and discuss the game's content, story, and world or setting. Then, we discuss what we would like the user or gamer to get out of this game and come up with several keywords to focus on. For example, the keywords that I was given for *Devil May Cry 3* were "an epic sibling fight"; in *Devil May Cry 4*, they were "love and friendship."

Especially for those games that have a strong storyline, I use the keywords initially to compose the main theme. Then, I arrange the main melody several times and disperse it here and there throughout the rest of the game. I do this to help build empathy toward the world of the game for the players.

Particularly in my case, before I compose anything I study the entirety of the game and all of the scenes that are shown to the audience and create a blueprint of the music.

I even go abroad for two weeks to observe the voice recording process to get a better understanding of the larger scenes. This helps me develop an even deeper understanding of the emotions and the attitudes of the characters as they interact with each other. I should add a disclaimer here: I have never met another composer who goes to the voice recording sessions, so maybe my method is unique.

3. Create an Asset List

Once you've determined your primary and secondary objectives, start planning the music asset list around them. A music asset is any cue that you'll need for the final game. If you're basing your music around character themes, then write out which themes you'll need and when you might use them in the game. Later in this book, we'll look at how best to determine the lengths of music for particular sequences.

4. Define Interactive Elements in the Score

The music score may contain additional interactive components that allow it to change in real time based on player decisions. In this step of the conceptualization phase, you want to define the parameters in the game that control the various elements in your score. These parameters might include AI behavior such as when an enemy attacks or when you solve a puzzle. These game parameters might be mapped to changes in the music.

See the previous "Synchronization and Integration of Music" section to help define the interactive elements. Throughout this book, you'll continue to learn about many interactive scoring techniques for use within your game.

5. Create a Supporting Audio Style Guide

A style guide is a tool that many designers use to help focus the direction of a creative element. In art, style guides are used to define the overall look and feel of a project. For a video game, an art style guide is made up of many different pictures representing the unified direction that the game should take.

An audio style guide usually consists of a variety of musical selections that represent musical genres and that help the design team hone in on the final direction of the music. It also helps the team identify criteria for judging whether a final piece is effective.

Generally, when groups listen to music for the first time, if they don't have a specific criterion on which to judge the music, they use their own music background to judge it. This can be difficult for a composer when presenting new music. For example, perhaps the game designer on the project broke up with his girlfriend while listening to music that had a saxophone in it. This association may have caused the game designer to hate saxophones. If this person is listening to the first presentation of the game music without the criteria in place, he's going to hate the saxophone no matter what, even if it's the best instrument for the game. In such a case, it's important to establish that the game designer doesn't like saxophone music before the composer begins working on a project.

The audio style guide helps inform the overall direction of the music before the composer begins writing. When each new piece of music is written, it can be compared to the initial style guide to determine whether you're making progress on your project or whether you need to rethink your initial approach.

Here is a list of criteria that you should establish with a style guide:

- Genre of the music (e.g., classical, techno, jazz)
- Tempo of the music (e.g., fast, slow)
- Instrumentation (e.g., orchestral, synthetic)
- Size of the group playing (e.g., intimate, grand)

You may need to have different style guides for different parts in the game. For example, if the character in a game is jumping around the globe as in *Uncharted 2: Among Thieves* (2009), each part of the game may need its own style guide.

6. Create an Audio Design Document

After you've done all of the work establishing your objectives, asset list, and style guide, it's important to create a document that you can share with your development team that outlines the overall creative strategy for your game. The audio design document is a compilation of the overall audio strategy for the game in written form. This document usually includes information about not only the music, but also all of the audio including sound effects (SFX), dialog, and music. In this book we focus primarily on the music aspects. The audio design document should contain information about the following music items:

- Overall creative direction for the style of music
- Music interactivity and implementation outline
- Preliminary asset list outlining the number and lengths of pieces
- The file names and formats that will be used

7. Revise

Throughout game development, you may find that some of your initial assumptions have changed. For this reason, it's important to update and revise your audio design document as the game progresses. Developing design documents is a standard practice in the game indus-try, as these documents generally contain all the information critical to the game development team and are considered a blueprint for how the game will be made.

> ### note
>
> On large games, the game publisher, franchise holder, or game developer may not involve the composer in many of the steps outlined in the music conceptualization phase. Frequently these companies employ audio directors or music supervisors who work to establish the overall creative direction of the music before hiring a composer for the project. These individuals then serve as the primary point of contact when conveying preproduction materials to potential or hired composers. Additionally, on large titles, the design documents are almost always drafted at the publisher/developer level and are not the responsibility of the composer.

Analysis and Critique of a Game Score

In this section, we begin to explore what makes a good game score versus a bad one. To ana-lyze game scores in any way, you'll need to form a language through which you can express your judgment of a composition's effectiveness within the context of gameplay. Developing this language is a key component in developing the most effective music for your game.

Composition is a purely creative endeavor; therefore analysis of the music is purely subjective. Decisions regarding music are qualitative as opposed to quantitative. Unfortunately, there is no right answer to the question, "Is this music good?" Therefore it's important for you to establish a set of criteria of what satisfies the needs of the story so that you can best judge the effective-ness and determine whether you've reached your goal after the music is written. A style guide is generally an excellent way to begin narrowing down which kinds of music work for your game. Better yet, it can define what's *not* appropriate for your game. In addition to the previous criteria, there are several other ways of determining whether a game score is effective:

- Do you notice the music, or are you enveloped in the storytelling of the world?
- Is the game succeeding in the goals outlined in the audio design document?
- Is the music score seamless, or does it jump from one piece of music to another without a transition?
- Does the music effectively enhance and support the overall story or experience?

Review

To build a language to use when describing video game music, it's important to understand some of the unique characteristics of the medium of video games. There are many important differences between linear experiences like film and nonlinear experiences like video games. These differences affect how the music is conceptualized, composed, and synchronized in video games. Some of the prominent differences include the following:

- Type of experience
- Length of experience
- Number of plays
- Game mechanics
- Pacing, synchronization, and flow
- Multiple story paths and repeatability
- Technology

Video games use music in different ways, including on a purely emotional level to increase empathy in the player, or as music that can be heard by the player in the game world itself. The important classifications of music within games include these four categories:

- Diegetic music
- Extra-diegetic (or non-diegetic) music
- Music as gameplay
- Player-customized music

Music can be a compelling and useful device to bring players into the game or to enhance the game's storytelling aspects. Music within video games can have many different functions:

- Setting the scene
- Introducing characters

serendipitous
sync.

- Signaling a change in game state
- Forging an emotional connection to the player
- Enhancing narrative and dramatic story arcs

To create successful music for a game, the game development team works with the composer to conceptualize the music. Conceptualization helps define the stylistic, creative, and functional goals of the music before the actual composing begins. The following steps are designed to help you keep focused as you determine which direction is the most effective for your game:

1. Gather and assess materials.
2. Prioritize primary music objectives.
3. Create an asset list.
4. Define interactive elements in the score.
5. Create a supporting audio style guide.
6. Create the audio design document.
7. Revise.

Exercises

1. Analyze a portion of any commercially released game by listing all the music cues and defining them in terms of function and categorization.
2. Broadly talk about any music triggers and music synchronization in any commercially released title.
3. Perform a critical analysis of the music in any commercially released game to determine its effectiveness.

CHAPTER 2

BREAKING DOWN THE LANGUAGE OF INTERACTIVE MUSIC

This chapter answers the question, What exactly is interactive music? It provides an overview of interactive scoring techniques commonly used in modern games and discussed throughout this book. Interactive composition has its own language and terminology. We begin to define these ideas and explore modern compositional approaches, the various ways in which interactive composition is used within games, and the creative and technological aspects that influence compositional approach.

What Is Interactive Music?

An interactive score is defined as music that can change dynamically based on some type of control input. This, in turn, means that the same piece of music may sound different at each performance or from listen to listen, based on changes to that control input. As you will learn, there are limitless types of control inputs available to composers.

As players make decisions while playing the game, they determine the pacing and flow of the game or influence various plot points or outcomes. These player decisions can have a direct or indirect relationship to how the music is evolving and shaped over time. The goal of these changes is to adapt the music in real time to enhance the specific emotional experience of the individual player.

In video games, composers work with the game developers to decide which game parameters will influence the music playback. These game parameters can be used to control, influence, or change the music score. Game parameters that affect the music might include progress in the story, location, time of day, presence of treasure or clues nearby, AI state (e.g., if the enemies are aware of the player), and many others. Composers are storytellers, and as such, it's important for them to capture the emotional changes in the gameplay based on the individual player decisions through control inputs.

ADAPTIVE VERSUS INTERACTIVE MUSIC

In the video game industry, *interactive music* is sometimes referred to as *adaptive music*. In this book we have chosen to use these terms interchangeably, even though there are subtle differences between the two. "Interactive music" is used more often when a player has direct control over the music, as in musical games like *Guitar Hero* (2005). "Adaptive music" is used when the player has indirect control over the music. Adaptive music may use other factors in the game world itself to change the music dynamically, including the time of day, weather, number of enemies, or player health.

In video games, changes to the control input are mapped to various aspects of the music. For instance, in the game *Uncharted 2: Among Thieves* (2009), the main character, which the player controls, is an archeologist searching for lost treasure. Throughout the game, the player explores various landscapes and comes across enemies in the archeologist's path. When the enemies get close to the player, the music changes from an explore cue to a suspense cue. When the player engages in battle with these enemies, the music changes to one of a number of battle cues. These battle cues may reflect varying degrees of combat intensity as they adapt to the game state. When the battle is over, the music goes back to its original explore cue.

Because the game's music is written in such a way to respond dynamically to these control inputs, the composer can customize the musical experience to better enhance the individual experience of the player. The changes in the music might include transitioning from one musical cue to another, manipulating the tempo, adding instruments to the music, and many others.

Throughout this book you'll learn about common practices that today's contemporary video game composers use within their games by learning where to place music, how to set up control inputs, how to compose interactive music that responds to this control input, and how to write transitions to seamlessly bridge from one piece of music to another.

> **note**
>
> What is a musical *cue*? A cue is defined as a complete piece of music having a beginning, a middle, and an end. Cues are written for a specific scene or a group of scenes that relate to one another. In video games, cues might be associated with emotional states (e.g., explore and battle) or a specific place or character. In classical music, symphonies are generally made up of shorter *movements,* which are very similar to what a cue represents in the modern language of films and video games.
>
> What is a musical *motif* or *theme*? A musical motif is a melody or specific musical passage that is associated with something in the story like a character, emotion, or place. Motifs are typically reused throughout the overall story to remind the player of various story elements and to maintain the continuity and emotional underpinnings of the story.

Types of Interactive Music

Where do you find *interactive music*? It may surprise you to know that interactive music isn't new, and it isn't found just in video games. Interactive music is prevalent in many different styles of music. Various types of interactive music have been evolving for well over a century, predating the introduction of video games into popular culture. In this section you'll discover what interactive music is, explore the myriad places where you'll hear interactive music, and examine why it's important in the evolution of music for video games.

Improvisational Construction: Variation and Form

Improvisation within music is defined as the ability to create or perform spontaneously, or without preparation. On the part of the performer, this means that the musician is composing new melodies or harmonies based on what's going on around him or her, whether it be what the rest of the ensemble or band is doing or how the audience is responding. This is a type of interactive music, as the music will differ from performance to performance based on the control input (the audience and the band).

One of the most popular forms of modern improvised music is *jazz*. When playing jazz, often the ensemble will begin by playing the head of a tune (the initial melody of the song along with its harmonies). Next, the musicians will improvise solos over those harmonies. Once the solos are complete, the ensemble returns to the initial melody (head of the tune) before ending the piece. In this instance the composer of the song has control of the harmonic structure and initial ideas, but the performers in the group take liberties with the melody, enhancing it and changing it as their own artistic representation.

Generally, *improvisation* is a term describing how the performers change the melody and harmony by slowly introducing new ideas to the composition. The musical key and harmonic progression inform the musical notes and improvisation that are being conceived. Improvisation is similar to the framework that many video game composers use when composing music for games. They create a framework and compositional structure for the music, but the control input (primarily the player's decisions) determines the final outcome of the music.

Another example of an improvisational style is a *drum circle*. A drum circle is a group of drummers who play together with a leader. This leader begins the music by selecting a rhythm, and the group repeats that rhythm. As the music progresses, the individual drummers augment and improvise slight variations on this original rhythm, gradually driving the overall musical progression forward. Similar to jazz, there is a framework that the leader begins, but that is then shaped over time by the control input: the creativity and perspective of the individual drummers sitting at the circle.

Within other styles of music, you can also find examples of a band leader shaping the song as the music progresses, either by allowing musicians to solo spontaneously or by changing the form of the song. For instance, funk artist James Brown might call out during a performance "Take me to the bridge," letting the band know that after the current section of music ends, they should play the bridge of the song. In this way, Brown changes the form of the song dynamically.

Video game music also uses musical form to shift the music based on what's happening to the player. If the player enters a battle state, this action could send a trigger to the music telling it to play the battle music cue after the current musical phrase ends.

Another important takeaway message for video game composers of improvisational styles is the importance of variation. Variation helps composers extend the length of a piece of music by adding alternative ways to play a melody using incremental changes in the melody and harmony.

Real-Time Composition and Arranging

Real-time composition is when the musician or ensemble makes musical choices while watching the events unfold in a story. In this section we'll examine two specific examples: music for silent films and circus music. Real-time composition incorporates many techniques that you can draw upon and apply directly to video game music.

While there are some parallels between real-time composition and improvisation, there are also significant differences that make each unique. With improvisation, the musical interactivity is determined by the group performing the music, and the control input is generally the musicians themselves or the audience. With this type of real-time composition, the control input consists of the story, scene, or narrative being shown.

Before the technological advances in film that allowed synchronization with sound, showings of silent films (1895–1930) were frequently accompanied by live piano or organ. Until the later years of the silent era, music was not even composed specifically for the film. Frequently, movie studios would send cue sheets known as *photoplay music* to theaters with their films; these cue sheets suggested musical accompaniments for various scenes in the film. Later (circa 1925–1930), big-budget silent films commissioned custom music scores from composers that were sent to theaters with the films, which the accompanist or ensemble would then play.

Film accompanists would actively score the film in real time, transitioning between musical cues using what they saw on the screen as a guide. The best of these musicians relied on a vast repertoire of memorized music in their heads, allowing them to move from one piece to the next while seamlessly representing the different emotions in the film: joy, sorrow, comedy, and so on. Oftentimes film accompanists would have the chance to see the film only once before having to perform live. These accompanists would compose and arrange the music on the fly based on the musical direction and cue sheets that were sent with the film.

Video games frequently rely on a musical repertoire from which pieces can be selected and played dynamically based on the story flow and architecture. However, instead of having a live accompanist play along with your video game, the computer processors tell the music engine what the player is doing, so that it can appropriately transition to the next musical cue or emotion.

Circus music is another excellent example of shaping real-time composition based on a performance or story. Frequently in circus performances there is an artist or ensemble that is performing a trick. Music typically accompanies these circus performances and is expected to enhance and synchronize with the tricks being performed. Because the synchronization of the music has to be performed in real time in tandem with the artist's actions, circus musicians have developed a lot of specific notations to help this process.

The circus band leader needs to watch the performance while cueing the band to repeat a section of music until the artist moves onto the next part of the trick. At that point, the band leader will cue the cadence to end the first section and move into the second. The music harmonic map must be extremely flexible to account for the variability in the individual performances. The circus performers themselves determine the pacing and outcome of the music, not the musicians in the ensemble.

Some tricks in a circus performance are actively mimicked by a specific instrument. Tricks that require this kind of synchronization are frequently improvised by the musician as he or she watches the performer. For example, suppose a tightrope walker is throwing things up into the air and catching them. A percussionist might use a drum roll to increase the tension, with the volume of the roll throughout the trick swelling louder and softer. Because anything can happen during the trick, the musician is frequently ad-libbing to the action. An ensemble of musicians would have a more difficult time synchronizing to the artist performing the trick with melody and harmony because of the enormous variability, whereas a single musician might be a better choice for mimicked synchronization.

When the circus band leader reviews the performance before the show with the artist, he or she will get specific information about how the trick is planned—for instance, when the first applause break will occur and how long the trick might last. The band leader then can adapt the written music in real time with the ensemble to best match the performance. Because smaller circuses sometimes use pickup musicians hired for just one or two gigs, the written music has to be extremely flexible and easy to read. This kind of music needs to clearly indicate the changes between sections, cadences, transitions, and loops for easy reading by the musicians.

Circus performers have consistently followed current trends in the popular music of the day, allowing circus ensembles to keep pace with the music industry. In addition, technology advances for playing music have been adopted by some big shows like Cirque de Soleil, which uses sophisticated software like Ableton Live to loop sections and to cue up segments at the end of a musical phrase or on a beat in real time.

Performance-Based Dynamics and Tempo Changes

Operas are also examples of story-driven experiences, and there is some interactivity in their very nature. The speed with which the event on the stage unfolds dictates how the conductor speeds up or slows down the musical tempo.

The same can be said of symphony performances. The conductor controls the speed of the musical tempo as well as dictates specific musical dynamics to the orchestra, such as the speed of a crescendo or the softness of a triple pianissimo marking.

Composers for video games can think about using control mechanisms in the game to change the dynamics of the music or increase the tempo in real time to escalate the tension in a scene.

Experimental Composition Techniques

Formal approaches to interactive composition in modern and post-modern music include *chance music, aleatoric music,* and *indeterminate music.* These interactive music approaches can control minute details of a musician's performance, whether it's dynamically changing the note

Table 2.1   Example Control Inputs That Influence and Change the Music

Musical Example	Primary Types of Control Inputs That Influence the Music
Video games	The player, the player's proximity to objects in the game world, the game's weather, and so on
Circus music	The performer executing the trick (i.e., how long it takes to complete a trick)
Silent film music	The film being shown in real time
Jazz	The band leader, the individual musicians, and the audience
Drum circle	The leader and the individual performers
In C by Terry Riley	The individual musicians in the ensemble and the conductor
4'33 by John Cage	The audience
Calder Piece by Earl Brown	The movements of Alexander Calder's mobile

length during the performance or adapting the overall form and structure of the music. Frequently these modern approaches to interactive music require the development of their own notation systems to convey the adaptive material to the conductor or the musician because it simply does not exist in traditional musical notation systems.

The principal takeaway behind this music stays the same: music changes dynamically each time it plays based on a control input defined in the composition itself. The changes in the control input directly change the music itself, making it dynamic and interactive. We can draw inspiration from this rich history of interactive music by examining various interactive scoring techniques to help foster ideas in our own scores.

Throughout Chapter 6, "Historical Perspective of Experimental Music," you'll learn more about the history of experimental music throughout the twentieth century and begin to familiarize yourself with the various types of interactive music beyond video games. As a result of this examination, you'll be able to add greater depth to your own compositions, as you can draw inspiration from the rich history of interactive and adaptive music and apply those techniques to modern video games.

Table 2.1 lists different types of interactive music and compares their primary control-inputs.

Instrument Design and User Interactive Performance

Many art installations create instruments (virtual or acoustic) allowing users to interact with and play the instruments. These instruments, by their very nature, have interaction as part of their design, creating a dynamic musical experience.

In New York City, on the Thirty-third Street subway line, there is a sound installation that is played like an instrument by reaching your hands in the air while you walk past. This installation, called "Reach," was created by Christopher Janney. The installation itself is mounted about seven feet off the ground and is located on both the downtown and uptown platforms. Thus, subway riders can play a duet between the two platforms. Similarly, at the MIT/Kendall station in the Boston subway, acoustic instruments sit between the northbound and southbound trains. The controls for these instruments are on both platforms and can be played by subway riders.

Video games that use music creation as a core mechanic can be inspired by real-world instrument installations and their design and interaction.

Control Inputs

Video game control inputs, in the general sense, refer to the mechanism of using external data to control game states, mechanics, and story. Typically, these player control mechanisms are converted into gameplay mechanics that are communicated to the music engine through messaging.

Game systems have many different kinds of physical control inputs that are used to control or change objects within the game:

- Game controllers
- Visual and motion sensors like Kinect or EyeToy
- Touch and pen controllers
- Computer keyboards and mice
- Steering wheels for driving games
- Guns for shooting games
- Microphone for voice input
- Specialized inputs specifically created for a game, like the instruments in *RockBand* (2007) or the bongo and shakers in *Samba de Amigo* (1999)

All of these devices can have either a *direct* relationship or an *indirect* relationship to controlling an interactive music score.

A direct relationship allows the game player to control the music directly, as in music-based games like *Rez* (2001), *Fract OSC* (2014), and *PaRappa the Rapper* (1996). These devices can control musical objects within the game itself, triggering musical notes or segments that play back based on the control input.

In an indirect relationship, the player uses these physical game controllers to change various elements or objects in the world (e.g., avatar location and actions, gameplay, story, mechanics), which then influence and control changes in the music. For instance, if a player uses her controller to move her character Link in *The Legend of Zelda: Ocarina of Tiem* (1998) closer to an enemy, the music system may change from playing an explore cue to a battle cue.

COMPOSER PERSPECTIVE

Akari Kaida

To assure the best work with the fewest problems, it is important to understand not only the music aspects but also the game development aspects, such as how a game is made and how the music is incorporated into the gameplay. The best thing for you to do is to find a job where you are able to study how a game is made from inside a game developer's office. Of course, you could learn a lot of technical skills in school, but, in my opinion, there are so many things that you can learn only through hands-on experience. Thus probably the quickest way is to work at a game company and be involved in a development process.

Music production within a movie or television series is not very different from video game music production, except that games are interactive so there are elements of musicality that you can incorporate in a game. Instead of being tied down by the restrictions found in movie and TV music, you are free to explore and try new things. If you enjoy this flexibility, you will really enjoy the field.

Throughout this book we use the term "control input" to refer to any piece of game data used to influence changes in the music system, either directly or indirectly. Any of the following gameplay elements might indirectly control the music system:

- Character location
- Enemy location or proximity
- Environmental effects like weather or time of day
- Level of suspense in a scene
- Emotion that the player should be feeling
- Health of the player
- Non-player characters (NPCs) that may interact with the player
- The action that the player is currently attempting
- How many puzzles the player has solved

Many different options are available to the music team based on the kind of game you are creating and the narrative and emotional experience that you want the player to have.

The Composer's Toolbox

There are many different ways for music to adapt in real time throughout a video game. Composers work with the game development team to decide which adaptive technique best suits the situation. The composer chooses how these game parameters might act as control inputs affecting the music. In this section we'll examine the toolset that the composer has at his or her disposal when composing an interactive score.

When scoring a game, it's important to consider the role that the music will play. This encompasses not only the control inputs but also other factors such as where the music will play, how often, how an individual cue may fit in context with the surrounding cues, and what the story is. All of these factors make up the overall interactive design, which in turn informs the use of the underlying musical technology, but is not necessarily married to it. This composer toolset is meant to be a guide for interactive music possibilities within the game.

COMPOSER PERSPECTIVE: COMPOSING AN ADAPTIVE SCORE—IMAGINE, DESIGN, INTEGRATE

Guy Whitmore

Imagine

Before concerning yourself with technical challenges, limitations, or design conventions, begin with an open book of possibilities. Imagine: how can the music best complement this game? Imagine: how can music flow throughout the game? Early on, I often capture gameplay footage and score it linearly, as if it were a short film. This allows me to explore creative avenues and visual synchronizations without worrying about design or technical issues just yet. Afterward, I ask myself, "Now how can I achieve this type of flow and synchronization in a nonlinear game environment?" And thus begins the music design process.

Design

Music design turns imagination into a conceptual plan. It defines where music will play and how it will function. Music design is highly creative and works best when it's a seamless part of the composing process. Rather than thinking in terms of one linear path for the music, design and create a range of potential compositional outcomes that align with the full range of gameplay. Being able to think about your music as flexible and nonlinear is critical to scoring a game, and consequently this is where there's vast room for innovation.

Integrate

Music integration is often thought of as a technical task, and composers often shy away from learning game audio tools. But we must learn to work creatively and compositionally within these new tools, just as we do in our linear DAWs. This is where music is synchronized with picture—where detailed "scoring" is done. What could be more important? These tools are now very capable and evolving at a rapid pace. So don't feel bound by the prescribed features of these tools; they can be bent to your will with a little ingenuity. This is where your score comes to life!

Cue Switching and Musical Form Adaptation

The simplest tool that composers have at their disposal when making music for video games is the ability to switch songs based on an event in the gameplay. This practice began in the 1980s with games like *Frogger* (1981) and *Super Mario Bros.* (1985). Based on the player actions, the game system would send a message to the music system requesting a change in the song. In these early arcade games, the method for switching from one cue to another involved simply turning off one musical cue and beginning a new one, similar to switching stations on a radio. Transitioning by this method can be very startling and surprising for players, possibly taking them out of the immersive experience.

As games evolved, the music systems became more sophisticated. The next step in cue switching was to fade out the initial track and fade in the secondary track. This method, known as crossfading, is used quite often in games. To hide the crossfade, some games use a sound effect or transitional musical element like a stinger to bridge these two cues. Many of the *Final Fantasy* titles use this method to switch from explore cues to battle cues.

A more advanced technique, introduced with the LucasArts iMuse system in the early 1990s, allowed the music system to wait for a musical phrase to end before transitioning to a new cue. This was used very effectively in *Monkey Island 2: LeChuck's Revenge* (1991), which has been updated to work on many modern platforms including iOS and Xbox Live. This technique ensured a seamless transition by waiting for the current musical phrase or melody to end instead of interrupting it. Interrupting a melody can be very surprising for the player. This technique can be very effective when trying to keep the player immersed in the experience. Most modern audio middleware packages (Fmod and Wwise) support this functionality.

With the introduction of intelligent music engines in games, markers can now be placed in the music that represent the different parts of a single cue. For example, a single cue used in a puzzle game might have a section that plays specifically when the timer is running out. The intelligent music system would loop in the less intense section of the music until the level started running out, then switch seamlessly (on the next bar or beat) to the more intense music of the same cue. In this book we refer to this technique as musical form adaptation.

In video games, the individual music cues can be divided up into different sections. The representation of the sections is known as the musical form. Generally, most composed music has a musical form and structure. In popular music, we can hear the musical form by dividing the song up into verses and choruses. The form might include an introduction, a less intense section, a more intense section, and an end. In a game, we might loop the less intense section while players are exploring; when they encounter an enemy, the music system would then transition to the more intense section. When the level ends, the players would hear the ending for that cue. Manipulating the musical timeline in a single cue is known as adapting the musical form.

These techniques are broadly characterized by the term *horizontal resequencing*—that is, we are resequencing the order of the form, or the order of the music horizontally against a time axis. This compositional process, as well as the various techniques used in it, is discussed in detail in Chapter 8.

INTELLIGENT MUSIC SYSTEMS

In video games, an intelligent music system is a system that understands and can respond to the music itself. Many intelligent music systems understand whether the current music is in the middle of a phrase or at the end, or where the next beat or measure begins. This musical intelligence allows the system to make more insightful decisions about when to transition, branch, or loop. This makes for a more immersive music experience in a game by transitioning more smoothly from cue to cue. Most modern audio middleware tools (e.g., Fmod and Wwise) used in gaming have an intelligent music functionality allowing for sophisticated musical form adaptation and transitioning.

Dynamic Mixing

Dynamic mixing within a game music system refers to changing the volumes of individual instruments that make up the music. For instance, in *Uncharted 2: Among Thieves* (2009), a suspense layer or instruments (usually light percussion) is faded in over the strings as the tension increases when the player sneaks up on an enemy. When the player goes into battle, a heavier percussion ostinato is brought in on top of the current music. These layers are then faded out when the player reaches a larger point in the story where a transitional element might play. *Batman: Arkham City* (2011) is another excellent example of a game that changes the tension level by adding and removing instrument layers as the flow of the game continues.

This technique is frequently used when the music must adapt between two states in short intervals. Instead of switching between two separate musical cues, it is more advantageous when switching between two states to change the instrument makeup within the same piece so you're not interrupting the musical flow.

In the game world, this is frequently known as *vertical remixing*, as you're dynamically changing the volumes of instruments stacked in the vertical space. Sequencers like Logic or Pro Tools look at instrument tracks vertically—hence the name. Chapter 9, "Vertical Remixing," details the use of this compositional technique as well as its advantages and disadvantages in games.

Tempo and Rhythmic Manipulation

As far back as the 1970s, games like *Asteroids* (1979) and *Space Invaders* (1978) were using their limited sound resources to adjust the music tempo in real time to push the player's excitement level and tension in the game. As the player advanced in the game, the short-looping two- or four-note melody would increase in tempo as the game difficulty increased.

Another example in a more modern context occurs in *Super Mario Galaxy* (2007), when Mario stands on top of a rolling ball. As the player controls Mario to roll faster, the tempo increases. The reverse is also true: when Mario is going more slowly, the music tempo decreases.

There are also many examples of this technique in music-based games like *Rez* (2001). *Rez* is a video game that can be described as a rave-based first-person shooter. As the game progresses, the tempo rises and falls based on how the player is doing. In addition, the player has control over building some of the rhythmic layers in the game. Rhythmic manipulation is a technique used in many music-based games that adds or changes the rhythm based on player interaction.

This technique can be an effective way to change the overall emotional perspective of the game. Today, it is found primarily in games that use real-time virtual instrument playback with MIDI, as opposed to games that use prerendered audio files. It's a fairly simple procedure to speed up a MIDI sequence, but it can be quite a hardware-intensive operation to speed up and slow down audio files without also changing the pitch of the audio. You'll find a more detailed look at how a musician composes for this technique in Chapter 14, "Real-Time Tempo Variation and Synchronization."

DSP and Effect Application

DSP refers to digital signal processing. In the audio world, it's also commonly referred to as effects. For instance, guitar players often carry around a lot of effects pedals (e.g., reverb, distortion, delay, chorus). These are similar to the kinds of real-time effects that we can apply to music within games.

There are several great examples of how real-time DSP is used within games to effectively enhance overall music. In *SSX Tricky* (2001), a snowboarding game, when the player begins a long jump in the game, the game uses a filter to turn off the bass (a high-pass filter). This small enhancement makes it feel like you're flying in the air whenever you go off a jump in the game. Another example of DSP application appears in *Call of Duty* (2003) and many other combat-based games: when your health decreases to near zero, the high end or treble of the music gets turned down as if you are entering a foggy area. This kind of low-pass filter can be effective at notifying players that they are near death.

You can use many different kinds of DSP effects within a game. Here's a list of some of the effects that may be available in your game engine:

- **Filters (Band Pass, Low Pass, High Pass):** These effects manipulate the overall frequency spectrum of the music by either increasing certain frequencies or decreasing them.

- **Distortion and Overdrive Effects:** Commonly associated with rock music, these effects add overtones that make the music more fuzzy or gritty.

- **Time-Based Effects (Reverb, Delay, Chorus, Flange):** These effects typically change the space in which we hear the instruments being played. Also, in rock and electronic music, delays can be added as a rhythmic effect.

- **Dynamic-Based Effects (Compression, Expansion):** These effects change the overall dynamic range of the music by either increasing it (expansion) or decreasing it (compression).

- **Pitch Shifting:** This effect manipulates the overall pitch of the music up or down.

Stinger and Musical Flourish Additions

A stinger or musical flourish is a short musical phrase or cue (usually less than 10 seconds) that emphasizes a gameplay event. A stinger can play on top of whatever music is currently playing or it can play by itself, depending on its function within the game. In a typical game, there are many different kinds of stingers, including musical flourishes for power-ups, game over, level finish, goal achieved, and plot point reached. Stingers and flourishes may also be used to begin and end a cue.

You can find these types of events in almost any game, but they are especially prevalent in casual games because so many types of scoring events in these games call for musical flourishes or sound effects. For example, stingers are found in casual games such as *Diner Dash* (2004) and *Peggle 2* (2013).

Most stingers are written in such a way that they don't need to fit into the overall rhythm of the underscore music. Nevertheless, certain musical games might need more synchronization of these cues. An intelligent music system can synchronize the stingers so that they play on a specific beat or marker in the underscore music of the game. The disadvantage of this approach is that the stinger might not play immediately.

Musical stingers or flourishes can also help bridge two pieces of music as a transitional element. When used with horizontal resequencing, this technique can be an effective way to smooth out the overall flow of a game. Transitions are very important to help bring together disparate visual screens, like the menu screen and the gameplay screen. In Chapter 10, "Writing Transitions and Stingers," you'll learn about the compositional process of writing these types of musical events.

Instrumentation and Arrangement Alteration

Changing the instrumentation in games refers to dynamically switching the instrument based on a player action. This technique is not often employed within games, but it can be very effective in setting the overall mood of a game.

Monkey Island 2: LeChuck's Revenge (1991) uses this technique very effectively on the docks. As the music cue plays, the primary melodic instrument and supporting instruments shift when the player moves from one location to another. The melody remains the same but it is picked up on another instrument. The advantage of this technique is that it offers a variety of musical palettes while using a single theme to hold the scene together instead of jarring the player by switching between separate themes.

Arrangement alteration refers to adapting a musical cue from one musical style to another. This is done by changing the instrumentation, but also by changing the rhythmic and harmonic frameworks of a piece of music. This technique is evident in *Legend of Zelda: Skyward Sword* (2011) when the player is shopping. The musical arrangement and style change as the character visits the different vendors in the marketplace.

The arrangement alteration technique is similar to using vertical remixing, which adds and subtracts various instruments from the mix. Instrumentation usually consists of the dynamic replacement of a specific instrument instead of a new addition to the track. Again this technique is typically used more often with real-time virtual instrument playback and MIDI, as opposed to streaming audio tracks. Instrumentation and arrangement alteration are discussed in more depth as they apply to composers in Chapter 13, "MIDI and Virtual Instruments."

Harmonic Approach, Melodic Adaptation, and Note Manipulation

Harmonic approach, melodic adaptation, and note manipulation are not widely used in video game music but can be found in many music creation games like *Rez* (2001), *Child of Eden* (2011), and *Fract OSC* (2014).

Changing the harmonic or melodic approach of the music in real time is unusual within a gaming context. This technique is frequently used in films to create different moods with the same theme. For instance, the hero theme might have two different versions: one in a major key and another in a minor, but more suspenseful key. The DirectMusic middleware engine introduced by Microsoft in the 1995 allowed for the application of different chord progressions on a melodic framework. This enabled composers to go from one musical mode to another, or from one key to another, quite easily. Two games that use this chord mapping feature are *Asheron's Call II: Fallen Kings* (2002) and *No One Lives Forever* (2000).

Different harmonic approaches within games are usually created as separate prerendered audio cues; then, using a technique like horizontal resequencing, the game transitions between the various cues. If your game is using real-time virtual instruments with MIDI, then it's fairly easy to transpose music at any time or to switch modes.

Many music-based games use melodic and note manipulation techniques; these methods are discussed at length in Chapter 15, "Advanced Dynamic Music Manipulation Techniques." Following is a list of popular techniques used in this area:

- **Real-Time Melodic Variation:** This technique allows a game to improvise on the note level to vary the musical phrases.

- **Shortening/Lengthening of Notes:** Changing the length of notes based on a control input can be an interesting effect during gameplay.

- **Transposition, Key, and Modal Changes:** Transposing the music to a different key or mode (i.e., from major to minor) can change the overall tension or signal a shift in the overall mood.

Review

An interactive score is defined as music that can change dynamically based on some type of control input. In games, player decisions can have a direct or indirect relationship to the music. Game parameters such as the location within the world or the number of enemies may be used to control, influence, or change the music score.

Music may sound different each time it is played, based on changes to the control input. The composer can customize the musical experience to better enhance the individual experience of the player by having the music react to these decisions. Dynamic musical changes might include transitioning from one musical cue to another, manipulating the tempo, and adding instruments to the music, among many others.

Numerous types of interactive music are used within video game music:

- Improvisational construction in which melodies, harmony, rhythm, and form are modified and altered

- Real-time composition and arranging in which the performer dynamically composes the music during the experience

- Performance-based dynamics and tempo changes in which the volume or tempo of the music is changed based on a control input

- Experimental composition techniques in which the music is changed using modern and post-modern classical methodology (i.e., chance music, aleatoric music, indeterminate music)
- Instrument design and user interactive performance in which the instruments can be played or changed during the experience

Video game control inputs are the mechanisms for using data to control game states, mechanics, story, and music. They can have a direct or indirect relationship in terms of coordinating changes in the music system. Game parameters that act as control inputs to the music system may include character location, enemy location, level of suspense, or health of the player.

When composing interactive music, the composer chooses which game parameters will dynamically change the music. The composer then writes the music in such a way that it will respond to these changes. Among the ways the music can respond to control inputs are the following:

- Cue switching and musical form adaptation
- Dynamic mixing
- Tempo and rhythmic manipulation
- DSP and effect application
- Stinger and musical flourish additions
- Instrument and arrangement alteration
- Harmonic approach, melodic adaptation, and note manipulation

Exercises

1. Find instances and examples of interactive music in your own world.
2. Analyze a video game for its use of direct and indirect controls of the music system.
3. Search out video game examples that have sophisticated interactive music systems and write a detailed explanation of how they work.
4. Watch gameplay videos with the sound removed, and write down the interactive scoring techniques that you might use if you were scoring the game.

CHAPTER 3

SPOTTING THE GAME

In games we try to create a single experience from the combination of senses: touching, seeing, and hearing. If the user "notices" the music as being apart from the story, the score is not working. This chapter focuses on the production of a game music score through game spotting, which explores the storytelling of each game level with the game developer. We begin by exploring the goals of the game score as well as commonly used interactive music scoring techniques.

The Game Production Process

Games can have long development cycles that can approach two or more years, whereas feature films are generally put together in less than one year. The longer development cycle is required because of all the different features that go into designing a game and because of the variability during gameplay.

Following is a game production timeline typical for a AAA console title:

1. **Initial Idea:** The initial game design idea is born by formulating the game concept and developing various paper and digital prototypes.

2. **Pitch Phase:** The game developer creates the initial design document and pitches the idea to various publishers looking for initial funding.

3. **Preproduction:** The initial idea has been funded and the developer begins building the team to make the game. The overall design continues, with music spotting being completed in conjunction with the creation of the game design document.

4. **Initial Development Stage:** The first real prototypes are created, and the full design document for production is finished. After this stage is complete, the publisher completes a final review before moving forward.

5. **Publisher Review:** The game publisher completes a final review of the initial materials and makes a "go" or "no go" decision on funding the game.

6. **Main Production Begins:** Music demos are written by composers bidding on the job. Composer decisions are made and the music team is hired. Music conceptualization begins.

7. **First Playable Prototype:** Creative direction of the music is finalized, and music composition for the game begins.

8. **Alpha Stage:** The game is playable and contains all the major features. The final music is recorded.

9. **Beta Stage:** The game is feature and asset complete, and only bugs are being fixed. The music is completed and implemented in the game.

10. **Gold Master Candidate:** All the bugs have been fixed, and the game is ready for release and distribution.

WHAT IS A GAME DESIGN DOCUMENT?

The *game design document* (GDD) is a guide that meticulously describes all of the features and assets of the game that is being developed. In addition, the GDD details how the game will be made, including schedules and timelines, and sometimes budgets. This document is often referred to by the game development team as the game's *bible*. The design document usually includes the following sections: overview, game mechanics, story, characters, user interface, interaction design, level/environment design, art, sound and music, game controls, and platforms.

Preliminary music work is done during the preproduction phase with initial music spotting. The primary music composition and production begins once the first playable prototype is finished (usually about halfway through the overall development timeline). The first playable prototype is typically a complete test level in the game, which may feature only five percent of the overall features of the game.

Much of the game may still be in early development when members of the music team begin their work. As a consequence, some of the cues that the composer may be writing will be composed before they can be seen in the actual game. Later in the game development process, these cues may have to be revised based on changes that have been made to the original design document. A disadvantage of composing for games is definitely the inability to play the game from beginning to end when the music needs to be produced.

Game music development has other unique characteristics that you should recognize:

- The music composition process is significantly longer than the music production of most films, typically ranging from 8 to 18 months for a AAA title. By comparison, music for a feature film is usually composed and recorded over a span of 2 to 3 months.
- Given the variability in individual players' experiences during the game, it's simply not possible to test all the different paths the player might take.
- Many of the cues may have interactive music components involving looping and real-time adaptivity, possibly increasing the composition time.
- An average AAA title has 2 to 3 hours' worth of composed music. Usually this music is extended during gameplay because interactive cues add variability to the players' experiences.

The Spotting Process

In film, *spotting* refers to the process in which the film director and the composer discuss the musical approach on a scene-by-scene basis. A similar approach has been adopted for video game music composition. Because of the length of the development cycle and the lack of a complete game, however, the challenge for a game composer is to figure out what the game is all about by using the available assets. Assets typically used to spot the game may include the following items:

- Story and scripts for the game
- Game design document
- Levels and maps
- Artwork

- Working prototypes of the game (if they exist)
- Overall structure of the game, and length of time needed to complete each section
- Core gameplay mechanics
- Any materials from the music conceptualization phase during preproduction (discussed in Chapter 1)

With these items in hand, the composer can sit down with the design team to discuss, level by level, the complete narrative and the emotional structure of what the player should be feeling at any given moment. This discussion should include a rough estimate of how long each level will last during average gameplay and the overall pacing of the game.

The next step is to define an overall creative vision for the music. First, it's important to establish what the "role" of the music will be by thinking of the music as an invisible actor. Will it be an active participant, or will it be part of the background? Next, the creative vision should include stylistic notes, plans for instrumentation, information about the genre, an outline for the main dramatic goals, the interactive plan, and the way in which the music will be structured.

The music structure is how the score is organized and broken down. For example, the score might be organized by overall themes and moods, or by levels in the game itself. This organization is key to the next steps of defining control inputs for the interactive musical structure and breaking the score down into individual musical cues.

After the creative vision is established, the goals for the interactive music system should be considered. Which control inputs will be sent to adapt the music system in real time while the game is being played? How will the music change when the music system receives a message? These considerations will definitely impact which musical cues the composer will work on and how they are thought out. The control inputs and music outcomes will be specific to the game that you're working on, but the examples found throughout this chapter offer some helpful guidance. As an example of a specific scenario, you may choose to intensify the music when players find themselves in trouble or are outnumbered in a battle. This choice might affect all the battle cues and how they are composed.

Many creative options may be dependent on other factors, such as technical issues or the tools being used. These factors need to be considered when working through the overall creative vision for the music.

With this information, the design team and the composer collaborate on the music, defining which cues should be written for the game based on the game structure. The music team goes through all the components of the game and begins to build the individual cue lists.

Cue sheets are an important part of organizing all of the music for a project. Although they are generally customized for each project, the following list identifies things you should include in your cue sheet:

- **Cue Number:** A unique identifier for each cue

- **Category:** The category of the music (e.g., gameplay music, music for a UI screen, a transition, or cinematic)

- **Cue File Name:** A unique identifier file name for each cue

- **Level or Scene:** Where in the game the cue plays

- **Cue Length:** The estimated length of the cue

- **Cue Description:** How the cue is being used

- **Starting and Ending Points:** Triggers that cue the music to play, and eventually end

- **Adaptive Characteristics:** Any interactive characteristics of the music cue

- **Control Input:** The control inputs for the interactive music

- **Version Number:** A number that tracks a specific asset through revisions

- **Notes for the Programmer/Implementer:** Any additional specific notes for the implementation of the cue

MUSIC AND GAMEPLAY STRUCTURE

When building a cue sheet, it's useful to categorize where the music might go in the game architecture. Video games are made up of various components that are typically divided into four broad categories:

- **User Interface.** UI screens usually contain information that is outside the main narrative of the story. These screens generally include a main menu or lobby, in-game status information like an inventory or a map, a pause screen, a game over screen, and saving and loading screens. The music on these screens is generally not intrusive, as the gameplay is usually paused while a UI screen is up. Sometimes whatever current gameplay music is playing is put through a filter of some kind, making it less intrusive and more of a background feature. The introduction screens may also include a two-minute sizzle reel or "attract loop" if the player sits idle for a set time.

- **Gameplay.** Gameplay is the heart of most video games. It's where the player is interacting with the game universe itself by possibly controlling a character or solving a puzzle. Because gameplay is dynamic, this is where most of the interactive music cues are placed. Most of the user experience of actually playing the game happens on the gameplay screens.

- **Cinematics.** Cinematics or full-motion video (FMV) generally consists of linear, noninteractive movies that give the player narrative and story information needed to play the game. An example cinematic (sometimes referred to as a cut-scene) might show the history of a particular character through flashbacks.

The player of the game generally does not have any kind of interactive control over the cinematic except to watch the story unfold. Usually these elements are placed at the beginning of a new section in the game, or they appear when you've completed a mission or goal. Music for cinematics is most often linear and can be scored like a scene from a movie.

- **Transitions.** Transitional screens and music cues help bridge scenes or screens that pull the user into the story. These transitions help weak points in the visual design by covering up jump cuts or filling time when the player has to wait for assets to load into memory.

These broad categories can be another way to identify the kinds of cues on your cue sheet.

Spotting and the creation of the cue sheet form an intensive process that will take time, but at the end of this process you'll be better organized and have a sense of the overall challenges of the project. When you're finished with the spotting process, you should have the following outcomes:

- Creative vision of the music with stylistic notes, instrumentation, dramatic goals, and structure

- Overall music plan and schedule

- Live musician production and recording plans

- A list of control inputs that might be used by the music system to adapt the music

- A music cue sheet that describes each music asset in detail (e.g., starting and ending points, musical interactivity, length)

Ideally, this spotting process should take place well in advance of the music composition and production; in fact, it is part of the game design process itself. These outcomes are usually integrated into the game design document, or into a related but separate audio design document.

The Goals of a Video Game Music Score

In this section, we'll explore the various goals associated with creating an interactive score for a video game as they apply to the end-user experience. In any narrative experience, there are a group of shared goals that the music may have:

- Driving the emotional experience by augmenting the storytelling aspects of the game
- Setting the location and time period

- Enhancing the overall aesthetic and creative vision of the game
- Synchronizing the music to react to the player's actions and support gameplay
- Representing characters, places, or storylines in the narrative to better communicate the story
- Helping bridge any leaps in the story by using musical transitions
- Notifying the player about a particular gameplay event
- Increasing musical variation of the gameplay experience so the game doesn't seem repetitive

The individual goals of an interactive score will change from game to game. In the rest of this chapter, you'll learn how to take a list of goals and integrate it into an overall music plan. The success of a music score depends on adequate planning, and outlining the dramatic goals from the outset will allow the composer and music team to have enough time to put together an awesome score.

COMPOSER PERSPECTIVE

Yoshino Aoki

It is very important to discuss the direction of the in-game music with the producer and the director. After the discussion, we can verbally determine the sound that they are looking for. Of course, every producer and director are unique. Some producers and directors are very knowledgeable with music terminology, some are partial to specific genres of music, and some are very open to letting you express your interpretations. No matter what kind of people they are, they always seem to have a lot of difficulty expressing in words which kind of sound they are looking for. Therefore, it is crucial that you as a composer really understand the plot of the game, the world in which the game is based, and the gameplay. On top of this understanding, you must decipher what is musically sought after based on the limited dialog that takes place between you and the director. It is very important that you strike a good balance among all of these considerations and make a decision about what you want to do and what you can do for the game.

Outlining the Emotional Context and Narrative Arc

With the creative vision in hand, it's very important for the composer to work with the game development team to define the overall narrative and emotional arc of the music throughout the game. Two key questions need to be answered to create an effective music score: "When is the climax of the story?" and "When are the low points?" The teams work together to figure out where the climax of the emotional arc should be and how to lead up to those points for the most effective score.

A music score needs to have both high points and low points—that is, both tension and release. Players tend to respond better to changes and shifts in the emotional arc of the musical composition as opposed to a singular emotion for an extended period of time. In musical language, this can be referred to as consonance and dissonance, stable versus unstable, or tension to resolution. This pragmatic thinking about the score before the composition begins will help the composer achieve his or her goals more readily and be more effective at augmenting the emotion in the game.

Many composers choose to draw out on paper the intensity of the music arc level by level, and throughout the game, to see where tension and release occur. In the composition process, they can then keep these points in mind to create the most effective music for each level. This process, which is known as emotional arc mapping, is common in narrative experiences.

COMPOSER PERSPECTIVE

Laura Karpman

My process in composing music for games is really the same as any compositional process that I embark on, and is the same for any genre I write music for. I always ask a basic question: What's the way in? That is, what will be the compositional basis for this music?

I like to come up with a conceptual core to a score; in other words, I need to have a central idea for how the entire score will fit together. This concept will be a dramatic one—what the game is really about; which kind or kinds of melodies, orchestrations, texts, and other elements will reflect those dramatic goals. Most important, I want to learn with every score that I produce. Of course, there's also the client—they need to be happy, too!

EverQuest 2 was really a dream job. I could write whatever I wanted, for however long I wanted it to be! I had some vague guidelines from the developers about locations within the game and about the atmospheres of those locations. But I was really on my own. So I decided to make the score a personal exercise in orchestration. I studied great examples of classical music—mostly mid-twentieth-century modern music—and used those pieces as a springboard for my own composition. For example, the "Sea Battle" cue was based on the "Four Sea Interludes" from *Peter Grimes* by Benjamin Britten. "Fallengate" was based on the second movement of Ludoslavski's *Concerto for Orchestra*. Every piece in that game had a very strong influencing composition that I admired for its orchestrational prowess.

Every game has its own unique requirements. *Kung Fu Panda* needed to combine the world of Carl Stalling with traditional Chinese instruments. In the Kinect Disneyland adventures, the challenge was trying to re-create the Disney sound without having the iconic Disney tunes to arrange. How do you write a great melody like "When You Wish Upon a Star" and make this new theme sound like it's always been a Disney tune?

I love what I do! I am musically and intellectually curious, and I find great joy and passion in every game score. I love writing music for games, and I find it to be the most satisfying commercial music that I write.

Structuring Interactive Music throughout Gameplay

Interactive music in gameplay can respond to real-time emotional changes of the characters in the game. Most often interactive music cues are written for gameplay sequences. The music team works out the emotional shifts that need to happen in a level, along with their control inputs.

Gameplay music can shift from one emotional state to another using a variety of techniques. One approach is to use a transitional piece of music to bridge between the first emotional state and another one. Another technique is to add a musical layer to the current music to increase the tension in the scene.

A game score should feel seamless when going from one emotional station (e.g., exploration) to another (e.g., battle). Composers typically write transitions, stingers, and music that is able to branch from one state to another without feeling like the game is switching abruptly to different radio stations.

Synchronization

For the music to follow the gameplay, the music must adapt and respond to the player's actions. This phenomenon is known as synchronization. If we analyze the medium of film music as a starting point, we can draw corollaries between movies and games in their use of music. In film scoring, the composer primarily writes music to enhance the emotional underpinning of a scene. For this to be effective, the composer must write the music in a way that is synchronized to each significant moment of the scene. If the music doesn't sync, viewers can be taken out of that experience as they begin to notice the music.

In Carl Stalling's scores for many of the Warner Brothers cartoons, every screen action matches up with a similar motion in the music. For example, if we see a mouse running up a staircase, we might hear a similar ascending string run. This technique is frequently referred to as Mickey Mousing and is commonly heard in early Disney films and in films from the 1930s and 1940s. In video games, you can find examples of Mickey Mousing in games like *Desert Demolition* (1995), which features the Road Runner from the Warner Brothers cartoons. As you might imagine, Mickey Mousing actions in a film are frequently associated with comedy.

Dramatic film and game scores often use subtler, less overt techniques to synchronize music events to the player or viewer. For example, they use evolving scores over longer periods of time and transitional materials to get from one cue to another.

Game music must synchronize to the player, adapting and evolving throughout the gameplay, to be effective. Otherwise, the music will seem out of sync with what's happening in the game and will take the player out of the experience.

Video Game Scoring Techniques

In this book you'll learn about many different scoring techniques used in video games. In this section we'll examine some of the most widely used techniques.

Noninteractive Game Score

The simplest type of game score does not have any interactive music at all, but just uses a linear loop of music. When a level starts, the music loop begins; when the level is over, the music stops.

This kind of score has some distinct advantages:

- These scores are very easy to compose and implement.
- Building a noninteractive score requires less time than building an interactive score.
- This type of score generally costs less than an interactive score.

There are also multiple disadvantages associated with noninteractive scores:

- There is no variety, so the music becomes very repetitious.
- The music has the same beginning, middle, and end, making the loop points more noticeable and repetitive to the player.
- There is no synchronization to gameplay, except for overall dramatic context.
- Harmonic, melodic, and tempo changes may miss the action.
- The score relies on serendipitous sync.

Horizontal Resequencing

Horizontal resequencing is a method of interactive composition where the music branches from one section to another once it reaches the end of a phrase. For example, when the music is playing underneath the gameplay, it may reach a decision point where it could go to a new section of music or it could repeat the previous section; the decision depends on the player's actions. The word "horizontal" is used to describe this technique because the game is frequently using time to determine the change in the music, and time is usually mapped to a horizontal axis.

This type of score has some advantages:

- Such scores are relatively easy to implement.
- The score is able to broadly switch musical ideas from one emotional context to another based on a game event.
- It can offer clean musical transitions.

Horizontal resequencing also has some disadvantages:

- Musical changes are sometimes not immediately realized so as to finish a musical thought or phrase.
- The transitions become more obvious when the game goes back and forth quickly between two musical states.

Horizontal resequencing techniques include branching, crossfading, and transitions. More information can be found about how to compose for horizontal resequencing in Chapter 8.

Vertical Remixing

Vertical remixing is a method of composition in which layers of music are added or taken away to create levels of intensity and emotion. For example, if the player is exploring a section of a level, he may hear a low drone; when an enemy approaches, the music fades in a percussion layer on top of the drone. The word "vertical" is used as a descriptor because that's how musicians typically see music in a score or a digital audio workstation; tracks are layered from top to bottom.

This method of scoring is useful for when the composer needs multiple quick changes to intensity in the score, where harmonic changes based on gameplay are not as important.

Some advantages of vertical remixing include the following:

- Vertical remixing is relatively easy to implement.
- You can quickly change the overall mood of the piece by adding or subtracting instruments.

Vertical remixing also has some disadvantages:

- The harmonic map is constantly looping, which disallows huge changes in the musical language based on a game event.
- The tempo map is also constant, which prevents the tempo from increasing or decreasing in response to the dramatic context.

More information can be found about how to compose for vertical remixing in Chapter 9.

MIDI Scores

MIDI scores (discussed further in Chapter 13) are not an interactive technique for composition by themselves, but because they are incredibly flexible in terms of what you can do in real time, we offer them up as an example here. MIDI scores offer the opportunity to have real-time control of music, including tempo shifts, harmonic adaptation, and instrumental rearrangement. These scores can also take advantage of the two previously mentioned interactive techniques, horizontal resequencing and vertical remixing.

MID scores offer the following advantages:

- MIDI scores offer lots of opportunities for real-time adaptive musical expression in a game context (e.g., transposition, tempo shifts).
- They offer more granularity in the music adaptivity because they are able to emulate real musicians changing their parts in real time.
- They are relatively easy to implement.

Disadvantages of a MIDI score include the following:

- The instruments are not as good as a real musician playing a real instrument (much of the nuance is lost).
- Generally these scores sound very synthesized; thus it's almost impossible to have a synthesized score sound like an 80-piece orchestra.

Advanced Interactive Scores

Throughout this book, you'll encounter numerous interactive music techniques, including the advanced techniques covered in Part III. On a more practical level, you'll find that horizontal resequencing and vertical remixing are the most commonly used methods in scoring today.

These interactive music techniques can be combined to create advanced interactive scores, but generally this requires a lot more participation from the programming teams. As a consequence, the planning, composing, and implementation of advanced interactive scores cost more than the same steps using other music techniques.

Advanced interactive music techniques are typically used when the interactive music needs to be much more detailed and precise, or when more control is needed. In particular, these techniques are used when developing music-based games or when creating algorithmic music for a game. You'll find more information about advanced interactive scores in Part III of this book.

> **note**
>
> As you begin to break down the interactive music structures within video games, you may start to recognize these techniques in the games that you play. This is known as hearing the "mechanics of the music system." The best interactive scores do a great job of hiding the interactive portions from the player. Even so, in many games it's easy to break an interactive score if you choose an action that was not well thought out in the design.
>
> For instance, suppose you set a trigger point to switch the music when the player enters the cave from the forest. If the interaction design is not well thought out, the player might go back and forth between the forest and the cave, causing a strange music glitch. In this instance, a timeout could have been used to not allow the user to play with the music in such a way. A timeout would be programmed so that the game would change the music every 15 seconds, ensuring that it doesn't sound like it's switching between songs on the radio.
>
> The music team essentially writes a set of rules for what the music will do, and then creates a smaller subset of rules that addresses specific cases (i.e., "In this case ignore the 'rules' and do this").

Music Control Inputs

In the previous chapter you read about how control inputs are changed into messages that are sent to the music engine. The music engine interprets these messages and adapts the music to synchronize to the player's actions. In this section, we'll briefly examine the practical side of setting up these inputs.

When game levels are being built, a music implementer may open the level map to add triggers at certain places within the level. When the game is played and the player goes from one area to another, he or she activates the trigger, which causes a message to be sent to the music engine. In addition to a specific switch, many level editors have the option to create entire zones (areas) that might send a message to the music engine.

Objects within the level editor can also have music attached directly to the object. This is useful in a game like *Portal II* (2011), where many of the objects actually emit music or sound, making up the overall ambience of the level. Likewise, this technique is valuable in a game like *Assassin's Creed III* (2012), which features actors singing an opera on a stage.

Other kinds of events may be accessible directly in the level editor, but many times a programmer may need to get involved to put hooks into the game program that send messages to the music engine. For instance, if the player gets ambushed by enemies—an event that should trigger a battle cue—the sending/receiving of the message is generally not done in a level editor, but rather needs to be implemented by the programmer on the team. These events probably also include world events (weather and time) and story development (plot point reached or puzzle solved).

> **note**
>
> The level editor is a tool that game designers and artists use to construct the levels in a game. These tools are built by the programming team to make it easy for non-programmers to create and change various aspects and parameters of the game.
>
> Sound designers and composers sometimes use these tools to place sounds within the game environment or world.
>
> Audio middleware such as Fmod and Wwise includes composer interfaces that can be considered a type of editor.
>
> These tools are generally not released with the game, but are used in the development process only.

Repetition, Randomization, and Surprise

Unfortunately, a game composer cannot write music for every single moment during which a player might be engaged in a game. There is not enough of a budget to individually score each player's experience. Consequently, the length of a player's game experience typically exceeds the length of the music created for that game. Many composers choose to write an interactive score that uses randomization and variation techniques to extend music cues without the need to write more music. Some of these techniques are highlighted here:

- Randomizing the order of the playback of different segments in the same cue.
- Creating alternate versions of the same cue. The game would pick randomly between the different versions. These alternate versions can have a varied instrumentation or a different take of a performance.
- Using a varying amount of silence in or between musical cues.

- Dropping out the music if a player is spending too long in a particular area.
- Composing secondary layers of music that may play on top of a cue during some of the performances, but not on others.

Whether you're trying to enhance the re-playability of your game or you have an open-world system that involves players coming back to the same area over and over, you have choices available that allow players to hear new versions of the same music, thereby increasing their enjoyment and avoiding repetition. Changing the music dynamically from play to play helps add the element of surprise in the music, extending the new gameplay experience.

On very large music teams, a music editorial and implementation team will frequently create alternate and derivative cues for variation editing from the music that the composer delivered. This is one reason that the composer frequently delivers full sessions of all the assets to the music implementation team. On smaller teams, the composer may personally build these derivative cues.

Review

The game production timeline is the overall flow from the initial concept of a game through its release. Spotting usually begins in the preproduction phase, while the primary music composition and production begin once the first playable prototype is finished (usually about halfway through the overall development timeline).

Game developers create game design documents (GDD) to use as a guide; these documents meticulously describe all of the features and assets of the game that is being developed. In addition, the GDD details how the game will be made, including schedules and timelines, and sometimes budgets.

Composers work with the game developer to spot the video game, discussing, level by level, how the music will be used to support the story. The spotting process includes defining the role of music, an outline for the main dramatic goals, points at which the music should play, the interactive plan, and notes on how the music will be structured. Cue sheets are used to describe and organize all of the music cues that will be used within a game, including start and end points, adaptive characteristics, and control inputs.

Video games are made up of various components, which are typically divided into four broad categories: user interface, gameplay, cinematics, and transitional elements.

The simplest type of game score does not have any interactive music at all, but rather uses a linear loop of music. Horizontal resequencing is a method of interactive composition where the music branches from one section to another once it reaches the end of a phrase. Vertical remixing is a method of composition in which layers of music are added or taken away to create levels of intensity and emotion. MIDI scores offer the opportunity to have real-time control of music, including tempo shifts, harmonic adaptation, and instrumental rearrangement.

Advanced interactive music techniques are typically used when the interactive music needs to be much more detailed and precise, or when more control is needed. In particular, these techniques are used when developing music-based games or when creating algorithmic music for a game.

Exercises

1. Interview a local game developer about the timeline of a project that this person recently completed. Make sure to inquire about when the developer hired the music composer and how the music timeline coincided with the overall schedule.

2. Create a cue sheet for a published game by collecting an inventory of music from a game, assessing the video game in terms of its structure, and categorizing the music assets by section.

3. Review game footage that uses the most common interactive music techniques and assess these techniques for their ability to engage the player.

4. Compare and contrast the music synchronization from a film to a game. Is one more successful than the other, and why?

CHAPTER 4

WORKING WITH A GAME DEVELOPMENT TEAM

The ability to work as part of a team is a vital trait that a video game composer needs to be successful. In this chapter you'll explore the relationship between a composer and a game development team. We'll begin by looking at the hierarchical structure in the game industry, then move on to the specifics of working directly with a team in terms of planning and organizing a project.

Who's in Charge?

A *game developer* is a company made up of experts who conceptualize, produce, design, and build games. It's not unusual for the development teams working on a large project to reach 100 or more specialists from all game disciplines. Experts who specialize in creating games include producers, artists, designers, audio specialists, and programmers.

Successful game developers include Blizzard (*Warcraft*), Naughty Dog (*Uncharted*), Bioware (*Mass Effect*), Maxis (*The Sims*), Bungie (*Destiny*), PopCap (*Bejeweled*), Zynga (*Farmville*), 2K Irrational (*Bioshock*), Harmonix (*Dance Central*), and many more.

A *game publisher* is a company that funds and oversees the development of a video game. Because publishers fund the game developers, they work closely with the developer to monitor the production and development of a video game to make sure it stays on track. In addition, they provide creative oversight and critiques of the ongoing development. Video game publishers are typically responsible for the manufacturing, marketing, and distribution of the finished video game.

Successful video game publishers include companies like Electronic Arts, Activision, ZeniMax, Konami, Capcom, Ubisoft, and Valve. These publishers usually own one or more game developers. Such so-called third-party developers include Infinity Ward (Activision), Bioware (Electronic Arts), and Bethesda Game Studios (ZeniMax).

A *platform holder* is a company that manufactures a game console, such as Microsoft (Xbox One), Sony (PlayStation 4), and Nintendo (Wii U). Platform holders issue licenses to publishers and game developers to develop games for the consoles.

These platform holders are also publishers that fund game development on their platforms. In addition, platform holders own their internal game development teams that design and develop games exclusively for their consoles, or assist with the production of games by an outside game developer. Developers that are fully owned by a platform holder are called first-party developers. Examples include Microsoft's 343 Studios (*Halo*), Sony's Naughty Dog (*Uncharted*), and Nintendo's Intelligent Systems (*Advance Wars, Fire Emblem*).

Game Development Teams

Although a small game can be made by a single individual working on all disciplines of the game, the creation of many games requires large teams with many people working together to use their individual specialties and expertise. In general, small casual and web games have teams ranging from 5 to 30 people, whereas a large console game may have a team ranging in size from 30 to 200 people. Specialties that make up the game development teams include the following:

- **Production:** Producer, Project Manager, Lead Tester, Game Tester, Quality Assurance
- **Design:** Design Director, Game Designer, Lead Designer, Level Designer, Writer/ Scriptwriter, Map Builder, Level Editor
- **Programming:** Lead Programmer, Graphics, AI, Multiplayer, Network, Engine, Tools Programmer, Systems Designer, Scripter, UI Programmer
- **Visual Arts:** Art Director, GUI Designer, Graphic Designer, Illustrator, Storyboard Artist, 3D Model Builder, 3D Cut-Scene Artist, 3D Character Builder/Animator, Level Builder, Art Director, Art Technician, Environment Artist
- **Audio:** Composer, Sound Designer, Audio Implementer, Audio Programmer, Dialog
- **Quality Assurance (QA):** QA Lead, Tester
- **Management:** Executive or Senior Producers, Owners and Partners

Audio Teams

The audio team for a AAA title is made up of many different specialists from music, sound design, dialog, and programming. Here is a list of the various roles across the entire audio department:

- **Publisher:** Audio Director, Music Director, Music Supervisor
- **Music Team:** Composer, Assistant Composer, Music Editor, Music Implementer, Music Recording Engineer, Orchestrator/Copyist, Musicians/Singers, Music Producer
- **Sound Design Team:** Sound Designer, Field Recorder, Foley Artist, Sound Implementer, Audio Programmer
- **Dialog Team:** VO Producer, Recording Engineer, Actors, Localization Team

On a small project with an overall game budget of less than $400,000, a single individual may handle all of the audio needs (music, sound design, dialog). On small to medium-size AAA console projects, there will be a small audio team consisting of a composer, several sound designers, and an implementer.

On extremely large projects (e.g., *God of War, Little Big Planet*) that involve multiple composers, the game publisher may have an in-house audio director who hires and supervises the overall audio production. There will also probably be an entire sound design team consisting of six or more individuals.

Finding the Composer

The composer is hired by the game developer or publisher. During the preproduction phase of game development, a call is sometimes made for composers to submit demos for the project. These composers submit reels and possibly demo material for the game. There are sometimes fees involved for writing these demos, but rarely does this token fee cover the time or cost of actually creating the demo.

On AAA projects, composers have been known to spend thousands of dollars on demos, using outside studios and live musicians to try and win projects. In contrast, small projects might not have a demo process at all. If the developer has already worked with a specific composer and they have a good working relationship, the developer may be more likely to hire that composer again without any kind of formal demo process.

If the composer writes a demo for a game, the publisher may ask that the composer to relinquish all rights to the work so that it becomes wholly owned by the developer. In these instances, the publisher pays full market rate for the music by the minute. In other cases, when the demo rate is smaller and the composer is not chosen for the project, the composer will usually be able to retain the rights to use the piece for other projects. Composers should always nail down the specifics of who will own the rights to the music before any writing begins on a project.

Along with the demo, composers may be required to submit an estimate of what it will cost to create the music for the game. In general, the developer/publisher will have already budgeted for the music, but depending on the company's experience that amount may or may not reflect the actual "market rate" for the composer or actual costs of production.

The game development team listens to the materials and reads through each composer's previous credits to determine which candidate is the best fit with the current project. The producer also examines the estimates to make sure it can afford the cost of the music composition process and then hires the best candidate.

This process of hiring composers and audio talent is discussed in greater detail in Chapter 25, "The Life of a Video Game Composer," and Chapter 29, "How Composers Find Work."

Collaborating and Approving the Music

The composer works with the game development leads from the various departments to start conceptualizing the overall creative vision for the music. Musical style guides are created to help establish the overall tone of the project. Frequently the composer will compose additional test tracks for various scenes to establish the overall creative direction. As the creative vision starts to take shape, the overall music schedule is worked through.

Composers generally meet with the teams once a week to go over the latest music cues, get the latest news and updates from the development teams, discuss challenges, and go over the upcoming schedule.

The lead game designer, director, producer, or business owner typically is responsible for approving any music cues. These individuals usually lead the overall creative direction of the project. If an audio director is working on the job at the publisher level, he or she will control the overall creative direction of the music and collaborate with the lead game designer or director.

When working with a developer, it's extremely important to know who the music decision maker is with regard to *signing off* or approving musical assets for the game.

Defining the Tone and Voice of a Game

It's important to ask tough questions when composing music. When you listen to your music, can you hear the characters, the locations, or the storyline in the music? Can you point to a specific instrument and say, "That instrument represents the protagonist in the story"? Many of the best composers write from the story itself. When you ask them about instruments or passages in the music, they'll describe a particular character in the story, or the scene where the music takes place.

The compositions that have this kind of depth leave players with lasting memories of the music. This is especially true of many of the *Final Fantasy* games composed by Nobuo Uematsu. These worlds come alive partly due to the fact that you can hear thematic material announcing characters or places in the game universe. Wataru Hokoyama's score to *Afrika* (2008) is also brilliant, featuring the use of animal themes in his music.

The composer and the game development team work together to establish the overall vision of the music, as well as the adaptive systems that control its interactivity.

Unique and groundbreaking scores may help sell more copies of the game. Fans of Nobuo Uematsu or Marty O'Donnell, for example, will buy video games just because they composed the music for certain games. In addition, Austin Wintory's Grammy nomination for the indie game *Journey* contributed to the wider recognition of the merits of game music, and may have been responsible for selling additional copies of the game.

In the case of *Journey* (2012), the overall role that the music has in the game greatly influences how it resonates with the player. There is very little sound design and no dialog in this game, so the music had the room to make a significant contribution to the gameplay experience.

Composers and game developers should strive to push the envelope in terms of both unique designs of interactive music systems and the quality of the music itself. Both large-budget games (*Bioshock*, 2007, by Gary Shyman) and small-budget games (*Vessel*, 2012, by Jon Hopkins) are making incredible leaps of innovation with music.

How does one create a unique music experience? This effort requires visionary composers and teams that are willing to take risks on music creation and design. It also usually requires some experimentation. It's easy to copy and steal ideas from other games; it's much more time consuming to be truly innovative. Make sure that you allocate some time for experimentation—doing so will pay off by improving the audience response.

Prioritizing the instrumentation (instruments and, equally important, the ways in which they are used) and the production applied (to affect timbre) can be just as crucial for creating a truly immersive and custom experience as the actual composition. Composers should be careful to not discount the importance of these factors, because in many instances paying attention to this kind of detail is what makes the score impactful and gets its author on people's radar as a composer who strives to rise above the noise of most music in the marketplace. Production can be a major differentiator of composers' skill.

COMPOSER PERSPECTIVE

Noriyuki Iwadare

Let's imagine you are requested to write a "happy" piece or a "sad" piece. The images of these emotions are probably different for everyone: for you, for your client, and for the general audience (gamer). Depending on our past experiences, times, places, and objects are all associated with various thoughts and feelings that differ from person to person. Considering all of these variables, it is a very difficult decision to choose the "right one" and create your piece out of it.

It is very important to first meet with the producer or the director face to face to discuss the project at hand. During this discussion, many of the vague or confusing factors should be addressed; oftentimes, the composer's goal becomes very clear by the end. In my case, many times during this initial meeting I pretty much finish composing in my head.

Also, to further narrow and define my understanding, I ask my clients to present me with a picture that best represents the music they are looking for. The impression that you construct from such a picture is very helpful because it narrows down your interpretations.

If the music is still difficult to define, I request that the client give me a few reference songs that fit the scene. However, extreme caution is necessary if you do this, because the piece that you write should not sound too much like the reference tracks. Be aware that the client may not necessarily be talking about the entire song. He could be saying that he wants the music to sound like one tiny part of the reference track.

It is also a good idea to submit multiple demo tracks to your client instead of just one. This way, instead of responding with a flat "yes" or "no," the client can tell you which demo track best fits his or her desired image.

Assessing the Music

At some point after the composer has written some music, he or she will need to get it approved by the client. As discussed previously, it's important to know who will be reviewing the music and deciding whether the music needs revisions or works well as it is. This person may be the lead game designer, game director, audio director, or producer of the project.

Music is incredibly subjective. This fact sometimes makes it difficult for a composer to get good feedback when presenting music to the client. For instance, if you ask clients whether they like a piece of music, they will use their musical memory to assess whether they like the music. If your music sounds like a song that reminds them of a breakup with a significant other, there is a good chance they might dislike the music.

A better question to ask when discussing music is, "Does this music fit the level and what we are trying to accomplish?" This takes some of the subjectivity of "I like it" or "I don't like it" out of the response. Assess music on based on its function instead of whether the client likes the piece.

Whenever possible, try to get your music heard in the context of how it will be used. There may not be an option to have it actually implemented, but you could have the cue delivered and synced to rough gameplay footage. Often, a client will react very differently when a cue is heard in context versus out of context.

In addition, many clients don't have a musical background—which means that when they give feedback on a piece of music, you'll need to reinterpret those comments as musical changes that you can make to your composition. Here are some sample questions you might ask a developer when listening to a musical cue:

- How well is the music telling the story or revealing the emotional state the player should be feeling?
- Is the piece unique and original?
- Does the music follow the initial musical vision?
- How well does the music sync to the gameplay?
- Does the musical ensemble feel right for the scene, or is it too intimate, or too large?
- Does the music develop nicely over time?
- How are the pacing and flow of the track? Are they too fast or too slow?

These questions will help eliminate some of the subjectivity and get specific feedback from the game developer, thereby allowing the composer to quickly produce the revisions needed. In many cases the contract between the developer and the composer may limit the amount of revisions to a piece of music before incurring additional costs.

What if the composer is not the right fit? Sometimes the game developer and composer just can't agree on the same vision for the music. If after several rounds of revisions the composer and developer can't agree, it may be time for both parties to part ways. If this is the case, generally the composer gets a fee for the work done up to that point, and then the contractual relationship ends.

COMPOSER PERSPECTIVE

Yoko Shimomura

Many different problems come up when working on a project [laugh]. When my opinion differs from that of the director, sometimes I have to argue head on, almost to the point of fighting. When that happens, that moment becomes very tense, but interestingly, afterward my relationship with the director becomes tighter and bound with more trust.

When I become discouraged because I find myself stuck on a piece that just doesn't work the way I want it to, I take an impromptu trip to change my mood. At other times, I just relentlessly distress myself to put a lot of pressure on myself. When the problem is technical, I ignore any rules or theories and just think of any possible solution that I can. I try methods that others might find surprising or unconventional.

Preparing for Music Production

Once the composer has been selected and the overall creative direction established, the primary music development and production begins. This section discusses the overall team workflow during the development process, the establishment of schedules, collaborative tools that game developers use on projects, and the process of implementation and testing of the music.

Team Workflow

Many game developers use *Agile software development* practices when creating a game. This method supports iterative and incremental development. Such company practices are supported with planning and organizational software. The Agile method most commonly used in video game development is *Scrum*.

Scrum is a method in which a project is managed through goals and tasks that are organized into timeframes called sprints. This method helps producers manage the project by tracking how many hours it takes to complete these tasks and goals, thereby giving the producers an overall picture of whether the project will be completed on time.

At the beginning of a sprint, all of the department heads (e.g., art, programming, audio, production) meet to plan out the next set of goals for the project and turn these goals into tasks. During the production, teams generally have short *standing* meetings every day until the end of the sprint. These daily meetings are called standing meetings because if everyone is standing, they'll be short (usually about 15 minutes). The task of the meetings is to communicate about the progress everyone made yesterday on the project, what they are planning to do tomorrow, and whether anything is blocking their progress.

At the end of any given sprint, there are two meetings: a presentation and discussion of the outcome of the sprint with the stakeholders, and a postmortem meeting to discuss how the sprint went and how things could be improved moving forward.

The audio director for the project is usually required to attend all the initial planning meetings, including many of the daily Scrum meetings. This audio director also will essentially have an audio version of the daily Scrum with his or her own audio team. The composer will probably be required to attend some of these meetings, and possibly the sprint planning and wrap-up meetings.

If you're a composer (without an audio director) on the project, you'll probably be attending the kickoff and concluding sprint meetings, and checking in at least once a week with the development team. As a composer, it's extremely helpful to be as informed as possible about the progress on a project.

When working with a developer, it's important to establish who the primary contact people are for logistics and for creative approvals. Then, find out how the company works internally so you can attend the appropriate meetings. Although it can be time consuming, the more contact you have with the developer through meetings, phone calls, video chats, and other means, the happier the developer will be.

For a contract composer, it may be challenging to fit into a company dynamic because you'll be working offsite. Generally, having more communication with the developer will result in a much stronger relationship and a better team dynamic.

Setting Schedules and Milestones

At the beginning of music production, one of the other items that needs thought and planning is the overall music production schedule. This should line up with the overall timeline of the project, and evolve from the working style of the developer. Whenever the game developer updates its schedule, the music schedule should be updated to reflect any changes. Generally music cues go through a review process and cycle that consists of the following phases:

1. Initial presentation and first review
2. Revisions and second review

3. Implementation in the game

4. Revision to match the gameplay

5. Live music recording

6. Final music mix

7. Final implementation in the game

There will often not be a limit on how many revisions are required. A composer should plan on revising music cues until they are approved and should make an effort to receive clear and consistent feedback on all versions of the music. The composer contract often includes a clause stating how many revisions are included (usually three), and the overage costs after that limit has been reached.

Along with the music production process, various milestones will signal the overall progress being made in the game's development. These milestones were discussed in Chapter 3, "Spotting the Game." Agile software development practices influence these milestone dates, as they are divided up into smaller sprints or goals. As a composer, you'll want to keep track of how the schedule may shift and notify the developer about conflicts well in advance if its timetable is starting to shift later.

Considering the Technology

Technology is an important piece of any game that's being made. Many composers have multiple computers in their studios that they use for creating and recording the music, as well as testing the playable game prototype that the game developer is creating.

Many games being created today are being developed in Windows environments. In contrast, many composers create their music in Mac environments. Because game composers generally work on multiple operating systems, they should be comfortable with both Windows and Mac systems.

Console and handheld game manufacturers typically create special versions of their products that are intended specifically for developers to make games with dev kits (short for "development kits"). Generally these dev kits can be purchased only by a licensed game developer; that is, they are not offered for sale to the general public. Games that will be released on a specific console or handheld are then tested with these dev kits. They allow the game developer to load and play builds of their games while they're developing the game test features and gameplay.

If you're an audio implementer at a game developer, you might work with these units while listening to and modifying the audio directly on the dev kit. If you're a composer working on a game project, you will probably have a lot less interaction with development kits.

Some games are not playable unless you have access to a development kit. Thus, unless you can be on site at the developer's studio with the development kit, you won't be able to play the game. In this scenario, the game developer may capture movies of gameplay and send them to the composer to allow the composer to get a feel for the game, as well as to hear how the music is working on a particular game level.

Obviously, the technology that the game is being built in has a great effect on the composer's working environment. For instance, if you're developing an iOS game or an Android game, you can use software emulators to play these games on standard computers.

Some games use specialized technology that may or may not affect how the composer approaches the music. For instance, if you're working on a music game with a specialized instrument controller like *Samba de Amigo* (1999), then having the technology available during the composition process may help the overall creative direction. If you're working on a game in which specialized technology will have a direct impact on the music, then you may want to see if you can acquire the technology.

The technology used will have other implications, as well, including dictating which audio file format to use and determining how much music you can have in a game. Chapter 22, "Mixing and Exporting Audio Files to the Game Engine," outlines the details of files you need to deliver to the game team based on the technology.

Sharing Documents

Many off-the-shelf technologies may be used throughout the game development process, including collaborative document sharing through Google Docs or Office365. Files are sent back and forth using technologies like Dropbox and YouSendIt. These technologies keep changing all the time, so it's important to keep abreast of the latest innovation—gamers are not afraid to use cutting-edge technology to help their workflows.

Because many game products are kept highly confidential, companies may choose higher security options with regard to files and their transfer. In these cases, companies may use virtual private network (VPN) technology, which allows vendors that are located outside of the developer to have direct access to the company's private network. Developers may also build their own proprietary software that they use to share files or use other technologies such as Secure File Transfer Protocol (SFTP). These technologies can be much more secure and successful at keeping files private than other methods.

If you're working as a composer on a project, you should coordinate with the developer to determine how they would prefer to send and receive files.

Collaboration Technology

Game developers also have a wide array of collaborative tools at their disposal, which allows teams to share game assets and update/make changes in games in real time. These tools make collaborating on a project a truly remarkable experience. When the artist updates the level backgrounds, for example, the composer can see the new images in the test build almost immediately.

In many settings, game developers use *source control technologies* like CVS, Subversion, GIT, and Perforce to work together. These technologies allow developers to download the latest build of the game and have the team members make individual updates to the game. The files are hosted on a server called a *repository*. This repository keeps track of all changes made to the game files by username, so that the developer can go back a step if needed.

You should be familiar with the following terms when using these technologies:

- **Check Out.** This term is used when a user downloads the initial build of the game to his or her local machine from a network.
- **Update.** This term is used when a user updates his or her local build of the game from the main repository. This action will download all the updated files from the primary server.
- **Add.** This term is used when you want to add a file into a project.
- **Commit.** This term is used when you copy your local file changes back to the main server to distribute them to all the other users on the project.

Sometimes there are conflicts between one user's files and the files already on the server. Such conflicts may arise if two people worked on the same file at the same time. These team members will need to resolve which file is the correct one before they can commit new assets back to the server.

When changes are made to the server, the user who is making the changes adds comments to the commit so that other users can see what he or she updated. Each update is also labeled with a version number to keep track of the builds.

Composers may sometimes be given access to the files on a server so that they can play the latest version of the game. In other cases, the developer may send builds or capture video footage of the game so that the composer can see the music integrated into the game.

Audio implementers are usually working with source control all the time, making changes to the actual game build. They update music and sound files, change when a sound might play in a game, and update the audio mix of the game. Composers who have the technical skills to use source control have an advantage because they are able to get the latest builds more quickly, see how their music is working in the game, and make any changes necessary.

Game Testing

One of the important phases in game development is making sure that the game is running the way it's supposed to. During the development process, game developers keep track of the features that aren't working through tracking software. Examples of tracking software include Trac, Jira, and Perforce.

Features that aren't working in a game are frequently referred to as *bugs*. When a bug is discovered (e.g., the music is playing at the wrong time), they are logged in the tracking software as a ticket. These bugs are then tracked with the ticketing system; each bug is assigned a priority and assigned to a person who will fix the bug. As each bug is resolved, the corresponding ticket is closed. This process continues until there are no more tickets.

Audio implementers use these systems to keep track of their progress in fixing bugs and issues with the music and sound effect systems. Composers who are working on a very small team may also be assigned tickets to fix an audio asset that won't play or some other audio issue. Although it's not a mandatory skill for composers to understand and be able to work some of these systems, it can be an advantage in some working environments.

Review

A game developer is a company made up of experts who conceptualize, produce, design, and build games. They employ specialists in the following areas: production, design and game design, programming, visual arts, audio, and management.

A game publisher is a company that funds and oversees the development of a video game. Small casual and web games have game development teams ranging from 5 to 30 people, whereas a large console game may have a team ranging in size from 30 to 200 people.

Audio teams are made up of many specialists in music, sound design, dialog, and programming. On smaller projects, a single individual may handle all of the audio needs (music, sound design, dialog).

Composers submit demos for projects; this process may or may not involve a demo fee. Once hired, composers meet with the development teams about once a week to go over the latest music cues, get the latest news and updates, discuss challenges, and review the upcoming schedule. The lead game designer, director, producer, or business owner typically is responsible for approving any music cues.

Creating an innovative and unique music score requires experimentation. The composer and the game development team work together to establish the overall vision for the music, and adaptive systems that control its interactivity. Whenever possible, the composer should try to get the music heard in the context of how it will be used in the actual game. Often, a client will react very differently when a cue is heard in context versus out of context.

When assessing music, it's important to avoid the question "Do you like it?" and instead focus on the question "Does the music fit the level and what we're trying to accomplish?"

Many game developers use Agile software development practices when creating a game; this popular method of development supports iterative and incremental development. An Agile method commonly used by video game developers is Scrum. With Scrum, a project is managed through goals and tasks that are organized into timeframes called sprints.

Schedules and meeting times need to be worked out with the developer. Whenever the game developer updates its schedule, the music schedule should be updated to reflect any changes.

Because games are usually created on Windows machines, game composers should be comfortable with both Mac and Windows operating systems.

Game developers that are building a game for a console use a modified console made specifically for developers called a dev kit (development kit). Often, the evolving game can be played only on this dev kit, so composers may need to visit the developer to play test builds of the game.

Many off-the-shelf technologies may be used throughout the game development process for sharing documents, including Google Docs and Dropbox. Projects with higher security needs might use custom sharing software or VPNs.

In addition, game developers may use source control technologies like CVS, Subversion, GIT, and Perforce to work together. These technologies allow developers to download the latest build of the game and have the team members make individual updates to the game.

Throughout the game development process, developers track the progress of features that aren't working through bug tracking systems like Trac, Jira, and Perforce. Bugs are managed as tickets, which are in turn assigned to individuals to fix. When a bug has been fixed, the ticket is closed.

Although it's not a mandatory skill for composers to know and use many of these technologies, it can be an advantage in some working environments.

Exercises

1. Go through some of the games that you own and identify the publishers, game developers, and creative leads who worked on the project.

2. Assess a musical soundtrack by asking the following questions:

   - How well does the music tell the story or signal which emotional state the player should be feeling?

   - Is the piece unique and original?

   - How well does the music sync to the gameplay?

   - Does the musical ensemble feel right for the scene, or is it too intimate, or too large?

   - Does the music develop nicely over time?

   - How are the pacing and flow of the track? Are they too fast or too slow?

CHAPTER 5

VIDEO GAME COMPOSITION OVER THE PAST 40 YEARS

Video game audio has come a long way since the first blips and bleeps of *Pong* in 1972. Although the topic of video game music history would fill several books by itself, this chapter aims to give you a short introduction to some of the highlights of video game composition and music technology over the past 40 years.

Why Video Game History Is Important

Why learn about video game history? There are a couple reasons. One is so that you're not walking in someone else's footsteps. Another is to learn about how limitations led composers to unexpected innovation.

Across the history of video game music, composers have faced many technological limitations that made it difficult to create music. Some of these limitations have included:

- Limited number of voices
- Inability to play certain pitches
- Lack of transitional events and traditional sync
- Limited synthesis
- Limited sequence and sample memory
- Difficult and time consuming to program

Because of these limitations, many composers were forced to innovate in unusual ways. Limitations allow many writers to concentrate their creative abilities on one particular aspect of composition. For instance, when there were a limited number of voices and timbres, composers focused their energies on creating memorable melodies because it was one of the ways they could innovate. Often video game composers speak about the fact that limitations actually allow them to center their ideas and write more quickly than if they had no restrictions as all.

Even today, many of these limitations still exist depending on the platform. For example, composers almost always face memory and voice limitations, and they lack adequate interactive music technologies. As the technology has advanced, composers have demanded more from each platform, including surround technologies, advanced interactive music capabilities, and real-time DSP. These demands force even the latest generation of consoles to work harder. Consequently, the composer must always keep the limitations of the platform in mind when composing for a specific system.

As this technology has advanced within video games, composers have been forced to adapt to new techniques and ways of working. This chapter breaks down music into several different eras representing a particular aspect of hardware or technological innovation:

- The dawn of coin-operated machines
- The ascent of the arcade machine
- The game console revolution
- The evolution of PC gaming
- The rise of handheld and network games
- The advancement of audio middleware
- The evolution of the modern gaming platform

Obviously, all the important advances in the area of music and sound cannot be covered in this short chapter. If you want a more complete perspective, consider reading Karen Collins's book, *Game Sound: An Introduction to the History, Theory, and Practice of Video Game Music and Sound Design*.

The Dawn of Coin-Operated Machines

Similar to the next chapter, which discusses experimental music, this section aims to give you some perspective on the role of nondigital games throughout the twentieth century and their part in informing and inspiring composers of digital games. Prior to the advent of video games with sound in the 1970s, companies built many games for novelty arcades throughout the twentieth century. These coin-operated devices included pinball machines, musical machines, gambling and slot machines, mechanical driving games, and shooting games, among others.

Companies like Gottlieb, Mills Novelty Company, Williams, Sega, Taito, Bally Entertainment, Midway, and Genco were popular manufacturers of electromechanical games. These machines frequently used sonic feedback to indicate to players how well they were doing. Many employed simple bells, ringers, electromechanical chimes, and buzzers for audio feedback. Since the devices were mechanical, many of the motor sounds (clicking, whirring, and sliding) could also be heard as the machine was being played, adding to the overall aural experience.

Although these electromechanical games were popular through the end of the 1960s, the introduction of computer-based games in the 1970s led to a decline of manufacturing in electromechanical games.

Musical Machines

Near the turn of the twentieth century, manufacturers created sophisticated self-playing mechanical musical instruments that would play when you dropped a coin into them. Similar to the pneumatic player-pianos that came before them, these new instruments primarily used electrical current to control the various instruments. For example, the Mills Novelty Company created the *Violano* (1909), which was a mechanical violin that was able to play back music similar to player-piano rolls. The Mills Company went on to create many of the subsequent novelty machines, including slots and games.

Gambling and Slot Machines

Gambling and slot machines influenced analog sound feedback in gaming. In 1895, one of the first mechanical slot machines, the *Liberty Bell* created by Charles Fey, included a bell that would ring if the player won by matching three or more shapes. By 1930, the Mills Company had introduced a secondary bell sound to indicate winning the double jackpot prize.

Slot machines continued to grow in popularity throughout the twentieth century with the introduction of the first electromechanical slot machine developed by Bally, the *Money Honey* in 1964. This device used an electronic bell to signal a win. In addition, the winning sound of the coins dropping into the coin catch pans helped attract players to the machines.

Novelty Machines, Shooting Games, and Racing Games

In the 1920s, several novelty companies included an internal phonograph for audio playback, including the fortune-telling machine *Verbille* developed by the Mills Novelty Company. Phonograph technology in coin-operated machines is prone to damage or malfunction, however. As technology advanced, the 1950s arcade machines began to use tape playback, including Prophetron Company's *Zoltan*, which delivered fortunes from these recordings, and Williams's *Peppy the Clown*, which danced to music. Tape playback was more reliable than the phonograph recordings earlier in the century.

The mid-1960s brought small electronic circuits to many mechanical shooting games to play back the various weapons sounds and emphasize feedback and engagement with the player. Sega's *Gun Fight* from 1970 was one such device. From 1969 to 1976, many electromechanical games used eight-track tapes to provide sound, including Midway's *Chopper* and *Haunted House* games. Many of these games had much better-sounding soundtracks than the games using the earlier-generation video game synthesizers. Several racing games also employed tape loops, including Sega's *Sand Buggy*.

Pinball Machines

Pinball has existed in various forms since 1770, when it was known as bagatelle. In 1871, the first bells were added to the pinball machine. Nevertheless, it wasn't until 1933 that Pacific Amusement's *Contact* introduced an electric bell into the game, with a solenoid being used to trigger it. In addition, the analog replay knocker was used to reward players for replaying the game. The addition of various sounds and lights helped attract players and spectators to the game. Bally's *Bumper*, introduced in 1936, was the first pinball machine to use pinball bumpers that rapidly accelerated the ball in a particular direction during gameplay. This game was also the first to introduce electromechanical scoring. The year 1947 saw the introduction of the modern "flipper," which expanded the game's popularity.

In the 1960s, many pinball machines added a three-tone chime mechanism to give player feedback such as scoring and game over. These chime mechanisms were used originally in Gotlieb's *Cleopatra*, *Sinbad*, and *Joker Poker* machines. It wasn't until the 1970s that pinball started using electronic sounds and digital scoring. These electronic sounds were produced by the same computer circuits found in many early arcade games. In 1979, Williams introduced the first electronic speech pinball game, *Gorgar*, which also featured a heartbeat sound that sped up during longer gameplay.

The pinball machine *Road Kings* (1986), from WMS, was the first game to use frequency modulation (FM) synthesis; thus it had a musical score. FM synthesis was replaced by sample playback in Data East's *Batman* (1991) pinball machine, which used a customized sample playback chip. WMS further pushed the state of the art forward with the first system of its kind to use completely digitized music; SFX led the way with a custom MP3-like audio compression system in a pinball machine.

Throughout the 1980s and 1990s, pinball machines continued to advance with emphasis on the latest sound technologies borrowed from popular computer-based arcade games.

The Ascent of the Arcade Machine

Ralph Baer's invention of the table-tennis–like game *Pong* in 1966 ushered in a video game revolution. Atari's release of the game, and its short audio blips and bleeps, into popular culture in 1972 paved the way for the career that many of us take for granted today—the pursuit of making video games for a living.

Circuits

In those days, computer games were built using multiple circuit boards, all of which worked together to feed an image to a cathode ray tube (CRT). The player interacted with the game using a small controller, while the CRT fed the player the game experience. These early circuit boards had some very basic sound capabilities that were able to play back basic waveforms.

As the computer game market grew throughout the 1970s and 1980s, the design of these circuits became more intricate as the games increased in complexity. In the early days, many of the sound circuits were custom built. For example, *Sea Wolf* (1976), a submarine game in which you targeted ships with torpedoes, used a custom sound circuit that played back various unique sounds.

Boot Hill from 1977 featured simple monophonic melodies that played before levels (the nursery rhyme "Pop Goes the Weasel"), when someone was killed (Chopin's "Funeral March"), and during the game ending (Bugler's "Assembly").

The game *Space Invaders* (1978) was created and designed by Tomohiro Nishikado. The game itself requires the player to defend his or her planet from space invaders that are slowly marching down to the planet. In this game, Tomohiro also created one of the first examples of an adaptive score. The background music is composed of just four quarter-note pitches that begin repeating at about the speed of your heart rate (60 bpm). Then, as the game gets more exciting, the tempo begins to increase, reflecting the impeding peril of the alien attack. This corresponds to the real-time player experience, having his or her heart rate increase as the danger nears.

Additional example games from this period include *Night Driver* (1976), *Asteroids* (1979), *Lunar Lander* (1979), and *Defender* (1980). Games such as *Defender* required very low-level assembly language programming for the sound—which was hardly musician friendly, and challenging even for the most experienced programmers.

The Programmable Sound Generator and the Rise of Melody

In 1980, several games released by Namco used a programmable sound generator (PSG), including the first arcade game to feature a constant melodic background soundtrack, *Rally-X* (composed by Nobuyuki Ohnogi). *Pac-Man* was also released at the same time with the same hardware; its soundtrack was composed by Toshio Kai. It was one of the first games to feature a prominent melodic theme when you started the game, as well as music during the interstitial vignettes that would play between levels.

With the introduction of dedicated programmable sound generators in the early 1980s by manufacturers like General Instruments, Texas Instruments, and Yamaha, sound generation was made easier. Game sound was still difficult and extremely time consuming to program. Many game composers throughout this period had to know how to program computers. The early PSGs typically had the capability of playing back three simultaneous voices at a time, which might alternate between the playback of sound effects and music.

Games increased in musical complexity because of the use of the PSG, while memory was still very limited. Games became more focused on creating short memorable melodies that would play back during gameplay. These sound generators had several basic sound waves that they could play, including the following options:

- Sine
- Sawtooth
- Square
- Triangle
- Noise

In addition to the basic waveforms, developers could access a volume envelope on each voice that provided for ADSR (attack, decay, sustain, release) to change the overall volume characteristics of a given sound.

Continuing the innovation on the musical front, one of the first games to feature adaptive song switching was *Frogger*, released in 1981. The game featured Japanese children's songs and would switch from song to song when the player reached the top of the screen with the frog after navigating a street and river. This expanded song palette enhanced the overall player experience and offered some relief to the more repetitive themes of other games.

In addition to PSGs, a few game developers were still experimenting with different ways to produce sound. In 1981, Pacific Novelty's *Thief* used analog tape loops to play back police radio chatter during gameplay. Tape loops allowed games to break away from their normal synthetic waveform boundaries. Other games that used tape loops during the 1980s included *NATO Defense* and *Shark Attack*.

Yuriko Keino's innovative score for the game *Dig Dug* in 1982 featured a song that would play only when the main character was moving around the screen. The player was able to start and stop the music by moving the character around on the screen.

In 1983, Bally Midway collaborated with the rock band Journey to create a video game based around the band. Instrumental arrangements of their music were played back during gameplay using a three-voice PSG synthesizer. When the player reached the end of the game, Journey's song "Don't Stop Believing" was played back using an audio cassette player within the cabinet. Although *Journey* is widely regarded as one of the worst games of all time, it is mentioned here because of its innovative use of licensed music during this time period and the way in which the limited technology played a role in its development.

Digital-to-analog converters in this period were sometimes used in arcade machines to reproduce sampled tones, but their usage was limited because of the high price of memory. The game *Gyruss* (1983), which featured J. S. Bach's *Toccata* and *Fugue in D minor*, used the DAC for the music soundtrack. Games also began using speech synthesis, which allowed games to communicate to the player; examples include *Berzerk* (1980) and *Q*bert* (1982).

Additional example games from this period include *Galaxians* (1979), *Donkey Kong* (1981), *Ms. Pac-Man* (1982), and *Mappy* (1983).

Laserdisc Games

Beginning in 1982, several video games were produced using laserdisc technologies. A laserdisc is a collection of prerendered audio and video segments that can be played back in random sequences. One of the first popular games to use this technology was *Dragon's Lair* (1983), whose soundtrack was composed by Chris Stone. The laserdisc technology was a precursor to the CD-ROM technology of the 1990s. Because the segments were prerendered, the composer could use any technology or live musicians desired to produce the music. In *Dragon's Lair*, Stone used the sampler Emu Emulator and the synthesizer Memory Moog for all of the music, giving it a distinctive sound for this generation of arcade games.

Additional example games from this period include *Astron Belt* (1983), *M.A.C.H. 3* (1983), *Space Ace* (1984), and *Dragon's Lair II: Time Warp* (1991).

The Golden Age of Arcades

The early 1980s saw enormous growth in arcade machines. The processors and sound circuits improved, allowing for better games at the arcade. In 1984, arcade machines began to use FM sound chips (YM2151), which replaced the PSG and allowed for eight simultaneous voices and much more sophisticated music. One of the first games to take advantage of this chip was *Marble Madness* (1984), whose soundtrack was composed by Brad Fuller and Hal Canon.

Many game manufacturers began to use these FM sound chips in their arcade games throughout the rest of the 1980s, including Namco, Sega, and Atari. In turn, many composers began to create scores that focused on melodic development and progression. Hiroshi Kawaguchi was one of the popular composers of that era, composing music for *Space Harrier* (1985), *OutRun* (1986), and *After Burner* (1987).

From 1988 through the 1990s, stand-up arcade machines continued to innovate, but faced a sharp drop in their profitability after the introduction of the home console and the rise in PC gaming. Until that time, arcade machines had used better graphics and sound technologies that made them worthy rivals of the first generation of home consoles (Atari 2700, Intellivision). As the home technology caught up with the arcade offerings, many of the denizens of the arcade in the United States shifted to playing at home.

Social Arcade Games

Although arcades declined in the United States throughout the 1990s, they remained a popular social retreat for young adults throughout Asia and Australia. This fueled innovation in many multiplayer social games, including fighting games, racing games, and rhythm action games.

In the early 1990s, multiplayer arcade fighting games such as *Street Fighter 2* (1991), *Mortal Kombat* (1992), *Virtua Cop* (1994), and *Tekken* (1994), became extremely popular. Music and SFX played an even more important role in many game studios. The game *Street Fighter 2* (1991), with a soundtrack composed by Yoko Shimomura, earned estimated revenues of more than $1 billion.

COMPOSER PERSPECTIVE

Yoko Shimomura

One of my earliest works is from *Street Fighter II*. I was quite young when I wrote the tracks to that, and I never in my wildest dreams thought that the music would still be listened to and rearranged today. At the time, I was still quite inexperienced and full of youthful recklessness. When I listen to the pieces now, I am quite embarrassed, but also filled with happiness to see that it has become a soundtrack that has been loved by many for so many years.

Recently, the titles that I have worked on have been the *Kingdom Hearts* series and the *Mario & Luigi: Superstar Saga* series. Up until then, I had been asked to do the sequel or have the sequel be done by somebody else, which I found to be a bit discouraging. However, I am thrilled that the entire series of these two titles are done by me. At the same time, the pressure of constantly delivering better and better works is building up. I will always give my best in all of my compositions, both now and into the future.

Although games since 1980 had been using digital-to-analog converters to produce sampled tones, their early limited memory allowed for only a very few samples. As memory became cheaper in the 1990s, many of the games began to feature a wider array of these samples for SFX and as music samples.

Racing games continued to be popular with audiences, including *Daytona* (1993) and *Sega Rally Championship* (1995), both with soundtracks composed by Takenobu Mitsuyoshi. Racing games had continuous music throughout the race, with stingers and musical events occurring when the race was finished or the player got to a checkpoint.

The enormously popular music game *Dance Dance Revolution* (1998) was the first in a long line of successful competitive beat-matching games. The controller for this game was a dance platform with colored arrows, which players would press with their feet in time with the music. Players would compete against one another, making for a popular social activity. Musicians would map out the levels against the licensed music in these games to make interesting levels for players. These songs were stored as digital files within the game itself.

Arcade games that promote social interaction are still popular in some circles today, with many titles being updated and rereleased for new audiences. Although the newer arcade machines are unlikely to reach the height of their popularity in the 1980s, they remain opportunities for innovation.

The Game Console Revolution

When home game consoles emerged in the late 1970s, they allowed people to play at home instead of going out to the arcade. Games that could be played at home on your television screen initially were much more limited in terms of technology than the games found at the arcade, but as the game consoles improved, the popularity of arcades began to decline as players abandoned them in favor of home gaming.

Games from 1977 to 1992 were primarily released through cartridges, with the game being written on to static memory. These cartridges had very small ROM, which limited the size of the overall game in terms of music and sound. Later, as the industry grew, the CPU power increased, allowing for better graphics and sound. With the invention of CD-ROM technologies, game publishers were able to distribute much larger games of about 600MB. In turn, composers could deliver much more music for a game, and include compressed audio instead of being forced to use synthesis for the music.

Cartridge-Based Consoles

Gaming consoles began invading the home in earnest with the release of the very popular Atari 2600 (1977) and Intellivision (1978). The Atari could play back only two voices at a time, so it would alternate playing back SFX and music. This limitation made it challenging for composers to conceive of music with any kind of complexity for such systems. In addition, the Atari could play back only certain sound frequencies, so some notes could not be produced. The Intellivision system had better sound specifications, including the ability to play back three channels at any frequency plus a noise channel.

Composers and sound designers from this era were more programmers than musicians, as the music needed to be entered into the game by hand in machine language. As technology grew, the number of voices increased. Colecovision (1982) supported four voices with a PSG chip, and the Nintendo Entertainment System (NES; 1983) featured five voices, one of which was capable of playing back digital audio.

As the sophistication of console technology increased, popular video game composers started to emerge. Koji Kondo, composer of *Super Mario Bros.* (1985) and *Legend of Zelda* (1986), brought strong iconic themes to two of the longest-running video game series. These melodic themes were created in part to overcome some of the limitations of the system. Because the voice capabilities were so limited, Koji focused on strong melodic and rhythmic motifs in his music.

In many cases, the number of voices on a console from this era had to be split between the music and the SFX. In *Super Mario Bros.*, for instance, notes in the harmony are frequently dropped out to play a sound effect. In a way, these soundtracks are adaptive, changing in real time based on other needs of the game. Essentially the sound effect needs act as a control input for the music adaptivity.

Nobuo Uematsu composed extensive thematic material for the original *Final Fantasy* (1987) on the NES. Nobuo's themes for the entire Final Fantasy series have earned him the moniker "The John Williams of video game music." Frequently Nobuo writes themes based on characters and locations within the video game.

Another successful series that began on the NES was *Metroid* (1986), with music composed by Hirokazu "Hip" Tanaka. His score was one of the first to blur the lines between music and sound design, allowing for the SFX from world elements to add to the overall suspense in the underscore. In contrast to Nobuo's and Koji's work at the time, the musical sound design in *Metroid* was featured over melodic elements.

The Sega Genesis (1988) shipped with a FM synthesis chip, and could also play one channel of digitized audio. The initial launch title, *Altered Beast* (1988), with a soundtrack composed by Kazuhiko Nagai, featured ostinato rhythms in a 2D side-scroller set in Athens, Greece.

Additional interesting scores developed for the Genesis system include *Toejam and Earl* (1991), composed by John Baker; *Sonic the Hedgehog* (1991), composed by Masato Nakamura; *Ecco the Dolphin* (1992), composed by Spencer Nilsen; and *Earthworm Jim* (1994), composed by Mark Miller.

Last, the Super Nintendo Entertainment System (SNES), released in 1991, offered eight simultaneous voices playback and featured games such as *Super Metroid* (1994) and *Donkey Kong Country* (1994) by David Wise. The SNES, unlike the Genesis (which used FM), used sample playback for its sound and music generation. That actually made it somewhat challenging to create a game for both systems, because the synthesis methods were so very different.

Composers Yasunori Mitsuda with *Chrono Trigger* (1995) and Nobuo Uematsu with the *Final Fantasy* series dominated the musical innovation on the SNES; they developed enormous musical scores that encompassed several hours of music for each game. Another innovative game to be released on SNES was *Mega Man X* (1993), with a soundtrack created by a team of composers working for Capcom, including Setsuo Yamamoto, Makoto Tomozawa, Yuki Iwai, Yuko Takehara, and Toshihiko Horiyama. Koji Kondo continued to evolve his *Zelda* themes in *Legend of Zelda: A Link to the Past* (1991). Last, the extremely popular series *Super Mario Kart*, with music composed by Soyo Oka, debuted in 1991.

CD-ROM–Based Consoles

With the advent of CD-ROM technology, games could take advantage of the much larger memory storage (600MB) that CD-ROMs offered. CD-ROMs became the preferred delivery mechanism for games because they were less expensive to produce than cartridge-based systems. This enabled composers to use all of the previous technologies, including synthesis and MIDI, as well as Redbook audio, which allowed the streaming of digitized audio directly from the CD-ROM. Also, cinematics with audio could be prerendered and placed on the disk for playback, permitting linear movie playback with high-quality audio within games.

Although both the Sega Genesis and SNES manufactured a CD-ROM expansion accessory, these units were not considered a success in the industry. Several companies then released CD-ROM–based consoles, which began to reshape the industry and move it away from cartridge-based delivery and toward disk-based delivery. Philips released the CD-i in 1991, 3DO released its home console in 1993, and Sega released the Saturn, its follow-up to the Genesis, in 1994. Even so, it wasn't until Sony entered the market with the original PlayStation (1994) that CD-ROM drives were considered a success in the home console market.

Nintendo released its N64 console in 1996 to compete with the PlayStation. The N64 was Nintendo's last console to support cartridges for game distribution. Among its standout titles known for their music were *Banjo-Kazooie* (1998), with an inventive score composed by Grant Kirkhope, and *GoldenEye 007* (1997), with music composed by Graeme Norgate, Grant Kirkhope, and Robin Beanland. Last, in one of the most highly regarded games in history, Koji Kondo continued to innovate with his music in the hit title *Legend of Zelda: Ocarina of Time* (1998).

Many CD-ROM–based games took advantage of the ability to offer digitized audio during gameplay, including *The Lost World: Jurassic Park* (1997). It featured one of the first full orchestral recorded soundtracks for a video game, composed by Michael Giacchino.

Resident Evil (1996), composed by Makoto Tomozawa, Akari Kaida, and Masami Ueda, and Konami's *Silent Hill* (1999), with excellent sound direction from Akira Yamaoka, introduced the world to the horror genre of video games. Horror games featured more silence in the music to provoke horror and included non-instrumental sounds as musical elements to scare players.

Final Fantasy VII (1997) is generally regarded as one of the best games in the series and was released on PlayStation across multiple disks. The compositions by Nobuo Uematsu continued to take thematic development to a new level. *Castlevania: Symphony of the Night* (1997), composed by Michiru Yamane, contained compositions from many musical genres, including classical, techno, gothic rock, jazz, and many variations of metal. *Grandia* (1999), with a soundtrack composed by Noriyuki Iwadare, featured an epic score featuring orchestral elements.

Inspired by Spielberg's movie *Saving Private Ryan* (1998), *Medal of Honor* (1999) boasts another excellent Michael Giacchino orchestral score that brought war simulation in video games to a whole new level.

128-Bit and DVD-ROM–Based Game Consoles

CPU advancement in the late 1990s allowed for more graphic detail and higher-quality audio. The increase in processing power allowed for more audio voices and more real-time DSP, including filters and reverb.

In 1998, Sega introduced its last console, the 128-bit Dreamcast, to compete against the dominant Sony PlayStation. Two excellent music releases for the Dreamcast were the rhythm action game *Space Channel 5* (2000) and the FPS music shooter *Rez* (2001), both from designer Tetsuya Mizaguchi.

Two years later in 2000, Sony updated its very popular initial game console by introducing the PlayStation 2 with DVD storage and playback technology. Then, in 2001, Microsoft entered the home gaming marketplace with its first console, the original Xbox; this system also included DVD technology and 128-bit technology. For the first time in game audio, both of these consoles included an optical audio output supporting surround audio playback. While the Xbox was able to encode 5.1 audio throughout gameplay, the PlayStation 2 could play back surround only with pre-encoded cinematics and DVD movie playback. Because the games were distributed on DVDs, game developers could increase the size of their games to more than 7 GB. This meant that composers could deliver more music, and music of higher quality, for their games.

Important titles for the PS2 from this period include *SSX Tricky* (2001), which used real-time DSP to filter the music when players launched themselves off snowboard jumps. The epic *Final Fantasy X* (2001), with a score composed by Nobuo Uematsu, Masashi Hamauzu, and Junya Nakano, featured more than 3 hours of music as an addition to this already iconic series. *Grand Theft Auto III* (2001) licensed more than 60 commercial music tracks for use on the in-game car radio. The score for *Kingdom Hearts* (2002) by Yoko Shimomura features one of the most well-known themes in video gaming. *Shadow of Colossus* (2005) featured an epic soundtrack composed by Kow Otani. Last, *Okami* (2006), which was inspired by Japanese folk tales, included more than 3 hours of music by Masami Ueda, Hiroshi Yamaguchi, Hiroyuki Hamada, Rei Kondo, and Akari Groves.

The Xbox had excellent innovations in music that included the incredible adaptive score for *Halo* (2001), composed by Marty O'Donnell and Michael Salvatori. Jeremy Soule's orchestral score for *Elder Scrolls III: Morrowind* (2002) has an emblematic and iconic theme. Jack Wall's beautiful cultural score for Bioware's *Jade Empire* (2005) has excellent lyrical themes for this epic RPG.

In 2001, Nintendo released its relatively inexpensive GameCube console geared toward family play, featuring many games intended for group play of two to four players. Another outstanding title in the *Zelda* series was released on the GameCube, *The Legend of Zelda: The Wind Waker* (2002), with a score composed by Kenta Nagata, Hajime Wakai, Toru Minegishi, and Koji Kondo. *Metroid Prime* (2002), with a soundtrack composed by Kenji Yamamoto and Kouichi Kyuuma, featured remixes of themes from past versions of the game. Last, *Animal Crossing* (2002), with music composed by Kazumi Totaka, Kenta Nagata, Toru Minegishi, and Shinobu Tanaka, provided an immersive score for the happy world of animals.

Consoles have gone on to improve by providing more storage, greater CPU power, and more voices. The modern generation of consoles is discussed in a later section in the chapter, "The Evolution of the Modern Gaming Platform."

The Evolution of PC Gaming

Throughout the late 1980s, the personal computer (PC) also started to emerge as a gaming platform. As the technology for PC improved, developers began to release more games for the PC. Many of these games initially relied on simple synthesis and MIDI to play back music, but later gained the ability to use more advanced synthesis and sampling techniques. The introduction of MIDI and the Standard MIDI Instrument set by the MIDI Manufacturers Association allowed composers to take advantage of these technologies on many sound cards and within operating systems.

MOD Files

With the introduction of the Commodore Amiga (1987), the MOD (short for "module") file format became more popular. The MOD file format had several advantages over MIDI. The instruments were embedded along with the sequence in the same file, so that composers could depend on the file playing back identically from platform to platform. The MOD file didn't depend on synthesis cards at the time, because the sequences played back built-in samples that were consolidated directly into the file. MOD files typically had more CPU overhead so that they could play back the samples, and were much larger than a standard MIDI file.

Prominent composers of MOD files on the Amiga include Martin Galway (*Comic Bakery*, 1984), Ron Hubbard (*Skate or Die*, 1988), and Tim Wright (*Shadow of the Beast 3*, 1989).

MOD files eventually became popular in PC games and were used in soundtracks for *Quake* (1996), composed by Trent Reznor of Nine Inch Nails, and *Unreal* (1998). *Deus Ex* (2000), with a score by Alexander Brandon, used MOD files and had an excellent adaptive music system based around combat and exploring.

MIDI Scores (SMF) and Sound Cards

In the early 1980s, the IBM PC and its variants didn't have the ability to play much more than a single monophonic voice—at least until sound cards made their debut at the end of the decade. There were several early developments in sound for PC computers, including the Apple IIe Mockingboard soundcard. EA, Origin Systems, and a number of developers took advantage of those developments with applications like Deluxe Music Construction Set (1984). It wasn't until the late 1980s that FM sound cards became standard additions to computers. Adlib and Creative Labs were among the first to begin offering FM sound cards to PC users.

As FM cards began to flood the market, companies such as LucasArts and Origin Systems developed many games that took advantage of these sound cards to create music for their games. These sound cards allowed for MIDI playback using the General MIDI Instrument Set introduced by the MIDI Manufacturers Association.

George "The Fat Man" Sanger composed MIDI opuses for games like *Wing Commander* (1991) and *7th Guest* (1993). Sanger used stylistic adaptations of a theme to identify each of the main characters in the game. These adaptations were then combined when two characters in the story interacted.

Among the first games to popularize the first-person shooter (FPS) genre were *Doom* (1993) and *Doom II* (1994) by id Software; their soundtracks, composed by Bobby Prince, also used a MIDI score. On the Mac platform, Bungie's *FPS Marathon* (1994) series featured music composed by Alex Seropian. It is considered by some to have eclipsed the original *Doom* on the Mac platform; *Doom* eventually spawned *Myth: The Fallen Lords* (1997), a game for the PC with a score composed by Marty O'Donnell and Michael Salvatori.

Throughout the 1990s, PC sound cards improved by taking advantage of different types of synthesis, including subtractive, FM, wavetable, granular, and built-in DSP effects like reverb.

Cards even began including memory slots for custom sounds through either DLS instruments or SoundFonts.

iMuse

Frustrated with the state of music in games at that time, two composers at LucasArts, Peter McConnell and Michael Land, created one of the first adaptive music systems, called iMuse. iMuse (Interactive MUsic Streaming Engine) let composers insert branch and loop markers into a sequence that would allow the music to change based on the decisions of the player. The iMuse engine was one of the first significant contributions to interactive music for video games. Its importance in shaping many of the techniques that you see in video games today cannot be overemphasized.

The first game to use the iMuse system was *Monkey Island 2: LeChuck's Revenge* (1991). As the player moved the main character from location to location, the music would seamlessly branch to a new section of the music after the current musical phrase ended. Almost every game released by LucasArts after the invention of iMuse used this system for the music.

Other excellent iMuse titles include *Grim Fandango* (1998), which featured an incredible jazz-based soundtrack composed by Peter McConnell, and *Day of the Tentacle* (1993), with a score composed by Clint Bajakian, Peter McConnell, and Michael Land.

CD-ROM/Redbook Audio

The use of CD-ROM technology in mid-1990s PC games allowed composers to stream preren-dered audio files from the disk. This allowed composers to record live instruments onto their pieces and have them play back during gameplay, as opposed to having to rely on the standard MIDI instrument set or MOD files. CD-ROMs had a memory capacity of 600MB, which was split among all of the game's assets. The streaming of game music from the disk meant that the music had almost no interactive characteristics at all except to stop and start the music. Despite this limitation, many composers at the time preferred to prerender their audio files using the higher-quality synthesizers and samplers available at that time to avoid using the lower-quality MIDI instrument set.

Notable titles from the CD-ROM era of video games include *Quake* (1996), with music composed by Trent Reznor; *Diablo* (1996), with music composed by Matt Uelmen; and *Warcraft II: Tides of Darkness* (1995), with music composed by Glenn Stafford.

Personal computers continued to evolve in power and available storage, offering more voices and greater CPU power for DSP and larger games. The modern generation of PCs is discussed in a later section of this chapter, "The Evolution of the Modern Gaming Platform."

The Rise of Handheld and Network Games

Many of the same challenges that affected early console development also shaped the introduction of handheld, Internet, and mobile gaming, including limited memory, voices, and CPU
bandwidth. These platforms essentially faced the same problems that consoles had encountered 10 years earlier. Handheld and mobile gaming also faced another problem not associated
with console or arcade games—namely, battery consumption.

Handheld Game Systems

Handheld electronic games were first produced in the 1970s by companies like Milton Bradley,
Coleco, and Mattel. These games had simple LED screens and a very limited number of sounds
they could play. They included sports games like football and basketball, racing, and matching games. In the 1980s, Nintendo began to release a series of electronic games called *Game
& Watch*, which used the technology from hand-based calculators at the time. These games
replaced the older LED technology with newer LCD technology. The sound in these devices was
very limited, consisting of a very basic synthesizer that was able to play one tone at a time.

Nintendo introduced one of the first successful handheld cartridge-based systems, the Gameboy,
in 1989. It featured two pulse wave generators, one wave playback channel (4-bit pulse-code
modulation [PCM]), and one noise generator for playing music and SFX. Nintendo bundled the
Gameboy with *Tetris*, which has a score composed by Hirokazu Tanaka that featured arrangements of folk and classical tunes. Soon after, Sega introduced its cartridge-based system,
GameGear, in 1990. *Sonic the Hedgehog*, with a score composed by Yuzo Koshiro, was bundled
with the system when it launched.

Nintendo continued to release many successful versions of its Gameboy system, including the
Gameboy Color (1996) and the Gameboy Advance (2001). The Gameboy Advance featured the
ability to play back two digitized audio streams in addition to the original playback scheme.
Because of the limited memory constraints (128–256MB maximum cartridges) on these early
devices, many games still had to rely on MIDI playback or MOD-style files.

The modern generation of handhelds began with the release of the Nintendo DS (2004) and
Sony's first portable gaming device, the PlayStation Portable (PSP; 2004). Both of these devices
had more CPU, memory, and voices for music playback. In addition, they offered networking capabilities, allowing for multiplayer opportunities and downloadable content. The PSP
included a UMD drive—an optical disk with a capacity of up to 1.8 GB. Unfortunately, this drive
demanded a lot of power and drained the battery quickly.

Nintendo's latest handheld at the time of this writing is the 3DS (2010); Sony has introduced
the Vita (2012). Both handhelds expand the sound capabilities of their predecessors with more
voices, DSP, and memory. In addition, both Nintendo and Sony have expanded their offerings
through network distribution of games through their online stores.

Internet Games

As the Internet emerged to a wider audience in the mid-1990s, publishers began to produce games that were played via the web. Internet games faced many of the same challenges that handhelds had, in that the memory footprints needed to be very small so they could be downloaded over slow connections.

Web browsers generally did not support sound playback on their own, instead relying on various web plug-ins. Popular plug-ins that were used in games included Shockwave (1996) and Flash (1996), which supported compressed audio file playback but did not have an option for MIDI. In 1998, the company HeadSpace, founded by Thomas Dolby, created an audio plug-in for the web called Beatnik that allowed for MIDI playback as well as custom sound bank creation for composers.

Companies such as Lego, Sesame Workshop, Cartoon Network, and Nickelodeon all developed a vast array of game titles for children that were playable on the web.

In addition to playing games on the web, the Internet has become a way to distribute demos of games to potential customers so that they can try out games before buying the full versions. These demos tend to consist of a only small section of the full retail versions of the games.

During the evolution of games for the Internet, the term *casual games* was coined to define games that were played for short increments of time. Many of the games developed for the Internet tended to be puzzle games because they had to be small in terms of memory; thus they were played in shorter increments than a game you would buy for a console. Advertisers also created many games online that promoted a specific product—so-called *advergames*. As social networks like Facebook emerged, game publishers looked to develop games that allowed players to play with friends, including the very successful *Farmville* (2009), with music composed by Steve Kirk.

Popular games from this era include Microsoft's *Netwits* (1996); Popcap's *Bejeweled 2* (2004), with music by Peter Hajba; *Diner Dash* (2004), with music by Michael Sweet; and *Plants vs. Zombies* (2009), with music by Laura Shigihara.

Mobile and Cell Phone Games

Games began to appear on cell phones in the late 1990s, but it wasn't until the year 2000 when users could download games to their cell phones. These early mobile games were allocated a tiny amount of space, forcing composers to use MIDI almost exclusively for music soundtracks and SFX. Many of the games of this early generation were advertiser supported and had tie-ins to other products or entertainment.

The first highly capable cell phone hit the market in 2008, with Apple's introduction of the iPhone. This new era of mobile design allowed game makers to create sophisticated games with much more memory and CPU processing power. With these smartphones, composers and sound designers could expect a dozen or more voices, plus the ability to stream audio from memory.

It wasn't until the launch of the highly successful iPhone and iOS App Store in 2007 that successful mobile games garnered both praise and large revenue shares. Between the constraints of small data plans and device memory, developers focused on making casual games for these devices. *Angry Birds* (2009), with a score composed by Ari Pulkkinen, and *Cut the Rope* (2010), with a score composed by Andrew Burmistrov, Ruslan Shafikov, and Michael Chertichev, were both extremely successful titles in this era. Android and Windows Phone have since developed their own successful stores through which games are distributed to players on their phones.

The Advancement of Audio Middleware

Programmers build reusable sets of code so as to simplify and reduce the amount of time required to program a game. These libraries of code are called application programming interfaces (APIs). In addition, game programmers build tools to help designers with the overall development and production of a game. These tools make the game development process easier by enabling nonprogrammers to help integrate assets, create levels, or test various elements of the game. Such tools are often called middleware.

Middleware is a package of tools and software libraries that facilitate game development. For instance, software libraries that help develop 3D games include UDK, Unity3d, and Source. Likewise, different companies have focused on building tools for audio developers to help them create better-quality aural experiences within games as well as to make it easier for audio experts to be involved in the integration process.

Audio middleware packages help game developers in the following ways:

- Simplify the audio programming for a game
- Provide specialized audio algorithms to mix and play back sound with very little CPU overhead
- Help the composer implement sophisticated musical structures without consulting the programmer
- Help sound designers create better-sounding worlds for games by allowing them to customize and randomize elements such as DSP, pitch, volume, and layers
- Make the delivery to multiple platforms easier
- Allow audio compression and decompression
- Use 2D and 3D audio in multichannel environments
- Ensure lower memory and CPU consumption by using optimized algorithms for each platform

In this section you'll learn about some of the more prominent audio middleware packages and the ways in which they affected video game composition and game audio.

The Beginnings of Audio Middleware

Middleware is designed to help with a specific problem that developers are having a hard time solving. One such problem arose in 1991, when programmer John Miles wanted to unify the implementation for all the different PC sound card manufacturers. The problem with PC sound cards at that point was that each had a different implementation; thus game developers had to code for multiple sound cards on every game. In addition, each sound card sounded slightly different, making it very difficult for a composer to know what his or her composition would sound like.

Miles began developing a custom set of libraries to standardize the sound of the many different FM synthesis cards on the market at that time. This way, composers wouldn't have to worry about whether their compositions were playing on an Adlib card or a SoundBlaster, as both would have a similar sound set. From his initial API until today, the Miles Sound System has grown to encompass many other different audio needs (e.g., playback, DSP, mixing, audio decompression, embedded instruments) within games across many platforms.

Publisher Tools

Publishers have also realized that the more tools they supply to game developers, the easier it is for them to create games. Many publishers and developers have either bought or created tools to facilitate the development of game software.

In 1995, Microsoft purchased a suite of applications and software developed by Blue Ribbon Soundworks that specialized in creating interactive music. These tools were then expanded and released as Microsoft's own DirectMusic engine. The DirectMusic engine had many unique features, enabling composers to create interactive adaptive music scores. Some of these features included dynamic instrument reassignment, real-time chord mapping, musical styles that could improvise melodies in a certain harmonic framework, and more. DirectMusic was a very advanced system that had a very difficult front-end user interface for composers. It was used very successfully in advancing adaptive music in games like *No One Lives Forever* (2000), with a soundtrack by Guy Whitmore, and *Asheron's Call 2* (2002), with audio direction by Jason Booth.

Because of DirectMusic's challenging UI, Microsoft moved to another adaptive audio system called XACT in the late 2000s. XACT (Xbox Audio Creation Tool) offered sound designers and composers sound file, pitch, filter, and volume randomization as well as segment and looping features, layering, and DSP options. This tool also allowed access to the very sophisticated audio chip on the original Xbox. Microsoft's current audio system is XAudio2, which doesn't offer a composer-based tool, only an API for programmers.

Sony built its own proprietary sound tool, which featured similar features, called SCREAM. This tool was used in many of Sony's published games, including the *God of War* and the *Uncharted* series.

Many other game developers have created sound and music tools to help game composers and sound designers implement music more rapidly and more easily. Companies with their own proprietary audio toolsets include Bungie, Bethesda, Ubisoft, DICE, and Electronic Arts.

Standards

Game composers and sound designers have been lobbying developers and hardware manufacturers to adopt standards in the industry, thereby permitting them to more easily develop for game platforms. Unfortunately, there has been little success in bringing rival hardware manufacturers together to adopt these standards.

The Interactive Audio Special Interest Group (IASIG) sponsored by the MIDI Manufacturers Association has helped to bring several manufacturers together to adopt the ID3L2 reverb standard as well as DLS (downloadable sound instrument banks). These standards have been used in DirectMusic software, Creative Lab's sound cards, and the audio middleware Fmod. IASIG has been working to define a standard format for interactive music and sound development called iXMF. The ongoing lack of agreement on standards makes it challenging for composers and sound designers because they need to become experts in many of these different implementations.

Modern Middleware

In addition to the publisher tools listed in the previous section, many other audio middleware tools have been developed for games. The lack of standards is actually one reason for the popularity of middleware. When a composer needs to ship a game on several different platforms (e.g., PS3, Vita, Xbox), it can be extremely time consuming to convert the soundtracks to multiple formats. Middleware can assist in delivering the product to multiple platforms all at once. In addition, middleware can help composers and sound designers build complex adaptive structures that can work directly in the game without having to involve the programmer.

The two most widely used game audio middleware software packages at the time of this book's writing are Firelight's Fmod and AudioKinetic's Wwise. Both middleware packages have an API for many different platforms and include software for composers and sound designers to build advanced interactive audio structures for games. Other audio middleware engines include RAD Tool's Miles Sound System, OpenAL , Tazman's Fabric for Unity3d, ADX2 from CRI, Un4seen BASS, and Unreal 3.

Audio middleware is discussed in depth in Chapter 18, "Using Middleware to Create Advanced Compositions."

The Evolution of the Modern Gaming Platform

The modern age of game consoles was ushered in first with Microsoft's Xbox 360 in 2005 and then a year later with Sony's release of the PlayStation 3. Each of these platforms offered much more RAM and CPU performance than previous generations of consoles. Both consoles could play back more than 100 voices if managed properly with regard to memory management and overall CPU demand. As a consequence, many of the limitations that composers had been shackled with over the last three decades were finally removed. Nintendo also improved its specifications for its game console in 2006. Nintendo geared its console toward families and chose to release a lower-cost console with less technical superiority, promoting innovative features like the WiiMote and the fitness game *WiiFit*.

In addition, game music finally began to receive attention from a global audience, with concert venues being the sites of symphonic performances of famous game music. Orchestral performances of video game music were highly promoted through *Video Games Live*, produced initially by Tommy Tallarico and Jack Wall; *Final Fantasy Distant Realms* performances; and *PLAY! A Video Game Symphony*. In turn, game publishers and developers recognized the value of better-quality music and began increasing their budgets to cover live instrument costs during game development, making it much easier for AAA console game developers to contract for and record live orchestras.

Prominent orchestral games from this period of games include *Everquest II* (2004), with music composed by Laura Karpman, and the *Uncharted* series (2007–2011), with music composed by Greg Edmonson. In addition, composers began to include more aleatoric orchestral elements into their compositions, including the groundbreaking scores to *Bioshock* (2007), composed by Garry Schyman, and *Dead Space* (2008), composed by Jason Graves.

Building on many of the interactive compositional techniques were excellent interactive scores, including *Mass Effect 2* (2010), composed by Jack Wall; *Batman: Arkham City* (2012), composed by Ron Fish and Nick Arundel; and *Portal 2* (2011), composed by Mike Morasky.

The latest generation of consoles also emerged from the three top manufacturers: Nintendo Wii U (2012), Microsoft Xbox One (2013), and Sony PlayStation 4 (2013). Pushing the technology further, these consoles have even more processing power than the consoles that preceded them. The video game industry is just beginning to test the audio limits of these new platforms. Composers and sound designers over the next few years will be asking for new features and innovating through use of new techniques within games to show off what these consoles can do.

Despite the advantages of these modern consoles, audio teams may still need to manage memory budgets and voice limitations—even on the highest-end consoles. The reason is that teams are pursuing innovations to make their music sound even better, whether that requires adding more channels in a surround matrix or adding more real-time DSP.

In terms of the DSP hurdles, for example, composers might be able to change the key of a piece of prerendered audio during gameplay if they were able to use a Melodyne-like plug-in. This kind of plug-in is not beyond the reach of modern consoles, but the graphic artists for the game would also be fighting to use the same CPU to make the visual world better. Composers must balance the needs of the entire game while pushing for the best audio they can create. It's likely that before long the industry will see more real-time DSP pushing the envelope once again.

One title that shows off some of the power of the real-time DSP and remixing capabilities of modern consoles is the RUMR (real-time user remix) system in the snowboarding game *SSX* (2012). This system allows dynamic remixing and DSP effects of user-imported music. These effects include sample-and-hold features played back in sync to the music, dynamic delays and reverb, and real-time pitch bends.

Game Engines, Indie Games, and Distribution

Today's game industry is seeing some standardization and consolidation in the tools that developers are using to create games. The emergence of common middleware tools for building games has allowed game developers to make games more quickly and easily than ever before.

Some of the more popular 3D game-making middleware solutions on the market today are Source by Valve, CryEngine by Crytek, Unreal Development Kit by Epic Games, and Unity3d. There are also plenty of tools in the marketplace for helping to build 2D games, including GameMaker, Construct, Stencyl, CoronaSDK, and Pygame.

The development of accessible tools has ushered in a revolution in the gaming world, allowing more and more people to make games without the kinds of related costs that would necessitate funding from a large game publisher. In a shift similar to what happened in the movie industry, independent game companies are able to make and distribute games relatively inexpensively and still be extremely successful. This trend has helped many composers and sound designers find steady work throughout the industry, whether they are working on large titles or smaller independent ones.

Game Distribution and Future Cloud Computing

The distribution model of buying games has already begun shifting from physical disks and cartridges sold in retail stores to online downloads through sites such as Steam, Xbox Live, PlayStation Network, and Amazon. As content is being distributed to a greater extent online, game developers can offer additional updates and extra content for games. This allows games to be expanded after the initial release, allowing for sales of expansion packs that might include additional music. This mechanism begins to redefine the boundaries of how much music you can deliver, as it is no longer strictly necessary to fit all of the content onto a single disk.

In the same way that we are able to stream movies to our homes, it will eventually be possible to use our laptops as a conduit to play our games on more powerful computers that might be in the cloud. Essentially your home machine may simply serve as a window into this other computer, meaning that you no longer have to worry about memory constraints, storage, and CPU power.

Review

Throughout the history of video game music, composers have faced many technological limitations that made it difficult for them to create music for such games. Some of these limitations have included the limited number of voices and limited sequence and sample memory. Even today, composers may face similar challenges with memory and voice limitations and a lack of adequate interactive music technologies.

Before 1970, electromechanical games frequently used sonic feedback to indicate to players how well they were doing. Arcade machines in the 1970s introduced circuits called PSGs to create the sonic feedback. Many of these sound circuits were custom built for each specific game.

Early sound generators had several basic sound waves that they could play, including sine, sawtooth, square, triangle, and noise waveforms. In the mid-1980s, machines began to use FM sound chips, which replaced the PSGs and allowed for eight simultaneous voices and much more sophisticated music.

The introduction of MIDI and the Standard MIDI Instrument set by the MIDI Manufacturers Association allowed composers to take advantage of these capabilities on many sound cards and within operating systems. Later, with the introduction of the Commodore Amiga (1987), the MOD ("module") file format became more popular. The MOD file format offered several advantages over MIDI. In particular, the MOD file embedded the instruments along with the sequence in the same file so that composers could depend on the file playing back identically from platform to platform.

Frustrated with the state of music in games, two composers at LucasArts, Peter McConnell and Michael Land, created one of the first adaptive music systems, called iMuse, in 1990. iMuse let composers insert branch and loop markers into a sequence, thereby ensuring that the music could adapt to the gameplay based on the decisions of the player.

The introduction of the CD-ROM allowed composers to stream prerendered audio files in games. At the same time, many of the same challenges that affected early console development shaped the introduction of handheld, Internet, and mobile gaming, including limited memory, voices, and CPU bandwidth.

Programmers build reusable sets of code to simplify and reduce the amount of time required to program a game. These libraries of code, called APIs, supported the introduction of common game-making platforms and software as well as audio middleware packages. Audio middleware allows composers and sound designers to create complex interactive music and sound without involving programmers.

The modern age of game consoles was ushered in with Microsoft's Xbox 360 in 2005 and Sony's PlayStation 3 in 2007. Each of these platforms offered much more RAM and CPU performance than previous generations of consoles. Both consoles could play back more than 100 voices if managed properly with regard to memory management and overall CPU demand.

The distribution model of buying games has already begun shifting from physical disks and cartridges sold in retail stores to online downloads through sites such as Steam, Xbox Live, PlayStation Network, and Amazon. As content is being distributed to a greater extent online, game developers can offer additional updates and extra content for games.

Exercises

1. Compare and contrast the evolution of a musical score in a long-running video game series such as *Zelda*, *Final Fantasy*, or *Super Mario Bros.*

2. Categorize and analyze all the musical components that make up one of the video game scores that was mentioned in this chapter. Discuss the limitations that the composer encountered during the composition of that score.

3. Compare the techniques used by a composer who has worked over several decades in the video game industry.

4. Pick a video game genre (i.e., RPG, FPS, racing games) and compare the evolution of that genre in terms of music and sound from the beginning of video games to the latest titles.

CHAPTER 6

HISTORICAL PERSPECTIVE OF EXPERIMENTAL MUSIC

Composers over the last century have done much to innovate and grow the world of interactive composition. There are many parallels that we can draw between nondigital experimental composers and the way modern video game composers approach their work. In this chapter we'll look at some of the innovation taking place in the music field and consider how it might apply to modern interactive music for video games.

The Beginning of Interactive Music

By examining the past, not only can you draw inspiration from these experimental compositions but you can also spark your own imagination in your writing.

The roots of interactive music date back many centuries to improvisational styles used in both formal studies, like counterpoint in Gregorian chant, and folk music such as madrigals and the songs of wandering minstrels. Although it is beyond the scope of this book to explore all the significant works in interactive music, in this chapter we'll survey some of the dominant changes and influences in the world of experimental composition throughout the twentieth century.

This chapter examines significant contributions by various nondigital composers and analyzes how they are influencing interactive music in video games today. All of the composers who are considered here have a wide repertoire of noteworthy compositions, of which only a small portion are mentioned in this discussion. It is recommended that you explore their work in more depth throughout your career to inspire and advance your own creative endeavors in interactive music.

Pre-Twentieth Century

Before the twentieth century, composers began to experiment with compositions by adding elements that would allow musicians to pick between different musical options at the time of the performance, including phrase order and choices made about the instruments that make up an ensemble. These early techniques paved the way for future composers to become more experimental with compositions techniques.

J. S. Bach: *The Art of Fugue* (1740s)

In J. S. Bach's late composition, *The Art of Fugue*, each voice is on its own stave without specified instrumentation. Composer and musical theorist John Cage referred to this in his lecture "Composition as Process" as an early example of indeterminacy. He wrote, "Timbre and amplitude characteristics of the material, by not being given, are indeterminate. This indeterminacy brings about the possibility of a unique overtone structure and decibel range for each performance of *The Art of Fugue.*"

Most scholars have now concluded that the instrumentation was meant for keyboard, but the idea that music parts can be adapted each time they are listened to is significant for creating music randomization in games. Variety and randomness within instrumentation are two musical components within video games that can extend the listenability of a track.

Although many games use this technique, here are some examples that capitalize on it effectively:

- In *Monkey Island 2: LeChuck's Revenge* (1991), the main theme modifies the ensemble that is playing when going from place to place. An example of this is on the wharf, when different instruments take over the lead melody depending on the location.

- Within the marketplace section in *The Legend of Zelda: Skyward Sword* (2011), the lead instrument changes based on the vendor you're interacting with. In addition, the melody is customized to each vendor.

- In the MMO *Asheron's Call 2* (2002), players are allowed to buy and play instruments with other players in the game. Players can interact with their instruments to play certain riffs and musical phrases. For the phrases of music to work well with one another, special care must be taken in the compositional process to match certain phrases with other phrases.

Amadeus Mozart: *Musikalisches Würfelspiel* (1787)

Musikalisches Würfelspiel by Amadeus Mozart is a composition made up of musical phrases that are played back in a random order based on the outcome of rolls of dice. These types of pieces were very popular in Western Europe in the eighteenth century. Dice are rolled to determine the playback order of the 177 different musical phrases. In fact, the translation of the words "Musikalisches Würfelspiel" is "musical dice game."

Randomization of the order of phrases is a common technique used in video games, especially when memory constraints limit the amount of overall music that can be used. This playback order randomization is similar to the shuffle feature in media players—except that instead of shuffling the order of the songs, you're shuffling the playback of individual musical phrases within the composition. This method is commonly used with horizontal resequencing, as discussed in Chapter 3.

This technique has been used in modern video games in several different ways:

- A variation of this technique is used in *Uncharted 2: Among Thieves* (2009), which has multiple starting points for each cue. When the player fails a level and restarts back at a checkpoint, the music randomly chooses one of the starting points to begin the cue.

- Because of the limited memory constraints of *Diner Dash* (2004), songs are kept more interesting by randomizing the order of the musical segments during each level. The phrases of the song are split up individually and played back in a random order. The music is written in such a way that each phrase connects with any other phrase.

1900–1950

During the first half of the twentieth century, composers began to develop and use unique systems to govern their musical compositions. In addition, composers began to ask the question "What is music?" from an aesthetic point of view as well as in terms of the interpretation and conveyance of an idea.

Marcel Duchamp: *Erratum Musical* (1913)

Marcel Duchamp was one of the first artists to put forth the belief that the *idea* behind the art was just as important as, or more important than, the actual aesthetic qualities of the art. One of Duchamp's art pieces, *Fountain* (1917), positioned a urinal in a gallery and called it art—a scandalous act for its time. Duchamp and other artists in the early twentieth century began to question the boundaries demarcating what art and music actually are.

Duchamp's composition *Erratum Musical* is a score written for three voices using chance operations. The score was composed by randomly drawing notes out of a hat, ranging from F below middle C up to high F. In video games, randomization of notes is a common technique in music games that use algorithmic composition models, like Brian Eno's score for the Maxis game *Spore* (2008).

Charles Ives: *Concord Sonata* (1919)

Charles Ives was an early American composer who pioneered many experimental compositional techniques, including polytonality, aleatoric techniques, and tone clusters.

In his piece *Concord Sonata,* Ives uses several interesting techniques. Much of the piece is written without bar lines or meter. Traditionally within music notation, bar lines symbolize divisions between musical ideas and phrases adding overall structure and form. In film and video game scoring, typically non-song–based approaches to tempo and rhythm are used to synchronize the music to the action on screen. The use of traditional form or a fixed meter is typically diverted.

In addition, during Ives's sonata there is notation for the performer to use a long piece of wood to play a cluster chord. Since this cluster chord cannot be played the same way twice, it is random each time the piece is performed. The idea of random notes has been used in many different games and applications, including the musical game *Bit.Trip Runner* (2011), where a series of random notes from a pentatonic scale is played when the player jumps or slides.

Last, *Concord Sonata* has optional parts for viola and flute. This is another technique that can be valuable for video game composers. Having optional instruments play when the composition is played multiple times will add variety and suppress repetition.

Arnold Schoenberg: *Variations for Orchestra, Op. 31* (1928)

Arnold Schoenberg was an extremely influential composer in the early twentieth century. Many of his students wound up as some of the twentieth century's most important composers, including Alban Berg, Anton Webern, John Cage, and many others. Schoenberg introduced serialism as a compositional technique. Serialism applies a series of numeric values to manipulate different musical elements in the composition. Schoenberg is most famous for his invention of the serial process known as the *12-tone technique*. The technique is an ordered arrangement of the 12 notes in a chromatic scale. The influence of math processes on music through serialism has been significant for composition in both the twentieth and twenty-first centuries.

One of the Schoenberg's significant contributions that uses the 12-tone technique is *Variations for Orchestra, Op. 31*. The main motiv used in the piece is B-flat, A, C, B-natural, spelling out the name Bach in German notation. Similarly, Jason Graves, in his score for *Dead Space* (2008), uses the notes D, E, A, D for the main motiv. Schoenberg's work uses his 12-tone technique throughout and is his first work to employ this technique with a large ensemble.

The 12-tone technique had various rules associated with its compositional process. Mathematical transformations could also be applied to the work, including retrograde, inversion, and retrograde-inversion of a passage. Serialism paved the way for other techniques used in the twentieth century, including being one of the origins of *process music*.

Henry Cowell: *Rhythmicon* (1930) and *The Banshee* (1925)

Henry Cowell made many contributions to experimental music, including an instrument he designed with Russian inventor Léon Theremin called the Rhythmicon. The instrument itself takes the pitch of the note and translates it into a rhythmic phrase. It can play 16 different rhythms at the same time. The pitches are related to rhythmic values by the overtone series, in which the fundamental beats once, the first overtone (if played) beats twice, the second overtone beats three times, and so forth.

Many games use the game interface (UI) as an instrument. Here are two examples of this technique:

- In the game *Chime* (2010), the payer places *Tetris*-like blocks on the game screen. When the timeline passes over these blocks, the game plays a note. The pitch of the note is directly related to its vertical position on the screen.
- In the game *Bit.Trip Runner* (2011), the character in the game is running at a constant speed. When the player jumps, slides, or picks up an object, a note plays. The fact that the speed is constant means that any object in the world will be hit at a specific time

during the level, similar to reading through a music score. These notes are timed to the background music, making the player act like the bow or pick on an instrument.

Henry Cowell's piano composition *The Banshee* (1925) uses many alternate playing methods, such as pizzicato and scraping and sweeping of the strings. Because these articulations can't be played the same way twice, the performance is ever evolving. Games can take advantage of this technique through the randomization of notes or phrases to avoid repetition within the music.

---

note

The word "indeterminacy" in music refers the capacity for composed music to be executed differently with each performance. Although certain factors affect the performance of any piece of music, including the musicianship and choices made by the performer or conductor, indeterminate pieces may include written notation for elements of randomness or chance directly in the music, making it impossible to duplicate the same performance twice. This method of music creation is also referred to as chance music or aleatoric music.

Indeterminacy can also refer to a piece for which methods of chance and randomization were used to create the composition itself. These techniques were popularized by Henry Cowell and his students, including John Cage and Earl Brown.

Paul Hindemith: *The Craft of Musical Composition* (1937)

Composer Paul Hindemith was equal parts prolific composer and systems thinker and designer. His landmark book *The Craft of Musical Composition* helped define techniques and practices of twentieth-century music. Although not considered experimental, Hindemith helped to establish a language of music composition. Throughout his career as a composer, he continued to innovate through his music, including in the opera and symphony *Mathis de Maler* (1938).

Frequently, composers who work in video games also need to help devise systems of musical implementation within video games. Being able to systematize and design the musical architecture of a game is very important. *Portal 2* (2011) and *Fract OSC* (2014) are excellent examples of designing a system based around musical objects in a 3D space.

Pierre Schaeffer: *Études de Bruits* (1948)

Pierre Schaefer introduced the world to *musique concrète*, which incorporated recorded sounds of nature and electronic sounds as musical elements into compositions. Like Duchamp, Schaeffer challenged audiences by asking the question, "What is music?" Originally a recording engineer, Schaeffer was influenced by early French impressionist filmmakers like Jean Epstein, who used the practice of recording and montage in cinema. Schaeffer began composing music using magnetic tape recordings by manipulating the pitch, speed, and direction of the recordings.

Schaefer's *Études de Bruits* (1948) had five movements, each of which used various recordings to create the composition. These recordings had a variety of sounds, ranging from piano and percussion to trains and toys.

In video games, composers frequently use nontraditional objects as musical elements to expand their musical ensembles and make their compositions unique. In *The Legend of Zelda: Spirit Tracks* (2009), the train's rhythm speeds up along with the music when the player controls the train.

Post-1950s

As many the walls separating traditional music genres began to fall, composers in the second half of the twentieth century began radically rethinking what music is and how to compose. Many new compositional approaches began to take shape, including chance music, open form, aleatoric techniques, and indeterminate music. These techniques are rich with interactive ideas for video game composers to bring to their scores.

John Cage: *Music of Changes* (1951) and *4'33* (1952)

More than any other composer in the twentieth century, John Cage promoted the theory that the idea behind the composition of music is at least equal to, if not more important than, the aesthetic qualities of the composition.

Music of Changes (1951) is often considered the first modern piece to be conceived through random procedures. Cage used *I-Ching*, a Chinese text in divination, along with random procedures like dice rolling, to create this composition. These inputs were then mapped to music through a large series of charts that determined the sounds, durations, dynamics, tempo, and densities within the piece.

There are obvious comparisons to gaming because of the use of dice, but also because many events that happen in games are out of the player's control. Randomization is commonly used in games to create game levels, to handle character responses and actions, and to vary the experience. Many games use random playlists in their music playback to vary the experience and diffuse the repetitive nature of game music. Cage's works often were not only conceived through random procedures, but the compositions also left many music decisions up to the players who performed the piece. Some of his more famous works that relied on this technique were *Number Pieces* (1987–1991).

Like Duchamp in the early twentieth century, Cage pushed the boundaries of what was considered music with his composition *4'33*. *4'33* is composed of three movements, all consisting of a single word, *tacet*. Tacet is musical notation for the player to remain silent. Cage was ridiculed by many of his peers for creating a silent piece of music. At the premiere of this work in 1952, the musician walked in front of an audience to the piano, sat down, opened his music, and waited for 4 minutes and 33 seconds before leaving the stage. Many presume that the audience is the music, but the composition goes beyond the simpler question of "What is music?" to the more evolved concept that the idea behind a composition is equal to, if not more important than, the composition itself.

> ## note
>
> *Open form* is often used by composers such as John Cage, Karlheinz Stockhausen, Terry Riley, and Morton Feldman. Open form is a notational and compositional style that gives the performer choices about the phrasing, pitch, and rhythm of the music. This style can look substantially different from the traditional notational styles, as it may feature specialized notation and no bar lines.
>
> Open form doesn't have a set structure like traditional notation, and much of the notation may be developed specifically for use in a single composition.

Pierre Boulez: *Structures I* (1952)

Building on Schoenberg's techniques, Pierre Boulez's *Structures I* (1952) uses serialism principles on many different musical parameters, including pitch, dynamics, density, durations, articulations, and the methods of attack.

Video game music can use serial techniques to help create variation in composition during gameplay, augmenting and extending the player experience. Whether this is done in prerendered audio files during the composition process, or in real time while the player is playing the game through algorithmic techniques, is left to the technology available to the game. Brian Eno's score for *Spore* (2008) is an excellent example of the use of these techniques in an algorithmic context.

György Ligeti: *Musica Ricercata II* (1953)

György Ligeti's *Musica Ricercata II* (1953) has a self-imposed limit on which notes are used in each of its eight movements. The first movement uses two notes, the second uses three notes, and so on. Ligeti's ability to think creatively within this limited framework produced an incredible piece of music. Ligeti forced himself to be creative with this limited set of pitches, allowing him to concentrate on the elements that he does have at his disposal, such as rhythm and dynamics.

Similarly, influential composer Elliott Carter composed pieces that focused on chords sets with a defined set of notes. His *Piano Concerto* (1964–1965) uses the collection of three-note chords; his *Third String Quartet* (1971) uses all four-note chords; his *Concerto for Orchestra* (1969) all five-note chords; and so on.

In the past, gaming composers were frequently faced with similar challenges, such as the number of voices that the game could play back at a single time. This constraint forced composers to be creative while working within these limitations.

Along with Krzysztof Penderecki, György Ligeti was also very influential in using aleatoric techniques in his scores. For example, *Atmosphères* (1961) uses tone clusters and micro-tonality.

Morton Feldman: *Projections* (1953)

Morton Feldman is a pioneer of indeterminate music who experimented with graphic notation, allowing the performers a substantial amount of freedom in the interpretation and performance of his scores. In his composition *Projections* (1953), Feldman creates his own notation scheme that relies on a series of graphs and rectangles. These specify the instrument, register, number of simultaneous sounds, mode of production, and duration.

Traditional music notation doesn't allow for variability in the performance. The idea of creating a new musical language to encourage musical variability in games can be extremely useful. Ambient music created through the spawning of musical events that have variable timing and length can be used to great effect in games that don't focus on melodic structures. In addition, the variable placement of notes can be used in composition as open form.

Karlheinz Stockhausen: *Klavierstücke XI* (1956)

A student of Pierre Schaeffer, Karlheinz Stockhausen was a composer who produced many ground-breaking compositions in serial and electronic music. *Klavierstücke XI* (1956) is made up of 19 musical fragments that are distributed across the score. These musical fragments can be played in any order. The dynamics and articulations of the notes are left up to the performers.

Video game compositions are frequently split up into fragments that are played only when a player makes a decision in the game. Many times these phrases must link up with the other phrases seamlessly.

Krzysztof Penderecki: *Threnody to the Victims of Hiroshima* (1960)

Krzysztof Penderecki's *Threnody* (1960) is an influential work of the twentieth century that uses many aleatoric performance techniques. Much of the score is composed on nonstandard notation, which allows passages to be played without the precision of traditional notation.

Penderecki's score features custom symbols that are associated with specific instructions at the beginning of the score. Many of the passages have a starting note for the performers, but they may then be followed by undulating lines that indicate where the pitch is supposed to go or how the dynamics should change.

These techniques, when Penderecki's music is played with an entire ensemble, introduce many clusters and microtonal differences, making for unique musical palettes that composers are unable to achieve using traditional notation. The sound is so unique and unusual that it's difficult reproduce identically from performance to performance. Video game composers such as Garry Shyman and Jason Graves have used many of these techniques to differentiate their scores.

Terry Riley: *In C* (1964)

Terry Riley's composition *In C* (1964) is set up very similarly to a branching composition using horizontal resequencing. The composition itself consists of 32 musical fragments. Starting at the beginning, each fragment is repeated until the group or an individual decides to move on to the next musical fragment. This means that the group is slowly shifting in waves from one musical fragment to the next. Thus, during each performance of *In C*, the listener enjoys a different experience because of the individual choices made by the performers.

Riley's *In C* also does not have a specified ensemble. Thus the composition can be played by a new set of instruments with each performance.

Similar to video games, *In C* has a control input that changes the music on each play through the music. What video game composers can take away from this composition is its ability to make minute changes over time to dramatically increase the player's experience by gradually shifting from one piece to another incrementally until an end point is reached. The idea at the heart of Riley's *In C*—that is, moving between small musical phrases—is an excellent minimalist technique to shift the player's awareness throughout his or her progress through the level of a game.

Earle Brown: *Calder Piece* (1966)

Earle Brown was a composer largely credited as the creator of open form in composition. His composition *Calder Piece* (1966) was derived from the motion of an Alexander Calder mobile. As the mobile moves, based on the wind and atmosphere in the space, notes are played. Essentially the mobile becomes the control input for shaping the performance of the musical piece. The score of the composition is made up of instructions that specify the instruments to be played, the density of the notes, the dynamics of the music, and the notes themselves.

One game that uses a variation on this technique is the Nintendo DS game *Electroplankton* (2005), in which players can manipulate the virtual objects in the game to change the music. In a series of music-derived activities, players are able to adjust the sounds and music without a musical interface.

Alvin Lucier: *I Am Sitting in a Room* (1969)

Lucier's brilliant composition *I Am Sitting in a Room* (1969) records the ambience of a poem read aloud in a room, then rerecords it being played back in that room, then rerecords it again and again. In the end, the poem is transformed into music. This transformation is an early use of effect manipulation.

Many video games use and manipulate space and, in turn, use effects like reverb and filtering for shaping the overall experience. The application of these effects as a musical effect has been observed in many games, including the *SSX* (2011) real-time remixing engine. These effects are sometimes referred to as DSP (digital signal processing).

Steve Reich: *Clapping Music* (1972)

Steve Reich, along with Lamont Young, Philip Glass, and Terry Riley, pioneered the use of minimal music throughout the 1960s and 1970s. Reich's *Clapping Music* (1972) is performed by two individuals or groups. The piece itself is a single bar in length. This bar is a single rhythmic motif that is repeated over and over again. The first individual or group performs this rhythmic loop as written over and over again. The second individual or group repeats the musical phrase eight times and then shifts the rhythmic pattern one eighth note later in time for the next eight bars. This process continues, delaying the phrase by an eighth note every eight bars, until the phrase is back in sync with the first individual or group. Another interesting aspect of this composition is that it can be scaled to groups of any size. This composition is known as process music because of the static mathematical manipulation of each sequence.

As in his other pieces, in *Clapping Music* Reich explores the phasing relationship of overlapping music when one or more parts are delayed in time. In video games, this is significant because many games have memory constraints that limit the amount of music that you can have in the game. Reich's *Clapping Music* consists of only one bar of music, making it captivating to listen to despite its simplicity, and this technique can be used in games to create similar kinds of experiences. Such a method of phasing allows the listener to hear 64 bars of interesting material as the second group offsets that bar by 18 notes every 8 cycles.

At a game developer's conference, Marty O'Donnell, the composer of *Halo*, described using a similar technique of phasing loops with different lengths for one of his compositions. This technique can be used to great effect in video games because of its power to use a minimal amount of music to create captivating compositions.

The minimalism movement also influenced many other composers, including Philip Glass (*Einstein on the Beach,* 1975) and John Adams (*Shaker Loops,* 1978).

> ## note
>
> *Process music* is the application of mathematical processes to a music phrase. The origins of process music lie in serialism, but process music is used most often with minimalism. It could be as simple as inverting a melodic passage or adding an extra eighth note each time the passage is played. These processes can be either added during the performance itself or built into the composition.

Review

Over the last century, composers have done much to innovate and grow the world of interactive composition. By examining the past, you can not only draw inspiration from these experimental compositions, but also spark your own imagination in your writing.

Experimental compositional techniques used throughout the twentieth century include indeterminacy in timbre, instrumentation, pitch, duration, dynamics, form, and rhythm. Indeterminacy can refer to variation in the performance, but can also refer to how a piece was composed, including using methods of chance and randomization to create the composition itself.

Randomization of the order of phrases is a popular technique in video game music, especially when memory constraints limit the amount of overall music that can be used.

The idea behind a composition can be just as important as, or more important than, the actual aesthetic qualities of the composition.

Process music such as serialism and the 12-tone technique applied various rules to the compositional process. Mathematical transformations can also be applied to the work, including retrograde, inversion, and retrograde-inversion of a passage.

Limitations can force a composer to look for new ways to be creative.

Randomized processes can help augment and increase the length of the music heard before repetition of a score begins.

Aleatoric compositional techniques can help create new avenues for sound palettes, including clusters and microtuning.

Effects and DSP can be used to create new and unusual music.

Process music is the application of mathematical processes to a music phrase. The origins of process music lie in serialism, but this approach is used most often with minimalism.

Exercises

1. How might the techniques used in an interactive nondigital music composition from the twentieth century apply to a modern game? Pick an experimental composition that hasn't been discussed in this chapter and outline how its interactive techniques might be applied today.

2. Compose a piece of music using the experimental composition techniques introduced in this chapter.

FUNDAMENTAL VIDEO GAME SCORING TECHNIQUES

CHAPTER 7

COMPOSING AND EDITING MUSIC LOOPS

Music loops are integral to extending music in a scene. Given that each gameplay experience is different for the player, composers must be able to write clean loops of music to let players extend their experiences through a level. Composing music loops is an essential skill that all interactive music composers need to know. This chapter describes best practices to create seamless loops from a compositional and technological perspective, including audio editing and musical considerations.

The Art of Looping Music

Many video games have variable-length scenes, which add constraints to how we compose music for those scenes. The first building block of creating music for games is creation of a seamless loop. Video game composers use musical loops to lengthen pieces of music to match and adapt to the pace of the player. There are many tricks and techniques to creating perfect seamless loops. In this chapter you'll explore the various ways to build them.

Creating seamless musical loops for video games is a fairly new art in which composers need to know not only how to write the actual music but also how to edit it on a computer to make a seamless loopable file. Many experienced video game composers learned the art of looping by a lot of trial and error. In fact, they probably can't even verbalize how they learned how to do this because it's rarely a skill that is taught in music composition courses. Unfortunately, there are not a lot of available texts on the subject. This chapter will help you along the sometimes bumpy road of creating these loops.

Music loop creation for games is a multidisciplinary skill combining both musical artistry and technical expertise within an audio editor. To build a clean loop, you need both of these skills. This chapter assumes that you are already proficient at sequencing within a DAW and that you've done some audio editing in the past.

Creating loops is not unique to video games. In written music, you've probably seen the various ways to notate repeats, bringing the performer back to an earlier point in the music to repeat either a phrase or a measure (Figure 7.1). Also, when creating software instruments, you may have used various tools to create a single note loop on a sampled instrument such as an arco violin. Knowledge of these techniques will help you better understand the process of creating musical loops for games.

Figure 7.1 Examples of the various repeat symbols in written musical notation

There is no standard industry software for creating and editing music loops. Indeed, composers working in video games use many different sequencers and audio editors. Use whichever software you are most familiar with to apply the techniques shown throughout this chapter. The examples are not specific to any one piece of software.

This chapter focuses primarily on one species of musical loops—namely, a continuous piece of music without silence to cover the loop point. With these loops, you typically don't hear the beginning or end of a piece; that is, the music continues seamlessly without stopping. In an actual game music environment, you may create the beginnings and endings as separate pieces that are attached to these looped pieces. For the focus of this chapter, though, it's important to be able to create these seamless pieces of music.

There are two types of music loops you'll create for games:

- **Nonsynchronized Loops.** These loops are played back alone (one at a time), and used typically when composing for horizontal resequencing (Figure 7.2). They provide more flexibility in terms of where you can trim the beginnings and ends of your loops.

- **Synchronized Loops.** These loops need to play back at the same time as another music loop (Figure 7.3). They are typically used when composing for vertical remixing (layering). Synchronized loops need to have exactly the same length (sample accurate), which means that clean seamless loops are more difficult to create.

In this chapter you'll explore the basic disciplines of audio postproduction and editing to help you to create better loops.

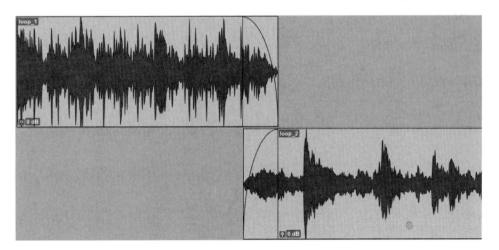

Figure 7.2 An example of how one loop fades out while another loop fades in. These loops have no rhythmic synchronicity and don't need to line up.

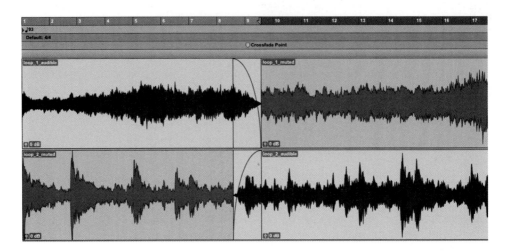

Figure 7.3 The two pieces of music match each other in terms of tempo and meter, so the timing between the two loops needs to be exactly the same.

> **tip**
>
> Recently, composing software packages such as Logic, Ableton Live, and ProTools have added fantastic features to help users create seamless loops. For instance, Logic has a feature called "Bounce 2nd Cycle Pass," which will stitch the end material to the front material to create a flawless loop. Consult your software manuals to see which options are available to you.

Musical Construction, Connections, and Cadences

Before we jump into a discussion of how to build musical loops for video games, it's important to break down some concepts regarding how a piece of music works.

If you analyze the structure of a piece of music, you'll notice that it likely has a beginning, a middle, and an end. The middle of the piece contains one or more sections of music that make up the main ideas of the composition. We can break this down even further to explore form in musical language.

Composers write musical ideas that form the musical sentences called phrases. Each musical phrase contributes to the overall musical cue. These phrases are then organized into sections. The overall musical organization of these sections is called the form of a piece. Many common

Table 7.1   Common Musical Forms

Form	Description
Strophic or Iterative	AAA
Binary	AB or AABB
Ternary	ABA
Rondo	ABACA or ABACADA
Arch	ABCBA

forms exist in music, ranging from the traditional, like the sonata form (exposition, development, recapitulation), to the modern, like the form in popular songs (verse, chorus, bridge).

In modern music, generally each distinct section of the form is given a letter: A, B, C, and so on. Table 7.1 shows some common forms in music.

Within video games, the idea of form comes into play when music phrases can be reordered or repeated based on the actions of the player. If you listen to a piece of video game music outside a game, you will hear it in order from the beginning to the end. A composer may compose the music this way, but when the piece of music actually gets put into the video game, we often break it into smaller sections with individual phrases. As the player controls the story outcome, these decisions in turn affect the order in which the music plays back.

Because this music is generally broken up into smaller chunks with individual phrases to customize the experience for the player, composers should know how a piece of music in a video game is played back. In most cases, composers break their scores down in the following way:

Introduction

Section 1 (looping)

Section 2 (looping)

Section . . . (looping)

Ending

Each section may then be broken down into even smaller individual phrases. For example, Section 1 may consist of four distinct phrases that may be played in any order. These details are left to the composer, allowing the composer to find the right voice and distinctive style for the game.

The parameters of the game itself may also dictate how the music is composed. For instance, if the memory footprint for the game must be small, as is the case with many Internet games, only a small amount of music may be included in the game. In such a scenario, adding a significant amount of randomness by mixing up the musical phrases might help the composer overcome the repetition problem.

On the one hand, because the music being written is so dependent on moving from one section to another, it's important for much of the music to be adaptable, so that it can flow smoothly from section to section. On the other hand, Section 1 may have to play for an extended period of time waiting for the player to reach a certain point. Writing Section 1 so that it can seamlessly loop will, therefore, be extremely important to fill that time.

Throughout this chapter, you'll break down all the musical elements of the creation of these individual sections or building blocks. You'll then see how these pieces are edited in your sequencer or digital audio workstation (DAW).

When composing a cue that needs to loop, make sure that you don't have any dramatic shifts in instrumentation, dynamics, or harmony at your loop point, as such a break will make the loop point more obvious to the player. For instance, if the entire instrument palette changes from the beginning of the loop to the end, a very obvious loop jump will occur once the music returns to the beginning. A better approach would be to extend the cue by reversing the instrument palette change before looping around to the beginning. If your musical cue needs to have a dramatic shift embedded in it for a specific reason, it's better to go over the top and use drums or percussion to emphasize the beginning of the loop.

Connecting the various cues together is very important. A mistake that composers frequently make when composing in various pieces is making the pieces too different from one another. Even though you're breaking down the musical cue into smaller sections, all of those sections should relate to one another—for example, by having a similar lead instrument or harmonic framework that brings them together.

Last, remember to use musical cadences effectively. Make sure that the end of your loop terminates with a musical cadence that resolves when it returns to the beginning. This will make the bridge more seamless.

> ### note
> Sometimes a developer may want to present the music in its original form instead of cutting it up into phrases, so as to preserve the integrity of the overall composition. In these scenarios, variety is generally added by increasing the number of cue variations. The composer or audio team will create many derivative cues based on the original. These creative choices are made by the music team in collaboration with the game developer.

Audio Editing

A little acoustic theory will help you understand why some music loops feel seamless, and why others don't. In this section you'll learn the basics of acoustics and audio editing—knowledge that will help you create better loops. It is far beyond the scope of this book to examine acoustics in depth, so we've limited the discussion here to a music-centric consideration of how acoustics is used within music.

Sound travels through the air in waves of differing pressure, ranging from high pressure to low pressure. This variation in air pressure causes the ear to perceive audio. Audio is measured in musical terms as volume (amplitude) and pitch (frequency).

- **Volume:** The amount of the variation in air pressure is representative of the overall volume of a sound. The greater the variation, the louder the sound will be.

- **Pitch:** The speed at which the air pressure fluctuates is representative of the pitch. Faster fluctuations in air pressure are perceived as a higher pitch, whereas slower fluctuations are perceived as a lower pitch.

When you examine a waveform digitally in an audio editor, you're looking at the increases and decreases in air pressure on the vertical axis versus time on the horizontal axis (Figure 7.4).

When the digital wave is translated back to analog so that it can be played through speakers, a change in the positive direction (vertical access) is represented by an increase in air pressure. Quite literally, the speaker pushes out toward you to create the increase in air pressure. Conversely, a change in the negative direction translates into a decrease in air pressure, with the speaker pulling in the other direction, away from you. Thus sound is translated from its digital form into electricity, which pushes the speaker back and forth to create the analog sound that you can hear.

How is this relevant to creating music loops in games? When an audio file is looped in a game, we want the end of the loop to line up exactly with the beginning of the loop, like in Figure 7.5.

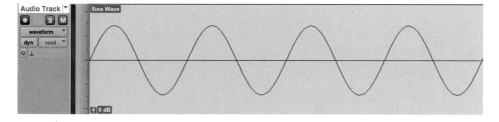

Figure 7.4 A single sine wave is turned into an audio signal by first increasing air pressure, then decreasing air pressure as the wave cycles.

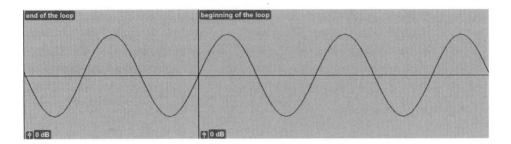

Figure 7.5   An example of a clean loop where the end of the loop lines up precisely with the beginning of the loop

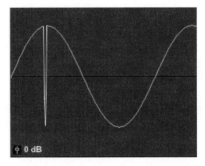

Figure 7.6   What the audio waveform would look like if it contained an audible pop. Audible pops are created by very quick changes in an audio waveform.

If our loops don't line up exactly, we'll experience a jump in air pressure. A rapid increase or decrease in air pressure will produce a high-frequency noise—that is, a pop. In Figures 7.6 and 7.7, you can see two examples of a pop in a music loop.

When editing music loops, it's important to take many different details into account. Throughout the rest of this section, you'll learn about each of the following factors and things to look out for when editing your audio loops:

- Zero crossing points
- Waveform shape and direction
- Transient and legato elements
- Music tempo, meter, and performance
- Reverb tails and long decays
- Crossfading

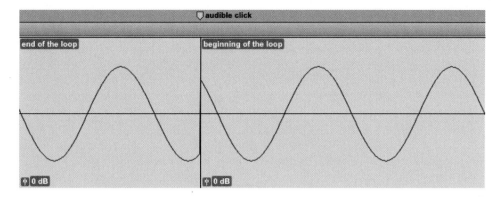

Figure 7.7   An example of a bad loop, in which the end of the loop and the beginning of the loop don't line up, causing an audible pop at the loop point

Zero Crossing Points

Many composers and editors choose to edit their audio files so that they cut only on the zero crossings. When looking at the visual representation of the waveform in an audio editor, the zero crossing point is the middle point on the vertical access, usually labeled with the number 0. At this point, there is no air pressure change in the waveform and the speaker is resting at its default middle position (not pushing outward or pulling inward).

If you edit both the beginning and the end of your files at a zero crossing point, the speaker is guaranteed not to make a large jump when starting or ending the file. As mentioned earlier, such an abrupt break would create a pop or audible click.

Many sound editing programs (e.g., Sony's SoundForge and Adobe Audition) allow you to select a portion of the wave to snap the edges of the selection to a zero crossing point. Unfortunately, there is a downside to enabling the zero crossing feature. If you are working in an environment where you must be sample accurate in the timing of your edits—for example, if two files must loop at the exact same time—the zero crossing feature in some editing programs will actually work against you by extending or shortening your editing length to reach the zero crossing.

When you are editing multiple files that need to be the same length, there is no guarantee that the separate audio files will all cross the zero point at exactly the same point. You should never use the zero crossing feature if the music file must sync exactly to the timing of another file, because your loops will gradually lose synchronization with one another. In these cases you'll need to sync to the music beats, rather than finding the nearest zero crossing. When faced with this situation, you'll need to hide the loop point using some of the other techniques described in this chapter.

If the zero crossing feature is left on while editing, the files might be out of sync. That means the files will play correctly before the first loop point, but gradually start to lose sync with every subsequent loop of the file. This discrepancy occurs because one of the files is shorter than the other.

When you are not synchronizing music files in the game engine (nonsynchronized loops), you can lengthen and shorten your music loop to get to a good zero crossing point without worrying too much about affecting the overall musical timing of the wave as long as it's less than 3 to 5 milliseconds. In turn, you'll be able to create cleaner, more seamless loops.

You can create your own zero crossing points by fading the end and beginning of the wave to avoid having a pop or audio click. This strategy doesn't always work, and generally it's better to use it with incredibly short fade times (less than 1 millisecond).

Waveform Shape and Direction

When choosing the beginning and ending points of your music loop, it's important to examine and match both the waveform shape and the direction in which the waveform is headed. This technique works primarily with nonsynchronized loops.

The larger the change in the waveform shape from the end of the loop to the end of the loop and back to the beginning, the more likely that a pop or click will occur when the music loops back around. Sometimes you can take advantage of this behavior, as transient material tends to hide your loop points. In most cases, however, you don't want to hear a click or pop when you loop back around. These transient pieces are much more common in techno music, but are rare in orchestral music, making the latter more difficult to loop. Try to match the overall amplitude and shape from the end to the beginning of your loop.

In addition, to minimize any clicks or pops at your loop point, make sure to match the direction of the waveform at the end of the loop. For instance, if the end of your loop is moving from high pressure to low pressure (positive to negative), you'll want the beginning of that loop to continue moving in the same direction toward lower pressure. Figure 7.8 shows an example of a loop that will create a pop because the waveform reverses direction at the beginning of the loop.

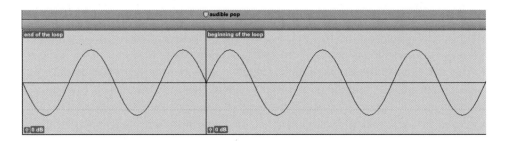

Figure 7.8   Even though the two waveforms match at the zero crossing point, the end of the loop is headed downward, and the beginning of the loop is going in the opposite direction. This creates an audible pop when the music loops back to the beginning.

Transient and Legato Elements

A transient is a high-amplitude, fast-attack, short-duration sound. Drums and percussion have sharp transients or high impacts when the sound begins, but then trail off. A high transient sound at the beginning of the loop will help disguise a bad edit. Because a bad edit usually contains a click or pop at the loop transition point, if the loop is composed in such a way that it has a transient (percussion hit) at the beginning of your loop, it will help hide the bad loop points.

Rather than relying on transients, many composers try to avoid using some musical elements at the loop point that are difficult to loop without an audible click. Sounds that have no transients are far more difficult to loop, especially when you need to use synchronized loops. Synth pads, arco strings, and delays or long reverb are also more challenging to loop.

There are several solutions for dealing with difficult looping elements in your mix:

- Move the legato elements to the middle of the audio loop instead of having them near the loop point.

- Fade the legato elements before and after the loop point. This is fairly challenging to do without the loop sounding awkward. In general, the longer the fade (1–3 seconds), the better it will sound. Shorter fades will typically sound like a drop-out in the recording.

- Overlap two separate loops with the legato elements that have different fade points so that one is always playing. This technique works only when you do not have to sync your harmonic content and is generally useful only with a drone or pedal that needs to play constantly through a scene. For example, if your first loop is 19 seconds and your second loop is 27 seconds, the loops would sync up only every 513 seconds (19 × 27).

- Use more silence in your music loops so that a fade at your loop point doesn't sound awkward. Silence is under-represented in most video game music and can be an effective tool for any composer.

Music Tempo, Meter, and Performance

In general, most composers edit their loops to begin and end on downbeats. It's far easier to remember to cut on the downbeats while editing instead of on an offbeat, but occasionally there are circumstances when it might be advantageous for the composer to cut the loops in another place. For instance, if the style is jazz and contains chordal anticipations, then it might be easier to cut all the loops on the anticipation before the downbeat, because that's where the chord actually changes. Alternatively, if there is some obvious rhythmic ostinato that overrides the meter, it might be a better place for the composer to cut. In these instances, remember to *be consistent*; that is, If you decide to cut some of your loops on beat 3, make sure to cut *all* of your loops on beat 3.

When using live instruments, if you look closely at the waveform, you'll notice that some of the players may have started slightly earlier or slightly later than their first note. This adds to the realism of having real musicians play the piece but may make it more difficult to cut up the music in the editing process. Also, as a composer/musician, you've probably heard of musicians playing "on top" of the beat or "in the pocket." These terms refer to the players performing slightly ahead of the beat or slightly after the beat, respectively. Because you don't want their performances to feel robotic, you'll want to let the players add their musicality to the music—which means that some of those imperfections in the performance are desirable. But what happens when you need to cut these performances up into loops?

When you're in the process of editing these loops, do you cut right on the beat (possibly cutting off the initial attack of one of your violin parts), or right when the first player comes in (before the initial attack)? Unfortunately, there is no right answer. The important thing to remember while cutting up the loops is that whatever you do, be consistent. If you edit slightly ahead of the beat, make sure your ending is also slightly ahead of the beat. Some composers choose to edit each of the initial instrument notes to be exactly on the downbeat of the phrase; they can then cut directly on the downbeat without having to worry whether the live player played early or late. In this scenario. the composer would likely leave the rest of the musical performance intact.

Reverb Tails and Long Decays

There are two additional stumbling blocks that we must overcome to create seamless loops: the reverb tail and the natural decay of certain instruments. These two challenges make it more difficult to create seamless-sounding loops.

When composing loops, try to have as few instruments as possible bleed across the loop point with long decays. If your piece is in 4/4 time and a crash cymbal hits on the end of the fourth beat, it's likely that this sound will be cut off when the music completes the cycle and loops back to the first beat. As a general rule, avoid having notes with long decays cross the loop boundary.

One of the difficulties with creating seamless loops is the *reverb problem*. When the sound loops back around, what happens to the reverb and ambience that was supposed to play from the end of the sound? Does it just disappear? Unfortunately, it does—you are no longer using your sequencer, but rather are dealing with a final mixed track. That split second of missing reverb is definitely noticeable. Most music has reverb on it to give it shape and ambience, so when you go from hearing reverb to the second when the reverb disappears at the beginning of the loop, it sounds unnatural. To overcome this problem, you'll need to take the reverb that was supposed to play at the end of the loop and merge it into the beginning of the loop before bouncing your final mix.

The next question you might ask is, "Won't I hear the extra reverb at the head of the loop?" The answer is that you probably won't notice it. If there is a substantial difference in the music at the end of the loop and at the beginning, the extra reverb will be very noticeable. But as discussed in the previous sections, the best way to create a loop is to match up the ending with the beginning. If you followed those guidelines, it's unlikely that you'll even notice the extra reverb at the front.

To copy and paste the reverb to the front of the loop, you'll need to have access to the raw materials that made up the mix in the first place: the individual instrument tracks, plug-ins, and mix. You won't be able to take just your final mix and extract the reverb from it. Composers create these assets while in the final mix stage, with the entire sequence open in their DAW. While in your mix stage, create a seamless loop with reverb by completing the following steps:

1. Insert several bars of silence before and after the section you want to loop.

2. Bounce down the section that you'll be looping, making sure to bounce it 5 seconds longer than you need so you'll have the extra reverb tail.

3. Copy that reverb tail to the beginning of the piece onto a new track.

4. Bounce down just the section that you'll be using in the game to the exact length of your loop.

The same considerations apply when you're working with long delays or echoes on certain instruments. If you choose to have longer delays on certain instruments, those delays will get cut off when the music returns to the beginning of the loop. Because delays are also more obvious than reverb in terms of their tonality, merging in the delay tails at the beginning of a loop may be impossible without the cue sounding strange. In general, with longer delays, you're better off letting the instrument end earlier and allowing the instrument delays to fade out before the end of the loop; that way, the delays won't be cut off unexpectedly as the delay crosses the loop boundary.

There is a shortcut to overcoming the reverb problem that is generally easier than copying the reverb tail of the mix and merging it onto the beginning of your loop. When you're done composing the section that needs to be looped, while still in the sequencer, take the very last bar of the music and splice it into the beginning of the music. Bounce down the entire piece of music, including the extra bar at the beginning of the music. Then open the final bounce in your audio editor and delete the first bar. This way you'll have the reverb tail already embedded into the front of your loop.

As previously mentioned, some modern DAWs (Logic, Ableton Live, ProTools) have special functionality built in to help you with creating seamless loops. Check your manual to see how that functionality works.

> **note**
>
> If you're using an audio middleware solution like AudioKinetic's Wwise in your final game, you might be able to bounce down your loops with the extended reverb tails (called the "post-exit" in Wwise) without merging them into the front of your loop. Markers within Wwise allow you to define where your loop and reverb tails begin and end. This incredible feature allows each loop to have its own reverb tail that plays when going from section to section. In addition, it's a valuable time saver for composers.

Crossfading

Throughout this chapter you've read about how fades on the loops can sometimes be used to minimize audible clicks in your loops. The downside of fading is sometimes audible: it might sound like a drop-out at the loop point. Some composers use another trick to fix these kinds of loop problems in complicated musical material—namely, crossfades.

In your sequencer, you may have used a crossfade to knit two pieces of music together seamlessly. You can use this trick to edit your loops for games as well. Basically you'll need to prebuild the crossfades into the loop directly by duplicating the crossfade that might happen if you did it manually in your DAW. This technique allows music that is typically difficult to loop (e.g., nontransient material, or music with delays) to be looped more easily.

The steps shown in this section enable you to create an eight-bar loop using the crossfade technique. Essentially, you copy the first bar of your music to the end of the loop before you bounce your virtual instruments. After you bounce down with the extra bar, you line up the mix as if you were repeating it three times, fading the edit points. You then cut out the middle eight bars to complete the final loop. Step-by-step instructions follow below.

While you're in the sequencer composing your loop, with your virtual and live instruments still separate, do the following:

1. Build your music cue so that it has a pickup measure before the cue starts (we'll refer to this as bar 0).

2. Copy the first bar of your actual loop (bar 1) and paste it at the end of your cue (bar 9).

3. Bounce the entire mix to a new track from bar 0 through bar 9—the silent bar 0 through the reverb tail in bar 9.

4. Create a new sequence with the same tempo map, then add three new audio tracks.

5. On the first audio track, paste the bounced mix at bar 0.

6. On the next audio track, paste the segment again, starting at bar 8, overlapping the two pieces.

7. On the third track, paste the mix again, starting at bar 16.

8. Next we create the fades between the three loops. Begin by fading out (using equal power) the first mix in bar 9 from beat 1 to beat 2.

9. Fade in (using equal power) the second mix on the pickup beat at the end of bar 8.

10. Fade out (using equal power) the second mix in bar 17 from beat 1 to beat 2.

11. Fade in (using equal power) the third mix on the pickup beat at the end of bar 16.

12. Bounce this new mix.

13. In a separate audio editor, delete bars 0 through 8 and delete bars 17 through the end.

This leaves you with a fully loopable eight-bar mix.

The advantage of using this technique is that you get a seamless loop, just as if you were editing it in the DAW with the power of crossfades at the loop points.

Auditioning Your Finished Loops

Once you've composed the musical cues and cut them up into loops, it's important to test them to make sure they play back correctly. The best way to do this is to actually listen to the loops in the game engine. Many times the game engine isn't ready to have sound placed into it, however, so you'll want to have some strategies for listening to how your loops play so that you can decide whether they're working properly.

The next best way to hear whether a loop is working is to paste the finished mix onto a track end to end several times. You can then listen to how it loops in either your DAW or an audio editor.

Although many audio editors (e.g., Adobe Audition, Sony's SoundForge) allow you to enable loop playback during listening to hear how a loop will sound, sometimes the loop playback may not be consistently reliable. There are a lot of technical reasons why this is true, primarily dealing with the way that the software interfaces with the hardware, by starting and stopping audio playback on the sound card.

The best way to audition your loops is to play them back directly in the game engine. Otherwise, the next best way to hear them is to paste your mix end to end in a DAW to see whether they are seamless.

> **note**
>
> If your final file format needs to be compressed, just the act of saving a WAV file in the MP3 format in Sound Forge may destroy your nice, smooth loop. Always test your loops in the game engine in the correct format to make sure that they loop properly, as audio conversions may affect your loop points. Middleware engines such as Wwise and Fmod usually don't lead to these kinds of problems because they include automatic loop compensation, but for people who are working on Flash games file conversions can be a significant problem.

Review

Music loop creation for games is a multidisciplinary skill combining both musical artistry and technical expertise within an audio editor.

There are two types of music loops you'll create for games. Nonsynchronized loops are loops that are played back alone. Synchronized loops are loops that need to play back at the same time as another music loop.

When you are composing a cue that will need to loop, make sure there are no dramatic shifts in instrumentation, dynamics, or harmony at the loop point. Such breaks will make the loop point more obvious to the player.

When you are editing music loops, many factors influence how well your cue will work. The following techniques can help improve your loops: (1) edit on zero crossing points; (2) make sure that the waveform maintains its shape and direction across the loop point; (3) use transient elements to disguise loop points; (4) match the musical characteristics at the loop point (e.g., tempo, harmony, density); and (5) add reverb tails to the front of your loops.

If your final file format needs to be compressed, just the act of saving a WAV file in the MP3 format in Sound Forge may destroy your nice, smooth loop. Always test your loops in the game engine in the correct format to make sure that they loop properly, as audio conversions may sometimes affect the loop points.

Exercises

1. Listen to any commercially released game and analyze the lengths of the loops in the game for duration and effectiveness.

2. Using music from several genres and styles, see how difficult it is to loop sections of the music.

3. Create musical loops from a piece that you've composed and for which you have the original sequence.

   - Were you able to make all your loops seamless?

   - Did you have to make any adjustments to the sequence to create seamless loops?

4. Create two sample accurate music loops using synchronized loops that must work together. Which difficulties did you encounter?

CHAPTER 8

HORIZONTAL RESEQUENCING

Horizontal resequencing is a method of interactive composition where the music is dynamically pieced together based on the actions of the player. For example. when the music is playing underneath the gameplay, it may reach a decision point in the music when it could either go to a new section of music or repeat the previous section depending on the player's actions. Horizontal resequencing is used to handle this kind of branching. In this chapter you'll explore the pros and cons of using this type of interactive scoring method and learn techniques relevant to writing for this medium.

Sequencing Music in Real Time

Horizontal resequencing is an interactive music technique that composers use to adapt music in real time within video games. This technique queues up the individual music cues dynamically based on player decisions and outcomes.

To sequence music is to arrange it in a particular order, similar to creating a playlist within iTunes. In a video game, these playlists are generated on the fly as the player makes his or her way through the level. In the beginning of the game, there may be an action scene, followed by exploration, then a battle sequence, then back to exploration, and so on. In many games you can't predict how long a player might spend in a particular state or which state might come next. With horizontal resequencing, you create this music playlist dynamically on the fly. Essentially, you shuffle the music cues around based on player decisions and outcomes.

Another way to think about this concept is to relate it to a *Choose Your Own Adventure* book. These paperback books for children have decision points on the bottom of many pages, allowing readers to construct their own story. When you get through reading a section of the book, you are asked to make a decision. Do you head into the cave and follow the Yeti (turn to page 87), or do you return to camp to get more gear (turn to page 101)? In a video game, music can branch dynamically moving from one cue to another based on decisions made by the player.

The term "horizontal resequencing" is derived from the fact that many music editing programs (e.g., ProTools, Logic) display the overall timeline moving from left to right, horizontally. As these are time-based changes, queuing up new pieces of music as the player moves through the story over time, it's a logical step to call this technique horizontal resequencing.

Recall the definition of a musical cue: a complete musical thought with a beginning, a middle, and an end. Horizontal resequencing is typically used when one idea has finished and a new one needs to begin. As a consequence, this technique is better suited for longer sequences (more than 20 seconds per cue) when you don't have to go back and forth between different states quickly. If your game changes emotional states in shorter intervals (less than 20 seconds), you may want to choose another technique. Given that a cue is a complete musical thought or idea, rapid changes between two ideas using horizontal resequencing are discouraged because they distract from the idea that a level has a central theme or idea.

As an example, at the end of a level in a video game, the music for that level may need to end and the music for the next scene begin. This may be done by using a hard edit—that is, stopping the first piece of music and beginning the next. More commonly, a composer might choose to write a transition to move from one cue to another more seamlessly by bridging them together. At other times, the transition waits until a defined point in the music (like a bar line or the end of a musical phrase) to better bridge the transition to the next piece of music.

> **note**
>
> Many of the large publishers and platform holders have audio teams that manage the interactive components, thereby freeing up the composer to focus on creating compelling content. It's a nice value add for the publisher when the composer is creatively aware of interactive scoring practices, but such knowledge is not absolutely necessary.

This chapter is devoted to horizontal resequencing and its use within video games. You'll learn the advantages and disadvantages of this technique, along with best practices. Once you've learned about the crossfading, transitional, and branching scoring models discussed in this chapter, you can apply the digital tools included with this book to test these techniques. The digital tools include an app for each one of these models.

Crossfading Scores

A crossfading score is a type of horizontal resequencing model that fades out one musical cue while fading up another musical cue (Figure 8.1). This type of score is probably the most common of all game scores because it is the simplest to implement from a programming point of view. Its biggest advantage is that the change from one cue to another is almost immediate, allowing for tight synchronization with the player's actions. The primary disadvantage is that the transition between one cue and another can feel a little like changing stations on a radio if the cues are very different.

There are two general types of crossfading scores:

- **Synchronized Crossfading Score.** In this score, the tempo maps of both cues are matched (Figure 8.2). For example, when the first cue is fading out on bar 4, the second cue is fading up on bar 4. This allows the composer to match the rhythm and tempo of the first cue with the second, making for a more seamless transition. In addition, the composer may choose to match the harmonic framework (or chord map), making the

Figure 8.1   An example of how one piece of music fades out while another fades in

transition from one cue to another even less abrupt. The disadvantage of synchronized crossfading is that you can't change the overall tempo of the piece based on some event in the game because the cues are locked together.

- **Nonsynchronized Crossfading Score.** In this kind of score, the two tracks do not share the same timeline or tempo map. When the new cue is faded in, it may not share any of the characteristics of the previous cue, thus making it less seamless and more abrupt to the player. The harmony may also clash between the two cues during the fade point, suggesting to the player that there may have been a mistake in the overall music. In addition, the score might be in the middle of a cadence or melody that will sound awkward if it's split when transitioning to a new cue. Of all the techniques discussed, this transition is the most startling for the player.

When writing for this framework, the synchronized crossfading score is preferred over the nonsynchronized score because the composer can tie both cues together in terms of rhythmic and harmonic progression, allowing for a seamless transition between cues. The synchronized crossfading score offers immediate transitions and musical coherence from one cue to the next because the cues share the same harmonic structure and tempo map.

Another disadvantage of the nonsynchronized score is that because the change from one cue to another is immediate, one cue may interrupt an important musical moment, such as the middle of a melody or cadence, making the player feel unsettled.

The template included with the digital tools that accompany this book has three different slots that you can assign to three different states (Figure 8.3). For example, you may choose to write an explore cue, a suspense cue, and a battle cue. When you start the template, you can then test how well your score works by clicking on the new cue and seeing how the cues fade against each other. You can set the crossfade in and out times to better customize the playback.

When choosing the fade times that establish how the new cue fades in and the old cue fades out, you'll need to experiment with your music to see what works best. In most circumstances, the fade-in sounds better with a shorter time. This is because music tends to be more pronounced

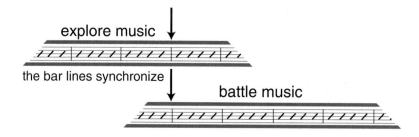

Figure 8.2   An example of a synchronized score in which one piece of music fades out while another fades in, and both pieces keep the same rhythm

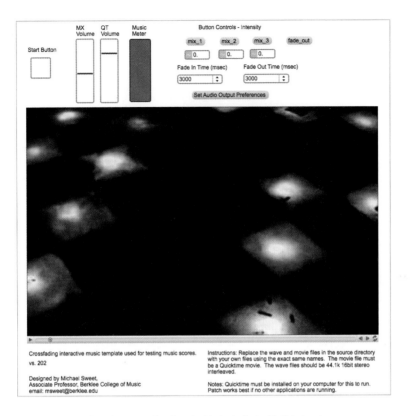

Figure 8.3   The crossfading demo application that is included with this book

as it enters, but tends to decay at a slower rate. The fade-out of the previous cue generally has a longer fade time, as we generally want the decay of the previous piece to last longer.

> **note**
>
> Audio middleware packages such as Wwise and Fmod allow composers and audio teams to customize with great detail the way music cues branch from one piece to another. Some of the details that can be customized are synchronization aspects, crossfade times, and playback of a transition (or not) before the next cue starts.

Transitional Scores

A transitional score is the same as a crossfading score but uses a transitional cue that bridges the two pieces of music (Figure 8.4). This transitional cue can be any length but generally works better if the cue is longer (10 or more seconds), allowing for a better bridge between the two pieces.

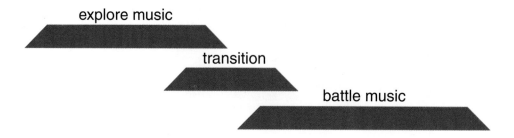

Figure 8.4   An example of how a transition is used to bridge two musical cues

Games like *Final Fantasy XIII* (2009) tend to use a sound effect as the transitional element to get the player from explore mode to combat mode. Other games, such as *Uncharted 2* (2010), use longer musical transitions to bridge the two musical cues.

Chapter 10 focuses on writing effective transitions that connect two musical cues together. In general, a well-written transition can bridge two different harmonic frameworks as well as two distinct tempos, allowing transitional scores for video games to be extremely flexible. Because the transition needs to be able to play at any time over the first cue, it's best to write the beginning of the cue without a tempo; then the first cue has time to fade out, before it is followed by the transition. Glissandos and crescendos, for example, are good ways to transition from one tempo to another.

The downside of this type of score is that because the two cues can be very distinct from each other, you wouldn't want to hear a transition between two cues in quick succession. This type of scoring technique works best if at least 30 seconds separates transitions.

Similar to the crossfading technique, another disadvantage is that the melody or cadence might potentially be interrupted by the transition.

Included with the digital tool set that accompanies this book is a template for testing transitional scores. The template provides two states (musical cues) and two transitions. The first transition plays between cue 1 and cue 2, and the second transition plays in reverse, from cue 2 back to cue 1.

> tip
>
> Although some games have made transitions or tension indicators iconic (e.g., the IE Metal Gear Solid (!) exclamation stinger, 1998), having the same transitional material appear between all music cues can get very old, very quickly. Games are often scoped to have composers create a wealth of transition variations to overcome repetition in the game.

Branching Scores

The last type of score in horizontal resequencing is the branching score, which waits for the first music cue to finish the current musical phrase before moving on to the next music cue (Figure 8.5). This is the most musical of all the interactive models explored in the book because you're guaranteed not to interrupt a music melody or the harmonic progression of your music.

The downside of this type of score is that the synchronization to the game may not be as tight. For instance, if your musical phrase has just started when the game calls for a music cue change, it may take a period of time for the phrase to end before it can transition into the new cue. You may have experienced this situation in a game, when you're fighting a boss monster and the music is full of tension and dynamics with the whole orchestra playing. Then you take out the boss, but the colossal music cue continues—so you think that you have another monster to kill. While you're looking around the level for another monster, the music finally reaches the branch point and transitions to a smaller suspense cue. At this point, you as a player hear the mechanics of the music engine making a mistake.

For this reason, branching scores tend to work best if the musical phrases are short (less than 10 seconds). This means that the musical genre can influence the effectiveness of a branching score. Classical melodies and phrases tend to be longer than 10 seconds, making it difficult to use them in a branching score. By comparison, rock and techno melodies tend to be shorter, making it much easier to implement this technique using those styles.

In many cases when a branching score is used, each individual phrase is bounced separately. That way, the score can be constructed in real time, allowing the game to mix and match phrases in a random sequence. For instance, suppose you're writing a suspense section that is 32 bars. There are 4 phrases, each 8 bars long, that make up the full suspense section. You can write the music in such a way that you split up those 4 phrases into their own files; then, when you play the suspense cue, you can play those files in a random order.

This method of scoring is useful when the composer wants clean musical transitions in the interactive score, or wants to change the emotional quality of the scene using harmony or a tempo change. Branching scores don't always change between two different states as quickly as they do with vertical remixing.

explore music

battle music

Figure 8.5   A representation of how one musical cue ends and another begins without using any fades

Random playlists allow the composer to deliver a lot of variety during playback of a limited set of assets. This branching technique helps games overcome the repetition problem. It is often used in casual and handheld games because there is generally less memory available for music on these platforms.

The digital tool set included with this book provides two branching engines in which you can test your scores. The first one is used for traditional cue-to-cue branching; the second engine has random playlists, allowing for multiple individual phrases per state. When you click a new state change, the engine will wait until the current file has finished playing before moving on to the next cue. A built-in timer shows the amount of time before the next decision point is reached, which would allow the engine to move on to the next music state.

When developing the framework for your composition, think about good places to divide up your music into these individual phrases. These phrases will be the markers indicating when your composition can move to another section based on the gameplay. In the composition process, think about how your musical cadences will be reflected when you exit one phrase and move to the next. Building an overall strategy for the natural tension and release of musical phrases will go a long way toward creating a great musical score.

If you're an astute reader, you may have noticed that a branching score is really a kind of crossfading score, but with notes that wait until the end of a musical phrase to do the cross-fade. Similarly, other variations on these themes exist—for example, crossfading at a "musically opportune moment" such as a measure or beat boundary, rather than waiting for the completion of the full musical phrase. Modern audio middleware accommodates many different ways to move from one musical cue to another. Composing an interactive score that is able to wait until the end of a phrase is different than writing a music cue that can be interrupted at any point. If your composition has strong melodies that shouldn't be interrupted, then branching at a musical point will work better than interrupting the music with a crossfade or transition.

tip

When using random playlists, you can achieve the most variety and randomness if the variations introduce slightly new ideas into the composition as they're played through. Each phrase within a section can extend the melodic ideas and have a different length to make the phrases more interesting. Think of each individual phrase of a section as part of a mini-form that might have heightened intensity in one variant and lowered intensity in another. You might even further the motiv by adding a bridge within a state. The utility of these techniques depends on how much music you can fit into your game or current level, but more variety is generally better for enhancing the player experience.

Composing for Horizontal Resequencing

When composing scores for games that use horizontal resequencing techniques, there are many musical considerations, including harmonic and tempo issues as well as decisions about how to set things up in your DAW for recording and mixing. The following subsections provide some advice about how you might approach these challenges.

Harmonic and Tempo Considerations

One advantage of using horizontal resequencing techniques in your video game score is that each phrase or cue can have its own tempo and/or harmonic framework. This allows you to radically change the music based on game events because the cues are different from one another. You could, for instance, change from one mode to another (e.g., from major to minor) based on some event within the game, or you could make changes to the tempo from cue to cue. These options aren't available when using the vertical remixing technique (discussed in Chapter 9).

On a cue-to-cue basis, having this much flexibility can also be a hindrance, as it's easy to write radically different cues that don't match up well with each other. This can increase the chances that the music will sound like a radio station has been changed when it moves from one cue to the next. Make sure that you stick to a single creative direction and have an element that links all of the cues together, such as a main instrument, theme, or harmonic or rhythmic device that remains consistent throughout all the cues.

Working within the DAW

There are several different ways to compose music for horizontal resequencing in a sequencer or DAW. Because it's easy to write radically different cues in this framework, many composers choose to write all the cues for a particular level within the same file, even if that file contains multiple sections. That way, the instrument palette tends to remain relatively static from state to state, helping to hold the overall creative direction together.

Lay out your cues back to back, with transitions (if you're using them) in between the sections. If there are tempo changes between sections, it is generally a good idea to insert 1 to 2 bars of silence so live players can adjust to the new tempo, and you have plenty of room to edit extended notes and reverb tails for mixing.

Delivery

There are several ways to deliver files to the development team if you're working with horizontal resequencing:

- **Individual Files.** This is the most common way to deliver all the individual pieces that make up your composition. Bounce down all the separate cues, taking into account any reverb tails and creating an individual file for each section.

- **Single File with Markers Separating Regions and Decision Points.** Less commonly, composers might deliver a single file with all the cues embedded into it back to back. Markers are then added to this file that represent decision points and points where cues start and end. This formatting usually adds more work for the programming side of things, but is an accepted way of delivering the files.

- **Multichannel Broadcast WAV Files.** You can embed as many as eight discrete stereo submixes in a single multichannel-broadcast WAV file. This file will likely be compressed for use within the game, but it's an excellent way to deliver multiple musical cues in a single file with layers if needed.

- **Audio Middleware Session.** If your team is using an audio middleware solution such as Wwise or Fmod, you can take your individual files and implement them directly into the middleware sound design tool that you pass to the development team. Both Wwise and Fmod have functionality that allows you to implement sophisticated horizontal resequencing compositions.

Review

Horizontal resequencing is an interactive music technique that composers use to adapt music in real time within video games. It queues up the individual music cues dynamically based on player decisions and outcomes.

The three primary ways to use horizontal resequencing are (1) crossfading, (2) transitions, and (3) branching.

When using transitions, be aware that repeating the same transitional material between all music cues can get very old, very quickly. Games are often scoped to have composers create a wealth of transition variations to overcome the problem of repetition in the game.

Each phrase or cue using horizontal resequencing can have its own tempo and/or harmonic framework, thereby taking advantage of tempo and harmonic changes synchronized to player actions. Make sure you tie all of your cues together by using a consistent instrument palette, theme, or harmonic or rhythmic device throughout all the cues.

When composing for this technique, lay out the cues back to back in the DAW, with transitions (if you're using them) in between the sections. Then, when you're doing the final mixing, you can separate each cue with a few measures of silence to properly capture the reverb tails and bounce the mixes to disk.

There are several options for delivering files to the development team if you're working with horizontal resequencing, including individual audio files, a single audio file with markers separating regions, a multichannel-broadcast WAV file, and an audio middleware session. Check with the developer to determine the best way to submit the files for the project you're working on.

Exercises

1. Analyze any commercially released game by listening for examples of horizontal resequencing techniques. List the cues that use these techniques, describing their use and measuring their length.

2. Find gameplay examples on YouTube that have at least three emotional levels or states. Using the digital template files included with this text, edit appropriate music for these examples within the branching template to sync with the video.

3. Using another gameplay clip from YouTube, compose your own transitional score for two states and two transitions to use in the digital template.

CHAPTER 9

VERTICAL REMIXING

Vertical remixing is an interactive composition technique in which layers of music are added or taken away to create levels of intensity and emotion. This method of scoring is useful when the composer needs multiple quick changes to intensify the score, where harmonic changes based on gameplay are not as important. In this chapter you'll explore the pros and cons of this type of interactive scoring method and learn about the best composing practices for this style.

Remixing Music for Intensity

Vertical remixing is an interactive music technique used in video games that uses different musical layers (or tracks) to alter the overall musical intensity. By adding more musical layers or taking them away, you can shape the music dramatically as the player experiences the game.

In general, when writing for vertical remixing, composers write a single piece of music that is divided into multiple layers. These layers then target various emotional states within the game. For instance, a composer might split up the music in the following configuration:

- Layer 1: ambient drone
- Layer 2: percussion
- Layer 3: string ostinato and melodic element

When the player starts the level, just Layer 1 (the ambient drone) plays as the player is exploring. When the player sees danger in the distance, the music engine fades in Layer 2 (percussion) on top of Layer 1 to increase the tension in the music. When the player encounters a battle with an enemy, Layer 3 (ostinato and melody) fades in. Then, as the player exits the battle and the danger ends, Layers 2 and 3 eventually fade out. This technique is shown in Figure 9.1.

This technique is used in many popular games, including *Red Dead Redemption* (2010), *Fallout: New Vegas* (2010), *and Mass Effect 2* (2010). It is relatively easy to implement. Another significant advantage of this technique is that there is a musical continuity between states, as the music is built from a single cue. This allows the music engine to fade in layers easily and quickly without the player becoming distracted by changes to the music.

Because vertical remixing uses a single cue, it usually begins at the start of a level. This single cue is then looped until the level or game sequence is finished. As a consequence, there is a linear framework to the harmonic structure and tempo map of the music. The dynamic and adaptive qualities of the music are simply fading in and fading out additional tracks of that same cue. Although this adds a cohesive quality to the music, it leads to some disadvantages.

One of the primary disadvantages of vertical remixing is the inability to sync harmonic or melodic changes to game events. The harmonic framework is static. For example, if you choose to use a 12-bar blues progression, the game will continuously loop through this progression

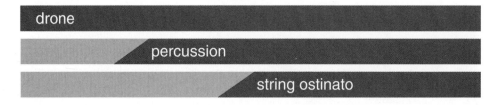

Figure 9.1   Musical layers of a score can be faded in over time using vertical remixing.

until the player reaches the end of the level. You won't be able to sync the dominant chord to a specific event in the scene, because there is no harmonic sync available. Harmonic sync is the ability for the music to change the current chord and key in conjunction with specific on-screen events. As vertical remixing uses a single piece of music with a single timeline, the chords play out in a specific linear sequence until the piece is stopped. Horizontal resequencing, in contrast, permits you to shift chords and keys based on screen events.

Similarly, because the music cue is static, with the exception of adding and subtracting layers, the tempo map is also static. Although the music cue can have embedded tempo changes, you won't be able to speed up or slow down the music based on an event that happens in the level. If it does sync, that matching will be accidental; that is, it will qualify as a serendipitous sync that is not likely to repeat on multiple play-throughs.

This technique is commonly used when the player goes between multiple states quickly. If the composer had chosen to use horizontal resequencing, the music would go from cue to cue, with each cue having its own unique tempo and harmonic framework. Using a single piece of music with vertical remixing won't sidetrack the player's experience as much as switching between cues.

Another disadvantage of vertical remixing relates to memory usage, buffering, and CPU processing. Every game platform has a specific amount of processing power and memory available for playing the game. Besides playing back the audio, this platform needs to render graphics, compute physics properties of the world, animate graphics, and more. With vertical remixing, the game engine is not just playing back one stream of audio; rather, it's playing back multiple layers of music, so it needs to load and buffer those layers to memory from the storage media. This may increase the demands on the platform and subsequently affect the overall number of voices you can use for music, SFX, and dialog.

Table 9.1 summarizes the primary advantages and disadvantages of horizontal resequencing and vertical remixing.

Table 9.1 Horizontal Resequencing and Vertical Remixing: A Comparison

Score Type	Allows for Immediate Musical Changes	Interruption of Current Musical Phrase	Tempo and Harmonic Changes Based on Game Events	Musical Transition Quality
Horizontal: branching	No	No	Yes	Excellent
Horizontal: crossfading	Yes	Yes	Yes	Low
Horizontal: transitional	Yes	Yes	Yes	Medium
Vertical remixing	Yes	No	No	Good

Many newer platforms, including Xbox One and PlayStation 4, have plenty of CPU and RAM. Games are able to use a full core or more for audio processing, allowing more streams and layers to emerge as the "new normal." This neutralizes a primary disadvantage of using vertical remixing scoring techniques within a game.

This chapter is devoted to vertical remixing, describing how you might use it within a game. You'll learn the advantages and disadvantages of this model, along with best practices. Once you've learned about the technique, you can use the digital tools included with this book to test the techniques introduced in this chapter. The digital tools include an app for testing your vertical remixing score.

> ### note
>
> In some modern games, vertical remixing and horizontal resequencing are used at the same time. In this book, these techniques are split into separate chapters to help you to understand the advantages and disadvantages of each and explore more complex scoring techniques. Having expertise in the individual components will help you when you start combining techniques together. Bringing these two techniques together in the same game can be really effective, although it increases the complexity for the programming team and the compositional process.

Deciding How Many Layers to Use

Every component that you include in a game adds complexity to the programming and design. Each layer that you create for the game means that you'll need to find a corresponding game trigger or control input to activate or disable that layer. In turn, if you present the game development team with multiple separate layers for each cue, you'll need to be able to describe when these layers turn on and off. Note that the level may not include enough triggers to provide for the level of detail that you want to include in the game.

In addition, every layer that you add to a cue has CPU and memory implications. These effects are platform dependent, so you'll need to explore the options with the development team regarding how many layers (voices) they can support based on the other specifications of the game.

Most vertical remixing in games uses two to four layers per musical cue. This makes it simple for the development team to undertake both design and programming. If you provide too many layers, you could potentially confuse the development team and increase the time it takes to implement all the components that you've planned.

With the newest game platforms, games are able to ship with many more independent stems. *Forza 5* (2014) on the Xbox One shipped with 12 discrete stems.

Types of Vertical Remixing

There are multiple approaches to implementing vertical remixing. The composer determines how each individual layer responds to a control input with the development team. In this section you'll read about two different techniques, additive layers and individually controlled layers, but you can customize and conceptualize your own techniques based on vertical remixing to suit the exact needs of your game. On large games, you'll find that the audio director manages the technical and creative considerations associated with various layering approaches.

Additive Layers

The additive layers technique adds music layers to the cue as the state changes, then removes them as the state reverts back again. Thus Layer 1 is generally playing all the time, and other layers are added in as the gameplay progress. This is a simple design for a programming team to implement, and requires the fewest control inputs. If there are three total music layers, for instance, Layer 1 would play all the time, and you would need a total of two control inputs to activate Layers 2 and 3.

Generally each layer above the first one requires one trigger or control input. For instance, in *Fallout: New Vegas* (2010), the control input is proximity to the center of a city. As you get closer to a city, layers of music are added to the music cue. The trigger point for each layer is a separate distance (in concentric circles) from the center of each city. In *Mass Effect 2* (2010), a single percussion layer is added when a player enters into combat.

Individually Controlled Layers

With the individually controlled layers style of vertical remixing, each layer has its own control input, allowing the layers to be faded in and out on their own. Unlike with the additive tracks technique, each layer is tied to a specific control input, so the tracks can be individually faded in and out based on a specific gameplay scenario. For instance, if a game has a running state and a flying state, you could use two layers to switch between these states. Then, when the player engages in combat, a third layer would play along with either the running or flying state, depending on what the player was doing at that moment.

Another way this technique could be used is to have a layer that is controlled by low health. When the player is nearing death, a layer of the music cue could be faded in that represents the player's impending mortality. *Red Dead Redemption* (2010) uses multiple layers that are faded in and out depending on player actions. One control input is whether you're in combat; another is whether you're riding a horse; and so on.

> ## warning
>
> **INTERACTIVE MUSIC AND THE GAME DEVELOPMENT TEAM**   On smaller game projects, the game development team may not have worked with interactive music before. In such a case, team members may not understand basic interactive music techniques or be familiar with this terminology. As the composer, it's up to you to explain the various techniques so that the developer can get the best music for the game.
>
> In addition, it's important that you be able to describe the interactivity that you plan to put into the game in a few sentences or less. If it takes a long time to explain what you want, it will add complexity for the programming and development teams. Implementation can be time consuming and the programming team always has a full plate of things to do, so you should try to minimize the amount of complexity that you add to the game. Time is critical (and expensive) to a game development team.
>
> The composer should also consider the QA process for ensuring that the music is playing back correctly. The developers or even the QA team assigned to the game most likely will not be completely informed as to what the music should be doing at any given state. The composer should be in the loop to make sure the implementation is working properly all the way through the development process. If you are fortunate, an audio director may handle these details, but even in this case the composer should take as much ownership over this issue as possible.

The Art of Fading Layers In and Out

In vertical remixing, you're frequently splitting up your music into different layers. These layers in the game engine will be faded in and out during gameplay. How do you decide which instruments go in which layers? How do you actually fade them in and out, and are there any parameters over which you have control? This section looks at those two questions and offers advice about what you should be thinking about when composing for vertical remixing.

Fade Times

Several parameters enable you to customize how your music layers fade in and out. In many engines, you can have a separate fade-in time as opposed to the fade-out time. In general, a fast fade-in time is less noticeable and is recommended when bringing in a new layer. The fade-in time often relies on the type of music that you're composing, but in general fade-in times are set between 500 milliseconds and 1500 milliseconds. A player is more likely to be so excited about the new addition to the music that he or she will ignore the shorter fade times.

When choosing a fade-out time, longer times are generally less noticeable than shorter fade times. If you quickly fade out a layer of music, it's much more noticeable than if you gradually faded out those elements. Fading out too abruptly will actually make it appear as though something is wrong with the music. In most cases, fade-out times for layers sound best between 3000 milliseconds and 5000 milliseconds, depending on the style and tempo of the music.

Layer Anatomy

When deciding how to compose the layers and which instruments to include, think about melody first. The melody is typically the most noticeable element in a piece of music, so it stands to reason that when you're fading the melody in or out, it will stand out more than a supporting instrument like a percussion element or a string ostinato. In general, supporting harmonic and rhythmic elements are easier to fade in and out of a mix without the player noticing.

Another factor to consider is that because the music is constantly moving forward in time, you can't guarantee whether you'll be fading up in the middle of the melody or at the end. Fading into the middle of a melody is more noticeable and less musical than fading up at the beginning of the melody. It's important to take this variable into account when constructing the layers.

Composers frequently will have a hint of the melody in the other layers, so the transition is not as abrupt when fading in a layer where it's prominently featured. This hint of the melody might be played on a secondary lead instrument. Another technique that is sometimes employed with melodies is to split the melody between two layers, alternating the phrases between them.

Last, when you have music constantly running through a level, you should think about incorporating silence into the layers. This type of quietude will help the piece be more musically dynamic.

> tip
>
> When composing, it's important to remember that games have a lot of sound at runtime. Dialog, music, and sound effects play most (if not all) of the time. Music layers are often informed by the complexity of the sound effects that surround them. The audio team needs to be aware of the other audio elements that will go into the game and carve out room for specific elements in the sound design, dialog, music, and other audio features. It's a team sport!

Nonsynchronization of Layers

In most cases, your layers will be synchronized to play back with one another. As a consequence, they share the same harmonic framework and tempo maps, allowing them to be easily faded in and out without the player noticing.

There are ways to use nonsynchronized layers that can be equally as effective. Composer Marty O'Donnell frequently uses nonsynchronized layers in his scores for *Halo* (2001). If you have two layers, one consisting of just a rhythmic track with no harmonic information and another that has a shifting ambient harmony with a loose rhythmic structure, these two tracks can play together and upon each play-through offer up a slightly different version. This is a great technique to overcome the repetition problem. There are several ways to create layers that will not sync with one another, including using differing overall lengths, alternating meters, and differing tempo maps.

Nonsynchronization of your layers could also allow you to experiment extensively with different ways of playing back the same music. For instance, you could use asymmetrical meters to shift the downbeats of your music against the other layers as the piece progresses. Typically one of the best outcomes is the element of randomness introduced into your music, as it extends the listenability of that music for a particular level.

Table 9.2 summarizes the primary advantages and disadvantages of horizontal resequencing and vertical remixing.

Table 9.2 Horizontal Resequencing and Vertical Remixing: Advantages and Disadvantages

Score Type	Primary Advantages	Primary Disadvantages
Horizontal: branching	Musical phrases are not interrupted.	Players may have to wait until the current phrase ends to hear the next music cue.
Horizontal: crossfading	The music can transition immediately into the next cue.	The music can be interrupted in the middle of a phrase and generally doesn't sound very musical.
Horizontal: transitional	There is a musical transition into the next musical cue that ends the current music while introducing the next cue.	The music transition can interrupt the current phrase, and the player might hear the transition frequently when going between states quickly.
Vertical remixing	There can be quick changes between one state and another without sounding like the music is going to a different cue.	The harmonic framework and tempo map are static and cannot change based on game events.

Composing for Vertical Remixing

Many composers who work with vertical remixing tend to overwrite their layers. As mentioned earlier, silence is an important ally in writing music, and a dimension that should be explored in your music. Not all the layers need to be playing all the time.

Generally, this goes against the traditional writing process. Intuitively, it seems strange for composers to write rests in their music if they've been contracted to write music; they believe that they are not doing their job. In reality, silence can be very effective in your score because it ensures that your music makes more of an impact when it actually does play. Jesper Kyd is a master of using silence to enhance the music in the *Hitman* (2000) series. *Hitman* is a game that involves a lot of sneaking around levels. The silence actually makes the levels creepier and makes the music even more effective when it does play.

Many composers who set out to write music using the vertical remixing technique encounter another huge pitfall—they rely on the control inputs from the game to create volume dynamics in the music. In this scenario, composers tend to overwrite all the layers to ensure that when the game requests to bring in a new layer, the player is guaranteed to hear it.

This may seem like a positive thing; when the game brings in the layer, you're always going to hear it. While this is not a bad goal to have, composers forget about how music is shaped—not just with parts, but through how those parts change over time. Rarely does a single instrument play through an entire piece of music. The music dynamics should change and evolve over time. Unfortunately, a game can't duplicate the composer's unique ability to create an emotional story through music by just fading in and out layers. Each layer should still have a complete musical thought containing dynamics and emotional levels. Simply put, as a composer you should never write an instrument loop that remains static through a music cue; instead, the tracks should all change and evolve over time.

The most effective scores that use vertical remixing start by being an excellent piece of music that has dynamics, swells in intensity, and offers harmonic changes and everything that a good piece of music has, before splitting it up into layers. This allows the writer to leverage the emotional musicality of the piece and its dynamics, but also allows the music to later be enhanced by the player's actions in the level.

note

While composing music for vertical remixing, writers often test their layers within the sequencer to see how effective they are. Within their DAW, writers may create separate buses (or pathways) for each layer they plan on using in their score. This way they can quickly hear what the layers would sound like if one is turned on or off.

Review

Vertical remixing is an interactive music technique used in video games that uses different musical layers (or tracks) to shape the overall musical intensity. By adding more musical layers or taking them away, you can shape the music dramatically to enhance the individual player's experience throughout the game.

One significant advantage of this technique is that it ensures musical continuity between states, as the music is built from a single cue. This allows the music engine to fade in layers easily and quickly without distracting the player by changing the piece of music. The disadvantages of vertical remixing include the inability to sync harmonic, melodic, or tempo changes to screen events.

Vertical remixing is commonly used when the player goes between multiple states quickly. Most video games that employ this technique use two to three layers per musical cue. For each layer that you create for the game, you'll need to find a corresponding game trigger or control input to activate or disable that layer.

The game development team may not have worked with interactive music before, so they may not understand basic interactive music techniques or be familiar with this terminology. As the composer, it's up to you to explain the various techniques so the developer gets the best music for the game. In addition, the composer should be involved in testing the music in context all the way through the development process until the game is ready to ship.

Many composers who work with vertical remixing tend to overwrite their layers. Silence is an important ally in writing music and a dimension that should be explored in your music. Not all the layers need to be playing all the time. When working in a DAW, many writers create a separate bus (or pathway) for each layer they plan on using in their score. They can then quickly hear what the layers would sound like if one is turned on or off.

Exercises

1. Analyze any commercially released game by listening for examples of vertical remixing techniques. List cues that use these techniques, describing their use and measuring the length of the cues.

2. Find gameplay examples on YouTube that have at least three emotional levels or states. Individually find an ambient drone, a vocal pad, and a rhythmic percussion from the music that you own. Using the digital template files included with this text, implement these three tracks into the vertical remixing layered project.

3. Using another gameplay clip from YouTube, compose your own layered score for three states for use in the digital template.

CHAPTER 10

WRITING TRANSITIONS AND STINGERS

In this chapter you'll learn about the importance and best practices of writing transitions to bridge two pieces of music during scene changes, loading screens, or horizontal resequencing. In addition, you'll explore the various types of stingers, including stingers that can either play on top of the current music or can be used to finish a piece of music.

Enhancing without Interrupting

In a game setting, it's important for music to reinforce the underlying emotional context of the scene. Video games use different musical cues to support the player experience during the game. Composers must find ways to connect these various pieces of music. In this chapter you'll learn about the techniques that composers use to move from one musical cue to another by using musical transitions. These techniques help keep the player fully immersed in the game universe without interrupting the experience. It is sometimes said that the best film scores are the ones that you don't notice. Similarly, the best video game scores enhance the entire experience of playing the game. Any music that does not support this goal will remind the players of the meta-reality instead of providing them with a cohesive immersive experience.

To enhance the player's experience from moment to moment, composers will also use stingers, or small musical phrases, to enhance the gameplay experience without having to switch to an entirely different musical cue. Stingers are generally played on top of the current musical cue signifying or supporting an event to the player. Examples of when stingers are used in a game might include winning a battle, finding treasure, losing a level, or entering a new area. The stingers enhance the moment while allowing the current music to continue without interruption.

Connecting Two Pieces of Music

Being able to connect two pieces of music is an important skill in composing for video games. In such games, the music may need to dynamically shift based on the real-time choices made by the player. There are two basic ways to connect two pieces of music in video games: the crossfade and the transition.

Crossfading

The simplest way to connect two pieces of music is to crossfade between them. Crossfading means that the source music (the music that's currently playing) fades out and the destination music fades in. Although this technique is used across many video games, it's an inelegant solution to bridging two pieces of music because it doesn't provide any kind of musical closure to the first piece or an introduction to the new piece of music.

> note
>
> Throughout this chapter, the word "source" represents the piece of music that we're coming from, and the word "destination" represents the piece of music that we're going to. The transition is the musical bridge that connects the two pieces of music.

If the tempo and harmonic progression are synchronized between the two pieces of music, then essentially you're using vertical remixing to go between the two pieces, allowing for a more seamless transition. This technique does suffer from the disadvantages discussed in Chapter 9, "Vertical Remixing"—namely, inability to shift tempo or harmonic context based on a player action.

Transitioning

To bridge two unique pieces of music more effectively, many video game composers will write a transition to seamlessly move from the source music to the destination music. The primary purpose of a transition is to close one musical thought and introduce a new one. Closing music and introducing new music are the most important elements to consider when composing a transition.

Transitions typically range in length from 3 seconds to 15 seconds. To emphasize musical closure from a theme, effective transitions tend to be longer in length and complete a musical idea or thought. Shorter transitions tend to sound more repetitive and less musical, taking the player out of the seamless experience that the video game score should support. Longer transitions tend to do a better job of satisfying the two main criteria of a good transition—ending one musical thought and introducing a new one.

Transition Matrixes

When composing music for a large game, composers will often be working with many different cues and transitions. In these scenarios, composers often create a giant table that describes which transition to use when going from each source to each destination. The role of the composer is then to completely fill out the source/destination table with appropriate transitions. Of course, many transitions will be reused in practice, and sometimes the transition actually may be nothing—that is, a direct transition from a specific source to a specific destination.

Audio middleware engines like Wwise allow very sophisticated usage of transitions by allowing you to create matrixes detailing how transitions will be used between cues. They help composers customize each transition by defining the exact fade times when exiting or entering another cue or specifying the precise timing of entrance and exit points. More information about audio middleware technology can be found in Chapter 18.

The Concept of Musical Interruption

A control input may request a change in the music in the middle of a musical phrase, at the end of a phrase, or the beginning of a phrase. When you exit the transition, you can specify where and when the destination music begins to play. The exit of a transition is much easier to connect musically than the moment when the transition begins to override the original source cue.

This musical interruption in the source music is more apparent when transitions cannot sync to a specific musical event (synchronized transitions). Whereas the source music can be interrupted by the control input at any point in time based on player action, the destination music can always have a specific entry point that is planned by the composer when using a custom transition. Therefore, the transition out of the source music is much more difficult to compose for than the entrance of the destination music, which is always known.

In a gameplay scenario, the composer can never know where the source music will exit because the player may make a decision at any given time that affects the music. For the composer, this means that the player's decision might interrupt the music in the middle of a phrase, melody, or harmonic progression that is not a musically appropriate exit point. How can a composer write a transition that interrupts a musical phrase yet retain some sort of musical coherence? Throughout the rest of this chapter you'll learn about the factors that influence how you write transitions.

Composing Transitions

There are multiple scenarios for how one might compose a transition to bridge two pieces of music. Factors that affect how the transition is composed include tempo, harmonic, and melodic variation between the two pieces of music. In this section you'll examine the different ways to compose the best transition for each of these scenarios.

There are two types of transitions: synchronized and nonsynchronized. A synchronized transition is played on a specific bar line, beat, or marker. To achieve a synchronized transition, the game must have some kind of musical intelligence, which knows the tempo and meter of the music, so that it can successfully play the transition on a bar line, beat, or marker. Far more common are the nonsynchronized transitions, which play immediately when called from the game without any kind of musical synchronization.

Audio middleware packages such as Fmod and Wwise include the musical intelligence needed for synchronized transitions as a built-in feature. If you are not using a middleware engine, it is far more common to create nonsynchronized transitions. Although a programmer could potentially build an intelligent music system without the use of middleware, it's likely that this would take eight or more hours to implement from scratch.

If the music engine that you're using has some kind of musical intelligence that can determine what the tempo is and where the bar lines fall, then it will be easier for you to synchronize when the transition occurs. If this synchronicity is possible, you can create much more elegant transitions to get from the source music to the destination music.

Synchronized Transitions

Synchronized transitions are much more musical because they can be placed at rhythmically and harmonically appropriate positions within the music. The length of time it might take for the synchronized transition to start depends on how the composer chooses to write the piece. If the composer decides that transitions can play only on the bar, then the player might have to wait just a few seconds before the transition might start. In contrast, if the composer chooses to wait until the end of the melodic phrase before playing the transition, the player could wait a longer time for the shift in music. This is the disadvantage of using transitions that sync with the music: the musical engine might have to wait for a musically appropriate place to play the transition. In turn, because the synchronized transition might not happen immediately, the delay might upset the visual synchronization of the game.

Nonsynchronized Transitions

When using nonsynchronized transitions, it may be much more difficult to bridge two pieces of music as effectively. Recall that when we refer to nonsynchronized transitions, we are referring to synchronization with the current musical cue in terms of bars or beats.

On the positive side, nonsynchronized transitions generally can play back immediately instead of having to wait for a musical phrase to end or the beginning of the next bar of music. If you need tight visual synchronization to a game event, the nonsynchronized transition is a better choice than using musical sync to time your transitions.

Transition Construction and Considerations

The construction of a transition has two important functions: closing the musical idea from the source music and introducing the next musical idea.

To appreciate how to write better transitions to bridge two pieces of music, it may be helpful to think about how a cue might end in a film score. Typically, musical cues use a cadence to wrap up a musical thought. The transition itself can be thought of as a kind of musical cadence or closure. The transition wraps up one musical thought before starting a new musical thought. For this reason, it's better to create some sort of finality before moving on to the next cue.

Musical closure can be envisioned as an exclamation point at the end of a musical phrase. Frequently composers use a crescendo or ramp to begin a musical transition, but then provide a musical cadence that wraps up the source music cue before introducing the destination cue.

When moving from a high-intensity piece to a low-intensity piece, it's generally better for the transition to actually increase in intensity to close the musical thought before going to the low intensity. This is a far more effective technique than using a decrescendo into the lower intensity.

When composing transitions, start by analyzing the source and destination music for tempo and harmonic content. This will inform your decisions about which key to use and how to structure the rhythmical variance between the two pieces.

Ultimately, when designing transitions, it may be difficult to build a transition that will satisfy all the different cases that the player might potentially create through his or her individual play style. Nevertheless, keeping some general principles (covered in the following sections) in mind when creating your transitions will go a long way toward ensuring a more seamless experience for the player.

Ambient (Rubato) versus Rhythmic

On the one hand, if the source music doesn't have an overt rhythm, then the transition can begin directly with the rhythmic motif because it won't conflict or interfere with any underlying rhythmic pattern. On the other hand, if the source music has a rhythmic pulse or percussive pattern, then the transition should start with a swell or other musical device that won't conflict with the rhythmic pattern in the source music. These ramps or swells in the transition are generally facilitated by a crescendo into a musical cadence that will provide closure for the source music. Once you have provided closure for the source music, you'll want to introduce the destination music.

The end of the musical transition can either introduce the destination music that is coming up next or end with a fermata that will create an overlap into the next musical idea, similar to a music overlap used in film.

Tempo Considerations

Bridging two pieces of music that have different tempos with a transition can be challenging. The easiest transition to write in this scenario is one that begins without a tempo. After the source music has faded, then a new tempo might be introduced to help bridge the piece to the destination music. Frequently transitions contain an accelerando or ritardando to transition more seamlessly to a new tempo.

Harmonic Considerations

When composing the transition, you'll also need to take into account the harmonic framework of the source music. Since the objective of a transition is to provide musical closure to the source music, the transition should provide a musical cadence and resolution. Many cadences use the dominant or possibly subdominant chords in the key of the source music. If your source music is using multiple keys, it may be easier to start your transition with an amorphous harmonic structure like a run or glissando. These figures at the start of a transition can help to mask any key changes between the source music and the transition.

Introducing Destination Music

Since the destination music will most likely loop, you can use your transition to introduce the destination music without having it replay when the destination loops back around. The introduction to the destination music is part of the transition, so the destination loop that follows will not play the introduction after the loop point. This technique also helps provide variety to the musical experience, thereby decreasing repetition.

Many games add variety to the music by having multiple start points for each musical cue. Establishing several different entrance points in the destination music will enhance the player experience by minimizing the repetition. This is an effective technique used in games like *Uncharted 2* (2009) to increase the variability across the same musical cue.

Repeating Transitions

If your transition will be used over and over again, you may want to consider composing multiple transitions to decrease the repetition associated with hearing the same transition on multiple occasions. Providing a variety of transitions when bridging the same two pieces of music repeatedly will enhance the player experience by not relying so heavily on the same material.

Example Transitions

This section lists some transition construction techniques that are widely used in games. These examples are meant to inspire you when you're constructing your own transitions.

- **Percussion Swell Transition.** The simplest type of transition is one in which there is no harmonic center or identifiable tempo. This might include a percussion roll like a symbol swell, bass, or snare drum roll. Although it's possible to use this technique to bridge two pieces of music, it's not as satisfying as providing an actual musical cadence to conclude the musical phrase. Transitions that are able to provide closure are significantly more effective at providing a transparent emotional experience with the music.

- **Overlap Transition.** Similar to the process used in film scoring, an overlap can be used when moving from the transition into the destination. An overlap in film scoring is typically used when one cue at a specific tempo ends, and another queue must start at a different tempo. The end of the first cue is often a sustained note such as a fermata. The new cue enters with a different tempo that begins underneath the sustained note, creating an overlap. Composers who have used this technique in film scoring will find it valuable in transitioning into the destination music.

- **Nebulous Chord.** When exiting the start music, you may not know which chord will be playing. As an alternative to using a glissando or other similar amorphous chord, you can choose to use chords that have nebulous characteristics in terms of whether they are major or minor, dominant or root. Chords that are amorphous or not identifiable in their harmonic structure can be excellent options to bridge two pieces of music more effectively. Amorphous chords can also include clusters, noise, cymbal swells, or tensions.

- **End Transition.** In addition to writing musical transitions that bridge two pieces of music, composers are often required to create transitions that will end a musical cue. Ending the musical cue will frequently involve a crescendo that completes a musical thought through a cadence that eventually leads to silence. Many of the same techniques that have been described here can be applied to transitions. Frequently the architecture of a transition begins with a crescendo, ramp, or swell, then creates a cadence that ultimately resolves into a fermata. The same rhythmic and harmonic considerations that were explored with bridge transitions can be applied to end transitions.

> **tip**
>
> In general, the more variation in the transitions, the better. The composer just needs to keep in mind the player experience—maintaining a signature transition style throughout the game will get old very fast. Ideally, the composer should have a few different kinds of transitions/transition styles for the same transition (e.g., Combat A transitioning to Ambient A). It's not much work from a compositional or implementation perspective to create this kind of variation, but it can have a big impact on the player experience.

Using and Placing Stingers

Stingers are short musical ideas that indicate a game event or change in state to the player. A stinger can signify the end of a level has been reached, treasure has been found, a clue is nearby, a boss monster has been killed or myriad other game events.

Although stingers can be synchronized to play on a specific beat, bar line, or marker, typically they are played immediately with no attention to where the music is. Depending on the specific gameplay situation, waiting for a specific beat to play the stinger might cause it to be too late to signal the change in state to the player.

Musical stingers are sometimes added on top of the current music to indicate a reward. These stingers can be synchronized to the current cue only if the system has musical intelligence, such that it knows where the beats are according to the tempo and meter of the cue. As discussed earlier in this chapter, having a programmer add this kind of musical intelligence to a game system may require many hours of work or the purchase of an audio middleware solution. This is beyond the reach of many smaller projects and projects that have limited resources. Also, on these smaller projects, the composer might be asked to sacrifice part of his or her own budget to help pay for the audio middleware license, again making this option less attractive.

When composing stingers, the composer must be aware that the harmonic context over which the stinger will play may change. This requires that the composer play the stinger in a variety of contexts.

Composers often choose to write stingers in the same key as the music, so that the rhythm of the stinger does not conflict with the underscore and create confusion in the player's experience of the music.

Synchronized Musical Stingers

The playback of a synchronized stinger starts on a specific measure or beat of the background music. Much as with synchronized transitions, the advantage of having the stinger play on a musical event is that it is more seamless and transparent to the player—that is, the stinger fits into the overall musical framework of the background music. The disadvantage is that because the stinger must wait to line up with a specific musical event (bar line or beat), the event may not be synchronized to a visual cue on the screen. Synchronized stingers are used most frequently in music-based games like *Bit.Trip Runner* (2010) and *Rez* (2001).

Nonsynchronized Musical Stingers

Nonsynchronized musical stingers play immediately, with complete disregard of the musical framework of the cue that is currently playing. They can be useful if the game needs to notify the player of an event immediately, instead of waiting for a particular musical event like the end of a phrase or the beginning of a measure.

The considerations discussed in reference to transitions also apply to building stingers: harmonic framework, rhythm intensity, and tempo. When constructing stingers, it may be useful to keep them in a neutral harmonic scale like pentatonic or to have a nonharmonic percussive event so there will be fewer conflicts with the underlying music.

Review

Being able to connect two pieces of music is an important skill when composing music for video games. The primary purpose of a musical transition is to close one musical thought and introduce a new one.

There are two basic ways to connect two pieces of music in video games: the crossfade and the transition. Crossfading refers to fading out the source music (the music that's currently playing) and fading up the destination music.

Since the source music can be interrupted at any point by the player, the entrance of a transition is much more difficult to connect musically than the moment when the transition begins the new cue.

Synchronized transitions are much more musical because they can be placed at rhythmically and harmonically appropriate positions within the music. A synchronized transition might not happen immediately because it's waiting for the musically appropriate event to occur. This can upset the visual synchronization of the game.

Nonsynchronized transitions play immediately when called from the game, without any kind of musical synchronization. Such transitions are less musical because they may play in the middle of a beat or melody, interrupting the overall musical flow.

When composing transitions, start by analyzing the source and destination music for tempo and harmonic content. This will inform your decisions about which key to use and how to structure the rhythmical variance between the two pieces.

Stingers are short musical ideas that indicate a game event or change in state to the player. A stinger can signify the end of a level has been reached, treasure has been found, a clue is nearby, a boss monster has been killed, or myriad other game events.

Synchronized musical stingers start on a specific measure or beat of the background music, which means they might not start immediately. Nonsynchronized musical stingers play immediately, with complete disregard to the musical framework of the cue that is currently playing.

Exercises

1. Analyze a video game for its use of transitions and stingers. Identify the following characteristics of each transition and stinger: length, effectiveness, tempo, synchronization, and key.

2. Construct each type of transition described in this chapter to bridge two cues of music you've written for a project. Analyze them for their effectiveness.

3. Compose several synchronized musical stingers and nonsynchronized musical stingers that can play back over a previously composed piece of music. Analyze them for their effectiveness.

CHAPTER 11

USING SOUND DESIGN TECHNIQUES IN MUSIC

As sound design has grown over the last several decades, the lines between music and sound design are being blurred in contemporary scoring. Sound design is used by composers to change the emotional intensity of a level and to add diversity to the palette of instruments, thereby enhancing the originality of a score. In this chapter we'll explore how composers have used sound design elements in their music in the practice of scoring video games. We'll introduce several easy techniques to create musical sound design and discuss ways to use interactive techniques with sound design to augment the experience of playing the level.

What Is Sound Design?

Sound design is the creation and manipulation of audio samples for use within instruments, scores, or sound effects. Frequently modern composers use sound design techniques to customize or create their own digital instruments. Through such sound design manipulations, composers are able to expand their sonic palette beyond the normal set of instruments in the composer's arsenal. The use of sound design elements can dramatically increase the uniqueness of a composition.

The challenge of being a composer in today's marketplace is that all professional composers own many identical sound libraries, making it difficult for composers to stand out in a competitive music marketplace. The creation of your own library of sounds can help your music sound unique among all the music that is written with stock libraries and plug-ins. Many professional composers, such as Jason Graves of *Dead Space* (2008) or Michael Giacchino from the *Medal of Honor* (1999) series, create their own instruments to build a more distinctive sound.

In film, many famous sound designers, including Walter Murch from *Apocalypse Now* (1979) and *The Conversation* (1974) and Alan Splet from *Blue Velvet* (1986) and *The Elephant Man* (1980), use sound design techniques to manipulate sound effects as a way to describe the emotional context of a scene. Using sound effects in an extra-diegetic context is a unique way to tell stories instead of, or in addition to, the use of music.

Games like *Amnesia: The Dark Descent* (2010), *Limbo* (2010), *The Swapper* (2014), and *Dead Space* all use sound design elements to make their scores more interesting and unique. Professional video game composers should be well versed in how to use sound design in their compositions if they want to compete at the top levels of our industry.

This chapter aims to educate you about the basic sound design techniques, including basic synthesis, and introduces additional sound creation techniques that can make your music stand out from the crowd.

> ### note
> To create harmonic continuity between sound effects and music in games, the audio team will often lock on tonal centers, or provide composer assets and related guidelines for use in production. This can provide balance throughout the game. It is prudent to recognize the need for both balance and progression throughout the game.

Basic Synthesis

In this section you'll learn about basic synthesis to help you customize the instruments that you purchased or created on your own. Synthesizers and samplers are generally divided into multiple components: the sound generator, filters, and envelopes, as shown in Figure 11.1. In addition, low-frequency oscillators (LFOs) are commonly used to modify these elements.

Sound Generator

On a synthesizer, the *sound generator* consists of one or more oscillators that are able to play back many different waveforms, including simple waveforms like sine, square, triangle, sawtooth, and noise, as well as other, more complex waveforms. The sound generator on a sampler can play back any digitally recorded audio, including notes recorded from a live instrument, sound effects, loops, or entire musical phrases.

The sound generator is generally in charge of pitch mapping, which means that when you connect the MIDI controller to your sampler or sequencer, it will correctly change the pitch of the

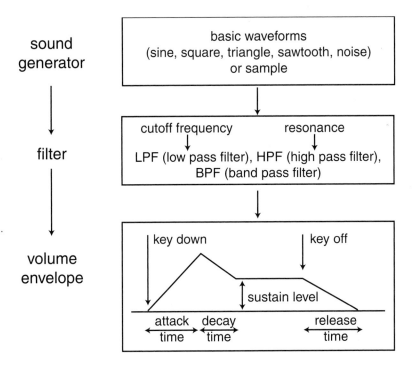

Figure 11.1 The basic components of a synthesizer. Sound traverses from the sound generator through one or more filters, then through a volume envelope.

note depending on the MIDI key that you pressed. Changing the pitch of a note is the first and most important tool in shaping sound design. If you're using a sampler with an audio recording, you must first make sure to map the audio sample to the correct pitch before the keyboard will play it at whatever key you press.

You can create myriad unusual sounds just by playing sound effects at different pitches. If this is the only tool that you have at your disposal, you will still be able to create a wide range of sounds. The importance of being able to pitch a sample cannot be overstated. The creation of musical sound design often relies on the ability to play sound effects at different pitches.

Filters

The word "filter," when talking about a synthesizer or a sampler, is a fancy way of saying "equalizer." In many ways a filter on an instrument is like the tone control of your car stereo, in that it allows you to increase the low, middle, or high frequencies. Several kinds of filters shape the frequency relationship within the sound itself:

- **Low Pass Filter (LPF).** A low pass filter is the most common of all filters; it allows the low frequencies to pass through the filter while reducing the number of high frequencies (Figure 11.2). This type of filter is often used in games when the player is going underwater, after a grenade has exploded next to the player, or when the player's health is low.

- **High Pass Filter (HPF).** A high pass filter allows high frequencies to pass through the filter while reducing the presence of low frequencies. This type of filter is used in games to simulate flying or jumping. One example is found in *SSX Tricky*: the low

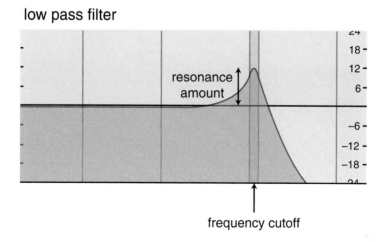

Figure 11.2 A low pass filter boosts frequencies with the resonance parameter at the frequency cutoff point.

frequencies in the music disappear when the player hurls his or her body into the air on the snowboard.

- **Band Pass Filter (BPF).** A band pass filter allows frequencies that are near the selected frequency to pass through, while reducing the frequencies above and below the selected frequency. This effect is used in games to make a sound "small," as if coming from a radio speaker in a diegetic context.

The two controls most commonly used on these filters are the cutoff frequency and the resonance amount. The cutoff frequency is the point at which all the frequencies above or below are reduced. In a LPF all the frequencies are reduced above the cutoff frequency, whereas in a HPF all the frequencies are reduced below the cutoff frequency. In a BPF all the frequencies are reduced both below and above the cutoff frequency, allowing just a narrow set of frequencies to pass through.

Most filters reduce the frequencies at either 12 or 24 decibels per octave. Thus, if you're using a 12 dB low pass filter, any frequency that is an octave above the cutoff frequency will be reduced by 12 dB.

The resonance control is used to provide an additional increase in decibels at the cutoff frequency. It is similar in sound to decreasing the Q on an equalizer. This control is used in conjunction with the filter cutoff frequency to create a wide range of sounds.

Envelopes

An envelope is generally used to shape and customize the volume curve of an instrument or sound. Envelopes can also be used to control the pitch of an instrument, although this scenario is observed far less often. Being able to shape the volume of a sound can be another very useful technique when shaping and customizing your own sounds. A volume envelope can, for instance, add a fade-in at the beginning of your sound or create a more transient attack. Most volume envelopes have four parameters to help you shape the sound: attack time, decay time, sustain level, and release time (Figure 11.3).

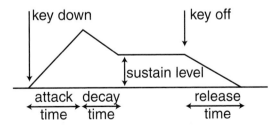

Figure 11.3 Volume is shaped over time using an envelope from when a key is pressed until after the key is released.

Complex synthesizers and samplers may offer many more parameters to adjust in their envelope structure, including hold and loop points. These additional parameters allow for more sophisticated volume shaping of a sound or instrument. The four basic controls described in this section are found on all synthesizers and samplers regardless of their complexity. Using just these four parameters will give you enormous flexibility in shaping your instruments.

Attack Time

The attack time is the amount of time it takes for the volume envelope to go from silence to full volume. If the attack time is short, then the sound is likely to have a sharp attack, or more transient front end. If the attack time is long, then the sound will have more of a crescendo, going from soft to loud when the sound is started. The attack time is usually measured in milliseconds. A practical example of using attack time is to decrease a sharp attack on a string patch by increasing the overall attack time to have a more legato feel.

Decay Time

The decay time, which follows the attack time, is the amount of time it takes for the volume envelope to change from the loudest points in the envelope down to the sustain level. Once the attack time portion of the envelope has reached its maximum level, the decay portion of the envelope starts. The time it takes to go from the maximum level of the envelope down to the sustaining level is called the decay time.

The decay time and attack time are generally used together to shape the initial envelope of a sound.

> ## warning
>
> **UNHEARD ADJUSTMENTS**   If the sustain level is equal to the maximum volume of the envelope, then adjustments made to the decay time cannot be heard. This lack of effect occurs because after the attack portion has completed, we are already at the maximum level of the envelope. If the maximum level of the envelope and the sustaining level are exactly the same, then no adjustments made to the decay time will be heard. If you want to hear what adjustments to the decay time are doing, the sustain level must not be at its maximum.

There are several practical examples of using decay time in a musical context. To increase the sharpness of a drum or the initial attack of a string marcato, for instance, you can set the attack time to short amount of time (0 msec) and the decay time to approximately 200 msec. With this setup, you will hear the initial transient loudly, with the level then immediately dropping to the sustain level. In this scenario, the sustain level should be set at about 50 percent. to make sure the volume decreases in the decay time to the sustain level from the maximum level of the envelope.

Sustain Level

After the attack and decay portions of the envelope have completed, the sustain level is the volume that the sound will maintain until a note-off message (or key-off) has been received. Unlike the attack and decay parameters, the sustain level will hold indefinitely until the key is released.

Release Time

The release time of an envelope is the amount of time that it takes for a volume envelope to go from its sustain level to silence. If, for instance, you are using a legato string patch and the end of the notes are not connecting well with the notes that come immediately after them, you could increase the release time, thereby allowing for more overlap between the notes. In most cases, adding more release time to a sound will make it more fluid, by increasing the amount of overlaps between notes.

Low-Frequency Oscillator

A low-frequency oscillator is typically used to modify the cutoff frequency, the pitch of a waveform, or the volume of an envelope. Such a device usually works at less than 20 hertz, out of the range of human hearing.

Since the LFO is flexible, it can be routed to either the pitch, the filter, or the volume. This control can be extremely useful in creating sounds. Most commonly, it modifies the filter cutoff; thus, instead of you having to automate the filter cutoff by hand, the LFO handles this task for you. An LFO that is applied to pitch will sound like vibrato effect; if it is applied to volume, it will sound like tremolo.

There are three basic controls associated with an LFO:

- **Waveform.** The LFO can usually be any one of the five basic waveforms (sine, square, triangle, sawtooth, noise/random) and can modify volume or pitch.
- **Frequency.** The frequency is the number of times per second the basic waveform will pass through a single cycle. The noise waveform is a special case where the frequency is the number of times per second that the LFO will pick a random number to modify the volume or pitch.
- **Range or Depth.** The range or depth control is used to tell the LFO how much to modify the pitch or volume. If the LFO's range is high, then the amount of pitch or volume change will increase. For example, a small value will change the pitch very little (like a vibrato effect), whereas a large value might change the pitch widely across an entire octave.

Audio Signal Processing

Audio signal processing, or effects, is another way to create distinctive and creative sounds. This section provides a primer on the different kinds of effects that are available. Sometimes these are known as DSP (digital signal processing) effects because most effects are processed in the digital (computer) domain as opposed to an analog chain.

Applying the following effects to your instruments and music is another way to customize your sound library to distinguish your compositions. Given that these effects rely on preset patches, if you really want your compositions to stand out, you should experiment with the various parameters you can adjust.

> **note**
>
> Video game developers may sometimes ask the composer to deliver drier, less effect-filled mixes because some effects (e.g., reverb, filters, and compression) are applied by a game-wide filter at runtime. Audio middleware such as Wwise and Fmod can provide these DSP effects while the game is running.

- **Time-Based Effects.** Time-based effects include reverb, delay, chorus, flanging, time stretching, and phasing. These effects generally shape the linear listening experience by adding echoes and spatial chambers to the sound or instrument. Time-based effects are the most noticeable of all audio signal processing and can change the overall sound more dramatically than any of the other effects listed here.

- **Frequency-Based Effects.** Frequency-based effects change the overall characteristics of the frequency relationships within a sound. They include equalizers, filters, pitch shifting, resonators, and vibrato.

- **Volume-Based Effects.** Volume-based effects are used to change the volume dynamics within a piece of music or are applied to an instrument by either expanding or compressing the dynamic range. They include tremolo, compression and limiting, gating, and expansion.

> **warning**
>
> **USING COMPRESSION**   Many new composers and musicians overuse compression effects because it may be difficult to hear what the effect is doing to the music. If you compress an orchestral piece of music, your *pianissimo* dynamics will change to *mezzo-forte*, but your *forte* dynamics will also change to *mezzo-forte*, leaving your piece without any dynamics at all. This leaves your piece sounding dull and without surprise. Be careful to not to use compression unless absolutely necessary, and choose specific instruments to compress instead of compressing the full mix.

Techniques for Creating Sound Design

Now that you've learned about sound manipulation techniques, we're going to explore ways to create your own sounds, including recording and using DSP to create sounds. The techniques described in this section are not complicated, so you'll be able to start creating your own sounds in no time.

Recording Live Instruments for a Sampling Session

One of the easiest ways to generate new sounds and instruments is to bring in one or more players for a recording session. During the recording session, the composer and musician work together to create new and interesting sounds on the instrument. On a trombone, for instance, the composer might choose to record the horn playing pedal tones or horn blatts, or use various mutes to capture some unique sounds. After the recording session, these captured sounds are used to build new instruments in a sampler like Kontakt. These instruments can then be used in your own compositions to give it a more unique and interesting sonic flavor.

This technique can be used with any instrument or ensemble size. In addition, some of the most unique sounds might be created by items that are not normally thought of as musical at all, including bowls, basement oil tanks, bowed cymbals, a bouncy ball being rubbed on a gong (a Michael Giacchino trick), or air-conditioning duct work. Be creative.

tip

Unfortunately, musicians as performers are a disappearing art. As electronic instruments have advanced, many performing musicians have found themselves in the unfortunate position of not being able to make a living. If you bring in live instruments for a sampling session, make sure the musicians know what they'll be playing. Most musicians will be annoyed by the fact that they are being recorded for the purposes of reusing the material over and over again without paying them for another session. Be respectful with your musicians. Either pay them really well for a sampling session, or pay them every time you use the samples on an actual paying gig. Musicians can be invaluable in elevating your compositions to a higher level, making them sound more professional and unique. Make sure you reward musicians in turn for helping you bring in work.

If you're working with union talent, the musicians union has guidelines and special rates for recordings made for the purpose of using them in sampled instruments. In these circumstances, make sure that you get the appropriate clearances from the union for the kind of recording you're planning.

Sending Sounds into Infinite Reverb

One of the easiest and simplest ways to create new sounds is to use a reverb that has an infinite time setting. An infinite time setting on a reverb allows a sound to continuously reverberate in a space for an indefinite period of time. When you play a sound into this infinite chamber, the sound quickly morphs into its own unique texture. Generally the most interesting part of the sound happens after the initial attack, during the time when the sound is reverberating in the space. This sound is then captured by a recorder or DAW, and subsequently used to create new instruments that can be played from the keyboard.

This technique can be used to create interesting sounds with almost any kind of input signal. Some examples might include a flute arpeggio to generate a chord in the reverberant space, an orchestral swell or hit, a sound effect like a screen or helicopter, or a single note from a violin. All of the sounds will create unique textures, giving your music a distinctive flair. Because you're making these sounds from scratch and they don't exist in a stock library somewhere, the compositions you create that incorporate them will have a fresh and interesting sound.

One of the unique advantages of using this technique is that you can create textures in a specific key or harmonic framework because you're able to choose the notes that you're sending into the infinite reverb. As a consequence, you don't have to spend a lot of time retuning a sample to get it into the correct key if you're working on a composition.

Using Speakers to Add Acoustic Resonance

Many sounds created with a synthesizer or artificial device lack a human quality. One of the ways to make an instrument sound more real is to add acoustic resonance around the sound. An easy way to do so is to record the playback of that sound through various speakers. The speaker itself will have an intrinsic resonance because the physical nature of the device adds a more acoustic quality to the sound. In addition, because you are using a microphone to record the sound, you'll be recording the ambient qualities of the space along with the sound being compressed by the air between the speaker and the microphone.

This technique isn't as dramatic as some of the other techniques mentioned in this chapter, but creative use of the types of speakers and the volume at which you play the sounds back will increase the uniqueness of the sounds.

Using DSP to Create Unusual Sounds

Composers can also use DSP effects to create new and unusual sounds. The idea here is that if you create sounds and instruments that exist only in your library of tools, then your compositions will also have sonic textures that will help make your sound more distinctive. Some simple DSP effects include reversing a sound, flanging with the feedback set really high, and using convolution reverb to create interesting sounds.

One of the most interesting things about using convolution reverb to create sounds is that you don't need to load an impulse response; instead, you can load any kind of sound, whether it's a loop or a sound effect. When you feed your sounds into a convolution reverb that is using alternative sources for the impulse response, you can achieve really unusual sounds.

In addition to the effects already listed, there are a wide array of interesting DSP options for you to explore, including distortion, filtering using resonance, pitch and formant shifting, and many others.

Review

Sound design is the creation and manipulation of audio samples for use within instruments, scores, or sound effects. Through such sound design manipulations, composers are able to expand their sonic palettes beyond the normal set of instruments in the composer's arsenal. The use of sound design elements can dramatically increase the uniqueness of a composition.

Professional video game composers should be well versed in how to use sound design in their compositions if they want to compete at the top levels of the industry.

Synthesizers and samplers are generally divided into four different components: the sound generator, filters, envelopes, and low-frequency oscillator. Envelopes have multiple parameters to help you shape the sound: attack time, decay time, sustain level, and release time. An LFO is typically used to modify the pitch of a waveform or the volume of an envelope.

Audio signal processing (effects) is another way to create distinctive and creative sounds. Effects usually fall into one of three categories: time based, frequency based, and volume based.

Four different approaches to creating sound design include (1) recording live instruments in a sampling session, (2) sending sounds into infinite reverb, (3) using speakers to add acoustic resonance, and (4) using DSP to create unusual sounds.

Exercises

1. Find three video game examples that use non-instrument sounds or SFX in an extra-diegetic context. Analyze them in terms of their effectiveness.
2. Modify several standard patches among your instrument library by using the basic synthesis techniques described in this chapter to create custom and unique versions of these patches.
3. Create four new instruments by using each of the four techniques described in this chapter.

CHAPTER 12

MUSIC AS A GAMEPLAY ELEMENT

Many modern games use music for diegetic or gameplay purposes. For instance, in music games, the gameplay mechanics directly affect and influence the music. In other games, musical events may occur when the player enters the proximity of an object in the game world or captures an object. These musical cues must be considered in the context of the entire musical landscape and the ways this audio might interact with any non-diegetic music in the scene. This chapter focuses on creating a strategy for unifying all the musical elements that might be part of a scene and discusses gameplay mechanics based on musical or rhythmic events.

Engaging Players with Music

Modern games employ many different ways of using music to immerse the player into the gameplay. Games often use music not only as underscore but also as a gameplay element or design mechanic in the world itself. In this chapter, you'll learn about the diegetic uses of music in games and explore how you might use music in alternative ways to engage the player.

Music can be used as a gameplay mechanic itself, where the rules of the music help determine narrative outcomes in the game. These so-called music games may include the beat matching mechanics used in games like *Dance Dance Revolution* (1998) or other types of music mechanics. Music can also be used as an interactive element in the design of the game world, whereby the world includes instruments that the game player can play, as in *The Legend of Zelda: Ocarina of Time* (1998). Last, objects or characters within the game world or user interface may create phrases, melodies, or tones, as in *Bioshock Infinite* (2013).

The composer's responsibility, along with the rest of the audio team, is to make sure that all of these unique elements help to unify the vision of the music for the project. All too often, sound designers and composers don't spend enough time collaborating throughout the project to make sure that the SFX don't clash with the music by, for example, being in the wrong key. The team needs to work together to solve these problems early in the development process.

This chapter explores non-underscore methods of musical engagement for the player, typical workflows, strategies, and development.

Music Games

For the purposes of this chapter, we will consider the definition of a *music game* to be any game that at least partly focuses on music as a prominent gameplay element. In most cases the music is prominently featured in a diegetic context—that is, the music not only serves as a means of emotional engagement, but also is used in the game design as an element that the player may interact with, manipulate, or control. In this section you'll learn about the different types of music games and see how the music creation process differs when music is a prominent mechanic used in game design.

Because the gameplay mechanics revolve around music, composers and sound designers typically work much more closely with a music game development team than on a normal project. In fact, on games such as these, composers and sound designers may actually make up most of the game development team. Specific knowledge about music construction and analysis is inherent in much of the production of these games, whether it be rhythmic tracking, melodic mapping of controllers, or real-time composition. These skills can be as important as game design skills when working on a music game.

The video game industry has used licensed popular music throughout the last 30 years. Many early video games were made as promotional vehicles for prominent musical artists such as Journey, Michael Jackson, and Peter Gabriel. This section focuses primarily on music games that center on the construction or deconstruction of music based on the gameplay itself—that is, games in which the music becomes a game mechanic.

Game developers really started to innovate with music games toward the mid- to late 1990s, exploring various approaches through games such as *PaRappa the Rapper* (1996), *Dance Dance Revolution* (1998), *Samba de Amigo* (1999), *Vib-Ribbon* (1999), *FreQuency* (2001), and *Rez* (2001). Each of these games pioneered new techniques with its direct use of music in the game mechanics. Performance-based music games exploded from 2005 through 2010, with successful titles including *Guitar Hero* (2005), *Rock Band* (2007), and *Dance Central* (2010).

Innovators in this field include companies like Harmonix (*FreQuency*) and Konami (*Dance Dance Revolution*), as well as individuals like Tetsuya Mizaguchi (*Rez, Space Channel 5*), Masaya Matsuura (*Vib-Ribbon*), and Toshio Iwai (*Electroplankton*, 2005). Music games frequently employ alternative controllers to help the player create or play along with the music. Examples include the maracas controllers for *Samba de Amigo* (1999), bongos for *Donkey Konga* (2003), instrument simulators for *Rock Band* and *Guitar Hero*, and the dance pads used in games like *Dance Dance Revolution*.

Many of these music games use licensed music from popular artists. For such music to be used in a video game, however, it needs to be deconstructed. This could be as simple as breaking down the rhythmic patterns of the song, or as detailed as re-creating the song from scratch to break the song into individual tracks. Later in this section you'll learn how the various music game models break down music by technique.

In addition to the music-centric games listed previously, many games include a section of the game that might have a music-related puzzle that the player must solve. Example games that contain musical puzzles include *Myst* (1993) and *Fallout 3* (2008). The puzzles in these games rely on simplified music mechanics. Thus the skills discussed in the section apply to both full-scale music games and smaller musical puzzles.

The production of music games requires some unique skills, including the ability to construct music or analyze music frameworks, as well as the ability to perform music in a rhythmic-based context.

Many different approaches to the integration of music mechanics into a music-based game are possible. In this section you'll learn about the following types:

- Beat matching
- Performance simulation
- Music mixing and adaptivity

- Memory matching
- Music creation and construction

Beat Matching

Beat-matching games include *Dance Dance Revolution* (1998), *Samba de Amigo* (1999), and *Dance Central* (2010). In these games, the game player is asked to play specific rhythms in time with the song. These rhythms generally have a relationship to the song, mimicking phrases and rhythms in the music itself. They are typically based off of rhythms that are played by various instruments in the song, including melodic rhythms or ostinato patterns.

Many of the songs used in beat-matching games are licensed from popular artists. Musicians are employed to go through these songs and develop rhythmic patterns based around the song itself. They create levels based on the rhythms found in the songs. In many cases, the musicians are creating three levels of difficulty for beginning, medium, and advanced players. The level design is based on the song itself, and the musicians who are creating the rhythms become the game designers.

Usually this process is accomplished by first creating a tempo map that matches the song in a DAW like Digital Performer or ProTools. Then, musicians build the levels around this tempo map, matching the various rhythms in the song by inserting notes that the player will try to match while playing the game. These notes are mapped to buttons on the game player's controller. The tempo map and rhythmic level design are then usually exported as an SMF (Standard MIDI File) for use within the game itself. In many cases, musicians also insert other notes and markers into the exported MIDI file to trigger visual events during gameplay, such as lighting effects, camera angles, or shifts in the visual palette. This process is frequently known as *note tracking*.

Developers like Activision developed proprietary tools for note tracking and for level-of-difficulty management. These systems sometimes involve nonstandard workflows and put extra responsibility on the composer/note tracker to learn new toolsets.

During gameplay, the game reads in the MIDI file and plays it synchronously with the original audio from the song. The rhythmic patterns are scrolled onto the screen several seconds before the player needs to play them on the controller. A representation of the current *music position* is displayed on the screen, and visual representations of the notes scroll toward this timeline. When the notes reach the timeline, the player tries to match the performance. The patterns and tempos increase in difficulty as the levels progress.

Player controllers for beat-matching games vary tremendously, from the regular game hand controllers used in *Space Channel 5* (1999), to toy instruments like the maracas used in *Samba de Amigo* (1999), to the physical foot pads used in *Dance Dance Revolution* (1998). These controllers need be taken into account when adapting rhythms from the original song to make sure that they are actually playable in the context of the game. Testing level difficulty is integral when designing a beat-matching game. The musicians who are creating these levels should consider the arc of difficulty throughout the game to make sure the game is playable and not too hard.

Performance Simulation

Performance simulation games simulate live musical performance using game controls. These games typically use custom toy instrument controllers to simulate what it's like to play real instruments. This game interaction is typically at a lower level than actually learning how to play a real instrument but offers a satisfying game experience that brings players closer to the music. Such games include *Guitar Hero* (2005), *Rock Band* (2007), and *PaRappa the Rapper* (1996). They use a variety of instruments, including guitar, keyboards, drums, and vocals.

Performance simulation uses all the same techniques as the beat-matching games described in the previous section, but adds the component that the music plays only if the player is able to play the notes correctly. If the player is unable to match a pattern with the game controller, the part will drop out for those notes.

In these games, the parts that are being replicated by the players need to be split out onto individual tracks so that the rest of the music will keep playing if an individual part drops out. With licensed tracks, the original multitrack sessions are often needed so that the game developer can ensure that this will happen. Before this genre of games became extremely popular, game developers like Harmonix would not be allowed access to the original multitrack masters, but instead would produce extremely high-quality reproductions of the tracks and then split out the parts for the gameplay.

Performance simulation requires musicians to create parts based on the original source music to simulate playing instruments. For instance, in *Guitar Hero* (2005), there are five buttons along the guitar fret board instrument and a separate button to simulate the picking action. Usually the musician who creates the parts knows how to play them on a real guitar, but simplifies the part to be played on the instrument controller. This brings the player into the music. The player is scored based on how well he or she matches the rhythms and notes patterned by the musician who designed the level. In the case of vocals, a microphone tracks the rhythm and pitch of notes in real time to score the performance.

In games like *PaRappa the Rapper* (1996), where the music is constructed from scratch specifically for the game, there is no need to obtain a multitrack master. Instead, the compositions are easily available from the composer because they are developed specifically in conjunction with the game itself. In this game, the game character PaRappa raps lyrics in rhythm to the music based on the performance of the game player. The lyrics are performed as the player presses buttons on the game controller. In this scenario the music is written first, and then the rhythmic patterns that the player will perform are generated.

Music Mixing and Adaptivity

Music mixing games include games like *Mad Maestro!* (2001), *FreQuency* (2001), *DJ Hero* (2009), *Wii Music* (2008), and *Kinect Disneyland Adventures* (2013). Similar to the techniques described in Chapter 9, "Vertical Remixing," these games combine rhythm action with the ability to adjust the volume of one or more layers of the music.

In *Mad Maestro!* (2001), the player controls the volume of the music through the amount of pressure applied when pressing the controller buttons. Similarly, volume is controlled in *Wii Music* (2008) by changing the angle of the WiiMote. In *FreQuency* (2001), phrases of music are layered on top of the current song when a rhythm action set has been completed. Last, in *DJ Hero* (2009), the player has a slider control to crossfade between mixes during the level.

Music mixing games require that each layer of music be split out into its own track for independent control and playback during the game. Care must also be taken to ensure the layers stay synchronized throughout play so they line up with the other tracks.

In addition to managing the volume, many of these games include other ways to adjust the music, including through the tempo. *Wii Music* (2008) allows the player to control the tempo by using the WiiMote as a baton for conducting. In *Kinect Disneyland Adventures* (2013), the "Disneyland Parade" section involves performance feedback to tell players how well they "conducted" the band. When the player is doing well, the band sounds good, whereas the band begins to fall apart if the conducting is not done well.

When planning for music to have a variable tempo, most games set limits on how fast or slow a tempo can go. Most games that use variable tempo rely on MIDI files and instruments to play back the music at runtime. Changing the tempo of a prerendered audio file can take up too much of a game device's CPU cycles at runtime and is usually not an optimal solution for gameplay.

Memory Matching

Although many of the music game categories listed in this chapter can be identified as memory games because levels can be repeated and the player begins to recognize the individual rhythms and patterns, memory games specifically refer to games where players identify patterns and pitches in a musical context. Game designers work closely with music professionals to build these aspects into a game. Education games use this mechanic to teach intervals, harmony, and theory to students.

Games in popular culture also use musical memory challenges, including the electronic game *Simon* (1978) invented by Ralph H. Baer and Howard J. Morrison. *Simon* had four buttons, each associated with a different color and musical note. Players had to remember the patterns that *Simon* played and repeat those patterns, which kept getting longer as the game progressed.

Other games, such as *Fallout 3* (2008) and *Myst* (1993), include musical phrases the player must repeat to unlock certain aspects of the game.

Space Channel 5 (1999) uses a call-and-response type of system similar to *Simon*, where a musical pattern is played back and then must be repeated using the game controller. The patterns grow in length and difficulty as the game progresses. In *Space Channel 5*, these musical patterns must play on top of the background music. Careful planning of the overall musical framework is necessary to achieve this musical interaction.

Music Creation and Construction

The category of music creation games includes *Rez* (2001), *SimTunes* (1996), *Fract OSC* (2014), and *Chroma* (2014). These games construct music on the fly as the players navigate their way through the levels. In this type of game, the player creates the score by composing pieces of music that can be broken down into individual parts (phrases, notes, instruments) that can be played back, reordered, and sequenced at runtime. These elements are controlled by the player through a framework that the composer and level designer have constructed.

Games in this category contain music creation tools for nonmusicians such as *SimTunes* (1996) and *Electroplankton* (2005). These games use interfaces whereby nonmusicians can create music by manipulating on-screen elements. Objects that play notes are placed around the screen and are triggered by either a timeline or autonomous objects that move through the environment itself. In the development of these games, composers plan out the instruments and the notes to which the player has access. In doing so, the composer may choose to simplify the number of notes to a pentatonic scale to limit the number of *wrong* notes that the player might hear.

Rez (2001) and its sequel *Child of Eden* (2011) both use a first-person shooter (FPS) mechanic at their core to create music. As the player moves through each level, he or she first targets objects, which play a corresponding note quantized to the underlying rhythm a moment after the targeting. A second note plays in rhythm as the objects are destroyed. The composer must plan how these notes will interact with the overall underlying framework of the music. The notes that are triggered by the player must work with underlying tracks both harmonically and rhythmically. In addition, these games use horizontal resequencing to move through the score. When the player reaches a checkpoint after destroying all the objects on a level, the music must branch into the next section of music.

Fract:OSC (2014) is a game where the universe in which the player exists is made up of many different musical sequencers and instruments. The player solves musical puzzles by activating these sequencers and changing the instrument sounds to unlock parts of the world. The music creation and game design in these worlds is built by the composer through a music framework that he or she has constructed. Game theory and music need to work together for these projects to be successful.

Level Design, Construction, and Adaptation

Many games use music as a mechanism to construct game levels and immerse players in the music. These games include *Bit.Trip Runner* (2010), *AudioSurf* (2008), *Chime* (2010), and *Rayman Legends* (2013). These games don't typically use the methods described in the previous sections of this chapter; instead, the game world itself might revolve around the music. That is, part of the world may be built around the music, which may influence the way that the game is played.

In *Bit.Trip Runner* (2010), the game levels are constructed based on the underlying rhythm and tempo of the underscore. In this side-scrolling game, the player runs at a fixed speed and jumps over objects in the world that are placed at specific beats in time. Many of the objects reach the player on a specific beat, as the object SFX is in time with the underlying music. Watching *Bit.Trip Runner* is a little like watching a musical score with notes moving across the screen.

The music-based levels in *Rayman Legends* (2013) rely on a similar mechanic, except that players have more freedom regarding the speeds at which they travel. If players slow down too much, they'll die; thus the players are forced to keep up with the music. Because of this mechanic, the music feels as if it's Mickey Mousing the players' paths, immersing them in the game world.

In both *Bit.Trip Runner* and *Rayman Legends*, the music had to be written before the game level was produced because the elements on screen need to sync to the music. With such a work-flow, the game developer and composer must work together to shape the overall gameplay of these levels.

Chime (2010) is a *Tetris*-like puzzle game that synchronizes its rhythm to the action on screen. A timeline moves from left to right, hitting user-placed objects in the world. This timeline has a grid and each space on the grid is an eighth or sixteenth note. The objects that the player places in the world are then automatically quantized to play on the grid. The pitch of the notes on this grid is determined by its vertical position. For example, if the object is placed high on the screen, the game plays a higher note. In addition, when the player completes a percentage of the level, the music branches to a new section.

In games like *Chime* (2010) that play notes as part of the user interface, the composer needs to consider the effect that the pitch will have when played on top of an existing harmonic frame-work. In this game, the composer chose to use primarily pentatonic scales so as not to conflict with the underlying song.

Games like *Audiosurf* (2008) analyze music that the player imports into the game for its tempo, rhythm, and accent points. These factors are taken into account when the game builds the custom level for the song. These points are then placed in a timeline and played like a rhythm action game. The level itself is created by the song. In creating this type of game, a musician works closely with the programmer to help the game understand how music works and to cre-ate a framework for analyzing the music.

DSP is another real-time element that is sometimes used on music throughout gameplay. For instance, in games like the snowboarding game *SSX* (2012), players can import their own music. Although *SSX* is not technically a music game as defined earlier in this chapter, the player is able to apply real-time effects to the music based on gameplay. A real-time remixing engine applies different DSP effects, such as delays and filters, to the music based on the player's ability to perform various tricks.

Instruments in Interfaces and the Game World

Many games create instrument palettes for some of the user interface elements in the world itself. Frequently, when a player scrolls through options on a UI screen or moves the cursor around on the screen, the game may trigger notes or phrases of music that relate back to the game world. Examples of this technique can be found in *Bioshock* (2007) and *Chime* (2010).

In addition, some games have chosen to give avatars in the game world instruments to play. In *The Legend of Zelda: Ocarina of Time* (1998), the main character Link uses an ocarina to play various melodies to make things happen in the game. These melodies are memorized by the player and must be played back at various points. For the composer, these melodies are significant plot elements in the game and must be well thought out, linking the different parts of the world together.

In the MMO *Asheron's Call 2: Fallen Kings* (2002), characters are allowed to carry instruments and get into jam sessions with other players. This was quite a task for the composers to take on, as the developers wanted to create a great experience for musicians and nonmusicians alike. In this case the developers had to make trade-offs between giving the player too much control or too little control, as well as account for the inherent latency involved in playing games with other players over the Internet. Timing issues as well as harmonic issues had to be thought out carefully.

Games may also place musical sounds on objects that can be manipulated in game worlds. In *Portal 2* (2011), the player can pick up various objects that create musical tones. As the player moves those objects around the world, the relationship between the tones and the overall musical architecture changes. This can also be a valuable technique to shape the musical engagement of the player.

Diegetic Music in Video Games

Bioshock Infinite (2013) provides several excellent examples of music embedded in the world as a diegetic element. During gameplay, the player encounters several musical ensembles that are playing instruments or singing. Because they are part of the game world itself, they need to be localized in that world positionally. As the player walks away from the ensemble, the volume will diminish and pan appropriately in the speakers. In addition, *Bioshock* features many elements in the world that have melodies, including the vending machines and public address (PA) system announcements.

Many games have scenes where a musical ensemble is heard, including *Contrast* (2013) and *Grim Fandango* (1998). In the latter game, there are several jazz bands playing in a club. As the player exits a nightclub, the sound of the band is equalized to make it sound as if it's coming from inside the club. In *Mass Effect 2* (2010), there is a scene where the main character walks into a nightclub. DSP is used to make this experience dynamic and shape the sound of the music for the space, as the protagonist is first outside the club and then inside.

Diegetic music can also be a powerful way to tell stories in video games. *Assassin's Creed 3* (2012) uses music from an early period authentic opera as the game opens in a theater. The singers and musicians are spatialized in the theater itself to enhance the realism of the experience.

In both the *Grand Theft Auto* series and *L.A. Noire* (2011), the player can enter various vehicles and choose which type of music to play on the radio. This feature is important not only to set the time period of the game but also to give the player choice in the type of music that he or she wants to listen to in the game itself.

Music Approaches in Other Games

There is no defined rule book or instruction manual that describes how you must use music in video games. Composers and game developers invent new techniques all the time. Most of them build on older techniques, but some approach the use of music from a completely new angle.

The lines between how we defined *music games* in this chapter and the rest of the game universe are constantly being blurred. Sometimes it's hard to tell if something is truly a "music game" or just a very interactive score.

Whether you choose to approach music as underscore in a game, use it as a diegetic or source element, or deploy it as a rhythm action mechanic, music can be a powerful element to immerse players in the gameplay.

Review

Modern games employ many different ways of using music to immerse players into the gameplay. Games often use music not only as underscore but also as a gameplay element or design mechanic in the world itself.

Composers and sound designers typically work much more closely with a game development team on a music game than on a normal project. In fact, in some such games, the composers and sound designers may actually make up most of the game development team.

The production of music games requires some unique skills, including the ability to construct music or to analyze music frameworks, as well as the ability to perform music in a rhythmic-based context.

Many different approaches to integrating music mechanics into a music-based game are possible, including beat matching, performance simulation, music mixing and adaptivity, memory matching, and music creation.

Games may also place musical sounds on objects that can be manipulated in the game world. As the player moves those objects around the world, the relationship between the tones and the overall musical architecture changes. These objects may be intrinsically musical (an instrument) or abstractions that emit music or a layer of an overall musical environment.

The lines between how we defined *music games* in this chapter and the rest of the game universe are constantly being blurred. Sometimes it's hard to tell if something is truly a "music game" or just a very interactive score.

Whether you choose to approach music as underscore in a game, use it as a diegetic or source element, or deploy it as a rhythm action mechanic, music can be a powerful element to immerse players in the gameplay.

Exercises

1. Harmonically analyze and deconstruct a music construction game for its assets (audio, instruments, SFX).

2. List and evaluate the different types of controllers used in music games.

3. Create a simple music-based game that uses proximity to objects in a 3D space that can be manipulated and carried around to change the dynamic audio of the game.

4. Find examples of diegetic music within video games and describe its use, along with its harmonic context with the underscore.

PART III

ADVANCED VIDEO GAME SCORING TECHNIQUES

- Chapter 13: MIDI and Virtual Instruments
- Chapter 14: Real-Time Tempo Variation and Synchronization
- Chapter 15: Advanced Dynamic Music Manipulation Techniques
- Chapter 16: Aleatoric Performance Techniques for Video Games
- Chapter 17: Algorithmic and Generative Music Systems
- Chapter 18: Using Middleware to Create Advanced Compositions
- Chapter 19: Creating a Custom Music Solution

MIDI AND VIRTUAL INSTRUMENTS

In this chapter we begin to focus more on the combination of MIDI and virtual instruments to create interactive scores. These interactive methods open up an incredible array of variable approaches to musical composition that are not typically associated with using prerendered audio to create a dynamic score.

An Alternative to Prerendered Audio

Many composers have pushed prerendered audio to the limit of how far it will go. If composers want more control and detail in their game audio with techniques such as real-time note manipulation and tempo variance, they'll have to rely on using MIDI for their scores rendered directly on the game platform with virtual instruments.

MIDI—an acronym that stands for Musical Instrument Digital Interface—was developed by the MIDI Manufacturers Association (MMA) in the early 1980s. Common MIDI commands include the following options:

- Note on/off
- Patch change
- Controller messages
- Pitch bend
- System-exclusive data

Composers often use MIDI as a language to communicate from their keyboards and controllers to their computer. Almost all DAWs such as Logic and Cubase support MIDI recording, through which composers can play back virtual instruments to create advanced sequences of music.

In this chapter, the term *MIDI* refers primarily to a Standard MIDI File (SMF), which contains a series of MIDI commands (e.g., note on, note off) in a sequence with a tempo map. SMFs can hold up to 16 channels of data. Channel 10 is usually reserved for drums and percussion, while the other 15 channels are available to play any instrument.

Composers have used MIDI sequences directly in games since the late 1980s. They are still used today, primarily on handheld gaming platforms or on the web where memory constraints are a factor.

For MIDI sequences to play back on a game console, a set of standard MIDI instruments is needed, or else the composer needs to provide a set of instruments to play. Some game consoles and mobile devices include a standard set of General MIDI Instruments for this purpose. The General MIDI Instrument Set was developed by the MMA and includes a set of 128 frequently used instruments organized into the following categories:

- Piano
- Chromatic percussion
- Organ
- Guitar
- Bass
- Strings
- Ensemble
- Brass
- Reed
- Pipe

- Synth lead
- Synth pad
- Synth effects

- Ethnic
- Percussive
- Sound effects

The challenge for a composer interested in using an SMF with these instruments was twofold: the General MIDI Instrument Set sounded different on every platform, and it didn't include many instruments. Composers would need to test their sequences on different sound cards and operating systems to see how their compositions would sound.

Toward the late 1980s, composers began to embed MIDI sequences into their games. This approach allowed them to write very long pieces of music while using very little memory. George "The Fat Man" Sanger became very famous when he used MIDI scores in games such as *Wing Commander* (1990) and the *7th Guest* (1993). Throughout much of the 1990s, many composers used MIDI and the General MIDI Instrument Set to create music for their games. As memory limitations decreased over time, composers were able to depend less on MIDI for their musical scores. Although the real-time data manipulation of MIDI sequences is powerful, the limitations of the General MIDI Instrument Set dissuaded many composers from using it.

Eventually, composers sought out a way to customize their own instrument sets that would replace the General MIDI Instrument Set. MOD files were developed in the late 1980s to include both sequence data (just like a MIDI file) and custom sample instruments. They allowed composers to create sequences that would sound identical on a range of platforms—that is, they eliminated platform-to-platform variations. MOD files are created with MOD trackers, which are available for cross-platform use. Both MOD files and MIDI files are still used in games today.

In the latter half of the 1990s, several other custom instrument standards emerged, such as SoundFont and DLS, which enabled composers to go beyond the General MIDI Instrument Set. Composers could create custom instruments to be used when playing back these MIDI sequences. These instruments may consist of a combination of sample-based instruments and basic synthesis.

> **note**
>
> In the late 1990s, two instrument formats emerged in the game world: SoundFont from E-mu and DLS from the MMA. Both formats allowed users to create sample-based instruments with key mapping, filters, envelopes, and low-frequency oscillators (LFOs). These instruments were then assembled in a bank to accompany MIDI files, which would play back these instruments.

Today, middleware engines can provide functionality for integrating instrument sets and support MIDI and MOD files playback.

In the rest of this chapter, you'll learn how MIDI is still used in gaming and how, in some cases, it can be more powerful when you're creating adaptive experiences than using prerendered waves. Prerendered audio limits the composer's ability to manipulate audio in real time. Even though MIDI was a predecessor to many of today's orchestral prerendered audio scores, it remains an extremely powerful tool for creating real-time adaptive music scores.

Working with MIDI-Based Scores

MIDI sequences offer many advantages over prerendered segments of audio. Because MIDI is composed of small commands (e.g., note on/off), the resulting data can be manipulated very easily with almost no CPU processing. Unlike prerendered audio, MIDI scores can easily shift in tempo or key during gameplay. MIDI scores also take up very little RAM—less than one percent of the space required by a prerendered audio file—allowing composers to create much longer sequences that can be loaded into memory more easily.

MIDI offers "granular" control over the composition. It can be compared to conducting a band or orchestra performing in real time, because it is being performed virtually in real time. Any individual part can turn on a dime, as can the entire piece. Many consider the combination of the capabilities of MIDI with the current and future advantages of streaming prerendered audio to be the next technical and creative frontier in video game music.

Although it's possible to take prerendered audio and shift the key or tempo using a real-time pitch-shifting plug-in like Melodyne, this kind of processing power is usually not available for audio that is processed in real time on a game platform. This limitation arises because the CPU on a game console must manage many other systems besides audio, including visual rendering, physics, character AI, visual effects, networking, and character motion.

Because the size of MIDI sequences is so small, composers can also use music in places where music is not normally possible with prerendered audio. For example, it is very difficult to play prerendered audio tracks on loading screens because, when these screens are visible, the game is clearing out RAM to load the next level. Because MIDI takes up very little RAM, however, MIDI sequences can usually play over loading screens, thereby seamlessly connecting two scenes. This is also one of MIDI's great advantages over prerendered audio files.

Although certain manipulations of music are very challenging with prerendered audio, including pitch manipulation, harmonic changes, muting specific instruments, and tempo manipulation, all of these techniques are relatively simple to implement with MIDI. MIDI sequences can take advantage of the following techniques in real time during gameplay:

- Tempo manipulation
- Note duration manipulation
- Note pitch manipulation

- Tempo synchronization
- Track muting and soloing
- Orchestration and instrument changes

Games that use algorithmic music composition techniques are more likely to take advantage of MIDI and virtual instruments because the need for note manipulation with real-time composition is paramount. Algorithmic scores are not possible within games unless virtual instruments are available. Algorithmic composition is explored in Chapter 17, "Algorithmic and Generative Music Systems."

> ## note
>
> In modern DAWs, MIDI is used to trigger high-quality sample and instrument libraries. Many games use the same MIDI technology to trigger instruments, but game platforms don't support the same types of virtual instruments that are supported in your DAW. Instrument banks for games are almost always custom created and, because of CPU and memory restrictions on the game platform, do not match the high quality that you encounter in your DAW. In games, MIDI sequences play back either the more generic General MIDI Instrument Set that may be embedded in the platform or the custom sound banks that the composer has created.
>
> Many games today do not use MIDI sequences in games to trigger instruments; instead, composers prerender their high-quality virtual instruments as audio files that can be used in the game. Sometimes they also add live instruments to these audio files. Although this approach allows composers to create high-quality, well-produced music, it does not offer the same flexibility as using MIDI sequences in game.

The disadvantage of using the General MIDI Instruments Set is that it doesn't sound anywhere close to the virtual instruments we typically hear when using our DAWs (LA Scoring Strings, East/West, Vienna Symphonic Library). In fact, most of the instruments encountered in games today do not have as much functionality and quality as many of the instruments that we use in our DAWs. Although the game consoles have enough CPU power to deliver the power of an instrument like Kontakt or VSL, music manufacturers have chosen not to port their instruments to game consoles. In addition, the standards for instrument banks on consoles (DSL, Sound-Font, MOD) are more limited than the refined instruments that composers buy with their DAWs.

Another disadvantage of using MIDI sequences that rely on custom instruments is that a sequence may use voices that the CPU needs to play back other sounds such as sound effects. As with any technique, you'll want to test how your game platform responds when you play back MIDI sequences coupled with virtual instruments.

Because there is still a trade-off between good-quality prerendered audio and the sophisticated note manipulation and higher quality associated with custom instruments, MIDI still typically takes a backseat to prerendered audio unless the needs of the game call for intricate real-time note manipulation. Nevertheless, several games intertwine MIDI with prerendered audio seamlessly, including *Super Mario Galaxy* (2007). Although this can be challenging for the composer to unify, games that mix MIDI sequences with prerendered audio can take advantage of all the benefits of both systems. Hybrid models that use MIDI sequences to handle tempo and note manipulation and prerendered audio to showcase orchestral and live instruments can be the most effective at immersing the player in the game world.

Using Virtual Instruments

The use of virtual instruments is probably familiar to anyone who has worked with a DAW. Video games can also use virtual instruments to create the score in real time via MIDI sequences. The advantage of using virtual instruments in a game context is that you're able to apply note manipulation and tempo changes in real time to customize each individual player's experience. In a game, this flexibility can allow for almost infinite variation.

As with using virtual instruments in the DAW, some technical considerations must be taken into account when using MIDI sequences:

- Memory
- Number of voices
- CPU processing power
- Disk speed
- Technical implementation

Each game platform will have unique technical specifications, allowing varying degrees of quality versus performance. These technical specifications will restrict the composer's ability to create some types of advanced instruments.

When using a sample engine inside a DAW like Kontakt or VSL, the samples are of high quality and many of them are streamed directly off of disk because of their size. These samples are often prebuffered in memory to allow the disk to stream the next part of the sample. As a result, the samples can be almost unlimited in length.

When you're using MIDI to trigger virtual instruments in a game, most of the virtual instruments will be custom created, as opposed to full commercial libraries. The latter libraries rarely ship within a game because of licensing, CPU, and memory constraints. Although it is possible to license the use of high-quality virtual instruments from the manufacturer, doing so may be cost prohibitive because special versions of the instruments would need to be created to support the specifications of the game platform.

In a game context, most instruments need to be loaded into memory because the disk or other storage medium is being accessed by many other systems on which the game relies. A larger instrument size (in terms of memory) usually equates to a better-sounding instrument. Because the memory of most games is much less than what's offered in a DAW, composers shouldn't expect the same high quality in the final product that they may have become accustomed to while creating the score.

When setting out to create your own virtual instruments for video games, you'll want to develop a plan for your sequencer to play back these instruments. At the time of this writing, the most widely accepted standard for instrument banks between games is DLS. DLS is supported by the Fmod audio middleware package. The DLS instrument banks are used in conjunction with standard MIDI files in the game itself. Both the Mac and the PC include software that can not only create DLS instruments but also be used for playback by connecting your DAW through a virtual MIDI router.

> ## note
> The use of MIDI and virtual instruments on the game platform does not preclude the use of prerendered audio files. In fact, scores that use MIDI technology on the game platform in combination with prerendered audio files can take advantage of the strengths of both techniques: adaptability on a note level and high-quality renders of live instruments.

The importance of being able to accurately represent what you'll hear on the game platform while you're developing the score cannot be understated. You'll save time and money by not having to transfer your materials to the game engine to hear what they will sound like.

Whether you are creating instruments for a DLS bank or working inside a MOD tracker, the fundamental principles of instrument design remain the same. As explored in Chapter 11, these instrument creators support many of the same basic synthesis functions, such as sound generators, volume envelopes, LFOs, and effects.

The outputs of sample-based instruments depend on variables such as sample rate, bit depth, and sample length. There is a trade-off between quality and size. As the quality of an instrument increases, the amount of memory that the instrument will take up on the game platform also increases. Most modern sample players like Kontakt or LASS maximize the quality of their instruments by increasing sample links and the number of instruments. This approach works well if all you're doing is creating music. When you add in all the other game systems that need CPU processing, however, you won't be able to sustain the high levels of CPU required to play back these instruments.

Within games, the instruments themselves need to be robust enough to provide the expected quality while fitting within the memory constraints of your game platform. Reducing the memory footprint of your instrument generally means reducing the amount of samples, the sample frequency, or the bit depth. When choosing the sample rate of an instrument, it's important to take into account the frequency spectrum of the original sound to save as much space and CPU as possible.

COMPOSER PERSPECTIVE

Yuzo Koshiro

In my case, I first meet with the director, who gives me documents. We broadly go over the general direction we will take. Within the documents are explanations of the in-game characters, the world/setting, and the overall gameplay. Also usually attached is a list of all the pieces that I will need to produce. While reviewing these documents, I will talk with the developer and discuss what sort of pieces he or she is thinking of and what he or she is looking for. Unless the developer has strong feelings of what he or she wants (in which case, I would follow their requests to the best of my abilities), I usually end up offering some of my opinions on what I think will best fit the game.

Once I start the compositional phase, I spend anywhere from 1 to 3 days writing up a demo. I send it in for review and await any feedback—for example, whether it is progressing in the right direction or if anything really needs to be changed. Often, the director is not fluent in music terminology, so I make sure to create a few samples so that he or she can just listen to them and let me know which one is the closest to the desired image.

Ten years ago, when everyone was using chiptunes, the music development process was easier because you just had to play back the sound from the actual console. More recently, projects have been using orchestras and orchestral sounds; thus it is more common to make a simplified demo using sequencing. However, this demo will sound very different from the finished piece, so it may be difficult for the director to get a clear idea of what you are intending. It is important to develop the techniques and the skills needed to make the best mockup in the shortest amount of time possible.

Sometimes after tirelessly working on a BGM track, you will notice that when it is synced with the game, an unexpected problem arises. Many times, the music sounds irritating after you listen for prolonged periods of time or you suddenly get a sync issue due to the data overload. To not waste music, I use only samples until all of the potential problems are completely ironed out. It is very important to create an environment for yourself in which you can readily handle any situation, like a sudden change of heart from the client or a last-minute change in gameplay.

Review

MIDI and MOD sequences open up an incredible array of interactive approaches to musical composition that are not typically associated with the use of prerendered audio to create a dynamic score. MIDI and MOD sequences play back custom instrument banks that the composer creates. During the video game, these sequences play back the virtual instruments at runtime.

A disadvantage of using a MIDI score is its lack of high-quality instruments, at least compared to the kinds of instruments with which composers become accustomed in their DAWs.

MIDI offers "granular" control over the composition. It can be compared to conducting a band or orchestra performing in real time, because the MIDI sequence is being performed virtually in real time. Any individual part can turn on a dime, as can the entire piece.

MIDI/MOD sequences can take advantage of dynamic music manipulation techniques during gameplay, including real-time control of tempo, notes, and instruments.

Games that employ algorithmic music composition techniques are more likely to take advantage of MIDI and virtual instruments because their need for note manipulation through real-time composition is paramount.

As when using virtual instruments in the DAW, technical considerations must be taken into account when using MIDI sequences, including issues related to memory, number of voices, CPU processing power, disk speed, and technical implementation.

Many consider the combination of the capabilities of MIDI with the current and future advantages of streaming prerendered audio to be the next technical and creative frontier in video game music.

Exercises

1. Compose an SMF for an 8-bit generation side-scroller using only the General MIDI Instrument Set.

2. Using a free MOD tracker (such as MilkyTracker), build a set of custom instruments, and then compose a piece of music using these instruments.

3. Find examples of note and tempo manipulation in games, and then analyze them in terms of effectiveness.

CHAPTER 14

REAL-TIME TEMPO VARIATION AND SYNCHRONIZATION

This chapter focuses on how real-time tempo manipulation and synchronization can affect players' experiences within games, and how we might use these variations in a game context. It explores different methods and techniques that rely on various gameplay mechanics to control tempo and synchronization within a game, and discusses best practices for composing musical cues with tempo changes.

Immersing the Player through Tempo

In video games, tempo variations based on real-time changes in gameplay have been around almost since the very beginning, with *Space Invaders* (1978) and *Asteroids* (1979). Tempo changes can be an exciting way for a composer to build the emotional tension in gameplay or to reward a player for playing well. The goal of using tempo variability within gameplay should be to ultimately increase the player's immersion into the experience.

Although it is fairly easy to adjust the tempo of MIDI playback in real time, the same cannot be said of changing the tempo of a prerendered audio file. As video game music has evolved to the point where the majority of video games use prerendered audio, it has become more challenging to explore real-time tempo changes within a score.

Tempo synchronization of gameplay events can also immerse the player not only within the game but also within the music itself. Types of event synchronization include having the visual events trigger on the downbeats of the music or dynamically speed up at the same time the game world increases in speed or action.

This chapter explores how to use tempo changes and ways to synchronize musical accents and events in your scores.

Varying Tempo Based on Game Events

In musical notation, there are various ways to notate changes in tempo, including the use of tempo markers, words like *accelerando* and *ritardando* (signifying a gradual increase or decrease in tempo, respectively), and tempo directions from classical music including *presto* or *andante*. Video games can employ similar events to vary the gameplay music.

In video games, the tempo of music can be manipulated to enhance gameplay. The control input for tempo manipulation can be the result of an action by the player, or it may come from the game world itself. Tempo changes can dramatically increase the player's engagement in a video game. Just as listening to music with a fast tempo while driving a car might make someone drive faster, so increasing the tempo of the game music can make the player react more rapidly.

There are many excellent reasons to use real-time tempo changes in your game and numerous examples of games that use them:

- Add emotional tension to gameplay (*Space Invaders*, 1978)
- Reward the player for playing well and collecting power-ups (*Super Mario Bros.*, 1985)
- Control or conduct the tempo of a musical ensemble (*Wii Music*, 2008)
- Signal when a timer is about to run out (*Mappy*, 1983)

- Indicate a change in health (*Street Fighter II*, 1991)
- Illustrate forward or backward changes to time events (*Braid*, 2008)
- Represent how fast a player is traveling (*Legend of Zelda: Spirit Tracks*, 2009)
- Indicate to the player that he or she has reached the next level (*Rez*, 2001)

In games, you'll see different implementations of tempo changes, but in general there are only two types of tempo changes within games:

- **Static:** Immediate changes from one tempo to another that are used primarily with prerendered audio files
- **Continuous:** Real-time variable tempo changes that are used primarily with MIDI or MOD files, similar to the musical terms *accelerando* and *ritardando*

The ability to adapt the tempo continuously can open up interesting game mechanics as well, such as the ability to control an orchestra's tempo through conducting in *Wii Music* (2008), or the ability to vary the tempo continuously by changing the speed that you're rolling around in *Super Mario Galaxy* (2007).

During game development, the composer works with the game development team to establish which control inputs from the game should influence how the tempo changes. This will inform decisions about whether to use a prerendered audio solution with less flexibility in tempo shifts versus MIDI/MOD files that offer continuous variable control over the tempo.

There are many creative ways to manipulate tempos within gameplay. When using multiple layers of music or vertical remixing, for example, the tempos of the individual layers could be manipulated as long as the layers don't need to be synchronized with one another. Thus you could compose a rhythmic layer and a harmonic layer and control the tempos independently.

While many interesting interactive music possibilities exist, if a particular feature (e.g., tempo ramping) isn't supported by the game engine/audio engine, then the composer can't use that technique. You should always work with the game development team to see which interactive music options are available before you begin writing.

Tempo Changes with Prerendered Audio

If you take a prerendered sound file and speed up the audio playback, two things happen. First, you'll notice that the tempo of the music has increased. Second, you'll notice that the pitch of the music has become proportionally elevated. This process is fairly simple and is associated with relatively low CPU load.

Through the use of time compression and expansion, you can adapt the music to change in tempo without changing the pitch. This process is relatively CPU intensive, however, and it generally produces various artifacts and distortions in the audio rendering of the file. There is a trade-off to having a better time-compression algorithm to reduce the audio artifacts: a higher-quality algorithm leads to more load on the CPU. Real-time tempo changes of prerendered music using a decent time-compression algorithm usually require too much CPU load to exploit during a game.

You are probably familiar with time compression and expansion, as these capabilities are incorporated into most DAWs, such as Ableton Live and ProTools. Many DAWs are capable of achieving real-time time compression and expansion of audio—albeit at the cost of using the entire CPU for audio. In a game, of course, the CPU must be shared among many different game subsystems, such as graphics, physics, and AI.

To use tempo changes with prerendered audio tracks, the files must be prepared by pre-rendering all of them with the tempos the game will use. As a consequence, the more tempo flexibility that you want to incorporate into your game, the more prerendered audio files you need to make.

When using prerendered audio files with multiple tempos, it's best to limit the number of tempos to only two or three because of the memory consumption issue. Ideally, you will also write transition clips that ramp up or down from one tempo to another. One transition clip might help link two pieces of music together by accelerating from one tempo to another; another might ritard from one tempo to another.

On the one hand, an advantage of creating prerendered tracks is that you can avoid audio artifacts produced by artificial time compression or expansion. In addition, you'll lower any CPU load on the game processor. On the other hand, each prerendered file at alternate tempos will take up a significant amount of additional memory.

An alternative approach is to create a multichannel broadcast wave file with various submixes and crossfade between each section at runtime. In this scenario, a tempo is assigned to two or more game states depending on how many tempos have been prerendered. Each tempo prerendering would be assigned to a specific game state.

For instance, if you're working on a FPS, you could assign three game states such as *explore*, *battle*, and *flee*. Each of these states could have a different tempo. The flee state could be the battle cue at a faster tempo. In such a case, you would need to compose transitions to make the tempo jumps less abrupt.

Because prerendered tempo shifts offer less flexibility than the MIDI model, it's important to consider implementing a timeout between these states. For instance, if the player enters into the flee state, the music should be allowed to play for a certain amount of time before entering a new state. Otherwise, the player will hear multiple tempo shifts with corresponding transitions quickly in succession, which would become very repetitive to the player experience and take the player out of his or her immersion within the game.

In other circumstances, it might be advantageous to have the pitch increase or decrease along with the tempo. MIDI and MOD tempo changes are easy to implement from a technical point of view and don't suffer from audio artifacts. A gameplay scenario that uses this model might be found in a game like *Braid* (2009), in which the player can speed up time and even reverse it.

Tempo Changes with MIDI or MOD

When the final music format in the game is a MIDI or MOD file, it's easy to adjust the playback tempo dynamically during gameplay. Unlike prerendered audio files with which real-time tempo adjustment may lead to audio artifacts, MIDI and MOD files don't suffer from a quality loss when you adjust the tempo.

MIDI and MOD files also have the advantage of being continuously variable in tempo, allowing for a range of tempo possibilities instead of just a few options as with the prerendered model. The control input for tempo with MIDI and MOD files can receive a continuously variable input as opposed to assigning the tempo to a specific game state, as in the prerendered model.

There is a trade-off between music production quality and the ability to be interactive (i.e., change tempo) if you use a MIDI/MOD-type system. The ease with which MIDI/MOD-based sequences can change tempo is offset by the inability to employ live instruments or use the same high-quality virtual instruments that composers have come to expect in their DAWs. These features are likely to improve in the future.

Composers should work together with the game development team to establish the control input for the tempo setting. Then, the teams should work out the slowest and fastest tempos that can be used with the file during gameplay. Once these details are settled, the programmer can establish the tempo limits for playback within the game.

Because of the ability to use a continuous control input for MIDI and MOD files, it's relatively easy to shift tempos quickly and easily, making for smooth tempo transitions. In other words, because of the variable tempo control, it's easy to create accelerandos and ritards in real time based on gameplay input.

Frequently, music games take advantage of the variable tempos that MIDI and MOD files can offer. For example, in games such as *Rez* (2001) and *Space Channel 5* (1999), tempos gradually increase as the levels develop.

The tempo flexibility of MIDI and MOD files can also help invite new gameplay mechanics. For example, in *Super Mario Galaxy* (2008), the speed of the character rolling around on a ball during the golf level controls the tempo of the music.

Tempo Synchronization

For a game like *Rayman: Legends* (2013) to synchronize the game's actions with the underlying music framework, the game development team needs to work closely with the composer. Music that is synchronized to gameplay in this way can be very exciting and immersive in regard to the player's experience. This type of level synchronization, where the actions in the game match the music tempo, is similar to the film technique called *Mickey Mousing*.

To create a high level of synchronization, the music must be written before the levels are designed. After the composer has worked with the development team to learn about the narrative structure of the level, he or she begins to write the music for the level without a game to actually play. The composer works with any temporary images and information that the game developer has supplied to get an idea of what the music should sound like for the level. Once the music has been created for the level, then the level designers who work for the game developer will synchronize elements and mechanics in the level design to the music. This method can lead to very tightly synchronized music that matches the mechanics of the level design.

Games that require tight music synchronization usually have a game mechanic where the player must be at a certain point in the level at a certain time. This creates the illusion that the music is in sync with the player's actions. Conversely, if the player fails to keep up with the music, the player loses the level and must restart at a checkpoint to allow the music synchronization to begin again, by lining up to a point where the level and music match.

The game mechanic that moves the player forward in the level in synchrony with the music usually gives the player limited control over the speed of the character on screen. The game forces the player to move at a constant pace to keep up with the music.

This kind of music synchronization in games allows the composer to create flourishes and other dramatic events in the music score that later can be synchronized with the level design. When composing this type of music, it's important to include these dramatic musical events in the composition to create fun levels for the player. Such dramatic musical events include accents, musical stops, flourishes, musical runs, and negative accents. In addition, musical phrases and cadences should be well thought out so that there are demarcation points for the music score to reestablish musical synchronization in the case that a player fails on the level and must restart.

This kind of music synchronization during gameplay can be an exciting way to immerse the player not only in the game but also in the music itself.

Phrase Synchronization

A complex problem that is difficult to solve in games is the ability to match a specific gameplay event with a musical accent that is synchronized in time with the music. If, for instance, you wanted to accent a sword clash between two foes on a downbeat, this is nearly impossible to do without the game knowing in advance where the downbeat will fall. Because the player has control over the flow of the game, these types of events can be very difficult to implement.

For downbeat and other musical accents to fall on specific gameplay moments, and for the musical tempo to remain intact, the animation for that event must wait for an appropriate point in the music to play. To do so, the animation engine must communicate with the musical engine, and the musical engine essentially fires cues to start animation events and synchronize them to musical moments.

In this scenario, there is frequently at least some latency in the animation playback, as the game has to wait for the specific musical accent to begin before playing the animation. Because of these challenges, it's rare to see games built with this level of phrase synchronization. A much simpler approach would be to play a musical stinger on top of whatever current music was playing to avoid the latency problem. Note, however, that a stinger playing on top of another piece of music will never feel as integrated as a specific musical accent that the music can lead up to.

In most scenarios, the music is following the actions in the gameplay. If we want a phrase or musical accent to play in the tempo of the overall musical framework, then the animations will have to follow the musical framework. This can be a challenging endeavor because the animation must respond to this musical framework and, in doing so, must have musical intelligence to know when certain beats and accents fall. In essence, the game itself must know how to read music tempos and meters so that it can provide accurate musical synchronization.

Middleware engines such as Fmod and Wwise have the ability to synchronize musical events by following the actions in gameplay. In the past, having the gameplay follow musical events usually required quite a bit of custom programming. More recently, improvements in middleware (e.g., Wwise, UE4, and Frostbite 3) have introduced per-event sound scripting, allowing developers to more easily synchronize these types of events to music.

Review

Tempo changes can dramatically increase the player's engagement in a video game. Generally, two types of tempo changes occur within games: static changes, which go immediately from one tempo to another, and continuous changes, which accelerate or slow the tempo down gradually to match another tempo.

Player immersion is increased through real-time tempo changes. Such changes may increase the emotional tension, reward the player, signal a change in the game state, or represent how fast the player might be moving.

Because it's difficult to change the tempo of a prerendered audio file in real time, the files are usually prepared by prerendering all the tempos that the game will use. Thus, the more tempo flexibility that you want to incorporate into your game, the more prerendered audio files you need to make.

MIDI and MOD files have the advantage of being continuously variable in tempo, allowing for a range of tempo possibilities instead of just a few options, as with the prerendered model. In addition, these files don't suffer from a quality loss when you adjust the tempo in real time.

If the goal is to create a high level of synchronization between the gameplay and the music, the music must be written before the levels are designed. The levels can then be designed with the music in mind, allowing for tight synchronization of events.

Exercises

1. Analyze and transcribe a game that uses tempo variation. Then do the same for another game that uses musical synchronization techniques as discussed in this chapter.

2. Compose music for a game that has two different game states, where one of the states increases in tempo by 15 beats per minute. Make sure to write at least two transitions to go from each state to the other.

3. Write a MIDI or MOD composition in which you can vary the tempo continuously across 50 beats per minute.

CHAPTER 15

ADVANCED DYNAMIC MUSIC MANIPULATION TECHNIQUES

The ability to dynamically change the harmonic or rhythmic context of the music based on player choices can radically change the way the music tells the story of a game. This chapter focuses on real-time music manipulation techniques, including dynamic melodic and harmonic changes, stylistic changes, ensemble-based changes, and building a small sequencer within the game itself.

Weighing More Expensive Options

Although horizontal resequencing and vertical remixing offer a variety of ways for composers to create interactive music for video games, these forms have limited flexibility in terms of dynamic variability and adaptability from moment to moment during gameplay. Horizontal resequencing and vertical remixing also rely primarily on the use of prerendered audio files, which suffer from problems related to looping and branching, making it difficult for notes to cross boundaries across segments or loop points. This also limits the flexibility of these two methods.

Game engines are beginning to inherit more of the features that composers find in standard DAWs, thereby allowing games to take advantage of more sophisticated real-time compositional changes and variability during gameplay. One factor contributing to the more robust system development is that the number of processors, RAM, and buffer sizes are growing exponentially with each console generation.

The adaptive techniques explored in this chapter can dramatically change the overall character of the musical score and decrease the repetitive nature of music in games. In addition, these techniques are much more reactive to control inputs, allowing scores to change more quickly with a finer level of detail.

Many of the techniques discussed in this chapter require a MIDI-based implementation scheme that can play back virtual instruments. Although there has been some progress over the past few years in the manipulation of prerendered audio segments using plug-ins such as Melodyne, the CPU cost is generally too expensive to use this technology during a game. MIDI manipulation has a low CPU overhead and is extremely flexible in terms of the range of manipulation you can achieve. Some of the techniques described in this chapter can be implemented through the use of prerendered audio instead of MIDI sequences, albeit with much larger memory demands.

These techniques are used far less often than the fundamental techniques discussed in Part II of this book, largely because of the greater amount of time and money required to implement them into a game engine. These techniques frequently require a game's audio engine to have musical intelligence; that is, the audio engine must be able to identify sections of the music, or the key or beat that is currently playing, and then adapt the music dynamically based on a set of musical rules. Few modern audio middleware engines support these techniques; thus many of these features need to be custom coded from scratch.

In this chapter, you'll learn about strategies for using dynamic reharmonization within a game context, including ideas about laying motivic elements on top of preexisting material, altering ensembles and styles, and building your own simple sequencer within a game.

Melodic Manipulation and Reinterpretation

Just as you might think about extending your composition by reinterpreting the melody in different ways, so a game engine could change the melody base by altering it in real time or by following a different harmonic framework. This would allow the melody to develop on its own, in turn extending the life of the melody by decreasing repetition. Here are some ways that you might want to think about altering the melody:

- **Transpose.** Move the pitch up or down by a constant interval.
- **Reharmonize.** Change the harmonic context by changing the chords.
- **Inversion.** Start on the same pitch but reverse the direction of the note leaps.
- **Retrograde.** Reverse the melody.
- **Permutation.** Change the note order.
- **Rhythmic Displacement.** Slip the melody forward or back in time by a rhythmic value.
- **Truncate.** Shorten the melody.
- **Expand.** Lengthen the melody.
- **Rhythmic Alteration.** Alter the rhythm but not the pitch.
- **Melodic Alteration.** Alter the pitch but not the rhythm.
- **Thinning.** Simplify the melody by removing notes.
- **Ornamentation.** Embellish the music by adding notes.

Many of these techniques are often used by composers in the composition process. For a game to interpret a score and make these changes in real time involves sophisticated programming. The game code must have enough musical intelligence to know how to apply these techniques in real time. These rules are taught to the game engine either through programming or through the use of a middleware engine that understands these concepts. More information can be found on this subject in Chapter 19, "Creating a Custom Music Solution." More commonly, the composer can provide alternate tracks within the MIDI sequences that embed these techniques. This allows the game to switch to a track or tracks that use the techniques without the programming required for the game to interpret the music in real time.

Ensemble, Rhythmic, and Style Alteration

When using MIDI, one of the easier adaptive music techniques to use within gameplay is to modify the instrument ensemble and the rhythmic makeup of a piece of music.

Dynamically changing the instrument ensemble requires that the gameplay engine switch the playback of a MIDI track from one instrument to another based on a control input. This can dramatically change the overall character of the score and decrease the repetitive nature of music in games. Many games use this technique effectively, including *Monkey Island 2: LeChuck's Revenge* (1991) and *Legend of Zelda: Skyward Sword* (2011). This technique can be used with pre-rendered files using vertical remixing but the result would take up substantially more memory.

Modifying the rhythm by muting and unmuting tracks within a MIDI sequence can be an effective and powerful way to change the context of a single piece of music. Secondary rhythmic tracks can be brought in to either intensify the rhythm of an existing piece or replace the original rhythmic framework for a more dramatic change. Combined with variations in tempo, rhythmic changes can increase the usability of your music for many different situations.

Along with changing out the rhythmic patterns, alternate MIDI tracks could contain style adaptations of the original piece. This would allow you to change the track configuration to go from one style to another, while retaining the original melodic and harmonic characteristics of the music.

Microsoft's deprecated DirectMusic engine lets you create musical style templates, which could be swapped while playing the music. These musical styles would inform decisions about the rhythmic and ensemble characteristics of the piece.

Embellishment and Fills

Musical embellishments and fills are another effective way of synchronizing the music to the gameplay. Musical embellishments emphasize a particular player action or game event, while fills generally assist in transitioning to a new piece of music. These fills and embellishments are typically played on top of the music that is currently being heard during gameplay.

Careful consideration of the harmonic content of the underlying music is necessary when composing fills and embellishments to ensure that they will fit the music when it is played during the game. If the fill or embellishment doesn't contain any harmonic information, then it will be easier to place at appropriate points triggered by the gameplay. If the fill or embellishment does contain harmonic information, then it might need to be transposed to the correct key and mode so that it will work with the underlying music.

Within the underlying music, the composer should place markers within the sequence that establish the appropriate places to play embellishments or fills. The programmer on the game development team would, in turn, create code that could read these markers and trigger the appropriate fills during playback.

Fills can be played to preempt and smooth an oncoming musical change. For instance, if the gameplay requires that the music switch from explore to battle mode two bars forward in time, the engine could play a musical fill in the next bar to facilitate the transition to the next piece of music. In the audio middleware engine Wwise, you could also accomplish this by using the "Pre-Entry" feature of a segment.

Russian Squares (2003) and *Peggle 2* (2013) are two excellent examples of scores, composed by Guy Whitmore, that use fills and embellishments that match the underlying harmony at appropriate gameplay moments.

Motivic Elements in a Running Score

In film, it's fairly common to use a theme or motif to identify a character, place, or idea. When a composer creates a film score, he or she considers the current key and harmonic framework, modifies the theme to work with that material, and places the theme on top of the current section. In games, this can be more challenging because the timing of a character entrance is never static, but rather is based on choices that the player has made.

You could use horizontal resequencing to interrupt the current music and play the theme desired. An alternative is to play the motivic material on top of the current music. In this case, the game engine would need to have some musical intelligence to determine the key and harmonic framework of the music currently playing and then modify and superimpose the motif on top of the music.

As an example, suppose that a game is based on *20,000 Leagues Under the Sea*, and the composer has written a theme for the giant squid. When the player sees the giant squid in the game, we want to play its theme. Without interrupting the current music cue, the game figures out an appropriate rhythmic point in the music to play the cue, while also transposing it to the current key and mode to match that music.

Composer Guy Whitmore used numerous themes in *No One Lives Forever* (2000). Employing DirectMusic, he was able to dynamically change the harmonic context of these themes based on the situations that the players find themselves in.

In a game that has this kind of musical intelligence built into the engine, you would be able to have your motif play back based on the harmonic context of the scene. Thus, if you have a character theme in the game, that theme would be able to go from major to minor based on the game context.

Superimposition of motivic events in a score can be achieved in several ways. The simplest solution is to place markers within the music itself where a motif can be played. These markers would be accompanied by the current harmonic context. The game engine would then pick the appropriate point to play the correct motif. This type of implementation would obviously require additional time on the part of the composer and the programmer to build it.

Dynamic Reharmonization and Chord Mapping

Using events within the game to drive the harmonic changes in the music can be another way to synchronize your score dynamically to the game world. These harmonic changes can range from a simple transposition up a key to indicate tension or story progression, to musically complex modal changes that alter the emotional state of a scene.

For instance, perhaps the game includes a section where the emotional content goes from glory to sadness to reflection. As a composer, you might want to change the theme from one mode (major) to another (minor). This would be a difficult challenge if you were using prebaked waveforms to create your music. If you are using a MIDI score, it's much easier to change the harmonic context dynamically within the gameplay. The programmer would map the notes in your MIDI composition to its related minor key in real time while the game was running. For instance, if your music begins in a major key and you need to go to a minor key, the game engine might remap the third, sixth, and seventh steps of the scale a half-step lower. This remapping involves simple math if you're using a MIDI-based engine.

Complex reharmonization is also achievable in this way by dynamically mapping a new chord framework to a piece of music. In this way you could dramatically change the original music by replacing the chord map entirely, substituting chords from the same harmonic family, or using modal interchange by borrowing chords from common minor keys, among other options.

As far back as 1989, some arcade games were using complex interactive techniques. The pinball machine *Black Knight 2000* (1989), whose soundtrack was composed by Brian Schmidt, included sound effects that could synchronize themselves to the underlying beat of the music. These effects would also transpose themselves (harmonically) to whatever chord happened to be playing in the background. The sound effect would even adjust itself in the middle of the effect, if the chord in the music happened to change while the sound effect was playing. In addition, the game provided callback and sync mechanisms, such that in some circumstances it would cause the game to wait a measure or half-measure before proceeding with gameplay. Last, the music system could even control the lights on the game, allowing for tight audio/visual synchronization. To pull off these kinds of complex achievements, the programmer generally needed to "buy in" to the vision of the game's sound.

The audio middleware engine DirectMusic, developed by Microsoft, had built-in dynamic reharmonization functionality that allowed the game engine to apply a chord map to a sequence. This changed the game's harmonic framework and the accompanying melody. To re-create this level in detail within a musical scheme would require a formidable amount of time but could open up new avenues for music innovation within video games.

In *Peggle 2* (2013), the player directs a ball at a group of pegs. When the ball hits a peg, a note is played. Composer Guy Whitmore designed the music so that these notes would ascend

BUILDING AN EVENT-DRIVEN SEQUENCER

incrementally based on the chord scale of the underlying harmony of the music. These scales change dynamically with each chord change.

Building an Event-Driven Sequencer

A challenging aspect of using prerendered audio files with traditional techniques like vertical remixing and horizontal resequencing is the difficulty involved in getting notes to cross segment and loop boundaries. This makes it difficult to overlap segments and rules out the use of certain types of sequencing.

An alternative to the dynamic MIDI sequences used in the previous techniques is to build a simple sequencer engine directly in the game, which controls the playback of individual prerendered audio segments. Instead of using virtual instruments that MIDI would trigger, the sequence would trigger individual audio segments and phrases. These short segments could play at the same time and overlap with one another, similar to how they would behave in a DAW like ProTools.

Having a sequence trigger prerendered audio segments and phrases is an excellent way to use actual audio recordings and still have the ability to change the audio from moment to moment as in a MIDI sequence. Put another way, this method uses audio, yet retains much of the flexibility for dynamic changes and overlapping segments that MIDI can offer. An example of this type of implementation is found in *Tom Clancy's EndWar* (audio direction by Ben Houge, score by Alistair Hirst and Matt Ragan).

In the game engine, this solution is fairly easy to implement. A metronome clock triggers the start of each of the individual audio clips; this clock is usually set to the smallest interval that the notes need to play.

Achieving sequencer-like functionality with a music segment triggering system can offer the composer a level of detail that allows control inputs to adapt the music in real time. This level of detail is much finer than could ever be realized through horizontal resequencing or vertical remixing.

COMPOSER PERSPECTIVE: CELL-BASED MUSIC DEPLOYMENT IN *TOM CLANCY'S ENDWAR*

Ben Houge

When I set about designing the music system for *Tom Clancy's EndWar*, I gave myself a clear directive: no loops and no fades. For me, these are the two phenomena that most clearly indicate that I'm listening to a game soundtrack, although they are relatively rare in most other genres of music.

To accomplish this, I devised what I describe as a cell-based system. The music is edited into short cells, a few beats long, and these cells are quantized to a common metronome. Cells aren't edited to loop; they contain the natural decay of the original recording, while duration (in beats) is defined in a cell's metadata. If a looping behavior is desired, the decay of one cell is mixed with the onset of the subsequent cell. When an event tells the music to stop, the current cell plays to completion, allowing for a natural decay with no need for a fade out.

A happy by-product of this functionality is that looping with variations (a process that would ordinarily require painstaking editing) becomes a trivial affair. It is similarly simple to introduce a random pause (within a range of beats) between cells. With several independent layers of this type of intermittent behavior superimposed, it is possible to create rich, evolving textures from an economy of musical materials.

Layers of cells with their intermittent properties can be grouped into pools, and our system allowed for a quasi-fractal organization into pools of pools; one subpool would play for a period of time (within a specified range of beats), and then switch to another subpool, providing a kind of mid-level coherence between the instantaneous and the global. Pool transitions were associated with changes in AI, and different layers of the music were associated with different parameters: general musical density indicated progress toward an endgame scenario, background tonality indicated whether the player was winning or losing, and percussion activity reflected unit movement.

The music system developed was a direct response to the game's needs. Our mandate on *EndWar* was to introduce first-person immersion to the real-time strategy genre. This cell-based approach allowed for the music to respond on a dime to the unpredictable vagaries of a strategy game, with a high degree of variation to match the game's replayability. The system was a perfect match for the soundtrack's rock-influenced style, mirroring the game's "down in the action" aesthetic, impeccably furnished by composers Alistair Hirst and Matt Ragan.

Review

Game engines are beginning to inherit more features that composers find in standard DAWs. These features allow games to take advantage of more sophisticated real-time compositional changes and variability during gameplay.

The disadvantages of using prerendered audio files include the following issues:

- Lack of dynamic variability
- Limited flexibility for adapting on a moment-to-moment basis
- Difficulty involved in notes crossing segment and loop boundaries

Adaptive techniques such as melodic manipulation, reharmonization, ensemble and style alteration, and embellishment can dramatically alter the overall character of the musical score and decrease the repetitive nature of music in games. In addition, these techniques are much more reactive to control inputs, allowing scores to change more quickly with a fine level of detail.

Real-time melodic adaptation techniques include transposition, reharmonization, alteration of the length of the phrasing, inverting, thinning, and ornamentation.

Musical embellishments and fills are another effective way of synchronizing the music to the gameplay. Musical embellishments emphasize a particular player action or game event, while fills generally assist in transitioning to a new piece of music. These fills and embellishments are typically played on top of the music that is currently being heard during gameplay.

Musical themes and stingers can be also altered to play in the current key of the background music, adapting to its harmonic qualities in real time.

These advanced adaptive techniques allow the composer to better synchronize the music with the game world. To establish this level of granularity in the music, many of the advanced techniques require a MIDI-based implementation scheme that can play back virtual instruments.

Exercises

1. Using an existing piece of music that you've previously written, compose multiple short embellishments and fills that could play at the end of phrases that might lead to a new piece of music.

2. Compose a piece of music with a harmonic framework but without a melody. Make sure the music has more than one key and a variety of chords. Then separately create an interesting two-bar theme/motif. Create all the variations you would need to play this theme anywhere on your original piece of music.

3. Advanced: Build a simple event-driven sequencer in Max or Pd (PureData) that can trigger audio segments every quarter note. Then write a piece of music with overlapping parts that you can import and play in your custom eighth-note sequencer.

CHAPTER 16

ALEATORIC PERFORMANCE TECHNIQUES FOR VIDEO GAMES

In this chapter you'll learn about aleatoric performance techniques, including how their variability can add depth to video game scores. Aleatoric composition incorporates an element of randomness in either the construction or the performance of the piece, which then changes the music from performance to performance. In video games you can harness the power of performance variability to dispel common perceptions about video game music, including minimizing repetition.

What Is Aleatoric Composition?

The word *aleatory* is defined as depending on the throw of a die, by chance, or random. *Aleatoric composition* refers to a technique used by many composers of the twentieth century that introduces variability or chance into the performance or composition of the piece. This chapter specifically focuses on aleatoric techniques as they apply to the performance of a piece, as opposed to the techniques used in the construction or composition of the work. Aleatoric techniques introduce variability into each performance of the piece, which can mean expressive changes to the music. Use of these techniques can also help to combat repetitiveness in game music.

Prominent composers such as Krzysztof Penderecki and György Ligety popularized these techniques in modern classical music. Contemporary composers have continued to apply and evolve these techniques for use within games and film. Modern film and game composers such as John Williams, Elliot Goldenthal, Garry Schyman, and Jason Graves have all used various aleatoric techniques within their scores.

Much of the motivation for the development of aleatoric techniques came from composers seeking out new sonic palettes and music that could not be achieved through traditional classical musical notation. Aleatoric innovation led many composers to create their own proprietary musical notation, which brought about changes in the ways that performers played scores.

This new notation needed to be explained on the parts and score itself. Writing specific instructions on the score to indicate the type of performance that the composers desired allowed them to create new sounds outside the bounds of standard musical notation. Traditional notation is useful for notating specific pitches, rhythm, form, and key, but if composers wanted to have variability in in any one of these elements, they needed to invent a new language of notation.

Compositions that can change each time they are played through the use of aleatoric techniques within the game are among the Holy Grails in game scoring. Aleatoric techniques can be used to combat repetition and enhance re-playability. Unfortunately, many of the techniques described in this chapter involve recording a specific performance of the aleatoric technique, which can eliminate the random nature of the piece by creating a static version.

When you record a composition that has been composed with aleatoric techniques, you're changing it from a variable event to a static event—essentially removing one of the key components of an aleatoric composition, which is that it changes each time it's played. This brings up the question of whether the event is still aleatoric once it's been prerendered for the game. Some composers would argue that once a performance has been captured by recording, it is no longer aleatoric because any randomness in the performance has been removed because the recording will remain static.

Aleatoric techniques used in conjunction with real-time rendering of virtual instruments, as opposed to prerendered audio files, can allow the piece to retain much of its randomness. These random elements need to be programmed into the music engine itself and are directly related to many of the generative and algorithmic techniques discussed in Chapter 17.

Whichever procedure you use (prerendered files or real-time MIDI rendering), introducing aleatoric elements into your compositions will yield new and interesting sound palettes to explore.

Although aleatoric music is typically associated with orchestral ensembles, the underlying principles can be applied to any size of group, from a soloist to a jazz ensemble.

In some cases it may be cheaper and lead to more distinctive results if you record your own aleatoric effects, rather than buy an expensive off-the-shelf library. Aleatoric samples that exist as part of an instrument library tend to be used and reused repeatedly in music because many professional composers own the same sets of high-end libraries. The advantage of creating your own library of aleatoric recordings using real musicians is that those samples are unique and no other composer can buy them from a sample library. This makes your music more distinctive and unique.

Aleatoric Techniques

Throughout the rest of this chapter, you'll learn about some of the more popular aleatoric performance techniques employed by composers. Aleatoric techniques are especially good at creating interesting music effects or textures including clusters, sequences, micro-tuning, or unusual articulations.

These aleatoric techniques are broken down into different categories that affect the various characteristics of the music, including pitch, rhythm, tempo, articulations, and form. Any of these aleatoric techniques can be combined and layered with other aleatoric techniques to create even more unusual sounds and effects.

Many of the aleatoric recordings that you can buy in commercial virtual instruments libraries are often overused and very identifiable not only in games but also in film trailers and television. By creating and recording your own aleatoric techniques, you will enhance your compositions allowing them to be more unique and hence more creative.

This chapter identifies only a limited subset of all possible techniques. For more information on aleatoric techniques, study the scores of popular composers who employ these methods. In addition, go out and invent your own aleatoric techniques that use variation in their performance.

note

Before you employ aleatoric techniques with a performer, you should be considerate of both the player and his or her instrument. For instance, if you're using an articulation such as *con legno* (with the wood of the bow), players may be uncomfortable with scratching their $80,000 bow. Or, if you ask performers to change the tuning on their instruments, it may damage the instrument itself. Sometimes there are simple solutions to these kinds of problems. For instance, Jason Graves went to a hardware store and bought dowels that the players could use instead of their bows when composing for *Dead Space 2* (2011). If in doubt, you should confirm with the players well before the session begins which kinds of aleatoric techniques you are planning.

Also, as mentioned in an earlier chapter, if you plan to use the session as a sampling session, make sure that your players understand that fact when you book their services. Musicians are generally uncomfortable with sampling sessions, as typically it means you won't call them again for another gig because you can just use their sampled performance instead. Be respectful of the musicians, because ultimately you are a musician, too. Be aware that the musicians union sets different rates for sampling sessions and the use of instruments in integrated products than for a regular recording session. Check with your musicians and local union to see if these rates apply to your session.

Pitch

Randomizing the performance of pitch can be an effective way to create clusters and produce microtonal and atonal effects in larger ensembles, and create strange individual sounds with smaller or solo performers. The following list identifies aleatoric techniques that use pitch as a primary tool to create the random elements. You should use this list to spark your own creative imagination:

- Use random clusters of notes within a particular range in which the performer chooses the specific note he or she will play when the music is performed.

- In your score, remove the absence of specific pitch and melody by leaving the music stems intact but removing the individual note-heads. Musicians then play a particular rhythm with melodic shape but the specific notes are left up to the performer.

- Use extreme vibratos or wavering pitches, which each of the musicians performs at a specific or random speed.

- On the score, create relative pitch changes for the musicians, indicating pitch melodic direction but leaving the interval up to the performer on the next note.

- Use synchronized or nonsynchronized individual glissandos or pitch bends, played extremely fast or extremely slow.

- Have the musicians tune their instruments using micro-tuning techniques or alternative tuning systems (e.g., tuning the strings much lower than their normal pitches).

- Employ atonal or non-melodic phrasing, in which the musicians are not playing the same parts.

- Have an ensemble play the highest or lowest notes of their instruments together.

- Experiment with graphic notation representing overall progression but not specifically defining pitches or rhythm.

Rhythm, Tempo, and Form

Varying the rhythm and tempo of a piece of music with aleatoric techniques can be an extremely powerful means of creating expression and variation. In addition, the form or order of particular phrases in a piece of music can be varied using aleatoric variation in the performance. This technique has been successfully used by many twentieth-century composers including Terry Riley and Karlheinz Stockhausen.

Here are some ideas taken from the aleatoric repertoire that focus on rhythm, tempo, and form. Use these examples as a jumping-off point to create your own unique techniques:

- Use free timing in your music—that is, music without a specific meter or tempo, or the absence of bar lines that defines a specific harmonic rhythm. The ensemble can play as a group or with individual tempos.

- Vary the start and end times of individual notes by giving the performer a range in minutes and seconds of when to start and end (á la Cage or Penderecki).

- Employ rhythmic patterns or fragments that can be repeated to create polyrhythms using frame notation. These fragments do not necessarily need to share the same tempo or length between instruments.

- Compose the music in such a way that the musicians play notes as quickly as possible on an instrument within a defined range of pitches; this is sometimes referred to as shredding.

- Within the score, quickly increase or decrease the tempo of a phrase of notes through the use of feathered beam notation.

- Use open form where the order of the individual music segments or phrases is left up to the performer.

- Make room in your score for free improvisation where the performer can play any rhythm or pitches he or she desires for a particular section.

Articulations, Instrumentation, and Dynamics

Playing instruments using unconventional methods or articulations can be another effective way to create unique and unusual sounds. The methods of articulation described in this section are not strictly aleatoric in the real sense of the word, but are often used in aleatoric pieces and can produce varied sounds and textures. The following list identifies some interesting articulations and techniques that composers have used in aleatoric composition:

- Employ string articulation effects like *col legno* (hit with the wood part of the bow) or *col legno tratto* (drawn with the wood part of the bow).

- Make use of sung vocalizations (or growling) through woodwind or brass instruments: hum, sing, or scream into the mouthpiece.

- Have the musicians play the pads of woodwind or brass instruments as a percussive element—a technique also known as key clicks.

- Try using flutter tonguing (rolling the tip of the tongue as rapidly as possible) on brass or woodwind instruments in your score.

- Use piano effects in your score, including plucking, scraping, hitting, or sweeping chromatically across the strings.

- Try knocking or striking instruments in a nontraditional way within your score.

Review

Aleatoric composition is a technique that introduces variability or chance into the performance or composition of the piece. Such techniques were developed by twentieth-century composers who were seeking out new sonic palettes and music that could not be achieved through traditional classical musical notation.

Aleatoric composition frequently relies on the construction of new musical notation, as traditional notation is useful for notating only specific pitches, rhythm, form, and key.

When you record a composition that has been composed with aleatoric techniques, you're changing the music performance from a variable event to a static event. Recording a performance essentially removes one of the key components of an aleatoric composition—namely, that it changes each time it plays.

Aleatoric techniques are especially good at creating interesting music effects or textures, including clusters, sequences, micro-tuning, and unusual articulations.

Randomizing the performance of pitch can be an effective way to create clusters and microtonal and atonal effects in larger ensembles, and create strange individual sounds with fewer or solo performers.

Varying the rhythm and tempo of a piece of music with aleatoric techniques can be an extremely powerful means of creating expression and variation in a piece of music.

Playing instruments using unconventional methods or articulations can be another effective way to create unique and unusual sounds.

Exercises

1. Analyze a written aleatoric score from the twentieth century and discuss how its techniques might be used in a modern score for a video game.

2. Record one or more musicians using aleatoric methods discussed in this chapter, and then build an instrument using the samples.

CHAPTER 17

ALGORITHMIC AND GENERATIVE MUSIC SYSTEMS

Generative music that is written while the game is being played opens up many opportunities for the composer to create rich, dynamic music. Algorithmic methods of composition are techniques in which the composer teaches the game engine about the rules of how music works, and the game engine then writes music as the game is being played. In this chapter you'll explore various approaches to algorithmic composition and generative music techniques within video games.

Using Algorithmic and Generative Music

The topic of algorithmic composition is so large that it would require several books to cover it in any kind of detailed way. This chapter is meant to give a general introduction to the topic as it applies to games. In Appendix D, you'll find additional book recommendations that will acquaint you with the topic of algorithmic composition in a more complete way.

Algorithmic composition is a method of music making in which the computer or game composes music in real time based on a set of rules that the composer or programmer has defined. These methods have been used successfully in modern gaming, as prominently featured in Brian Eno's score for the game *Spore* (2008) by EA Maxis, and in the music puzzle game *FRACT OSC* (2014). Many instances of generative music engines can also be found in other non-game interactive disciplines, including art and museum installations and mobile apps.

Algorithmic composition—also described as automated composition—has existed for hundreds of years. The method of creating compositions through the use of algorithms or formulas could certainly describe *Musikalisches Wurfelspiel* (dice music) in the eighteenth century or serialism (the 12-tone method) in the twentieth century. During the mid-twentieth century, composers began to use computers to generate music through algorithms, including early pioneers such as Lejaren Hiller, Leonard Isaacson, and Iannis Xenakis.

Creating an algorithmic music engine for a game generally requires both the expertise of a composer and the implementation skills of a programmer. In rare instances the composer and the programmer are the same person, but in most cases the composer must work closely with the programmer to create the algorithmic engine that is able to successfully satisfy the creative needs of the project.

There are several advantages of using algorithmic composition practices within a game:

- This technique applies perpetual variation or originality in the music that is generated, so it is possible for a player to never hear the same piece of music twice.
- It creates a reactive score that can react to and change incrementally based on the subtlest of game changes and player decisions.
- It offers the most detailed level of flexibility when it comes to controlling adaptive music parameters and transitioning from one musical direction to another.

Audio middleware engines have a very limited toolset for algorithmic composition, so teams frequently prototype creative ideas by using established music and sound programming languages. With Wwise's recent inclusion of support for MIDI (beginning in 2014), it may become easier to create algorithmic scores using middleware.

Universities typically use music- and sound-based programming engines like PureData (Pd), Csound, Nyquist, Symbolic Composer (SCOM), and SuperCollider as research and design tools. These simplified programming languages allow composers to more easily implement an algorithmic composition model than if they had to write that model from scratch in a language like C++.

These music- and sound-based programming languages sometimes can be integrated into the game engine itself. Several open source libraries have been built to facilitate the integration of these engines into game frameworks, such as Unity.

More often, once an algorithmic composition model or concept has been tested and approved by the game development team, the programming team is tasked with re-creating the music functionality directly in the game itself. The time the developer needs to allocate for this process depends on the musical complexity of the generative music engine.

Generative music within games generally relies on the use of virtual instruments. Instruments are either custom designed by the audio team or derived from the General Midi Instrument Library for algorithmic playback. Alternatively, the composer could rely on a series of prerendered audio samples to produce a generative score; however, in that case the adaptive options would be limited to rearranging the order, pitch, tempo, and duration of the samples. Virtual instruments used in conjunction with an algorithmic engine are far more flexible, allowing for much more dynamic melodic, harmonic, rhythmic, and ensemble options at runtime.

Generating Music

A lot of computer-generated music relies at least partially on random models. Other generative music systems may comprise a set of completely nonrandom processes, albeit derived from different control inputs. The output from these systems depends on the sophistication of the music knowledge and rules on which the system is based.

There are many different ways to generate music, ranging from randomly picking notes to applying sophisticated mathematical procedures and generative models such as Markov chains, Gaussian distributions, and stochastic algorithms. As stand-alone processes, these models may not produce output that sounds like the music you typically hear. Once you begin to incorporate the rules of music (e.g., harmonic theory, rhythm, cadence, counterpoint) into these random algorithms, they're able to generate unique music that is closer to what we typically perceive as music.

Which parameters of the music are affected (e.g., pitch, duration of notes, articulations, dynamics, harmonic framework, counter melodies, counterpoint, form, ensemble) is up to the creative framework that the composer and the game developer have chosen. Most games have at least some randomization in their music playback, while more detailed construction is achieved through the inclusion of more variability in the music. More detail and control of a music system requires more programming time to develop and implement.

The musical rules that govern an algorithmic music system can be derived in two ways: by composing defined rule sets and by using knowledge-based musical intelligence.

Composer-Defined Rule Sets

In this scenario, the composer defines the relationships between notes (e.g., harmony, rhythm, melodic progression, counterpoint) by implicitly inputting music rules into a system. The composer or music team defines the kinds of interactive music elements over which they want to have control, and then sets up rules in the system to properly satisfy that creative vision.

Knowledge-Based Musical Intelligence

Knowledge-based systems gather historical data from compositions from a particular style, then analyze them in the aggregate to find commonly used harmonic progressions, melodic techniques, and rhythmic frameworks. Rules are then derived from these pieces and used in the process of generating new pieces. Knowledge-based rules are generally more difficult to modify for a specific function within the game because they rely on previously collected data.

This type of generative music system is generally not used for gaming, because the music for a game typically needs to adapt in real time to support the emotional experience of the player. Knowledge-based systems need time to analyze a selection of pieces to derive the rule sets. Consequently, these systems are used more often to support diegetic instances of music used within games. As this technology evolves, composers might be able to leverage it for games. At the time of writing, however, it was typically used for generating a specific style of music as opposed to being able to adapt in real time to a player's experience.

The Rules of Game Composition

This section describes the basic principles of teaching music intelligence to a generative music engine. Because generative systems rely on random values to create music compositions, the composer should begin by mapping these random values to basic music mechanics. As more rules are put into place, the complexity of the music begins to grow and the output sounds more like music instead of a computer's interpretation of music.

There are many early historical examples of computer-generated music based on rule sets, including William Shottstaedt's automatic species counterpoint (1964), Kemal Ebcioglu's system for generating four-part chorales in the style of J. S. Bach (1986), and Iannis Xenakis's stochastic music generation GENDY3 (1991).

The construction of a piece of generative music largely depends on the musical style or genre desired. If tonal music (either classical or popular) is desired, then there are more defined rule sets governing musical construction than apply to nontonal music. Nontonal music is typically built using stochastic or mathematical procedures, similar to a 12-tone row progression. Random mathematical music generation can also be used to create tonal music, but the rules of musical construction must be applied to make it sound more tonal.

Many film scoring devices, such as pedal points, ostinato patterns, multiple key centers, and modal interchange, can also be used to effectively develop the harmonic framework for a generative music system.

There are many different ways to teach musical rules to a generative music system, and the order of defining these rules is also important. If the harmonic framework is built first, the melody is constructed based on this framework. Conversely, if the melody is built first, the harmony must support it. These systems need to work together to produce tonal music. The following sections explore the principles that you should consider with each system when constructing a generative music system for tonal music.

Mapping the Harmonic and Rhythmic Framework

When you are setting out to create a piece of tonal music, the key center, type of scale or mode, and meter are essential ingredients. From these three building blocks, you can derive many other components of the music.

This harmonic center may change over the course of the piece, but from moment to moment there is usually an identifiable key center. The algorithmic engine must have a place to store the current key center, and must pick appropriate notes within that key to support that music.

Each genre of music has its own common chord progressions that should inform the desired musical outcome. The generative music engine may rely on these fundamental chord progressions as its basic framework, yet allow for some improvisatory elements to keep the music sounding fresh. The harmonic layout of the chords should have an appropriate narrative arc that defines the beginning, middle, and end of the piece through tension and release—that is, harmonic dissonance to resolution, cadence to harmonic center.

The harmonic framework informs the overall rhythmic pulse, which in turn defines which beats are strong and which are weak. In turn, downbeats usually mark the beginning and ending of musical phrases. The chord progression informs the overall narrative direction. These building blocks help determine the framework for how the melodic material is built.

In a game context, musical movement from tension to release (e.g., battle to explore) can be emphasized and built in real time by the algorithmic generator. This allows player decisions to influence the overall shape of the harmonic framework, which in turn influences the melodic development. These game factors can play a central role in the development of the score on a moment-to-moment basis. Similar to film music, this type of generation uses non-song-form–based narrative development because the form is based on the action playing out on the screen.

The harmonic and rhythmic framework also needs to reflect the mood or emotional map of the player. This could mean employing a more long and languid framework with a slower tempo, or a short and aggressive framework with a faster tempo. These factors would influence the rule sets that govern the generative music engine.

Melodic and Thematic Development

Constructing a tonal melody or theme relies heavily on the harmonic context and rhythmic framework of the game, whereas strictly stochastic or mathematical methods of melodic development (e.g., 12 tone) typically create nontonal music.

A theme is a series of notes played in sequence. Many games use themes to characterize different parts of the story or game. For an algorithmic music engine to use themes, it must remember the themes that it generates. These sequences of notes can then be repeated to emphasize a specific story element or give context to the player.

Melodic construction is based on a series of notes and rhythms that should have an overall shape and harmonic context. For a computer to generate these melodies on the fly, the harmonic construction plays a significant role in determining the notes, overall context, and phrase length. Melodic notes that are chord tones tend to be emphasized on strong beats, whereas passing tones (non-chord notes) help build the melodic development over time. As with chord mapping rules, melody should emphasize tension, suspension and release, moving from dissonance to resolution.

Stochastic and mathematical procedures can also be used to change tonal music through the use of modulation and key change, or procedural generation such as inversion and retrograde on the melody.

Chord Construction, Counter-Melodies, and Supporting Instruments

The instruments that support the melody and harmonic framework also need musical intelligence in tonal music. Chord inversion, voice leading, the rules of counterpoint, and melodic harmonization are other key components that can support the music generated by an algorithmic composition engine.

Orchestrating and arranging techniques also help develop and build a musical experience over time. The appropriate instrument additions or reductions can help immerse the player emotionally into the experience, whether it is an intimate scene that involves just one or two instruments or an epic score involving an entire orchestra.

Mapping Control Inputs to Music

Many of the dynamic music manipulation techniques discussed in Chapter 15 are directly applicable to generative music systems. In fact, with a generative music system, there is almost an infinite amount of musical control on a moment-to-moment basis for changing the music in real time. This is because the rules for the system can change, with those changes then propagating to all of the other music construction systems. For instance, if the harmonic framework changes from a major key to dorian mode, the melodic and chord progression will change accordingly, depending on the rules that govern the generative music system.

As an example, in the game *Spore*'s creature creator, even minute changes in the character shift the harmonic mode to indicate the behavioral changes of the associated creature. For example, if you added sharp teeth or horns to your creature, the music would change to a more aggressive harmonic context.

Since the generative musical framework is built on rules, these rules become the objects that can be manipulated at runtime by various control inputs from the game. Subtle changes in the story can affect the various rules, including whether a section is more dissonant or consonant, which harmonic scale or mode applies, and which rhythmic parameters are relevant.

Applying Algorithmic Composition

Like computer-generated characters within a game, music that is created via a generative music engine can sometimes seem soul-less or bland, lacking the creativity and originality that a composer can bring to a score. Computers lack the same emotional sensitivity and the ability to make bold choices that only a human composer can bring to the score.

Generative music systems are only as good as the composers who program the algorithms and rule sets that create the score. As composers are able to communicate and program their ideas more effectively to computers, better scores will be generated by these systems.

Through the use of music programming languages such as Pd (PureData), Max, Nyquist, SCOM, and SuperCollider, composers are able to quickly construct and test rule-based generative music systems. The complexity of a music system grows exponentially as you add more rules to the system. Of course, adding more rules to a system increases the amount of time that it may take to program it into the game. Once the game development team has signed off on the decision to use a generative music system, the composer works with the team to define the control inputs for the system and to determine how those controls will change the rules of the system.

The practical implication of using a rule-based system to create tonal music is that it can make the music sound more artificial and robotic, whereas music that is nontonal and stochastically generated can sound more "real." To overcome this problem, the rules need to be complex enough that the generated music isn't simplistic.

In addition, the developer needs to take other technical considerations into account, including the platform and processing requirements. Memory budget implications may also arise if the system needs to stream or load banks of sampled sounds.

Review

Algorithmic composition is a method of music making in which the computer or game composes music in real time based on a set of rules that the composer or programmer has defined. Creating an algorithmic music engine for a game generally requires both the expertise of a composer and the implementation skills of a programmer.

Using algorithmic composition practices within a game offers several benefits, including perpetual variation, a reactive score that can change incrementally based on the subtlest of game changes and player decisions, and the most detailed level of flexibility when it comes to controlling adaptive music parameters. Many generative music systems within games rely on virtual instruments to perform the music.

Audio middleware engines have a very limited toolset for algorithmic composition techniques. Consequently, teams frequently prototype creative ideas by using established music—for example, by using PureData (Pd), Csound, Nyquist, Symbolic Composer (SCOM), and SuperCollider.

There are many different ways to generate music, ranging from randomly picking notes to employing sophisticated mathematical procedures and generative models such as Markov chains, Gaussian distributions, and stochastic algorithms.

In a composer-defined rule set, the composer establishes the relationships between notes (e.g., harmony, rhythm, melodic progression, counterpoint) by implicitly inputting music rules into a system.

Knowledge-based systems gather historical data from compositions in a particular style, and then analyze them in the aggregate to find commonly used harmonic progressions, melodic techniques, and rhythmic frameworks. Rules are then derived from these pieces and applied in the process of generating new pieces.

The following principles serve as a basis when defining a rule set for constructing a generative music system for tonal music:

- Map out the harmonic and rhythmic framework.
- Ensure melodic and thematic development.
- Provide for chord construction and counter-melodies, and arrange supporting instruments.

Generative music systems are only as good as the composers who program the algorithms and rule sets that create the score. As composers are able to communicate and program their ideas into computers more effectively, better scores will be generated by these systems.

Exercises

1. Analyze a game that uses algorithmic composition techniques to define the control inputs to the music system and determine which transformations in the music occur when the variables are changed.

2. Build a simple random note generator within a music-based programming language such as Pd (PureData), Max, Nyquist, SCOM, or SuperCollider.

3. Building on Exercise 2, add rules to the generative music system to pick only notes from a specific key and mode. Then integrate the ability to change the key in real time.

CHAPTER 18

USING MIDDLEWARE TO CREATE ADVANCED COMPOSITIONS

Audio middleware allows composers to implement complex interactive scores more quickly and easily by starting with an intelligent music system. Audio middleware has opened up many opportunities for composers to add more musicality in their interactive scores by branching in the middle of a phrase or on a specific beat. In this chapter you'll learn about audio middleware, including its advantages and its functionality within games.

Simplifying Composition with Middleware

Middleware helps developers make games more quickly and easily. Middleware engines aim to put more of the actual implementation into the hands of the designers instead of sequestering it among the programmers on a team. These middleware engines generally have a visual interface that allows the designers working on the game to interact with the game instead of having to use a programming language.

Many different kinds of middleware solutions are available to developers: some help build 3D worlds, some are physics engines, and some help composers and sound designers create complex audio worlds for games. This chapter focuses on the use of audio middleware engines such as Fmod and Wwise, which enable composers to design and implement complex musical scores for games.

Many of the interactive compositional techniques discussed throughout this book become easier to implement when you use an audio middleware solution. Interactive compositional techniques such as horizontal resequencing and vertical remixing can be quickly implemented in a game using these audio middleware solutions. Audio middleware often allows the composer to use many different techniques at once, creating very complex intelligent musical scores with large transition matrixes to go from one cue to another.

In addition, the use of an audio middleware system allows the composer to create significantly more complex musical cues without requiring more of the game programmer's time. In general, when a composer would like to build special music functionality into the game, such as transitioning on a specific musical beat or at the end of a musical phrase, the game programmer must spend hours creating an intelligent music framework for the game. Audio middleware can make life much easier for the programmer, and it greatly reduces the amount of programmer time required for creating these special music functions. Nevertheless, it doesn't completely eliminate the need for programmer assistance. Specifically, the programmer still needs to add hooks to control the music (i.e., set variables, specify that it's time to make an interactive transition).

Audio middleware engines have essentially prewritten an intelligent music engine for use within a game, thereby freeing up the game programmers to work on game design, AI, physics, or many of the other game systems. The use of middleware allows game developers to avoid the many hours of programming that it might take to implement a sophisticated interactive score into a game.

Because the audio middleware engine has sophisticated musical functionality built into the system, the composer needs to learn how to use these tools so as to write more sophisticated scores. As has been mentioned in other parts of this book, development efforts for large games may hire audio integration specialists, who may assist in this process. Some publishers only require finished music from the composer as opposed to delivering Wwise or Fmod projects.

It is to the advantage of composers to learn about the tools available in middleware, or at least to understand the tools' functionality, irrespective of whether they will be the people actually using the tools to implement the score. Having this knowledge base allows composers to understand interactive music scenarios on a deeper level, allowing them to write more sophisticated interactive scores.

The use of audio middleware can also make porting from one gaming platform to another easier. Wwise and Fmod both have features that allow the audio team to scale the audio appropriately based on the audio capabilities of the target platform. High-end consoles such as the Xbox, PlayStation, and Wii can use larger audio banks with better audio quality than a handheld device such as an iPhone, Vita, or DS. Composers and sound designers do not have to re-author their audio content for each platform because the middleware is able to adapt to each platform.

All the composition techniques discussed in Part II of this book can be implemented within an audio middleware solution. In fact, many of these techniques can be used in conjunction with one another in middleware. For instance, it's easy to have a layered score that also branches and triggers stingers on a specific beat.

The choice to use audio middleware in a game depends on many different factors:

- The overall budget of the game
- A lack of in-house programming resources with which to develop a custom solution
- The feature set of a given middleware solution
- The need to support multiple platforms
- Prior experience
- The complexity of the desired audio framework for the game

Middleware engines have tiered license structures, such that their makers charge smaller-budget games a smaller fee, whereas larger titles pay a higher license fee that permits the game developer to include the full technology within the game. This license fee increases for each additional game release platform—for example, a game that is released on two platforms (e.g., PlayStation and Xbox) would require two licenses. Discounts are generally available for each platform after the first.

On larger projects, the game development budget may include a line item for the license to use middleware. In other cases, the fee to use audio middleware needs to be subtracted from the overall audio budget. Because of this, if the complexity of the music score is not especially difficult to implement (e.g., by layering), then developers generally choose to have the game programmer implement the music instead of using middleware. Other factors related to the usage of a middleware engine are discussed at length in Chapter 23, "Implementation and Progamming."

The audio middleware engines Wwise and Fmod use different terminology to describe much of the same functionality. For instance, what Fmod refers to as a *reverb tail* is called a *post-exit* by Wwise. This chapter tries to focus on the overall concepts, as opposed to the individual software features, to illustrate techniques that can be used in both of these middleware engines. The companion website for this book includes both Fmod and Wwise examples using similar techniques customized for each middleware engine; you can use these examples as templates for your own projects.

The rest of this chapter focuses on the additional functionality that many of these audio middleware engines bring to games.

COMPOSER PERSPECTIVE

Vincent Diamante

Sometimes, you go into situations you are perfectly prepared for. At other times, you're in game production.

Before I began work on what would become *Flower*'s interactive music soundtrack and sound effects, I had a strong idea of how it could be done using the Fmod Designer tool. Parameters, envelopes, layers—it all made a great amount of sense.

Of course, Fmod was not the tool that we had at our disposal.

Early on, we (Sony's audio department, thatgamecompany, and myself) ended up exploring a number of interesting tools that were being developed elsewhere in the Sony pantheon. But it wasn't long before we decided to do things in our own way.

While the multiple MP3s that made up each level's background music were spooled up to play in sync with each other, a combination of a time-aligned MIDI file dotted with NRPNs (Non-Registered Parameter Numbers), a Lua script, and various Maya level design nodes provided information to the music playback system on the mix levels of these MP3s. For the communication of harmony and tempo information between the music and the sound playback system, those same MIDI NRPNs would change SCREAM parameters in the active sound bank containing the musical flower "bloom" sounds.

In the end, the sound and music system looked rather unlike the Fmod-ish mental model in my head, but the actual execution ended up as I had expected. Beyond just knowing how to do something with de facto industry standard tools, it was important to (1) understand the low-level potential power of all the individual components I was working with as a musician and audio designer and (2) work with my colleagues to unleash that potential, communicating audio possibilities clearly in a tool-agnostic fashion so that we could create what we wanted.

You don't really know how to do something until you do it the way that you've never done it.

Using Multiple Interactive Techniques

Since each fundamental interactive composition technique outlined in Part II of this book has advantages and disadvantages, why settle on just one technique for your game? Audio middleware allows composers to use multiple interactive and adaptive music techniques at the same time. For instance, it's fairly easy to implement a score that has multiple layers that can fade in and out, then branch from the musical cue on the appropriate musical measure to the next cue.

The challenge in composing this type of score is that because there really are no limitations, it may be difficult to answer the question, "Where do I start?" Limitations force us to write in a particular way, but once many of those limitations are removed and anything is possible, composers sometimes have a more difficult time knowing which direction to choose.

When composing scores for an audio middleware engine, much more time is spent in the initial planning stages to figure out which interactive and adaptive scoring techniques best fit the game. Sometimes a game composer wants to use a particular feature that the audio middleware provides, but it may not be appropriate for the game. If you create a strategy and set some initial goals for your score before you begin writing, then the process of composing your score will be far easier than when you're trying to use all the bells and whistles that a middleware engine can provide.

Many composers initially underestimate the amount of time it takes to implement and iterate music cues. Unlike with linear media, when planning an upcoming interactive project you'll need to allow time for creating a music strategy, researching the techniques offered by the middleware engine, actually composing the cues, implementing those cues into the engine, revising stem mixes, and iteration. The iteration process can take as long as the initial composition as you refine each musical event so that it plays properly in the game.

Creating Scores Using a Middleware Engine

To create a score that will use an audio middleware solution, start by learning what the audio middleware software can do. By exploring the features supported by each system, the composer becomes more informed about the benefits and limitations of each individual system and can take full advantage of those features when writing the score.

Audio middleware is not a substitution for a DAW. You'll still need to compose your pieces using virtual and live instruments within a DAW, and then export the individual music segments required. For vertical remixing, you'll be exporting layers from your composition as long loops; in horizontal resequencing, you'll need to bounce all the segments and phrases as loop-able pieces. Once you've finished the exporting process, you must piece those segments together inside the audio middleware engine for use in game.

When working with a new audio middleware engine for the first time, try out the core fundamental interactive techniques laid out in this book: looping, horizontal resequencing, vertical remixing, random segments, and transitions. This experimentation process will give you excellent knowledge about what is possible, and help you understand how to implement the various techniques in each engine before you start the composing process.

Take advantage of sequences that you've previously composed for other projects by using them as a starting point to get yourself up and running quickly with the audio middleware engine. Export these sequences and begin to implement this material in the middleware engine as if the pieces would be used in an actual game.

Once you've learned how music is implemented in the middleware engine, including the advantages and limitations of this process, you can use that knowledge to compose in your DAW.

When writing with an audio middleware engine in mind, composers start by sketching their ideas for a project in a DAW using virtual instruments. They then bounce these sketches and begin to test them inside the audio middleware client by creating a rough sketch of the implementation while they are in the composition process. This is one of the most important methods in creating an effective interactive score: iterating the composition after hearing what it will sound like once it's implemented in the middleware engine.

Many composers realize too late that what they thought might work in the engine actually won't—something discovered when the approach fails after implementation. This is why it is extremely important to iterate during the composition process by checking whether a particular technique will work. Implement your sketches early, then go back to fix things in your sequence, and repeat the process over and over again.

Intelligent Music Engines

For a game to understand music concepts such as when a specific musical phrase begins or where the beats fall, programmers need to teach the game these rules through code. Games by themselves don't understand anything about music. Many audio middleware engines bring this musical intelligence into the game via software libraries that are loaded into the game—that is, through an application programming interface (API). This API ensures that the game is familiar with some basic musical concepts, thereby allowing the composer to write more sophisticated scores. Musical features offered by middleware engines include the following abilities:

- Insert tempo and meter markers laying out when the beats fall, and then transition on a specific beat or play a stinger in time with the music.

- Insert markers that indicate the beginning and ending of musical phrases or indicate loop and branch points.

- Play back randomization of phrases or notes.

- Create a transition matrix in which you can map out every musical switch possibility and customize the transition for each instance.

- Apply custom fades when transitioning between cues.

- Use advanced loop features, including reverb tail playback.

- Combine multiple compositional approaches, such as layering and branching, within the same musical cue.

- Play back multiple tracks of synchronized music simultaneously.

All of these features would be difficult and time consuming for a game programmer to implement from scratch, making audio middleware a good investment if you need to use these features.

One of the best features offered by an audio middleware engine is the ability to transition more seamlessly between two pieces of music by customizing the transition. This includes using fades or musical segments serving as bridges between two pieces of music.

The use of a modern audio middleware solution gives the composer and sound designer much more control over the audio, freeing up the programmer's time because the programmer no longer has to build these complex audio systems for the game from scratch. For instance, a composer who wants to build a unique transition matrix to go from one piece of music to another doesn't have to spend hours sitting with the programmer and tinkering with the code to get the solution to work. Using a middleware engine, the composer can lay out the transition matrix within the middleware clients; all the programmer has to do is call the correct music at the correct time, and the correct transition will play automatically. This frees up the programmer to work on other parts of the game.

Without the use of an audio middleware engine, many of the techniques described in this chapter would be very difficult and time consuming to implement in a game. The time it takes for a programmer to implement the adaptive features you want should be weighed against the cost of licensing an audio middleware solution. For example, if you want to use a layered score within the game and the programmer can put that together in an hour, then that option is much less expensive than licensing a middleware engine.

Many of today's modern audio middleware solutions include an application specifically designed for the composers and sound designers who build these complex audio systems. Using this so-called client application, composers can build complex interactive compositions that can be loaded into the game and allow for sophisticated musical transitions and other advanced music structures.

Looping within a Middleware Engine

As discussed in previous chapters, looping musical segments can be a time-consuming and frustrating process. Audio middleware engines like Fmod and Wwise have some extra features that are specifically designed to create more seamless loops within a game.

The framework of the loop is still created within the DAW, but you generally don't have to copy the reverb tails to the beginning of the loop and rebounce. Instead, you can either bounce the reverb tail as part of the end of your musical segment or bounce it as a separate file altogether. Within the middleware engine, you can set up the loop points to play back the reverb tail at the correct time.

Each individual segment can have its own reverb tail, which allows for better transitions when branching from one musical segment to another. For example, if you have a phrase of music in D-minor and you want to go to an A7 chord, you'll hear the reverb from the D-minor chord when the A7 chord begins.

Typically, when you aren't using a middleware engine, these reverb tails need to be bounced to the beginning of the loop. The disadvantage of this scenario is that the harmony of the reverb tail may not match the previous segment, making for a less seamless transition. Reverb tails within an audio middleware engine can be customized for each musical segment, making for a more musical composition.

Additionally, audio middleware engines allow you to define a custom introduction for each musical segment. Thus the segment may begin with a musical introduction, then loop through the main part of the piece, and finally play a reverb tail when it either loops or branches to a new piece of music.

> **note**
>
> Wwise uses the terminology *pre-entry* and *post-exit* to refer to a loop's introduction and reverb tail, respectively.

Variation and Randomization

Composers often rely on variation to extend the listenability of the video game score. Audio middleware engines enable composers to implement these variations in various ways. In this section you'll learn about randomization provided by audio middleware. The two basic types of randomization used in such middleware are *playlist randomization* and *time randomization*.

Random Playlists, Track Variation, and Alternative Start Points

If a musical cue is split up into various phrases, the order of the playback of these phrases can be randomized. This feature is similar to the shuffle button found in many music players, except that the phrases in a middleware engine are played back to back. The random playback order of these phrases provides variety in the music, which can help minimize the repetition of a particular cue.

Audio middleware engines like Fmod and Wwise allow you to also set the weighting of these phrases, so that one phrase plays more often than another. Randomization doesn't need to occur on just one track, but can occur independently on multiple tracks if you're using vertical remixing.

In a layered score, random playlists can be particularly effective because the composer can randomize the playback of multiple layers. For instance, if you have a drum layer with three variations and a bass layer with three variations, you can exponentially increase the number of various combinations as you increase the variation count. This technique is also referred to as track variation and is quite common in game scores.

For layered variation to work properly, the phrase lengths must match up in a musically correct way. For instance, in the preceding example, the drum phrase could be one measure long and the bass phrase could be four measures long. These phrase lengths need to be sampled accurately so they don't fall out of sync during playback. If you are using layers with two or more layers that need harmonic or melodic synchronization, then it's recommended that you keep all of the phrases the same length to minimize the overall complexity of the score.

A variation on the idea of random playlists is to have multiple start points for the same cue. This is key in a game where a character might have to restart the level multiple times. If the music is beginning from the same place on every restart on a difficult level, this can be extremely irritating to the player. If the phrases are not split up, you can also insert markers into the music indicating appropriate places to start the cue.

Time Variation

Audio middleware engines allow musical segments and phrases to be played back at random times. Sound designers commonly use this technique to create background ambiences in game levels. For instance, a sound designer creating the ambience for a beach location will begin by creating the individual sounds for that location: seagulls, wind gusts, waves hitting the rocks. Then, in the game level, these sounds are triggered at random times, creating a more successful audio environment than if the composer used a single 30-second audio loop of beach ambience.

Composers can realize this approach by using precomposed musical phrases that play back at random times during the level. There are many different ways to implement a score that uses time variation, ranging from simple to extremely complex. Using time variation for the playback of phrases in a game is similar to the algorithmic and aleatoric processes discussed in Chapters 16 and 17 but lacks the coordination between layers that would develop a specific musical pattern.

Following are a few examples:

- Phrases can be written with nebulous harmonic content, allowing them to be played randomly over any part of an underlying musical cue, thereby adding suspense, mystery, or variation in the musical cue.

- A musical cue can be written specifically to use time variation only. In this scenario, many musical segments are split up and played randomly, with a variable amount of silence in between the phrases.

- Complex musical ambiences can be created by using multiple layers of musical material. Building on the preceding example, additional layers of phrases would be applied to the mix. Each layer would have a variable amount of silence between the phrases that would play. For instance, Layer 1 could be bass drone phrases, Layer 2 could be percussive flourishes, and Layer 3 could be short string phrases. This scenario requires extra planning because any harmonic narrative would be displaced during the playback of each phrase—an outcome best suited to a modern or aleatoric composition.

Review

Middleware engines aim to put more of the actual implementation into the hands of the designers instead of the programmers on a team. Some middleware engines help game developers build 3D worlds, others are physics engines, and some help composers and sound designers create complex audio worlds for games.

Two popular examples of modern audio middleware used in games are Fmod and Wwise. The use of an audio middleware system allows the composer to create significantly more complex musical cues without increasing the demands on the game programmer's time.

The choice to use audio middleware in a game depends largely on two factors: the overall budget of the game and the complexity of the desired audio framework for the game.

When planning an interactive project that uses audio middleware, the composer needs to allow time for creating a music strategy, researching the techniques offered by the middleware engine, actually composing the cues, remixing audio stems, implementing the cues into the engine, and iteration.

Audio middleware is not a substitution for a DAW. You'll still need to compose your pieces using virtual and live instruments within a DAW, and then export the individual music segments required.

Audio middleware engines such as Fmod and Wwise have some extra features specifically designed to create more seamless loops within a game.

Composers often rely on variation to extend the listenability of the video game score. Audio middleware engines allow composers to implement variation in both the timing of events and the randomization of the musical phrase.

Exercises

1. Using Fmod, write and implement a score that has layers with a variable amount of silence between the phrases that play. Hint: use the Fmod *scatterer* event for phrase playback.

2. Using Wwise, write and implement a score that has multiple cues that use the pre-entry and post-exit features.

3. Using either Fmod or Wwise, compose and implement a score that can transition between cues on the measure downbeat or at the end of a musical phrase.

CHAPTER 19

CREATING A CUSTOM MUSIC SOLUTION

Although you've explored many different fundamental techniques used in video game music throughout this book, sometimes you might need to break the conventions and rules to create something totally new or solve a particular design constraint. In this chapter you'll explore different ways to develop new interactive music techniques for games.

Solving Problems with Custom Solutions

The conventions of scoring a film have basically remained the same for the past 80 years. The development and implementation of a video game score, by comparison, changes for each game. This dynamic nature arises because the game design, mechanics, and story influence how the interactive music is thought out, composed, and implemented in the game. It would be far easier for composers to use one technique in all video game scoring, but as you've learned in previous chapters, each technique has advantages and disadvantages associated with it.

The techniques described in Part II of this book are relatively easy to implement and do not require a lot of time and money. Horizontal resequencing or vertical remixing doesn't take an enormous amount of time for the programming team to implement in a game. This chapter focuses on building more complex solutions that wouldn't be achievable through an off-the-shelf audio middleware solution.

Although the use of middleware such as Fmod and Wwise has begun to standardize the way we think about interactive music, these engines also possess many limitations that don't allow composers to create new kinds of structures and models for interactive composition use within games. There are many problems related to real-time interactive music for which the industry has yet to find convenient solutions. Standardization also means that composers are less likely to create new and more interesting ways of approaching an interactive score. From the developer's perspective, however, part of the drive toward standardization comes from the need to control costs and development risks. After all, it is much easier to tackle a project with known solutions than it is to accommodate new feature requests.

Another major challenge in today's video game scores is that although there is a lot of communication from the game to the music engine, there is relatively little communication from the music engine back to the game. As a consequence, it can be difficult for visuals to sync up, for example, to downbeats in the music. The music is always playing catch-up to what is happening on the screen. If the music is trading information with the game itself about what beat it's on, then the visuals can also better sync to the music, including having a stinger perfectly in sync with a visual event. Challenges like this are difficult to overcome, and there is no middleware engine that takes these kinds of events into account. Instead, such situations require a custom music solution that talks back to the visual engine. Although some recent developments made in this area have improved communication, including the latest versions of Unreal 4 and Electronic Arts' Frostbite engine, much room for improvement remains.

This chapter focuses on how to think outside the box by developing your own techniques, prototyping them, and then selling the idea back to the game development team.

Limitations of Interactive Techniques

Both Fmod and Wwise primarily use prerendered audio files for much of their interactivity. Many of the interactive techniques discussed in Chapters 13 through 17 are made more challenging or impossible without the use of MIDI. If composers want to experiment with real-time music manipulation including dynamic reharmonization or algorithmic compositional techniques, for instance, they may need to look elsewhere or build their own custom solutions through programming. The easy math required to manipulate MIDI files to adjust the key, mode, or tempo in real time has not been readily available for use since DirectMusic. In 2014, Wwise introduced MIDI functionality in its engine and client software, so we may see lots of growth again with MIDI over the coming years.

Current audio middleware technologies are also not well suited to creating a game in which music is the primary game mechanic. Music games that generate music scores on the fly like *Rez* (2001) or *FRACT OSC* (2014) are almost impossible to author with current audio middleware engines.

Many top interactive game composers, such as Guy Whitmore, push the limits of off-the-shelf solutions. For example, Whitmore's creative use of Wwise in *Peggle 2* (2013) allowed him to have game event stingers and SFX play in the same key as the underlying music. The level of music complexity in *Peggle 2* is at the very cutting edge of music innovation within today's generation of games.

To ensure synchronization of the music, the game engine must send messages to the music engine about the game state. The music engine then must respond to this input signal. Because of this back-and-forth conversation, the music typically lags behind the action as it catches up to the latest state change. Current audio middleware doesn't communicate especially well with the visual engine about which beat the music is on or whether the music is ending a phrase—information that would allow the action to better sync with the music.

Most audio middleware engines provide basic building blocks for audio file playback and mixing optimized for low CPU overhead, allowing programmers to build advanced music engines on top of the basic middleware framework. Authoring the content for music games usually cannot be achieved by composers using the tools that modern middleware ships with.

In the past, various audio middleware solutions focused more on MIDI interactivity in their scores, including DirectMusic and iMuse. Unfortunately, much of the flexibility of these engines has been lost in modern middleware solutions because of the current approach of focusing solely on prerendered audio.

Teaching a Computer the Rules of Music

Designing a music system typically involves teaching the rules of music to a game. It's a fairly simple task to trigger music to play when something happens in a game, but it's much more difficult for the game to trigger a piece of music on the next downbeat of a measure. For this to happen, the game would need to know the tempo and meter of the piece as well as the beat it is currently playing. Essentially, when you begin your journey down the road of building your own music system, you'll need to teach that system how music works—everything from the basic building blocks of beats and measures, to more complex harmonic theory involving dominant and subdominant chords.

Many of the reasons why composers pursue the creation of their own music engines revolve around the goal of making the music system smarter, which in turn means teaching music theory to the game itself. Current audio middleware has a little bit of music knowledge, including bars and beats, but such programs don't know anything about harmony, counterpoint, or even the difference between melody and rhythm.

Once these rules are integrated and taught to a music system, the composer has much more flexibility in terms of creating more seamless music experiences for the player.

Selling the Idea to the Developer

Writing a custom music solution for a game requires money for design, development, programming, and testing. Unless this custom music solution is part of the primary game mechanic, these resources are generally not allocated in the main budget for the game. The music team, therefore, needs to lobby the developer to undertake the endeavor.

The best way to sell the idea to the developer is to prototype it. The creation of such a small-scale model allows you to show the developer your concept and hear an example of how it will work in the game. In many cases, composers don't have the programming skills to prototype the idea in the main game itself. Instead, they use visual programming languages to develop prototypes and demonstrate their ideas to the game development team.

The developer must be convinced that the time and effort put into this solution will make the game better, ultimately leading to the sale of more copies of the game. If developing a custom music solution doesn't help the publisher sell more copies, there is really no reason why the developer should spend extra funds on the idea.

Shaping an Interactive Musical Engine

Building your own interactive music engine for a game can be a daunting prospect and usually requires the knowledge and skills of several people. In this section you'll learn about prototyping your idea, planning your design, and implementing it in the game.

Prototyping the Idea

New music frameworks are usually created through prototyping and experimentation. This activity usually takes place outside the game engine and may be as simple as showing how the idea might work within your DAW. Other, more complex designs may need to be demonstrated by programming the idea in a musical programming language. Prototyping and designing is a cyclical and iterative process, as you refine your original concept by finding out what works and what doesn't.

Prototypes can be built in many different programming languages. Given that composers may need to sell the idea to the development team, they are usually the people responsible for prototyping the idea. To demonstrate ideas to the team, many composers use music-based visual programming languages like Cycling 74's Max or the open source Pd (PureData) to prototype those ideas. These simplified coding languages allow for rapid prototyping of audio playback, DSP algorithms, MIDI manipulation, and synthesis. Other languages that are sometimes used in prototyping include C-Sound, SuperCollider, and Processing.

Sometimes programming languages like Pd have been ported for use directly in the game itself, including in *FRACT OSC* (2014) and *Spore* (2008), to provide advanced music functionality. If the code can be ported to the game itself, then the work that went into building the prototype doesn't need to be repeated in the game engine, thus saving time and money.

The prototyping phase takes the initial ideas and builds an actual working prototype so that the team can listen and evaluate how the music will sound in the game. Once the initial prototyping has been done, it's important to test the idea to confirm that the creative solution will be valuable to the game.

The development team can then assess whether the idea adds enough value to the game to pursue it further. If the prototype stage is approved, it becomes the initial framework for the specification and ultimately leads to the actual implementation in the game.

COMPOSER PERSPECTIVE

Richard Vreeland

We spent months prototyping a music system for a series of rain levels in *The Floor Is Jelly*. The system played an individual note for each drop as it hit a surface. These drops generated harmonies that changed as the player moved. We even made an in-game editor. Unfortunately, playing a sample for each drop was too CPU intensive. Our system trashed the frame rate. The issue crept up on us because we prototyped the idea using a sparse amount of rain. When we found we couldn't increase the notes and droplets together, we had to scratch the whole system.

Instead, we created short loops of rain-like music that change as you progress through the world. The frequency of rain is great enough that synchronizing with each droplet was unnecessary.

For *Cannon Brawl*, we prototyped another system. The music consisted of four bars: two for the blue team on the left side, panned to the left, and two for the red side, panned to the right. The concept seemed sound—that is, the notion of two marching bands, in a never-ending call and response. The intensity of each team's band fluctuated, depending on the game state. While this idea seemed great on paper, "trading twos" turned out to be annoying.

The final solution involved a longer piece of looping music, made up of many stems. Certain instruments represent each team, and are often panned to their respective side. When either team gains a level, the appropriate stem gets added to the mix. The concepts of our first prototype informed the simpler solution we reached.

In both cases, our "what if" approach created useful roadblocks on the path to the final solution.

Design and Specification

The game development team needs to assess which game-specific problem the custom music solution would solve and determine why it is important for the outcome of the final game to build such a solution. Team members should outline the exact details of what they're trying to achieve.

Next, the composer and game developer need to investigate why an off-the-shelf system wouldn't work for their game. Audio middleware solutions are generally cheaper than building a system from the ground up. The time and money involved in designing a new system can be quite daunting depending on the complexity of your project.

After this evaluation, if the team decides to build its own system, the team should create a very detailed document describing how the new music system will work. This document, which the game development team will use as the framework for its system, is called the *specification*. The specification must unambiguously describe every behavior in the new audio solution. Without it, the programmer won't know what to code and the tester won't know which behavior is correct.

A complex music engine may take the programmer several weeks or more to implement, test, and debug. If the development of such a custom solution is approved, the producer of the project will need to schedule the programmer's time, and assign people to help debug the implementation.

Implementation in the Game

Once the game development team has given the green light to the new music system, the actual programming begins to implement this system in the game itself. The producer of the team needs to allocate the necessary time and money for the development. The composer works with the team to ensure that all the features of the prototype are properly implemented in the project.

A programmer working on the game development team writes the implementation of the music engine into the game. Once the programmer has implemented the feature set, the composer will need to help debug the engine by evaluating whether it's working as specified. The programmer will then fix any bugs that have made their way into the code.

Most games are programmed in C++, although some games use a combination of a scripting language (Lua, Python, C#, JavaScript) and a deep programming language like C++. Scripting languages are generally easy to learn, and parts of the audio system may be implemented in a scripting language. This may allow for audio implementers and sound designers to add functionality directly into the game without the help of the programmer. Composers, too, may be able to help with the implementation if they have some prior programming knowledge. More important, if a composer has programming knowledge, he or she will also be able to assess how long it might take to implement a project and whether the idea is even feasible.

Review

The use of middleware such as Fmod and Wwise has begun to standardize the way we think about interactive music. Standardization means that composers may be less likely to create new and more interesting ways of approaching an interactive score.

A lot of information is sent from the game to the music engine, but there is much less communication from the music engine back to the game. This makes it difficult for visuals to sync up to specific beats in the music.

Both Fmod and Wwise primarily use prerendered audio files for much of their interactivity. If composers want to experiment with real-time music manipulation, including dynamic reharmonization or algorithmic compositional techniques, they need to look elsewhere or build their own custom solutions through programming.

Most audio middleware engines provide basic building blocks for audio file playback and mixing optimized for low CPU overhead. Programmers can then build advanced music engines on top of this basic middleware framework.

Writing a custom music solution for a game requires money for design, development, and programming. Unless the custom music solution is part of the primary game mechanic, these resources are generally not allocated in the main budget for the game. The music team needs to lobby the developer to undertake the endeavor.

The process of developing your own music engine involves three phases:

- Prototyping the idea
- Design and specification
- Implementation in the game

Exercises

1. Research a game that uses a custom music engine (e.g., the original *Halo*, *SSX*). Create a design document that describes the functionality, or do an analysis of the gameplay.

2. Analyze the score for a game that was composed using a custom music engine. Then create a design document for the music system as if you were building it from scratch.

3. Learn a scripting language like C# or JavaScript and implement your own vertical remixing score that uses layers of music.

4. Interview a game programmer about how he or she implemented sound on a recent project.

BRINGING MUSIC INTO THE GAME

CHAPTER 20

COMPOSING MUSIC WITH A DIGITAL AUDIO WORKSTATION

Over the last 25 years, the digital audio workstation (DAW) has revolutionized the way the music industry creates music. Scoring music for games requires expertise in both composing and sequencing music within a DAW. Setting up a DAW for video game sequencing is different than composing for linear media, and requires composers to test and assess music cues while in their DAW. This chapter suggests common DAW workflows for games scoring, and explains how to organize a score to more easily convert and transfer it to the game itself.

Getting Started with a DAW

Approaches to video game scoring are radically different than composing a linear score because of looping, interactive scoring techniques, and ability to transition from one piece of music to another. This has implications for how you set up and lay out your sequences in a DAW. Most important, you'll want to hear how the interactive score will work in your sequencer (as much as is possible) without having to wait for the music to be implemented in the game.

This chapter is not a tutorial on how to use your sequencer, nor is it meant to replace your sequencer manual. Before reading it, you should already be very familiar with the capabilities of your sequencer, as this chapter details the specifics of using a sequencer to compose music for games. Some of the things you should already know how to do within your sequencer include setting up multiple virtual instruments, routing and busing audio streams, editing MIDI and audio data, and bouncing and exporting audio.

When working on a game, scoring is an iterative process in which the composer tests looping and transitions in the DAW, then makes further revisions once he or she hears the score within the game. Being able to test transitions while writing can eliminate some of the actual game-play testing later. Of course, there is no substitute for in-game testing: even though the music may play back correctly in the DAW or even in a middleware solution like Fmod, it's always possible that it isn't working in the game correctly.

This chapter aims to guide you by identifying some best sequencer practices and introducing the audio formats you might encounter in the game industry. Although this chapter focuses primarily on the creation of prerendered audio files from a sequencer or DAW, the first two subsections talk about the use of MOD files and Standard MIDI Files within games.

Choosing a Sequencer

Within the video game scoring community, composers use almost all of the various DAWs available on the market. There is no *standard* composing tool that suits all needs for all video game composers. At the time of this book's writing, popular sequencers used in composing music for video games included ProTools, Cubase, Logic, Sonar, Digital Performer, and Reaper.

Many composers find themselves mastering several different sequencers and then using the best one for the specific project that they are working on. For instance, Ableton Live might be a great solution if your game music style is techno or beat driven, whereas Cubase or Logic might be a better solution if your music style is orchestral or has a lot of tempo changes.

The choice of a sequencer is driven primarily by your personal working style and the game platform. Most DAWs (e.g., ProTools, Digital Performer, Cubase) have cross-platform capabilities, but some (Logic, Sonar) do not. Each DAW has certain pros and cons that make it more suitable for one composing style over another. Most game composers are fluent in more than one sequencer, and if your career spans multiple decades you may see some sequencers disappear and new ones appear as technology shifts and improves. Once you've mastered one sequencer, it will definitely add to your value as a composer to learn another.

Almost all commercial recording studios support ProTools for recording live instruments; other DAWs are supported strictly on a case-by-case basis. You should definitely call the recording studio that you are working with to determine which sequencers it supports. If the studio doesn't support your DAW, then you'll need to export your materials to an appropriate sequencer for recording.

No matter which sequencer you currently use, it's usually a good idea to also learn to use ProTools because of its omnipresence in recording studios. Many composers export their materials to ProTools for recording, and then reimport the recorded materials into their sequencer of choice to finalize and mix once the recording process has been completed.

COMPOSER PERSPECTIVE

Akari Kaida

I own two PCs as my main work machines, an 88-key MIDI controller, a physical controller, two sets of monitor speakers, three mics, a mic pre-amp, the latest version of Cubase, SoundForge, Vienna Ensemble Pro, a lot of VST instruments (there are too many to list them all), and some instruments like a guitar and bass.

First, based on the type of song request, I develop my own image of the song. If the director gives me a reference track, I listen to it carefully. Then I establish a general tempo for the piece. Especially if there is a video that I am scoring to, I determine the tempos that fit with the footage and figure out the length of the piece (probably around 3 to 4 minutes). I tend to use my DAW to determine more or less how many measures, not just the tempo, I will need to complete the scene.

After this initial outline is established, I decide the instrumentation and think about the entire shape of the music and development with the song image. I usually start by choosing some sample rhythm loop that kind of matches my image. After that, I write the chords and bass line before writing the melody. Then I take out the preinserted loop and actually write my own out. Last, I add the remaining sequenced instrument parts as well as record live instruments or vocals if needed.

At this point, I present the demo to the director to get a reconfirmation of the direction of the piece. However, some directors will request to hear everything once it is finished before they can make a decision, so this step is often conducted on a case-by-case basis. If the director approves everything, I move on and start doing finishing touches on the piece.

Sequencing Standard MIDI Files

As discussed previously in the book, using MIDI with virtual instruments can offer excellent real-time adaptive capabilities, including note manipulation, ensemble adaptation, and tempo variance. If you're working with MIDI, the final music file for your game is typically a Standard MIDI File (SMF). Almost all sequencers can export an SMF. The important thing to remember when creating an SMF is that you must initialize each MIDI track at the beginning of the sequence with the following control items to ensure proper playback:

- Patch change
- Pitch bend
- Volume (MIDI controller 7)
- Panning (MIDI controller 10)
- Sustain pedal off (MIDI controller 64)

If you don't initialize the MIDI data at the beginning of your sequence, then whatever MIDI file was previously playing on the device may have left some of these values in a state that won't work with your music.

MOD File Sequencing

If you're composing MOD files for your game, you'll be sequencing and building instruments in a special application called a *MOD tracker*. MOD trackers exist on many different platforms, including Windows (ModPlug Tracker, Madtracker, Skream), OS X (MilkyTracker), Linux (SoundTracker), and game platforms like the Nintendo DS (Nitrotracker). Most of these trackers are based on the original trackers created for Amiga and DOS, so their front-end interfaces are typically old-school text interfaces. Each standard MOD file type (XM, MOD, IT, S3M) offers various features. Check with your developer to determine which file type is compatible with the game engine and make sure you author files in that format. Although more modern MOD trackers may take advantage of advanced features such as VST instruments and Rewire (e.g., Renoise), the games themselves typically do not support these more modern features.

When you're using MOD files within the game, you'll usually need to be concerned with the overall memory footprint of the final files. Check with the developer to determine how much memory you have available so you can plan your composition around it. Samples within MOD files take up the most space, and you can customize the sample rates for each individual sample to minimize the memory footprint of the file. Most MOD trackers will allow you to change the sample rate on a per-sample basis after you've completed the project, so you can master and finalize the files after you've composed your piece.

Several middleware engines allow you to compress the embedded samples within a MOD file to MP3 (Fmod's OXM format) or Ogg Vorbis (BASS's MO3 format). These compressed files are able to play back at runtime and have much smaller memory footprints.

Sequencer Setup and Track Layout

There are many different ways to set up your sequences, and as you become more familiar with the techniques used in the gaming industry you'll develop your own techniques and ways of working. Following are some suggestions for beginners that will help you begin to think about ways to audition different techniques within your sequencer.

Sample Rate and Bit Depth

Currently, many composers work at a sample rate and bit depth of 48 KHz, 24-bit. There is a trade-off between the number of virtual instruments you can use and the sequencer settings. The four settings in a DAW that are all interconnected are sample rate, bit depth, sample buffer size, and number of playback tracks (audio, virtual instruments, and effects). A larger sample rate and higher bit rate will offer higher quality, but will decrease the number of virtual instruments you can use. You can use more virtual instruments if the sample rate and bit depth are set lower.

Increasing the sample rate or bit depth will decrease the number of playback tracks but increase the quality. Increasing the buffer size will also increase the number of playback tracks but will incur more real-time audio latency. Audio latency is the time gap between when you physically press a MIDI key and when you hear the corresponding note.

The sample rate, bit depth, and compression used in your own sequencer may differ from that of the files that you deliver to the developer. For instance, if the game is being developed for the Xbox One or Xbox 360, you'll need to deliver uncompressed 48 KHz, 16-bit files, so you may need to dither down from a 24-bit to a 16-bit depth.

It's always a good idea to have the highest possible sample rate and bit depth for your own archives. Then, if the publisher is interested in remaking the game later using a more modern console, or if an advertising agency wants to use your music in a commercial for the game, you can provide high-quality files.

> **tip**
>
> While composing and creating mockups, composers sometimes reduce their sample rate and bit depth even more to apply a small buffer time for low audio latency. Longer buffer times lead to greater latency, so the MIDI keyboard you're playing will feel spongy as it triggers your samples later. When you're ready to finalize your mixes or record live instruments, you'll need to bump up the sample rate, bit depth, and buffer size to record the highest quality before bouncing mixes or recording live instruments.

Track Layout, Submixes, and Stems

The track layout and routing for a game project proceed in much the same way as you would lay out a film score. Film scores frequently lay out sequences in multiple submixes called stems. These stems represent different groups of instruments (e.g., high strings, low strings, woodwinds, percussion) that can be balanced quickly and easily. Stems have a logical comparison to the way games use vertical remixing and layers. Most game composers set up their sequences with stems to listen to volume configurations between the various stems, simulating how layers would work in the game with an individual fader per stem or group.

A typical sequence is set up using the following paradigm (Figure 20.1):

1. MIDI tracks trigger virtual instruments.

2. Instruments are routed to audio submixes called stems.

3. Audio tracks from live instruments are also routed to stems.

4. Each stem has its own individual DSP effects chain so that the reverb of one audio submix does not end up on a completely different submix.

5. Stems with their effects are recorded onto separate audio tracks so you'll have a recorded master for each stem.

6. The stems are routed to a final mix audio track, which is used to bounce any final mixes.

7. The final mix audio track is routed to the speakers.

The number of audio stems that you will use will be determined by the individual needs of the project:

■ If the game developer will use your original sequence files to edit new cues and submixes, you'll need to provide as many options as possible. This means each individual instrument group should have its own stem and corresponding audio track.

■ If you and the game developer have decided to use vertical remixing, then the number of stems will probably equal the number of layers you plan to use in the game.

The more audio stems you include in the framework of the project, the more flexible it will be in terms of creating new mixes, creating arrangements, and building new cues from the original source materials quickly and easily. Although having more stems increases the overall flexibility, it also increases the amount of time you'll need to set up the individual tracks and buses associated with the stems. You'll need to assess the needs of the project and the overall budget to determine the balance between flexibility and the work involved.

Many composers use their downtime when not working on projects to create efficient working sequencer templates to use on various types of projects. You might consider making a template for each genre of music that you typically compose for (e.g., orchestral, electronica, children's music) with premade buses, virtual instruments, and audio tracks.

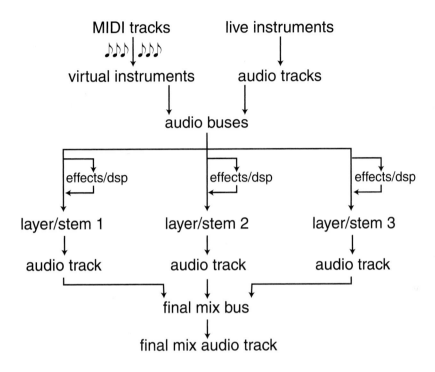

Figure 20.1 The DAW signal flow of tracks in a typical game project.

While you are composing using this model, the stem audio tracks and final mix should be set to *input monitoring* until you're ready to record live instruments. Once the basic sequencing is done, the live instruments are typically added. If you are recording instruments one at a time at a private home studio, these can be recorded directly into the sequence. If you are recording in a vendor's recording studio, a secondary sequence is usually created just for the recording. This procedure is discussed at length in Chapter 21, "Live Recording, Session Preparation, and Mixing."

COMPOSER PERSPECTIVE

Yoshino Aoki

Nowadays, samples have improved greatly, and you can make your sequence seem like real live instruments. However, in the end, if you do not understand the musical style or how the instruments work, you cannot write well for them. Particularly for orchestral or live band music, it will be of great help to you to go to as many live performances and live shows as you possibly can. Of course, it will be beneficial for you yourself to perform live as well.

It is also a good idea for you to note-for-note transcribe many different styles of music to learn more about them. Even if it is an instrument that you cannot play, if you transcribe music for it, you will gain a deeper understanding of how that instrument produces a sound and the capabilities/limitations it possesses. You will understand how to write for the instrument so that it can sound the best. The more times you repeat this process, the faster and better you become at sequencing, too.

Always keep an open mind and do not lean too much in one direction. Many different requests will be made of you while you are working on a game soundtrack, but as long as you can be flexible and listen well, you will be able to combat any problems smoothly and efficiently.

Planning for an Interactive Score

When sequencing in a DAW, it's important to be able to test the various ways the music might play back in a game. In this section you'll learn about various ways to set up your sequencer to test different interactive scoring techniques.

Create a final stereo mix audio track that allows you to bounce all your materials to one place. You'll use this track for the final pieces that you want to import into the game as well as for testing materials during composition and assessment.

In addition to the final stereo mix audio track, create three audio tracks in your sequencer to audition various events:

- **Loop Test Track.** This track is used to test end-to-end looping of the music segments.
- **Audition Tracks 1 and 2.** These two tracks are used to test how one piece of music may transition from one piece to another using crossfading, branching, or some other horizontal resequencing technique.

Once you have recorded or bounced your sequence to the final stereo mix audio track, you'll want to copy these pieces to the loop test track and audition tracks to test the various scenarios planned for the game itself. These tracks should be presented as solo tracks when auditioning so that you do not hear the rest of your sequence—just the pieces you want to audition.

Looping

Many sequencers allow you to loop a section of your sequence during playback while composing. Although this will give you a rough idea of how your piece will flow musically during a loop, it will give you a false sense of how it will loop once you export it. DSP elements that you've added (e.g., reverb tails) will automatically wrap around the loop point only while you're working in the sequencer. Once you export the loop, generally the reverb tail and other DSP will disappear at the loop point. A few exceptions to this may exist depending on your sequencer (e.g., the special export loop option in Ableton Live, the second cycle bounce feature in Logic). Refer to the sequencer manual to see if the device offers specific features to help with loop exporting.

The best way to audition loops in your sequencer is to actually bounce or record your loop to disk or a track, then use the loop test track of your sequence and paste the bounced segment end to end and see how it will play back. Repeat this process while following the guidelines from Chapter 7, "Composing and Editing Music Loops," until you have a loop that works.

In most circumstances, you'll need to embed the reverb tails in the first part of the loop. The easiest way to do this is to copy the last bar of the music and splice it into the beginning of your sequence. Then, bounce the segment to disk and delete the first bar from the bounced file.

If you're working with a game audio middleware engine like Fmod or Wwise, you'll want to audition your loops directly in the middleware client. Both Fmod and Wwise support extra features related to creating clean loops, as described in Chapter 18, "Using Middleware to Create Advanced Compositions," including pre-entry and post-exit regions.

Ultimately, it's important to listen to your final loops in the game itself. Although there are substitutes listed in this chapter, hearing your loop in the game is the best way to hear how it's going to sound to the player. After hearing the results, you can go back and iterate the files in your sequencer to make sure your segments loop perfectly.

Vertical Remixing

With the track layout illustrated in Figure 20.1, each stem can be used like a layer or mix. That is, as tracks and instruments are routed to the stems, they are included with that layer or mix. Testing the layers is relatively easy, because the audio track associated with each stem can be individually adjusted with the fader control.

When building a layered score, testing and assessment are important steps in creating a successful experience for the player. As you test the different possibilities in your DAW, you'll gain greater insight into what works in each layer or mix. For example, you might discover that moving one or more instruments from one layer to another results in a better musical experience.

When planning your score. you may decide that you want to add the same instrument to several different audio stems or layers. For instance, you could plan a score in which the first layer has an instrument play only in the first measure, and then rest for three measures. In the second layer, you might have that same instrument play in the remaining measures (two through four). In the actual game, when the first layer is activated, you will hear a reduced version of the piece. When the second layer is brought in, you will hear the full version. When setting up this scenario, make sure that the effects that are applied to this instrument are sent to the correct layer.

> **warning**
>
> **VOLUME RELATIONSHIPS**   Normalization will change the overall volume relationship between your stems. The DSP command *normalization* will determine the loudest point of an audio segment, then measure it against the maximum possible volume of that wave file, and finally increase the gain of that wave file by that amount. This essentially increases the volume of a particular audio segment to the maximum extent. If you're exporting layered stems from your DAW, you'll want to avoid applying any normalization or volume effects on these files after they've been exported because it will change the volume relationship between the files, destroying your overall mix.

Horizontal Resequencing

When creating pieces that need to connect with one another through horizontal resequencing, you'll be composing multiple different cues. There are two key components to creating a successful score that use this technique:

- Ability to audition, assess, and revise how each section of music will transition to another section of music quickly.
- Ability to organize the different musical cues. This is a key component not only for keeping track of the various cues that you're composing for a game level, but also for recording live instruments in the future.

Auditioning the Transitions between Cues

Composing successful transitions relies on the ability to audition them directly in the sequencer so that you can revise and modify any transitions that are not working properly. Using the extra tracks that you created in the previous sequence setup section, you can drag the mixes onto these tracks to audition and assess these transitions.

If you're lining up transitions to cue on a specific measure or beat, as is common in many audio middleware engines, quantizing the placement of these clips can help better identify how they will work in the actual game engine.

Because gameplay varies based on the player's choices, testing every music scenario that the player might experience in the game may be impossible. For instance, there can be hundreds of different options for which cues and transitions might play next to each other in a game, which would make it exceedingly difficult to test each one in your sequencer. Even so, it's important to test a wide variety of scenarios that might arise in the game engine to better understand how your music will sound once it's added into the game.

Organizing the Musical Cues

Composers typically use the same set of instruments (ensemble) for a game level that has multiple cues. Because of this, composers will use the same sequence to line up one cue after another in the sequence file. If these pieces need to connect with one another in an end-to-end fashion, then it's best to line up those cues end to end in the sequence file.

The various cues should be placed in the order that you would typically hear them in the game engine itself, even if they don't connect musically in the sequence.

If there are tempo and/or complicated meter changes between cues, then the composer will typically insert several bars of silence in between cues. This will allow live players time to adjust to a new tempo if the recordings are done in a single take.

When musical sequences are split up using multiple bars of silence, your clips may stop at the end of a measure because they wrap back around to make a loop. To create more seamless loops, it can be extremely useful for musicians to play the downbeat that follows at the beginning of the next measure to complete the phrase, even if it's not an ending that you would hear in the game. This allows you to cut and edit your loops more effectively based on the live performances you record by showing exactly where to play the downbeat. Such a practice is extremely helpful if the players are either playing on top of the beat (a little early) or more in the pocket (a little late), as opposed to directly on the quantized beat.

> ### tip
> You may find it very helpful to create an extra audio channel that contains either an actual click track or a click sound on beat 1 measure 1, and on beat 1 of the first measure after the end. Then, during editing, you can easily and precisely determine the correct position to cut the loop by using this visual reference.

Transitioning between the DAW and the Game

No matter how much planning goes into composing the perfect score for a game, you are likely to encounter some speed bumps along the way. Even though you've tested every transition in your DAW, the transitions may still play back differently once you've exported the files and gotten them into the game.

Auditioning transitions within your DAW is only half of the equation. The other half is listening to how the music works once it's actually implemented in the game. It's incredibly important to hear how the music works in the real game as early as possible in the development process so that you can make the necessary adjustments in your score to account for these changes.

For instance, when you begin composing your score, you may be told by the development team that you can branch from one cue to another on a beat. Later, once you've handed off the music for them to test in the game, the development team may realize that they underestimated the capabilities of the programming team—and then you'll be faced with the prospect of creating transitions that can happen anytime as opposed to happening more musically. The earlier the composer has this information in the development cycle, the better planning he or she can do in regard to creating additional musical cues.

If you can't get access so that you can play the game yourself in your studio, have the developer record and send you as much game-capture footage as possible. It's easy for members of the development team to capture footage as they are playing and testing the game.

Review

Scoring music for games requires an expertise at sequencing and composing music within a DAW. Setting up a DAW for video game sequencing differs in important ways from composing for linear media, and it requires composers to test and assess music cues while in the DAW.

Within the video game scoring community, composers use almost all of the commercially available DAWs. There is no standard composing tool that meets all the needs of all video game composers.

Composers generally set their DAW sample rate and bit depth to 48 KHz, 24-bit. Increasing the buffer size will increase the number of playback tracks but will incur more real-time audio latency. Increasing the sample rate or bit depth will decrease the number of playback tracks but increase the quality.

Many game composers set up their sequences with audio stem submixes to simulate how layers would work in the game with an individual fader per stem or group. The more audio stems you include in the framework of the project, the more flexible it will be in terms of creating new mixes and arrangements, and building new cues from the original source materials quickly and easily. Unfortunately, this practice also increases the amount of time you'll need to set up the individual tracks and buses associated with the stems.

In addition to having a final stereo mix audio track, it's useful for a game composer to set up multiple audio tracks to test audio loops and transitions.

Audition your loops in a program that will play them back precisely, such as Wwise, Fmod, or SoundForge. Consult the manual for your DAW to see how best to do this. In addition, you can audition loops in your sequencer by pasting looped segments end to end, but be aware of the potential for pasting errors.

When composing a game score, testing and assessment are important ingredients in creating a successful experience for the player. It's critical to hear how the music works in the actual game as early as possible in the development process so that you can adjust the score as necessary to account for these changes.

Do not normalize your stems: normalization will change the overall volume relationship between the stems.

Multiple musical cues used in the same game level should be placed end to end in the sequence. If there are tempo and/or complicated meter changes between cues, the composer should insert several bars of silence in between cues; that will allow the live players to adjust to a new tempo if the recordings are done in a single take.

Exercises

1. Create a sequencer template within your DAW setting up MIDI tracks, virtual instruments, buses, and audio tracks; include stems for three layers for a score that uses vertical remixing techniques.

2. Write a score that uses horizontal resequencing techniques. Pick gameplay footage that has two different emotional states; then, following the sequencer layout suggestions, write a score that has two cues and two transitions.

3. Write a score that uses vertical remixing techniques. Pick gameplay footage that has two different emotional states; then, following the sequencer stem suggestions, write a score that has two different layers that can play together.

CHAPTER 21

LIVE RECORDING, SESSION PREPARATION, AND MIXING

There have been many different attempts to write down interactive music on a score, from traditional notational methodologies of repeats and codas, to more experimental postmodernism approaches to scoring. In this chapter we focus on techniques to help prepare and record scores for live musicians. We give practical advice for how to notate, record, and mix the various interactive scoring techniques described in this book to take them into a game.

Elevating the Score with Live Musicians

Recording live musicians for your project can have a profound impact that raises your music to a new level. You can harness the artistry and creativity that performers have spent many years developing. Cues that have live musicians also differentiate themselves from the enormous bulk of synth music in the marketplace. Musicians can help elevate the creative depth of your pieces as well as provide the listener with palettes that no electronic instrument can duplicate.

Some composers in the marketplace do not have the skill to write music down for musicians. These composers sometimes are able to create amazing pieces, but the study of written music allows composers to bring in a much wider array of unique palettes and different techniques to their musical scores.

Recording can range from being a simple undertaking with only one musician, to quite a challenging endeavor with a larger ensemble or orchestra. Both types of sessions require planning, organization, efficient use of time, money, and the ability to communicate with the musicians about your piece.

In this chapter you'll learn about the preparation and logistics of recording live instruments for video game scores.

Preparing, Orchestrating, and Arranging

Large ensemble recording requires a wide array of skills. Some composers orchestrate, arrange, and conduct their own pieces for live instruments, while others hire specialists to handle these responsibilities. Your overall budget will influence whether you're able to hire specialists for your project.

When choosing an orchestrator, arranger, or conductor, it's important for the composer to evaluate that person's experience working with video game scores. Since many of the scoring techniques for video games involve interactive music, the challenges increase for orchestrators and conductors. The more experience that they've had with interactive scores for video games, the easier it will be for them to grasp the structure and nuances of how to prepare the score, saving you both time and money.

If you are preparing the parts and score yourself, you'll want to double-check your music along every step of the composition. At the very least you'll want to print a score that contains the instruments that you'll be recording at the session. But, to more easily and quickly correct mistakes during the session, it's also definitely helpful to have all of the instrument parts printed on the score. Following is a checklist of the items that you should include when you are putting together your score and parts for a session:

- A title, cue number, and initial tempo at the head of every cue

- Instrument ranges for the level of musicians you're working with

- Transposition for the instruments

- Dynamic markings on every part

- Clear marks on the score and each part for all tempo, key, and meter changes

- Thorough instructions for aleatoric sections for the musicians

- Measure numbers on each bar line for both the score and the parts (these measure numbers should line up with the measure numbers in your session files)

- A score for the conductor, the recording engineer, the score reader, and one for yourself as composer

- A list of all the cues that need to be recorded, along with notes about which sequence file the engineers will be using and which bar they'll be starting at

After you've created all the parts for your session, make sure to play through every individual part at the piano to double-check for mistakes. If a musician won't be playing on a particular cue, make sure to include a part that simply reads *tacet* so you don't have to spend time explaining to the player that he or she isn't playing on that cue.

COMPOSER PERSPECTIVE

Yoshino Aoki

I had the opportunity for a particular project to record part of my pieces with live instruments. Overall, the musical style could have been categorized as ambient, with a minimalistic usage of live instruments. I was so caught up with creating the right atmosphere while sequencing that I hadn't put enough thought into the actual recording that was to happen after that. As a result, despite the musicians delivering a fine performance, I feel as though I was not able to use the instruments to their fullest capacity. The reason we use live instruments over samples is because they are able to express that which cannot be expressed with a computer. However, I feel that during the production phase of the live recording sessions, I did not sufficiently devote myself to the part writing, so it didn't come out as well as in my mind.

After this incident, I decided to take out this sort of mediocrity from my working attitude. I now think about the "sound" of the live instruments more deeply. When I listen to my finished pieces, I try to listen to them as if they were not my pieces but rather were composed by someone else. By switching my mentality, I am better able to analyze the meaning of each sound the instruments produce or whether the transitions are really working out well.

> It is important to really think about what you are composing. This may sound obvious, but I think it is actually rather difficult to see things from an outsider perspective. If you take out the "I" from your compositions, you may be able discover new things and your music could potentially evolve in a good way.
>
> Maybe I am becoming a little too philosophical, but composition is really a battle with yourself. The moment you believe that the piece is good enough, it is done. But you have to keep striving and keep thinking until you can absolutely believe that the piece is great. Even once you are working professionally, there is still a long journey ahead.

Preparing Sequences for an Orchestrator or Arranger

An orchestrator usually requests that the composer send rough mixes along with the original sequences. In many cases the orchestrator will not have the same instrument plug-ins as the composer, so the rough mixes will be extremely useful for the orchestrator to interpret your sequence. Before sending materials to the orchestrator, the composer should clean up the sequence as much as possible both for readability and to save money with the orchestration fees. Cleaning up sequence files usually includes the following tasks:

- Labeling tracks clearly
- Moving each instrument articulation on to its own track (for example, if the composition has both string pizzicato and arco articulations)
- Removing all key switches so they don't accidently show up in your score
- Double-checking to make sure you haven't written outside the instrument ranges
- Including written notes about what you're intending with each cue and how to perform dynamics and any special articulations

Session Preparation and Planning

When prepping your sequences within a DAW for recording, organization is one of the key factors in guaranteeing a successful outcome in the recording studio. This section focuses on how to determine the order of the cues, how to multitrack smaller ensembles, what to include in your sequences, and how to prepare for what can go wrong at a session.

Determine the Recording Order of Cues

When determining the overall order of the cues that will be recorded, there are many factors that you should consider.

First, you'll need to examine which musicians will be playing on which cues. Order the session so that you have the least downtime for each musician. For instance, if you have several cues that are strings only, you wouldn't want to be paying the woodwinds to stand around waiting to record.

Second, if your score has multiple layers, then you might need to record the cues in multiple passes because instrument groups can bleed into the microphones of other instrument groups. Frequently in video games each section of instruments is recorded at a separate time (e.g., brass on one day, strings on the next) for maximum flexibility when dynamically layering instruments or constructing alternate cues from the source material.

Last, you should analyze the difficulty of your music cues. During the session you'll want to start with a few warm-up cues before tackling the more difficult pieces. In general, it's recommended that you complete the more difficult cues early in the session while your musicians are fresher. Ideally, then, you should front-load the difficult cues after the warm-up cues.

Once you've looked at these factors, create a rough schedule of the order in which you'll record cues and the instruments.

Multitracking

Multitracking is the recording of additional passes of the same instrument group playing the same parts to layer on top of one another. It is often used to try and achieve a bigger sound with a smaller ensemble. For instance, if you have a limited budget, you could augment a section violin part with a single violin player recording the same part over and over again, and then add it to the synth instrument.

It's difficult to create the sound of a full section of musicians this way, because a section is made up of individual players, each with his or her own vibrato, tone, ambiture, and so on. When recording the same individual or small group, these characteristics tend to phase with one another because of the similarity between the performances.

Because of the decline in budgets for live musicians, this technique is widely used by composers. Frequently union rules mandate an additional fee with each multitracked performance, so make sure to either budget it into your project or work out an agreement with musicians before they come in and play.

Sequence Preparation

How do you format and prepare your sequences for live recording in the studio? Recording studios are set up to specialize in recording, so they will not support a lot of the virtual instruments and specialized effects that you'll be using in your home studio. You'll want to bounce these virtual instruments and effects to audio tracks in addition to providing the studio with a full mix track, mix-minus, and bounced audio click track (as described later in this section). These extra tracks can help you rebuild a corrupted sequence if the DAW won't load the files at the studio.

Here is a checklist for prepping your sequence files for the studio:

- Organize your session by labeling all tracks clearly.
- Bounce your virtual instrument and MIDI tracks on to audio tracks. Then, disable all virtual instrument tracks.
- Bounce any specialized effects and DSP that you're using to audio tracks within your sequence.
- Conform your sequence to the correct DAW, sample rate, and bit depth you'll be using at the recording session.
- Write detailed notes to the studio regarding the order and organization of the cues that you'll be recording.
- Include any video files that you might need as reference.

Following is a description of the extra audio tracks that you'll want to include in the sequence files that you deliver to the studio:

- **Full Mix.** A full mix of your mockup includes all instruments, even the ones you plan on replacing with live instruments. This is tremendously useful for producers, engineers, and even your musicians to understand the scope of the piece. Since many musicians are recorded at different times, it will be difficult for them to know exactly what you're looking for unless they hear the complete mockup or are able to look at your score. If you are recording all live instruments on your piece, it is still useful to include the full mix mockup so that the musicians can match the tuning of your piece.
- **Mix-Minus.** A mix-minus is the full mix of your mockup minus the instruments that you plan on replacing. It allows the players to perform alongside the instruments that are not being recorded at the session. When replacing the entire ensemble, you wouldn't need to include a mix-minus.
- **Audio Click Track.** The audio click track can be customized to include only a specific number of count-off clicks before the cue begins, or to remain silent on a fermata or diminuendo so you don't hear the click from headphone bleed. An audio click is especially important if your sequencer files become corrupted, as it can substitute for your MIDI tempo map. The sound of the audio click can also be customized for the particular piece of music, such as a traditional metronome click, high-hat, or shaker. Also, due to certain sync/jitter problems with ProTools (and other DAWs), it is a best practice in session preparation to bake the click track as a bounced audio file to ensure accuracy and no lag or loss of sync during recording.

Although you can record without a click track, it is generally not recommended in video games unless you're working with rubato tempos, recording aleatoric passages, or recording a sampling session. Frequently video game composers need to record projects in layers using vertical remixing techniques. If a click track is in place, the musicians will have a much easier time locking to the tempo than if they have to just follow a previous performance. In addition, it makes editing performances and creating alternate cues much easier overall.

> ## tip
>
> While it might seem obvious that you would include reverb when exporting a full mix, should you export the reverb on individual tracks when exporting to another sequencer? Much of this decision-making process has to do with personal preference. A lot of mix and recording engineers would recommend that you keep everything dry when exporting so you have more control in the mix. Others would argue that leaving these decisions for the mix just ends up extending the mix.
>
> If you like the reverb, then you should print it to the tracks. The mix will be a long process, after all, and it's better to make decisions along the way. If your effect is more specialized and the facility where you'll be mixing doesn't have those plug-ins available, then it's definitely a time saver to print the effect directly to the tracks so you don't waste time trying to re-create the effect at the mix.

Preparing for What Can Go Wrong

When using an outside studio to record, there is always a risk that somewhere between the composer's studio and the recording studio the sequences will be corrupted. Here are a few suggestions that may help ward off chaos and mitigate any damage, staving off a disaster in the studio:

- Schedule a meeting well ahead of the recording session to talk with the recording engineer. At this meeting, describe what type of session is planned, how many musicians will be recording, and what kind of setup they'll need to prepare for. In addition, the engineer should be made aware of any layering that you'll be doing as well as limits on multitracking and multiple takes. Last, you'll want to discuss what you'll be sending ahead of the session (typically your sequences with cue lists and descriptions) and what you'll be leaving with after the recordings (e.g., the recorded sequences or final mixes).

- Get the materials to the recording studio at least a day in advance so that personnel there can check them.

- Always include a full mix, mix-minus, and audio click track for every cue. If the sequence or session file won't open at the last minute, it can be easy to create a new session with just these raw audio files.

Exporting a Sequence to Another DAW

Many composers work in their preferred sequencer, and then record in another sequencer because of what the recording studio offers. The ability to move materials from one sequencer to another is an invaluable skill. In this section you'll learn about some of the best practices for moving from one sequence to another. Following is a list of steps you should perform for each cue you plan on recording in the studio:

1. You'll need to transfer your tempo and meter map into the new sequencer by exporting a Standard MIDI File (SMF) from your original DAW, then importing it into your new DAW. This will allow your materials to have proper bar and beat alignment in the new sequencer.

2. Bounce or export an audio track from each instrument in your sequence. Make sure to start each of the audio files in the same place, even if these tracks have large blocks of silence at the beginning. Then import these onto separate tracks in the new DAW with your tempo map. Alternatively, you could export stems or groups of instruments that are similar, but make sure to separate out any instruments that will be replaced with live instruments.

3. Similarly, export or bounce a full mix of the demo tracks, and a mix-minus if needed. Start them at the same time as your other instrument tracks. Bring these audio files into the new DAW with your instrument tracks.

4. Bounce an audio version of the click track, including count-off, from your original DAW to import into your new DAW. Again, make sure this track starts at the same place as your other audio tracks.

5. Check your sequence in the new DAW to make sure the click track and all other instruments line up together, and then correct any mistakes that you hear.

> **tip**
>
> A two-beep (or two-pop) is an audible beep at a specific moment in time; it is usually placed exactly two seconds before the cue is supposed to begin. Originally used in film, commercials, and television, it is a way to line up audio recordings for which the start times are not exactly the same. Many professional composers embed two-beeps in all the audio file exports so they have an audio and visual representation within the DAW to show where the files line up. This process acts as a safety mechanism in case one of the audio exports didn't start at the right place. If you follow the adage, "If something can go wrong, it will," the two-beep will be your best friend in trying to resolve timing issues between tracks.

Session Flow and Practices

Time is of utmost importance at a recording session, as each second represents money spent on the musicians and facilities. Organization and time management are key elements to coming away from your recording session with all the elements recorded successfully in the time allotted. In the booth, a session manager needs to make the team aware of the following factors in the session:

- Which cues have been recorded, and which cues are remaining

- The pace of the session, including how many minutes of music the group is recording per hour, and how many minutes of music remains

- Whether the group needs to increase the pace of recording, or if they can spend a longer time recording a specific section

On larger sessions, this information is typically stored in a database so that calculations can be made in real time about how far along the session is and how to plan the remaining time.

The recording session itself can be broken down into several activities:

- **Setting Up the Studio.** The setup is done before the players arrive. Microphones, chairs, and music stands are placed in the correct positions. Music parts are distributed to the individual musicians via their corresponding music stands before they arrive. The sequences are tested and set up for recording by adding new tracks and routing instrument microphones to the correct tracks.

- **Rehearsing the Cues.** Before each cue is recorded, the composer describes the cue to the musicians and has them take note of any difficult passages. The musicians should tune their instruments, and then the conductor runs through a rehearsal with the group while the composer addresses questions, comments, and mistakes that may appear in the score. Ideally, the recording engineer will record rehearsals just in case the performance is one the team wants to keep.

- **Recording the Cues.** Once the recording begins, the composer listens for the best performance. The amount of time that the team can spend on a specific cue is a balance between how much time is remaining in the session and whether the performance works for the game. In evaluating each take, it's important to listen to (1) the overall performance, (2) tuning of the instruments with each other and the synth tracks, (3) note entrances and cut-offs for future multitracking, (4) overall dynamics, (5) timing against the click, and (6) specific articulations.

- **Exporting the Final Elements.** Once the session is complete, the recording engineer hands over any notes and sequences to the composer for final editing and mixing. The composer reviews all the takes, choosing the best ones to take into the mix. The composer either exports the materials back to the original DAW or continues to use the recording studio DAW to finish off the tracks.

Time Management

How much time do you need in the studio? As a general guideline, with a 60-piece orchestra, you can reasonably expect to record between 3 and 5 minutes of music per hour depending on the complexity of the music. Thus, if you have a 40-minute score, it would take a minimum of 8 hours of recording time.

Here are a few general suggestions for making the most of your time and having successful recording sessions:

- **Be prepared.** Preparation will save you time in the studio and get more out of the orchestra.

- **Work with people who are experienced.** Working with experienced people who are excellent at their craft (engineers, orchestrators, copyists, conductors, players) will guarantee not only a great product but also the best value for the resources spent.

- **Gather real-time feedback on takes.** Writing down specific feedback on cues as they are being recorded will save hours in post-recording editing.

Final Mixing and Editing

The final mix of the cues involves picking the best takes from any live recordings that were done, creating an appropriate balance for the music, and editing the materials for use within the game. Mixing can be particularly challenging, as the composer mixes the music by making the best guess about how the music will interact with the surround sound elements, such as ambience, SFX, and dialog, within the game.

Following are some mixing tips for making games sound great:

- A/B your music mix with a similar game's finished music. This is a great way to hear dynamics and frequency levels in your own music and to determine how it matches up against a piece of music that you feel works.

- Listen to your music with sound effects and dialog during the mix to better balance the elements that might conflict with one another.

- Mix with stems grouping your instruments together and recording each to their own track. That way, if you or someone else has to revisit a mix because the brass wasn't loud enough, for example, it's an easier fix than loading up the entire mix with plug-ins.

- Listen to the music within the game if possible. Mix, export, implement, listen, and then repeat until it sounds flawless.

When editing the cues recorded by live musicians, it's important to zoom in on the waveforms to make sure that you don't clip the beginning of the cue if they played a little on top of the beat, or clip the end of a cue if they played in the pocket. Frequently composers have to make small adjustments on a recording level to fine-tune any loop or branch points.

Musicians and Recording

Over the past four decades, demand for live recording of musicians has dwindled as a direct result of the increased use of synthesizers and virtual instruments. In addition, the perceptions from employers that it's easier to compose music through these means have led to tighter budgets for composers and live instruments.

Recording live instruments can be as inexpensive as recording a single musician in a composer's home studio with just a microphone and a pair of headphones. By comparison, on the largest projects there may be several large ensembles booked to record in several different cities around the world. Given these extremes, there is an enormous range of budgets and fees for live recording.

On larger-budget projects, musician and recording studio fees might have their own budget outside of the creative fees that the composer is paid. On lower-budget projects, musician fees typically come out of the composer's own pay, making it a difficult choice if you need that money for next month's rent. That being said, if you want your pieces to stand out so that you can move up to larger and better projects, live recording is a worthwhile investment. Pieces that have live musicians recorded on them are usually showpieces for your reel.

Calculating the amount of time that you'll need for the musicians and studios can be challenging. As composers have more opportunities to work in the recording studio, they'll be able to better plan the pacing of the session. Following are some of the factors that influence the amount of time you'll need for recording:

- Length of the cues
- Difficulty of the cues
- Experience of the composer, musicians, and recording engineer
- Use of nonstandard notation such as aleatoric or improvisational elements
- Use of vertical remixing techniques (layers need to be recorded in separate passes to avoid microphone bleed)

Union Contracts

Union contracts guarantee a standard hourly rate for musicians to be paid when recording on projects. Unions also help with various benefits, including health insurance options and retirement benefits, for musicians who work on union projects. Musicians who have joined the American Federation of Musicians (AFM) are required to work only under union contracts; otherwise, they may be asked to leave the union.

In the United States, the current AFM contract for video games (established in 2012) is rarely, if ever, used. The contract is known as the Videogame/Interactive Media Agreement (VIMA). The terms of the VIMA are not favorable to video game developers and publishers because of the high rates. This factor has forced a lot of video game publishers to look to non-union orchestras throughout the United States and overseas.

Video game developers and publishers have different needs than the film industry, in which future royalties are paid out to musicians. The video game industry prefers to buy out performances so that developers and publishers don't have to pay ongoing royalties on any project. This has pushed up rates for video game contracts.

Most game publishers have had to work with non-union orchestras unless they were able to set up another one-time agreement with the AFM. Most of the best musicians in the United States belong to the union (especially in Los Angeles), making it challenging to record musicians in the United States for games. Consequently, composers are often forced to look elsewhere to record. There are excellent orchestras in Europe, for example.

Because of the exodus of musician work from places like Los Angeles to Europe, there is an ongoing negotiation with several publishers and the AFM to set up a new video game contract to bring work back to the United States. There will likely be a ratification of a new contract within the next year.

Musician Expenses

Musicians' rates vary tremendously for each type of project (film, jingle, song). When they work through the AFM union, musicians make an average of $120/hour. In some European orchestras, musicians can make much less, closer to $30/hour. Many other variables are associated with these fees, including the expertise of the player (some musicians get paid double or triple scale) and fees for carting their instruments to the gig. When the AFM has a final video game agreement with musicians, you'll be able to use those rates when hiring them.

If the musicians you've hired are non-union, you'll need to negotiate with them to find a mutually agreeable rate for the amount of work. If your parts are not very complicated, then you might be able to find college students to play your parts for $25–$50/hour. If your parts are particularly challenging or if you need an uncommon instrument (e.g., didgeridoo, duduk), the rates will reflect the particular expertise of the player. Professional players will command a much higher rate, $150–$500/hour. These higher rates also reflect the fact that the musician will not receive any additional compensation after the initial payment. Essentially this payment is a *buyout* of the musician's performance on the project in lieu of receiving additional royalties later.

The compensation should be representative of the kind of work that musicians are providing for the composition. Composers are dependent on musicians to play their work, so you should treat them with respect and gratitude when it comes to compensation. In turn, musicians are reliant on composers to provide them with gigs. Because the relationship is mutually beneficial, we need to promote the use of more live instruments on our projects and encourage publishers to increase music budgets to accommodate better music scores in our industry.

When calculating time for your musicians, make sure to include any video game–specific expenses, such as multiple takes for building a section with few players, individual passes for better track separation, and possibly playing many different cues. If you're working with a union contract, there may be guidelines for additional payments for multitracking parts or having instrumentalists double with another instrument. Make sure you investigate the union contract carefully to properly prepare the budget for your project.

If you're hiring more than 10 musicians for a gig, you may want to hire a contractor to arrange the availability of all the musicians. Contractors are typically paid double the musician's rate.

Last, regarding unions, you cannot contract with the AFM without the use of a designated signatory. A signatory is a group or individual who has agreed to the terms of the contract. Given that almost no video game publishers have signed the current agreement with the AFM, third-party signatories are mandated for all union contracts as a practical matter. The orchestral contractor is often the signatory, because it is almost impossible for the composer to act as a third-party signatory and sign an AFM assumption agreement with the AFM's consent.

warning

LOOPS AND SAMPLE-BASED INSTRUMENTS   If you're going to bring in live musicians to record samples or loops that you can use in future projects, make sure to inform your players of your intention before they arrive at the studio. Many musicians feel that composers take advantage of their talents by using their performances in virtual instruments on multiple projects without inviting them back for an additional session. Musician compensation should reflect the fact you might be using their performance across multiple projects through loops or virtual instruments; that is, you should either pay the musicians a higher rate or possibly pay them a royalty every time you use their performance on a project. The AFM does provide a special session rate for sampling sessions if your project is working under union guidelines.

Musician Releases

An important document that all musicians should sign at the end of the recording session is a *musician waiver and release* form. This document authorizes the composer to use the live performance and states that the musician can claim no ownership over the performance. The musician signs this form is in return for whatever compensation the composer has agreed to with the musician.

Many publishers collect the musician release forms at the end of a project so that they will not be held liable for claims against their games by musicians and other performers. Composers sign a similar agreement that is usually embedded in the project contract assigning the rights of a composition and recordings over to the game developer or publisher.

Recording Studio Expenses

On smaller projects, the composer can usually make do with recording a single musician at a time in a home studio. Once the live instrument needs become large enough to be called an ensemble (four or more musicians), the composer may need to bring the musicians to a recording studio so they can play together at the same time.

A recording studio offers many advantages over a home studio, including sound isolation, an excellent microphone selection, an experienced recording engineer who has an expertise in recording, and a relaxed environment for creativity.

Most studios support ProTools for recording, but some other studios may support other software. Make sure that the studio you choose has a software solution that works for you. Depending on where you live, there may not be a choice of where you can record, limiting your DAW choice. This is one of the reasons why it's important to have experience with a variety of different sequencers, onward and upward.

Recording studios fees vary widely, depending on how large they are and where they are located. Expect to spend $50/hour at a small studio and up to $400/hour at a large studio. Most studios allow you to book long segments of time for discounted rates.

When choosing a recording studio, start by researching the needs of the project—for example, how much recording studio time you'll need and how many musicians you'll be recording. This will inform the decision about which kind of studio you'll need. Next, explore any project-specific needs. For example, you may want to record at a studio that uses ProTools. Look at the studios in your area to determine the best fit for the specifics of your project.

As noted earlier, studio recording for video games sometimes involves recording each section of instruments in separate passes either for a layered score or to have the flexibility to edit the various takes into new and rearranged cues. For instance, if one of your music layers has a violin section and a different layer has brass, you wouldn't want to record these at the same time as the microphone bleed would ruin each of the takes; instead, you'd need to record them separately. When calculating the overall studio time and budget, make sure to include these factors.

Review

Musicians can help elevate the creative depth of your pieces as well as provide the listener with palettes that no electronic instrument can duplicate.

Among the factors that influence the amount of time you'll need for recording are the length and difficulty of the cues, the experience of the team and musicians, and the use of interactive techniques such as vertical remixing.

When you're preparing the score and parts for a recording session, make sure to (1) double-check all the parts; (2) include dynamics; (3) include clear marks for tempo, key, and meter changes; (4) bring multiple scores to the recording session; and (5) provide clear notes about the cues you need to record and the sequences that they correspond to.

During the session, you'll want to start with a few warm-up cues before tackling the more difficult pieces. In general, it's recommended that you complete the more difficult cues early in the session while the musicians are fresher.

Before sending materials to the orchestrator, the composer should clean up the sequence as much as possible for readability and to save money with the orchestration fees. This process includes (1) clearly labeling tracks, (2) moving individual instrument articulations to their own tracks, (3) removing key switches, and (4) including any notes about the parts and an audio mockup.

Multitracking refers to the recording of additional passes of the same instrument group playing the same parts to layer on top of one another. Multitracking is often used to achieve a bigger sound with a smaller ensemble.

When preparing musical cues to be recorded at a studio, it's useful to include a full demo mix, a mix-minus, and an audio click track along with your sequence.

The ability to move materials from one sequencer to another is an invaluable skill that you'll need if you're recording live musicians in studios. Moving a session from one sequencer to another involves transferring the MIDI and tempo maps, bouncing all virtual instruments, and importing all of the audio tracks in the new sequencer

The recording session itself can be broken down into the following activities: setting up the studio, rehearsing the cues, finding the best recording, and exporting the final elements.

Union contracts guarantee a standard hourly rate for musicians to be paid when recording on projects. Unions also help musicians with various benefits, including health insurance options and retirement benefits. Video game publishers almost exclusively prefer that musicians are hired under a buyout contract, meaning that they will owe no royalties to the musicians after the initial payment.

Exercises

1. Observe a recording session for a game or film score.

2. Record three separate instruments on a music cue that you've written.

3. Write a cue that uses a small live ensemble exclusively, and then record and mix your cue.

CHAPTER 22

MIXING AND EXPORTING AUDIO FILES TO THE GAME ENGINE

All of the interactive scoring methods described in this book cannot come to life without actually being harnessed and implemented in the game itself. Once a composer has created a musical asset for a game, what is the process of actually exporting the music for use in the game itself? This chapter introduces composers to the file formats and procedures for exporting audio to the game engine.

Considerations for Mixing Music for Games

Many questions arise after you've composed a music cue for a game, including the proper format that the game might need, and concerns about mixing. Once you've composed a music segment for a video game, how do you create a file that will work in the game itself? Video games use multiple types of audio files and compression that you'll need to be familiar with to export the correct files for use within a game.

This chapter overviews the process of mixing, exporting materials from your DAW, and readying audio files for use within the game. You'll learn about the various formats you'll encounter as well as techniques for making your music sound great.

Mixing music for games can be especially challenging because of the variability of elements not only in an interactive music score, but also across other audio disciplines in the game that affect how we hear the music, including sound effects and dialog.

Music is almost always premixed for the game in the DAW. This means the composer won't be able to hear the music mix against the SFX during the gameplay until after the music files are implemented. Then once the score is implemented, if the composer needs to make changes, he or she must go back to the original sequence files, remix them, export them, and then put the new files back into the game. This is a time-consuming process and not very intuitive or easy.

On large games, publishers often allocate months of time to mix games, and coordinate with internal test teams to track bugs along with content tweaks needed after mix passes. In these instances, it's rare for the composer to be on site during the entire burn-down and mix process. Outstanding mix issues can be addressed through redelivering music cues through change orders to the composer who works remotely.

Being able to mix to a temporary audio file that contains some of the SFX and dialog can help tremendously in carving out frequencies that allow both the SFX and music to be balanced correctly and heard within the mix. If there is a conflict in the frequency ranges, music is frequently turned down so that the dialog can sit in the forefront. Thus, in many cases, the music gets buried underneath the SFX and dialog. If you're able to balance the frequency ranges between the music, SFX, and dialog, you'll end up with a much better mix, allowing the player to hear all the audio elements.

Mixing has been a huge area of growth both in terms of software tools and the increase in work for audio professionals in video game development. Although mixing within a DAW is facilitated by the availability of robust tools and plug-ins for controlling a mix, mixing within a game is incredibly challenging because of the lack of intuitive and useful tools. Most game engines still have primitive interfaces for changing the levels of the audio. To add to this frustration, these controls are typically not available while the game is actually running. Many audio implementers need to change the values, load the game to check the levels, stop the game to edit the values, and then repeat. This can be an extremely time-consuming process.

Audio middleware engines such as Fmod and Wwise have only recently begun to add real-time tools for mixing audio while the game is running. These recent advances should help pave the way for better tools for mixing music in the future.

Like many of the techniques in the book, mixing requires iterative changes—that is, reviewing and assigning the assets within the game, then applying the appropriate mix changes before repeating the process.

Mixing also needs to take into account how the music will play back in the game. For example, the placement of source music (diegetic) in a 3D game will shape how the player hears the sound. Many games dynamically add reverb to diegetic music to fit the 3D space in which the player is hearing the music. In addition, if the music source is located behind a wall in the game, the game will have to add the appropriate obstruction and occlusion filters to make the music sound as if it's coming from behind a wall. Then, as the player moves and the music source comes into view, these filters need to change dynamically. The composer won't be responsible for this implementation, but it may affect how he or she chooses to mix the music.

Bouncing and Exporting Master Files

Once you've finished composing, recording, and mixing a music cue, you'll want to first export a high-quality uncompressed master file to be used for all future file conversions.

Whenever you work on a project, it's important for you to store and archive the master files uncompressed at the highest possible sample rate and bit depth. The two most common uncompressed audio formats are WAV and AIFF. At the time of this book's writing, it was standard practice to archive master uncompressed audio files in a 48 KHz, 24-bit format or better for professional quality.

It is recommended that you export and bounce all final materials in real time so you can listen to the final mix and make sure everything sounds the way it should. If you take shortcuts by bouncing offline to save time, your work might have more errors that you'll need to go back and fix later. In addition, if you don't check your files after you've exported them, the client could hear something you didn't anticipate that could possibly misrepresent you or your work. Always check everything before you deliver it to minimize any mistakes.

If the music cues are 100 percent live source, the recording or mix facility may bounce the final content to delivery specifications. This type of mix collaboration is also commonplace on hybrid scores that ingest stems and premixed layers from the composer, which are then mixed next to live elements recorded in the studio.

File Formats and Compression

Each game engine will have its own set of guidelines with regard to the music formats it accepts. This section discusses the various types of audio files that you will encounter during the game development process.

Although composers and sound designers would rejoice at the idea of using uncompressed WAV files during a game, this technique is generally not possible for a variety of reasons—most important of which is overall memory footprint. Compressed audio files are typically 80 to 90 percent smaller than the original uncompressed file:

- 1-minute stereo WAV file uncompressed = 44.1 KHz, 16 bit ≈ 10MB
- 1-minute stereo MP3 file compressed = 128Kbps ≈ 1MB

Because memory is always a constraint when making games, even on larger console games, the audio team needs to work with the game development team to plan for the overall memory footprint of the music, sound effects, and dialog. If the game will be deployed to a handheld device, the memory constraints will be tighter than if the game is an Xbox or PlayStation title. Higher memory constraints will be correlated with lower bit rates for music and audio files, decreasing the overall sonic quality.

Memory and size constraints are discussed at greater length in Chapter 23, "Implementation and Programming." That chapter will help you develop a strategy for the overall music memory footprint for the game.

After you have bounced your music segments inside your DAW, you'll need to export them to a format that the game engine will use. DAWs usually support a handful of different audio formats and compression settings. For alternative formats like Ogg Vorbis, you may need to look elsewhere to compress your audio files. Applications that support a wider range of audio formats include Sony's SoundForge, Adobe Audition, Audio Ease Barbabatch, and Max by Sbooth.

> ## warning
>
> **AUDIO VERSES FILE COMPRESSION**   Unfortunately, the term "compression" does double duty in video games. Audio compression refers to the manipulation of the dynamics in a piece of music. For instance, if you use DSP to compress a music track, then you can change your *triple-pianissimo* dynamic to be *mezzo-pianissimo* and your *triple-fortissimo* dynamic to be *mezzo-forte*. File compression refers to how the audio is stored on disk. For instance, an MP3 or AAC file is a compressed audio format that takes up less space than an uncompressed file like an AIFF or WAV file. Compressed audio file formats will never sound quite as good as the uncompressed original files, but today's compression algorithms are quite robust and are of excellent quality.

Audio File Compression Formats

Uncompressed formats generally have two adjustable settings: sample rate and bit depth. The higher the settings you use, the better sounding the resulting files. Simply increasing the rate of a file doesn't gain any quality; the original recordings and virtual instruments need to use the higher rates to hear an increase in quality. There are two major types of uncompressed audio file formats you'll encounter:

- **WAV (also called WAVE):** Ubiquitous uncompressed audio format originally developed by IBM and Microsoft
- **AIFF:** Less common Audio Interchange File Format originally developed by Apple Computer

There are two types of audio file compression: *lossless* and *lossy*. Lossless data compression will decompress to produce an exact replica of original file. The resulting file has a much larger memory footprint than the corresponding lossy compressed file. An example of a lossless audio compressed file format is the FLAC format. Lossless compression retains all the fine details of the original file, but lossy compression is used much more frequently in games because of its huge memory savings.

Lossy compression is able to create significant memory savings by creating an impression of the original audio with coarser details. Once you've converted an uncompressed audio file to the lossy compressed audio format, you cannot create an uncompressed version of that file without some loss in quality.

The following compressed audio formats use lossy compression and are commonly used in video games. All of them have an adjustable control measured in kilobits per second or a "quality" parameter. The higher this rate, the better the audio quality. Compression algorithms that support variable bit rate encoding use a "quality" parameter to adjust the audio settings. Many games use a 128Kbps rate to achieve a balance between size and quality, although many more recent games use higher bit rates to ensure better quality.

- **MP3:** Audio format that is part of the MPEG2 compression specification originally developed by the Moving Picture Experts Group; used on virtually all game platforms
- **AAC/MP4:** Successor to MP3 that is slightly higher in quality; used primarily on iOS games and Apple games
- **Ogg Vorbis:** Open source compressed audio format; used on most game platforms, including handhelds
- **WMA:** Windows Media Audio file developed by Windows; used in Windows games only
- **XMA/XMA2:** Compressed audio file format; used on the Xbox platform

> ## warning
>
> **WHY DON'T MY MP3 FILES LOOP CORRECTLY?** MP3 files sometimes pad the end of the files with silence. The original MP3 specification didn't account for looping, which designates the file to be a certain length related to its frame size. Certain tempos will loop correctly but many other tempos will not. Some MP3 playback codecs and middleware (such as Fmod) will compensate to create gapless MP3 files, but others will not. Check with the software manufacturer and your game developer to see whether you'll be able to use gapless MP3 files. One reason for the popularity of the Ogg Vorbis audio compression format in video games is that it can create gapless loops automatically.

The following video compression standards are widely used, so you might run across them either when delivering rough audio embedded into a cut-scene to a client or when you receive game capture video from a game developer. You may need to convert these files to another format to work in your DAW with a software tool like MPEG Streamclip by Squared5.

- **H.264:** MPEG4 video compression standard
- **MPEG2/M2V:** DVD video compression standard originally developed by the Moving Picture Experts Group

Media container formats can hold multiple mixed data, including video and audio encoded with various types of compression discussed previously, but may sometimes include additional elements such as text, closed captioning, button hotspots, and other interactive features. Following are the most common container formats:

- **MOV:** QuickTime movie container format developed by Apple Computer
- **MPEG2:** Container format for audio/video created by the Moving Picture Experts Group; commonly used on DVDs
- **MPEG4:** Updated container format commonly used on Blu-Ray disks
- **AVI:** Older Audio Video Interleaved format designed by Microsoft
- **WMV:** Modern container format developed by Microsoft
- **BINK2:** Common video delivery format for consoles created by RAD Game Tools

Game Audio Formats

Although it is beyond the scope of this book to list all the different file formats used by every game engine, you'll often encounter the following formats when working with these popular game engines:

- **Crytek:** Fmod or Ogg
- **Unity:** WAV, AIFF, MP3, or Ogg files (Ogg is recommended)
- **Unreal:** Uncompressed WAV files (44.1 KHz, 16 bit), outputs Ogg Vorbis
- **GameMaker:** MP3
- **iOS:** AAC or MP3
- **Android:** Ogg Vorbis
- **Flash:** MP3
- **HTML5:** MP3 or Ogg, depending on the browser
- **XNA Game Studio:** XACT file, WMA, or MP3 files

Several of these game engines support audio middleware integration (Fmod, Wwise), including Unity, Unreal, and Crytek. If this middleware is being used in the game, then the game engines can accept prerendered banks that the middleware produces. More information is provided about middleware solutions in Chapter 18, "Using Middleware to Create Advanced Compositions."

Audio middleware such as Fmod and Wwise can both import and use original uncompressed audio WAV files. When these engines build banks for use within the game, the middleware will customize the output file format for the targeted platform, thereby saving the composer a significant amount of time. For example, if you're working on a game that will be deployed on both the PlayStation Vita and the Nintendo DS, you can set up two separate targets in Fmod, then build a bank for each of the targets with separate format and compression settings.

> ## tip
>
> When faced with the prospect of using really low bit rates for a game (less than 32Kbps), it can be very challenging to make an orchestra sound like a real orchestra. In contrast, if you compose music with instruments that players are less likely to identify, they won't be making the comparison, "Why doesn't this violin sound as good as the violin I heard at Carnegie Hall?" Imitating known instruments at low bit rates can make your music sound inferior, so picking less commonly heard instrument palettes can sometimes work to your advantage with these highly compressed audio files.

Surround Mixing within Games

Much of the audio in console games is played back in surround systems. Surround systems in home game audio systems commonly use 5.1 channel systems, with channels arranged as follows: left, center, right, left surround, right surround, and LFE. LFE—that is, low-frequency effects—is usually played through the subwoofer speaker.

Other surround configurations such as 6.1 (additional back channel) and 7.1 (left and right back channels) are also possible, but 5.1 channel systems are by far the most common. Console games commonly premix their music in quad format, keeping the center and LFE channels clear for dialog and SFX.

The diegetic sounds in the game, SFX, and dialog are usually specialized into the surround audio system by their placement in the 3D universe. For example, if a monster in the game is situated behind the player, those monster sounds will play out of the rear surround speakers. As the player turns to face the monster, those sounds are dynamically panned to the front speakers. The audio implementer and programmers do not need to worry about implementing these features themselves, as they are usually built into the 3D middleware technology used by the game. Extra-diegetic music, in contrast, usually doesn't pan dynamically around the 3D space unless the music is part of the scene itself (diegetic music).

At one time, underscore (extra-diegetic music) primarily was relegated to the front left and right speakers, with some additional music reverb in the surrounds. In recent years, movies, television programs, and video games have gotten more adventurous with panning elements of the music into the surround speakers. Immersing the player emotionally into the game experience is the primary reason why music is used during gameplay. Because music is an emotional component, there is really no reason that it needs to be relegated to just the front speakers.

That being said, music in the surround speakers can be distracting to the player if it covers up the footsteps of an enemy who is sneaking up on the player. Discretion should be used in creating the immersive experience for the player. As with the actual composition of the music itself, it's better to start with the idea you're trying to get across, as opposed to implementing a technique just because you can.

Recently, more cut-scenes, loading screens, and menu screens have placed music across the surround speakers, enveloping the player in the excitement of the world. Situations during gameplay that use music in the surround speakers are still relatively rare, with the notable exception of during music games.

The LFE channel (which is usually played from the subwoofer) should be used only for special events. If the LFE is overused, then it won't have the impact for highly emotional events when it's needed. For example, using the LFE channel for a constant drone is definitely not recommended, whereas using the LFE to augment a musical stinger that plays after killing a boss during a level is more appropriate.

On non-surround systems (e.g., a normal stereo TV downmix), the LFE is completely discarded, so you shouldn't put anything critical in the LFE. This channel is designed solely to improve the experience for a 5.1/7.1-equipped game player.

Review

Video games use multiple types of audio files and compression that you'll need to be familiar with to export the types of files that can be used within a game.

Music is almost always premixed for the game in the DAW. As a consequence, the composer won't be able to hear the music mix against the SFX during the gameplay until after it's implemented.

Audio middleware engines such as Fmod and Wwise have only recently begun to add real-time tools for mixing audio while the game is running. These recent advances should help pave the way for better tools for mixing music in the future.

Once you've have finished composing and mixing a music cue, you'll want to first export a high-quality uncompressed master file to be used for all future file conversions. Compressed audio files are typically 80 to 90 percent smaller than the original uncompressed file, offering significant memory savings for video games. The quality of the compressed audio is proportional to the disk space it takes up. Uncompressed audio file formats include WAV and AIFF. Compressed audio file formats for games include MP3, AAC, Ogg Vorbis, and AC3.

Surround technology is frequently used when mixing music for games. Home audio surround systems commonly use the 5.1 channel format, with speakers arranged as follows: left, center, right, left surround, right surround, and a subwoofer for low-frequency effects (LFE).

Exercises

1. Convert a music cue to each of the following formats: WAV (44.1Kpbs, 16 bit), AIFF (44.1kbps, 16 bit), MP3 (32Kbps), and Ogg Vorbis (32Kbps).

2. Analyze and assess the surround mixes of music from several different console titles. Describe how they use surround mixing in all the different parts of the game, from the menus, to the loading screens, to gameplay and cut-scenes.

3. Mix a music cue that you've written for use in a 5.1 surround setting.

CHAPTER 23

IMPLEMENTATION AND PROGRAMMING

Once a composer has created a musical asset in the correct format for a game, what is the process of actually implementing the music to play and change at the correct times within the game? This chapter aims to answer that question whether your game development team consists of 80 people or just one or two. In addition, you'll learn about the different types of tools game developers use to collaborate with one another.

Defining the Music Framework

When developing a game, the composer and development team strategize an overall musical framework. As the composer begins writing cues, this musical framework needs to be integrated into the game so that any interactive musical cues that the composer has written will actually work in the game.

In addition, the composer works with the game development team to advise the programmer where music events need to play, change, and stop. The programmer will then find the correct place in the code to add these events to the gameplay. This process is known as adding a sound hook—short for "attaching a sound to a specific event in the game." For a composer, the sound hook is a line of code that calls a musical event within the game at the appropriate time. The amount of time that it takes to put the sound hooks in a game is proportional to the complexity of the game and music framework.

Very large publishers and game developers may have teams of in-house audio integration specialists who manage and define the music framework. They also manage the content and editing so that the composer can focus on composition and the emotional efficacy that drives narrative. This allows the audio team to focus on the implementation side instead of distracting the composer from the compositional work.

Some game engines, such as Unity, Unreal Development Kit, and Crytek, have level editors in which the artists, programmers, and designers collaborate to create levels for the game. Sound playback capabilities are typically built into the game-level editor itself as well, allowing for the composer or sound designer to place audio objects or events directly in the level or world itself.

Sound designers are frequently asked to place sounds directly in the game world or level. Learning how level editors work is a valuable skill. Since many games that are released today are in 3D, the level editors used to build these 3D worlds are fairly complex, requiring many hours to become fully acquainted with their capabilities. In some companies, dedicated individuals place sounds into game worlds, making sure that they play correctly, they are positioned in the right place, and the playback volume is adjusted appropriately. This role on a game development team is frequently known as the audio implementer.

On smaller game development teams, it can be an extremely valuable contribution if the composer or sound designer can not only create the sounds but also implement them. Implementing sounds into a game, whether through a level editor or a scripting language, can be incredibly valuable to a composer or sound designer, allowing him or her to gain knowledge about the limitations and possibilities for sound in the game engine.

The two best ways for a composer to get familiar with audio implementation are as follows:

- Download and learn a game engine that is freely available. Examples include Game-Maker, Unity, and Unreal Development Kit.

- Learn how to modify (mod) existing games. Many games allow players to create their own levels and make changes to the game, a process known as mod-ing. Games that include tools for editing and making levels include Crysis, Unreal Tournament, and Skyrim.

Many game engines use scripting engines like JavaScript or C# that allow game developers to provide unique functionality and customization of their game. Scripting languages are much easier and more forgiving to learn for nonprogrammers than languages like C++ or Objective-C. Although many games are written in complex languages like C++, they often are written in such a way to include the capability of using a scripting language so that the rest of the members of the game development team can customize parts of the game that don't require a detail-oriented level programming language. For instance, *World of Warcraft* (2004) is written primarily in C++ but allows scripting of scenes and changes to the game through the scripting language LUA.

On large projects, composers are usually asked to collaborate with a music director or audio director, and content integration and how things are implemented are usually kept behind an iron curtain by audio integration specialists. At high levels, it is rare for composers to interact directly with engineering teams and code specialists.

On smaller projects, composers may need to meet with the programmer multiple times over the course of the development of the game to work out when and where the sounds will play and any other audio functionality needed. Because of the reliance of the audio team on the programmers for the game, it's always a good idea to establish a rapport and make friends with the people who are programming and implementing the game. Composers and sound designers often hear sounds that they created in the wrong place when playing the game during the development process. Having excellent communication with the game programmers and implementers will minimize the number of sound-related bugs. The complexity and depth of the game will determine the amount of time you'll need to spend with the programming team to place the sounds correctly into the game.

The Implementation Process

Once the composer and the game development team have defined the overall music framework, a specification document should be written describing all the features that have been agreed upon by the team. This document should live where the entire team can have access to it and should serve as a bible describing how the music will be implemented in the game.

During the actual game development, the composer should consult with the game developer on the progress on implementing this framework and provide the development team with as much support as possible, including temporary and placeholder assets for testing. In addition, the composer should review the builds at regular intervals to hear the implementation and comment on whether it matches the original specification.

The size of the game will largely determine the methodology through which music assets are put into the game. If the development team includes an audio director, the composer will be frequently insulated from much of the implementation, but a composer's better understanding of this process will allow him or her to write better cues.

Each musical asset that you plan on creating should be included on a master music asset list, along with a description and a plan for how it will be implemented. Here is a list of procedures that every asset should go through to get it into the game properly:

- Write specifications for the sound, including what the sound or music cue is and when it will play.

- Develop a placeholder element or temporary sound asset that will play while waiting for the composed asset under development.

- Have the programmer code the sound hook so that the game will play or change the sound at the correct time in the game (at this stage the sound hook generally plays the placeholder asset).

- Create the sound or musical event.

- Iterate the sound and placement within the game based on creative feedback from the team and testing within the game.

The music asset list should be updated as the development process continues and more features are added to the game, until the entire project is complete.

Game Production Methodology

Game development teams use different methodologies to produce games. One popular methodology used throughout the game industry is Agile's Scrum. Teams using this model work toward goals called sprints. These sprints are several weeks long and represent stages in the overall development of a game. That's one of the distinguishing factors of Agile development (as contrasted with "normal" development, where milestones can be months apart). Teams that use this methodology usually meet once every workday to update everyone on the latest progress, the next steps, and any obstacles that are stopping them from getting their work done.

If you're working in-house with a game developer, you'll probably be working within a similar production model. If you're an outside contractor, you probably won't be checking in every day with the team, but rather once or twice a week to update the team on your progress.

The production of a game can last anywhere from a few weeks to several years. During this process, keeping track of every team member's progress is the responsibility of the game producer.

The composer should be proactive about staying in the loop on asset deliveries, implementation, and feedback. In the development process, a lot of time can be wasted waiting around for feedback. The more ownership the composer can take in getting information from the team, the more effective the composer will be.

The video game and technology industries have developed many different collaborative tools that are essential to working on projects. These software tools help teams work together by sharing information with the entire team and allowing teams to review assets and give feedback. These tools also support contractors and employees who work remotely with the game developer.

Although some of the collaborative tools are proprietary to a specific developer, many game companies use off-the-self or open source solutions to work with vendors as long as they meet any privacy and confidentiality requirements for the project. At the time of this book's writing, some products that are frequently used within the game industry include Google Docs, Skype, Google Hangouts, Dropbox, and Microsoft Office.

Collaborative tools are built around the many game production processes, including scheduling, sharing files and game assets, music review and feedback, and version control.

Scheduling and Milestone Delivery

As a part of the production process, game developers frequently use project-tracking systems to keep them on schedule and within budget. Some of the systems that are used by game developers include Jira, Agile/Scrum, Trac, BaseCamp, Assembla, Fogbugz, and Redmine.

Many of these project-tracking systems track all the elements of the production of a game, from the design, programming, audio, and art assets, through to quality assurance and bug tracking. Many tasks are assigned through tickets. A ticket is a specific task related to the project. Tickets are assigned with a due date to the team members.

Contract composers rarely work directly with these project-tracking systems. Instead, milestone dates and a calendar will be distributed to the composer by the game producer, which uses these systems to manage the overall production timeline. In-house composers are more likely to be more involved directly with a project management system, being assigned tickets and checking them off as they complete those tickets.

Managing Assets and Files

Games are built with assets that live as files. Since many people might be working and collaborating on creating assets for a game, software has been created to help developers manage assets that are accessed by large groups of people. These so-called asset management systems help distribute the latest version of the game to all the team members over a network like the Internet.

With larger projects, the developer usually sends the composer video captured from the game to review. On small to mid-size games, the composer may have access to the latest game builds so he or she can play the game and hear the assets being used. Some development teams may also let the composer actively add his or her own assets to the server and make changes in real time, thereby allowing the composer to work on the game while it's being developed.

In this process, as content developers submit files to or change files on the server, the asset management system keeps track of all the changes. If the developer needs to go back to an older version of a file or a build, the asset management system handles all of the data retrieval. The asset management system archives all the files from all the different versions that are written to the server.

Popular asset management systems for games include SVN, CVS, GIT, and Perforce. Here's a list of some terminology you might see while working with asset management servers:

- **Check Out.** Create a mirror of the build on the asset server by checking out a copy of the latest game build to store it locally on your computer so you're able to play it. Depending on which system you are using, you might also be able to mark files so that the rest of the team can't change them while you're working on them.

- **Commit.** The content developer or composer commits a change to the assets in a build of the game and uploads the file back to the asset server, allowing for distribution to the rest of the team. This is sometimes referred to as "checking in" a file.

- **Add.** Add a file to the game build and upload the new file from your local build to the server.

- **Update.** Copy any changes that have been made to the server to your local copy of the build. This allows you to have the latest assets from all the content developers working on the team.

These tools can be very useful in reviewing the latest changes and builds of a game. Contract composers and sound designers are given access based on their technical abilities and interest in working on the game directly. Many composers rely on the production team to get their assets into the game.

If builds of the game need to be distributed to the composer via snail mail on storage media, it can take a long time to hear your hard work actually incorporated into the game. Many game composers now request access to real-time game builds through the game's asset management system to ensure that they have immediate access and the ability to make changes directly.

Tracking Asset Reviews and Feedback

When presenting work to a client, it's important to keep track of feedback from the developer so that the composer knows which assets need changes and which are final.

Some asset management systems and ticket-based systems have built-in notes for tracking and indicating feedback. Depending on the composer's comfort level with these kinds of technologies, the simplest approach may be to keep a shared Google spreadsheet among the team members that keeps track of the music assets.

The composer and the producer of the game usually work in tandem to work out where and how feedback is delivered. Establishing a virtual paper trail is of extreme importance on projects requiring hundreds or even thousands of music assets. Knowing which one of these assets is approved or needs revisions is important to keeping a project organized and on track.

Naming Conventions

For game design teams to keep track of and organize assets, it's very important to establish naming conventions for all of the assets. If an asset is mislabeled in the game, the error could crash the game when it tries to load that asset. The composer needs to work out a naming strategy for all the music assets that he or she will be creating. Consistency and organization are key aspects in having a naming convention that works.

Most file systems recognize files named with lowercase letters as different assets than files named with uppercase letters. Thus, if you try to replace an asset called "level_01_music" with "Level_01_Music," the whole game might crash when it tries to load the asset and can't find it.

Over the course of the development cycle, the composer may potentially create many variations of the same music cue before it's finally approved. Keeping track of which version is the final asset that needs to be put in the game is crucial. The composer and the game development teams should meet and define a strategy for naming files.

Balancing Compression with Quality

Every game platform has a limited amount of memory and CPU power. These resources are generally divided up between the various game systems, including code, art, sound, and music. Even on the latest generations of consoles, the composer needs to meet with the development team to talk about memory and CPU constraints of the game.

When working on a project, it's important to know the estimated size of the entire project and how much of that memory will be dedicated to music and sound. Although this is largely dependent on the type of game, most games use somewhere between 20 percent and 40 percent of the overall memory footprint for audio assets.

The earlier that the composer begins comparing the size of the music assets against the memory constraints of the game platform, the earlier he or she will be able to develop an appropriate strategy for memory allocation related to the music. Far too many composers have gotten to the end of a project, only to have a portion of their music removed from the game because the music assets proved too large for the platform.

Large games that employ an audio director in addition to the composer will put in memory budget requests well ahead of production. If memory budgets decrease, it is usually due to an emergency in another content discipline—or failure of the developer's audio infrastructure to accurately scope memory allocation.

Composers and sound designers need to balance the memory constraints of the game with the overall quality of the files. Because the quality of the sound files is proportional to the size of those files, composers need to find a good balance between quality and the memory constraints of the game. On games that have limited memory footprints, you may need to squeeze out every last kilobit of each sound file to get it to fit. This may mean adjusting the file compression individually for each sound based on the frequency content in each sound file.

Working out how memory is handled for the music requires discussions with the game developer about the overall resources, memory constraints, and media footprint of the game. During the game development process, it's likely that these discussions will continue and influence the development of the score.

The following sections discuss several different types of memory that composers need to be concerned with.

Physical Removable Storage

Games use a variety of storage devices to deliver content to players. Most retail games are available on a disk-based storage mechanism for consoles, and on cartridge-based memory devices for handhelds. These devices vary widely in how much memory they provide. Following are approximate values for commonly used storage media in games:

- CD: 700MB
- DVD Single Layer (Wii uses a hybrid proprietary DVD): 4.7 GB
- DVD Dual Layer (Xbox 360, PlayStation 2): 8.5 GB
- Blu-Ray Single Layer (PlayStation 3 and 4, Xbox One): 25 GB
- Blu-Ray Dual Layer: 50 GB
- Nintendo DS Cartridge: 8–512MB
- PlayStation Vita Cartridge: 4 GB

Downloadable Games and Onboard Media Storage

Many games in today's marketplace are distributed via the Internet (Steam, Amazon, Xbox Live, Apple's App Store). Hard-core gamers are much more likely to download large games from the Internet (4 GB or more), whereas casual gamers using Apple's App Store are less likely to download games with large memory footprints. According to a 2012 survey that sought to determine iOS game sizes, the average game for iOS has a memory footprint of 60MB.

The overall media storage for a device is also a factor. Low-end iPads have an onboard memory capacity of 8 GB, whereas a typical PC game machine has at least 1 TB of capacity.

Onboard storage is also sometimes used by retail console games because the game may copy elements from the disk over to an internal hard drive or Flash memory storage. When games are able to cache some of their assets on faster memory devices, they can load much faster and composers are able to stream assets more efficiently. This method is used only on very large titles. Since distribution models are moving more toward digital distribution via the Internet, most games are played from the local media storage after they've been downloaded to the device.

In the future, assets for games may exist entirely in the cloud, so that the player doesn't need any onboard memory storage. We probably won't see this model dominate the marketplace for at least 10 years, though.

Onboard Working RAM

The onboard working RAM is one of the most important items that composers need to be concerned with. Music is generally loaded into RAM at the beginning of a level. This RAM also needs to hold other assets in the game, such as art, architecture, code, sound effects, and more. The game development team will work together to allocate these resources based on the type of game.

As a composer, it's extremely important to know how much music you can put into a level based on these memory constraints. Once you know how much RAM is available for music, then you can calculate the minutes of music possible based on the type of compression that you'll be using.

Some games can stream music directly from the hard disk or the removable storage. This ability generally depends on which other elements are part of the game and whether they also need to be loaded from disk during gameplay. Such streaming is more likely to be available when your music is linear and non-interactive.

Online Network Storage

Many Internet-based games load parts of the game as needed by the game itself. For example, while the player is playing Level 1, Level 2 may be loading in the background. Music can be loaded in the background for playback later in the game. The programmer must design this sort of resource juggling into the architecture of the game, but it's a useful strategy when your game has to be loaded in smaller chunks.

If you're loading music from another source—for example, from the Internet through a cloud-based solution—the music constraints are determined by the speed of the Internet connection, rather than by how much disk space is available with a console title.

Voice Considerations

Voice refers to the CPU power needed to play back a single monaural (mono) audio file during gameplay. The number of voices that you'll be able to play back at a single moment will depend on the CPU power of your game platform. Stereo voices increase the CPU load more than mono voice playback; 5.1 surround mixes increase the CPU load even more. If you have a layered score, you'll be increasing the number of voices exponentially for the music.

Sound designers will most likely use more voices in the game than the composer. Consideration needs to be given to reserving voice channels for the music so that the music doesn't disappear when too many sound effects play.

The composer, sound designer, and game development team should customize the voice allocations to suit the game by balancing them with the capabilities of the game platform. These discussions should happen early in the development cycle so that the composer does not create a game score that is impossible to play back due to the constraints of the CPU of the final game platform.

Allocating Time for Programming

No matter how simple the music is for a game, there will be some programming involved in implementing music cues. As the music becomes more complex using interactive music techniques, the programming needs will increase.

In general, two basic processes need to have time resources allocated to the programmer or sound implementer:

- Setting up the overall music framework and interactivity
- Implementing the hooks to play music and change the music at the correct points within the game

Setting Up the Music Framework and Interactivity

Simple interactive music techniques like layering or branching are relatively simple for a beginner programmer to implement into a project. As you add musical complexity and start combining interactive music techniques, however, the amount of time the programmer has to spend creating the overall music framework for the game can grow exponentially.

Programming time can also vary tremendously based on factors such as the experience of the people, the technology, the robustness of the codebase, and a thousand others. Also, debugging can range from a trivial matter to a thorny problem that requires spending several days to track down an issue. The time estimates presented here for the example scenarios are, therefore, only approximate.

A simple-layer music framework may take 3 hours of an experienced programmer's time to implement and debug within the game. A simple crossfade for a branching framework will likely take a similar amount of time. If you want to combine these musical interactive solutions, the time that a programmer will need to spend on them increases at least twofold.

If the music complexity grows large enough, it may save the team money to license the use of an audio middleware engine such as Wwise or Fmod. You can estimate a programmer's time at $100/hour when doing the math about whether licensing an engine is right for your project.

During the game development process, these solutions need to be weighed against the overall budget and time constraints of the project. This requires several planning discussions with the game developer and programmers for the project to assess the needs of the music system.

Implementing the Hooks

No matter how simple or complicated the audio framework for a game is, implementing hooks that trigger or stop music cues takes time. Putting in the hooks is not a complicated process for the programmer, but the more events that trigger sound in a game, the longer it will take the programmer to code those events. Unfortunately, the use of an audio middleware engine generally does not decrease the amount of time needed to place these hooks within the game. This time needs to be outlined in the overall schedule for the game by the game producer and the programmer as early as possible in the development cycle.

As mentioned earlier in the chapter, some game engines have level editors in which audio implementers, sound designers, and sometimes composers can add sound hooks directly in the game editor. Frequently this approach is less expensive than using the programmer's time to add these sound hooks to the game.

Integrating Middleware Solutions

The use of an audio middleware engine such as Wwise or Fmod can decrease the amount of time spent by the programming team to implement a music framework, but it does not eliminate the time the programming team needs to implement this framework or to add the music hooks to the game. Implementation of a middleware framework requires at least 3 to 5 hours of programming time initially to get the middleware solution working in the game. Then, additional time needs to be allocated to debugging. Time also needs to be allocated to add the music hooks throughout the game. Depending on the level of experience of the programmer and team, these times may need to be increased and should be planned for early in the development process to keep the project on schedule.

The use of an audio middleware solution generally lightens the load on the programmers, but it will have the opposite effect on the composer. Unless the game developer provides additional audio resources to support the composer (i.e., audio implementers), the composer's workload will increase, as he or she will be in charge of implementing the musical assets and cues in the middleware engine. The advantage is that the composer will have much more control over how the music is shaped in the game in its musical complexity without having to bother the programmer with a bunch of small requests.

Mixing and Real-Time DSP

Once the assets have been integrated into the game, the composer needs to review those assets to see whether they're playing at the correct volume. In-game mixing of music assets against SFX and dialog is very challenging. There are not many tools that allow you to play the game and change the various levels of the assets in real time. Quite often composers and sound designers change the levels of the sound assets either by changing a variable in an XML document or by loading the sound asset into a sound editor and changing the volume. This is a time-consuming and often frustrating process.

Audio middleware has begun to give audio creators more control over the overall sound mix by being able to run alongside a working build of the game so the composer can mix the game audio assets in real time. These tools are very much in their infancy and should see many advances in the coming years.

Games sometimes also create busing structures for ducking music under dialog using DSP compressors in real time. If your game has this kind of complexity, middleware allows for multiple bus structures and the ability to add DSP on a specific set of audio assets (i.e., SFX, dialog, music).

Another common use of real-time DSP on music used within games is related to a player's health status. If the player's health falls below a certain level, a low pass filter may be applied to the audio of the game to signal that status.

Audio middleware supports a wide range of built-in DSP options, making it easier to create these kinds of effects. If more specialized plug-ins are needed, manufacturers like iZotope have begun to license their plug-ins for use within games. Contact individual software manufacturers to explore the details of such possibilities.

Creating dramatic emotional moments during a game in which the music becomes the focal point while the SFX fade out at a specific time can be time consuming to implement and program. Real-time dramatic mixing within games is at the forefront of the next wave of advances in game audio.

Review

Implementation of music into a game involves setting up the overall music framework and interactivity, as well as implementing the hooks to play music and change the music at the correct points within the game.

Many game engines have sound playback capabilities built into the game level editor itself. This allows the composer or sound designer to place audio objects or events directly in the level or world itself.

Music assets are tracked through asset sheets. Each musical cue should have a description and a plan for how it will be implemented. When creating music assets, you should define when each piece will play, develop a placeholder asset, and have the programmer create a sound hook that will play the asset in the game.

Development of musical assets is an interactive process, in which revisions are made as sounds are tested and heard in gameplay.

Collaborative tools are built around the many game production processes, including scheduling, sharing files and game assets, music review and feedback, and version control.

Every game platform has a different amount of memory and CPU power. These resources are generally divided up between the various game systems, including code, art, sound, and music.

Composers and sound designers need to balance the memory constraints of the game with the overall quality of the files. Because the quality of the sound files is proportional to the size of those files, composers need to find a good balance between quality and the memory constraints of the game.

The use of an audio middleware engine such as Wwise or Fmod decreases the amount of time spent by the programming team to implement a music framework, but it does not eliminate the time needed to implement that framework or add the music hooks to the game.

In-game mixing of music assets against SFX and dialog can be very time consuming and challenging. Audio middleware has begun to allow audio creators more control over the overall sound mix by being able to run alongside a working build of the game so the composer can mix the game audio assets in real time. These tools are very much in their infancy and should see many advances in the coming years.

Exercises

1. Download a middleware game development tool like Unity or GameMaker, and build a simple side-scroller with sound to learn how games are built from the ground up.

2. Visit a local game development company or game jam to shadow a programmer or game producer for a day to learn about how the game development process works on the inside of a game development team.

CHAPTER 24

LARGE-SCALE MUSIC DEVELOPMENT

Composing for a game that requires 15 or more hours of gameplay to finish the experience can pose unique challenges for a composer, owing to the need to score the game as one unified experience. In this chapter we discuss the process of creating a unified compositional experience and presenting it to the player.

Establishing a Unique Creative Direction

Mapping out the score for a AAA game that has 15 or more hours of gameplay is extremely challenging. Many AAA games have between 2 and 3 hours of composed music. If you have a budget to compose 2 hours of music, how would you map this music to the gameplay experience? Games of this scope can also have extremely long development cycles of two years or more. Even if you do your best to map out the music at the beginning of a project, many games will change quite a bit during such a long development cycle.

This chapter focuses on establishing a unique creative vision for your project, setting up criteria for making musical decisions, planning and organization, mapping a musical arc, and meeting the challenges of interactive music on large-scale projects.

The best music scores are the ones that are so inseparable from the game experience that it's almost impossible to play the game without the music, or conversely to listen to the music without thinking of the game. Examples of games with especially memorable scores include the *Mario* series (Koji Kondo), the *Zelda* series (Koji Kondo), *Kingdom Hearts* (Yoko Shimomura), *Dead Space* (Jason Graves), *Halo* (Marty O'Donnell and Michael Salvatori), *Bioshock* (Garry Shyman), *Journey* (Austin Wintory), and the *Final Fantasy* series (Nobuo Uematsu).

The best compositions are not just about musical aesthetics. Compositions in which all musical decisions are based on the story of the game have much more depth than compositions that are solely based on whether you've written a great melody. To use an analogy, it is similar to buying a beautiful apple at the deli, only to find out once you bite into it that the fruit tastes like plastic. The best compositions start with the seed of an idea and build outward. If the vision is purely aesthetic, your composition will not have the same lasting impact as a composition that is well thought out and for which the musical decisions are built around the framework of the story.

Before you begin composing the music, write down in words how you'd like to construct this score. Identify how you might represent the story with your music by including ideas about the tempo, instrumentation, and thematic ideas. Too many new composers begin at the keyboard and find a nice melody before considering what that melody will represent. This process may produce an adequate piece of music, but it will not have the depth and character of a great piece of music. All of the musical decisions that you make for a game—from the tempo, to the ensemble choice, to the articulations—should have a purpose as they relate to the story. These choices will help you create a more effective score that is more integrated into the story instead of listening only for the aesthetic qualities of the music.

There are many ways to innovate compositionally for a game—melodically, harmonically, rhythmically, through the use of dynamics and articulations, through instrument and ensemble choice, through the use of DSP and effects, and many more. In addition, throughout this book you've learned about a variety of compositional techniques that can help you develop a unique vision for the music's interactivity.

Innovation takes time, research, and experimentation. When setting out to create the defining characteristics of your score, take the time to experiment to find the best character and voice to tell the story through music. Many great ideas come from experimentation and failing in a few directions before settling on the one that really works for your game.

The task of composing music for a large game can be extremely daunting. Moreover, if the game developer has given you total creative control over the music, the limitless options can sometimes handicap a composer's ability to write. Begin by setting up a framework for your ideas and tackling smaller pieces or chunks that might define a specific storyline or main idea. Once the ideas or themes are in place, it will be easier to write the majority of the cues based on that framework.

Unification and Planning

Unification is the ability for a score to work seamlessly from beginning to end without the cues sounding as if they were written by multiple composers or came from different albums. The unification of a large score is one of the most difficult challenges for a composer. If the composer and development team agree on an overall creative framework and structure at the beginning of a project, before the first cue is even written, the score is much more likely to function as a single cohesive work that satisfies all the creative goals.

Setting up the overall framework for a successful video game score involves multiple parts:

- Written documentation, including descriptions of the creative direction and the interactive music framework
- Audio style guides, which indicate the overall musical direction of the project
- Asset lists, which identify all musical cues that need to be written for the project
- Overall timeline and schedule
- Mechanism for collaboration and feedback, including a way to share files for distribution and review

This planning should include a clear plan for who will act as the day-to-day contact for composer communication at the developer/publisher, how often the composer will interact directly with the creative stakeholders on the development team, and how and when in-person meetings will take place, if possible. Often, the creative stakeholders may have the final approval in terms of creative direction, but those people will most likely not be on the front lines of providing day-to-day feedback, as they have many other responsibilities vis-à-vis the game.

Once this framework is in place, any asset that is created by the composer needs to be reviewed against the original framework to see whether it satisfies the creative criteria.

If the game developer is reviewing musical cues solely based on whether the individuals of the team like a track or not, instead of basing decisions on whether a piece matches the overall musical framework, it's likely that the project would come off track and the score will feel disorganized. Musical cues should be reviewed with one question in mind—"Does this cue effectively match the overall story we're trying to tell?"—instead of based on whether the individuals on the team like a cue from an aesthetic point of view.

The schedule of the game will be based on milestone dates determined by the senior producer at the game publisher in collaboration with the game developer. The composer's schedule should be mapped out to coincide with those dates. The following steps suggest a typical calendar that a composer might use for a game:

1. Initial planning, including the creation of the audio design document, music framework, and audio style guides

2. Music development, along with in-game implementation and testing of the music

3. Team approvals and revisions requests

4. Continued music development and implementation addressing any revision requests

5. All music assets approved for recording

6. Live recording

7. Preliminary music mixes

8. Ongoing implementation of the music into the game for review

9. Final music revisions

10. Final mixing and implementation of the music assets within the game

Every project will have its own unique needs that will change the way a schedule is built. For instance, the composer may need to record earlier in the development cycle to build instruments that use those recordings, as was the case with Jason Graves's score for *Dead Space* (2008). Usually the live recordings are done after most of the music mockups have been approved to consolidate all the recording sessions together and avoid having to rerecord music because of a revision.

Organization, Revisions, and Backups

In a large AAA title, there may be hundreds of musical assets that you'll need to create. Keeping track of which musical cues have been approved, need revisions, or have yet to be started is incredibly important. Shared documents like the ones that are stored within Google Drive can be an excellent way to share information between the composer and the game development team. But how does the composer keep track of the private sequence files that he or she uses to create these assets?

Everyone who works as part of an audio team must be ultra-organized in keeping track of every file that went into the creation of an audio asset. Musical cues that may have been previously approved may need revising weeks or months later. The composer will need to reload these files and sequences, make changes, and deliver the assets to the client.

Most composers develop a naming scheme and folder structure to organize all the materials for a game. In addition, composers generally keep track of every revision, as a client might request to go back to a previous version of a musical cue later in the project. Defining the naming convention is essential to keep track of these sequences and revisions.

A typical music folder structure for a project might include the following:

- Final Audio Assets
- Work-in-Process Audio Assets
- Audio Style Guide
- Builds of the Game
- Demos
- Instruments
- Movies
- Reference Art
- Samples
- Scores
- Sequences
- Project Documents
- SVN or Perforce Directory

When developing your folder hierarchy, you'll likely need to customize it for the specific project you're working on, adding folders when needed.

warning

BACKUPS!   Many composers have learned the hard way that project backups are essential at every step along during the project. Hard drive failures, broken sequence files, or any number of other problems *will* happen at the most inconvenient times. Composers should be prepared for the worst and make sure that they back up all their files, preferably in multiple locations, at least on a daily basis. Semi-regular *off-site* backups also protect against tragic losses due to theft, fire, or water damage. Likewise, composers are advised to keep a file folder (actual paper) with valuable information like the serial numbers of all their software, iLok passwords, and so on, in case something happens to the studio.

Mapping the Overarching Emotional Arc

When working on a large score, it's easy to get lost in the myriad cues you need to write. Once you've created an asset list in the preproduction phase for all the music cues that you'll be writing for the game, it's important to tag each music cue with the order of playback during the game and its emotional intensity level. This will help you map out the overall emotional arc of the story for each cue that you plan to write.

To create an effective musical score for a game, you need to provide the player with the emotional context of the overall story. If all of your music cues have the same intensity, the player will not be as emotionally involved in the storyline. Music needs contrast: tension and release, loud versus soft, open versus dense. Music is most effective when you show this contrast. For example, players won't perceive something as being loud unless they hear a quiet sound before it.

Put simply, the musical experience must illustrate both the high points and the low points of the emotional arc. Once you've planned out the score, you should graph the musical experience from the beginning of the game to the end, making sure there is contrast in the score.

All of these decisions should be informed by what the game director or lead game designer envisions for the score. Sometimes the game director is happy to take a back seat and let the composer drive this process, so the composer just needs to be clear on how much autonomy he or she has. It's always a balance between the composer's vision based on what he or she understands the director to want, and what the director actually envisions the role of the score to be.

Integration and Follow-Through

Once the composer has completed a musical asset that has been approved by the game developer, it's important for the composer to follow that asset through implementation and hear the music cue in the game itself.

Composers in the video game industry sometimes don't find out that music assets they've created for a game have been implemented incorrectly, don't play at all, or were removed entirely from the game without their knowledge until after the game is released to the general public. It can be extremely frustrating for composers to see their vision of the music destroyed by the implementation.

Usually the responsibility for making sure the sounds are implemented in the right place falls on the sound supervisor, who reports to the audio director of the project. On small projects, the composer and the programmer may be responsible for sorting out placement of the music.

Quality assurance (QA) teams often won't report or track music-related bugs, even when they're provided with instructions and notes from the composer. This is due to the fact that QA testers generally won't recognize if the wrong musical cue is playing in the build. Either the composer or someone on the audio team needs to be responsible for making sure that all music assets play the way that they were designed.

Composers need to be vigilant about tracking each music cue to make sure that it's implemented correctly in the game. Audio QA is generally not an item that a composer thinks to include in an audio proposal, but it is an essential part of making sure that the sounds play as they were designed in the final implementation.

When considering working on a project, the composer should ask the game development team who is responsible for making sure the audio is implemented correctly and whether the composer will need to provide supervision and oversight for this task. These answers may have implications for how the composer budgets the project if the responsibility falls on the composer.

Large-Scale Interactive Music Challenges

Several challenges are unique to creating interactive music frameworks for large-scale games. Although many different genres of video games exist, in the following sections you'll learn about three common AAA game scenarios and the musical challenges associated with each.

Closed System (Games on Rails)

In a closed-world system, the music is created around a story-driven game that has a rail style framework, which allows the player to go down only a single pathway, usually accompanied by checkpoints. Examples of this type of game include the series *Halo*, *Call of Duty*, and *Uncharted*. These games have a sequenced narrative design and allow the composer to create a music score with a set playback order for the musical cues.

Music frameworks that are designed around closed-world game systems are generally excellent at emotionally connecting the player to the story but have more difficulty managing the moment-to-moment experience of the player. Music is generally started at the beginning of an event and fails to respond to the emotional changes within the game until the next checkpoint is reached.

In addition, music frameworks that are built for closed systems tend to push the player out of the experience if the player is stuck on a level or isn't following the path that the game designer expected the player to follow. In these scenarios, the game player typically will break the music engine because the composer had not considered a play tactic that the game player is using.

If the player is stuck in a level, he or she may be forced to listen to a specific piece of music over and over again until the player is able to move forward in the game. This can be exasperating for beginning players, as the music emphasizes their inability to reach the end of the level. Marty O'Donnell, composer of the *Halo* series, has devised a useful solution for this problem: fade out the music if the player is not making progress in the level.

Although technology exists to deal with these kinds of situations, sometimes the implementation fails because the people in charge of designing the adaptive music and scripting system didn't anticipate all of the potential scenarios and develop plans to handle them. Thorough testing after the implementation and any revisions is essential to create the best interactive music score.

Open System (Open-World Games)

In an open-world game system, the player has greater flexibility in terms of changing the order and outcome of a story. Open-world systems generally have a large world that the player can explore at his or her own directive. Examples of this type of game include *World of Warcraft* (2004), *Fallout: New Vegas* (2010), *L.A. Noire* (2011), and *Grand Theft Auto V* (2013).

In an open system, the composer is tasked with creating a music system that will apply to various parts of the game universe. For instance, in *World of Warcraft*, the music system is largely based on the player's location within the game. The music itself acts like background ambience to give the player a feeling of being in the universe but doesn't heighten the emotional connection as events play out—for example, those that might lead to the character's death in the game.

In a game like *Fallout New Vegas*, the music system is location aware. That is, the music is specific to how close the player is to the center of town, and is driven by events that happen within the game world.

Games that trigger music based on game events such as combat or exploration tend to inform a player about a game state through the music. The player, having figured out how the music works, then uses those music mechanics to determine whether there are enemies left to kill instead of the music simply supporting the game's emotional framework.

Combat-Triggered Musical Interactivity

Many games trigger special music cues based on whether the player has entered or exited combat. The question that many music frameworks ignore is how to handle the drama that happens in a fight itself. For instance, many games that have a single battle state cannot change to heighten the emotional level when the player is about to die, or when the player is definitely going to win a battle and has just one enemy left. How should the music engine handle these scenarios?

Because of broad state shifts from a generic explore state to a generic combat state, players are frequently faced with a generic event-driven music score that doesn't emphasize the subtlety that a good music score can provide. To overcome this problem, composers need to spend more time in the creation of a more complex score that can react to a range of subtle changes within states. This complexity in developing a music score is much more time consuming for the composer, but also more satisfying to the player.

When composers are educated on these potential scenarios within games, they can be proactive about making good choices in the creation of an interactive score. They can also follow up with someone on the development team who is working on solutions on the implementation side.

The problems outlined here are challenges that face today's video game composers but will likely be solved by the next generation of composers. Of course, these composers will probably encounter a whole new batch of problems once the current set is resolved.

Review

On large projects, establishing the overall creative framework and structure at the beginning of a project, before the first cue is even written, will lead to a single cohesive score instead of a disparate set of musical cues. Once the framework is in place, any asset can be reviewed against the original framework to see whether it satisfies the creative criteria.

Uniqueness contributes to creating a music score that becomes so identified with the game that it's almost impossible to play the game without thinking about the music, or conversely to listen to the music without thinking about the game. As a composer, you should be able to defend each musical decision that you make by relating it back to the story. The music needs to match the emotional arc of the story.

Organization is key to creating a successful score for a large AAA title. A composer may need to create hundreds of musical assets in such a case, so it's important to keep track of which musical cues have been approved, need revisions, or have yet to be started. Make sure to have a backup system. Hard drive failures, broken sequence files, or any number of other problems *will* happen at the most inconvenient times.

After the music has been implemented in the game, the composer needs to review it and see if it needs revisions. QA teams often won't report or track music-related bugs, even when they're provided with instructions and notes from the composer. Thus it frequently falls on the composer to debug the score once it has been implemented.

Creating excellent interactive scores that include subtle changes can be challenging and time consuming. Broad state changes (i.e., from explore to combat) limit the amount of subtlety in the music. Scores that adapt from moment to moment based on the action instead of broad state changes are more effective at bringing the player into the experience.

Exercises

1. Take an existing AAA game and write down all the music cues heard in the game, mapping their emotional intensity (on a scale of 0–10), the placement of the cue, the duration, and any interactive music components.

2. Compare the cues on the released soundtrack for a game with the game itself. Identify how the cues are used within the game by location, type, function, and interactivity.

3. Generate three interactive music design solutions that creatively solve the problems related to interactive music design in large-scale titles.

4. Play several AAA games and assess their interactive music approach. Discuss how you might improve on the design.

THE BUSINESS OF SCORING MUSIC FOR VIDEO GAMES

CHAPTER 25

THE LIFE OF A VIDEO GAME COMPOSER

Pursuing the career of a composer of video game music requires passion, dedication, and a wealth of knowledge. This chapter focuses on setting your expectations about the industry and explaining what it is like to be a composer. In addition, you'll learn about the various entry points for a composer into the industry and some of the skill sets that a composer will need to succeed in this industry.

A Day in the Life of a Game Composer

This chapter begins by setting up expectations of what it is like to be a composer working in video games. Composers who choose to work in films and games must keep in mind at all times that they are writing music for someone else, not themselves. In the case of games, they are typically writing for the game designer. If they are able to compose a piece of music that matches the vision of the game designer, then they'll be successful.

Some composers are better off as a songwriters or as writers of classical music, where the composer's vision outweighs any other opinions. Successful composers know that their vision is not necessarily as important as the person who is ultimately paying for the music. Composing music for games entails a delicate balance between offering a creative vision and melding it with the overall vision of the game.

Beyond the collaborative process of working with a team, successful composers have many entrepreneurial skills. Many composers have to spend much of their time networking and selling themselves to game developers for project opportunities. On average, composers may spend as much time looking for work as they do composing. Ultimately, success as a composer in the gaming industry means being able to do what you love (composing music) and being able to pay your rent every month.

> ### note
> Direct solicitation of work is sometimes not an option with mid-size to large projects. Having good representation or business development help can be essential to freeing up the composer's time. Cold-calling an audio director during crunch time usually leads to bad results. Most composers who are starting out have to wear many hats, and representation may not be an option at this stage in their careers. In these cases, it's important to develop business acumen and good sales and marketing skills. These skills are discussed in detail in Chapter 29.

More specifically, what is a composer focused on at any given time while working? What follows is a general list of tasks that a composer may face, from meeting contacts in the beginning, to pitching a job, to dealing with setbacks encountered when working in the industry. To make this list slightly more fun, I've added points to show the value of each task like an RPG (role-playing game) would do:

1. Network to meet possible future clients. Pitch your compositional skills. +10 points.
2. Call your contacts to search for games that are starting up. +10 points.
3. Get rejected; try again. –30 points.
4. Convince a client to pay you for your music. Collect self-esteem and go directly to the next step.

5. Meet with the client and conceptualize the music. +2 points.

6. Experiment with musical ideas. +2 points.

7. Establish creative direction for the music. +10 points.

8. Write music. +5 points.

9. Meet the client and review the music. +5 points.

10. Revise, revise, and revise. +10 points.

11. Get rejected on a piece of music. –20 points.

12. Meet the client and get assets approved. +50 points.

13. Write music, revise, and repeat. +30 points.

14. Supervise the implementation of your music. +100 points.

15. Finalize all assets. Level up!

16. Bill the client. +5000 points.

17. Wait for the check. –200 points.

18. Organize yourself. +1 point.

19. Create new instruments, and optimize sequencer template. +1 point.

20. Buy new software. +1 point.

21. Pay taxes and contribute to retirement. +5000 points.

22. Give back to the industry by speaking at an event. +2000 points.

23. Repeat.

The Business of Scoring Games

To help you better understand music composition within games, this section explores the video game industry in terms of market share, game production and development, and education as it relates to video game music composers.

Size of the Industry

The video game industry currently earns $60 billion in annual revenues on a worldwide basis. Included in that total are revenues from games of many different sizes and genres. Game consoles like the PlayStation, Wii, and Xbox offer players a wide range of games. Social media sites like Facebook embrace games such as *The Sims* and *Farmville*, which have millions of daily users. There are more than 500,000 mobile apps for iOS, half of which are games.

The 2014 Game Developer's Conference hosted more than 24,000 game professionals. Almost 1,000 of these attendees worked in audio. The AES Game Conference in London hosted more than 300 audio professionals in 2013. The video game industry directly supports several thousand audio professionals at any given time.

As the game industry grows, composers and game designers need to know about the latest techniques to create interactive scores for games. Composers for these games need to be ready to deliver advanced interactive scores to keep pace with the rest of the industry. This book aims to be a reference point to bring the music aspects of modern gaming into focus.

Music is about the emotional storytelling in games. Many prominent directors in the film and game industries stress the importance of music to the experience, and are quoted as saying that the audio component represents at least 50 percent of the experience.

Beyond games, composers can also look to many ancillary industries that use interactive music techniques. For example, such techniques may be encountered in museum installations, websites, theme park rides, children's toys, computer and mobile UI, and live ensemble shows (circuses and dance theater), among others.

Game Development

High-end game budgets rival film budgets, approaching $60 million to $80 million. As game budgets have grown over the last 30 years, the investment in audio budgets has grown as well. This has allowed many contemporary console titles to use live orchestral musicians to play their scores.

Platform holders like Sony, Microsoft, and Nintendo grant licenses to developers to work on their game platforms (Xbox, PlayStation, Wii). Publishers like Ubisoft, Electronic Arts, and Sega provide financial and production support to game developers. Game developers such as Bungie, Naughty Dog, and Irrational employ creative and production talent to make the games. Sometimes the lines are blurred, as game publishers and game developers might be one and the same (e.g., Microsoft Studios).

Game budgets range from amateur games created at home for next to nothing, to small web games ($20,000–$30,000), to large casual games ($100,000–$500,000), to mega-console games that can have enormous budgets ($30 million or more). Although there is an emphasis in the media on big-budget titles, large console games represent only 20 percent of the entire games market. Social, mobile, and casual games all have incredible needs for audio and music.

COMPOSER PERSPECTIVE

Yoshino Aoki

I would like to take this opportunity to speak from a female perspective, but in actuality, while I am working, I do not think gender matters so much. Oftentimes, I probably forget about it. I do not think gender matters when you are creating something, and luckily for me, I have not felt any gender bias at my workplace.

In that respect, I think the industry is very straightforward, making it a comfortable work environment for women. However, I do think it is an occupation that is very difficult and demanding if you are also raising a child. I think in the eyes of those composer mothers, I have not had a very challenging time in my career. I really admire the strength of these women.

I believe if you want to be in this industry for a long time, you need a lot of mental and emotional strength. Many of the women in this field possess a sort of "chivalrous spirit" in a good way. You do not need to distinguish or separate yourself based on femininity in this industry.

In a typical budget, audio may account for 5 to 10 percent of the overall cost to make the game. The audio team for a game encompasses a wide array of expertise, from music to sound design. The percentage of the overall development budget dedicated to audio varies significantly depending on the platform and the size of the game. The following list identifies some of the related creative and production costs associated with each game audio discipline:

- **Music:** Composers, musicians, orchestrators, copyists, recording studios
- **Sound Design:** Sound designers, field recording, editing, studio time, specialized equipment rentals (e.g., period weapons, race cars)
- **Dialog:** Acting talent, recording, engineering and editing fees, localization costs for multiple languages
- **Implementation:** Audio programmers, scripters, mixing engineers

With the enormous growth of the game industry, the market has also become crowded with talented composers and sound designers looking for success in these careers.

note

Leading independent composers may come with entire teams of people who help them execute on projects (e.g., assistants, mixers, orchestrators). That makes it easier for the composer to provide a package price to a developer or publisher, which includes both the normal fees associated with these other individuals and a production fee for handling the logistics of coordinating these individuals.

Game Development Education

As an outgrowth of the commercial success of video games, universities have begun to develop courses for teaching the skills necessary for game development and offering degrees for about the last decade. Universities with successful game design programs include the University of

Southern California (USC), Cornell University, New York University (NYU), Savannah College of Art and Design (SCAD), Georgia Tech, and many more. Beyond the subject of game design, these programs include courses in many of the disciplines of game development, including art and illustration, 3D modeling, programming, and game production.

In addition, music institutions have followed suit by offering game audio courses to cater to the needs of the game industry. For example, Berklee College of Music, Ex'pression, USC Thornton, University of California at Los Angeles (UCLA), Pinnacle, NYU Steinhardt, Pacific Northwest Film Scoring Program, Leeds College of Music, and The Arts Institutes all offer game audio and/ or scoring classes. Game development education is an excellent way to learn about the game industry and gain specific skills necessary for working in games.

Because game audio is such a diverse field filled with many different skill sets, it is particularly well suited for master's degree programs. The field of game audio development generally requires all the knowledge that a person needs to be a professional composer, but then the composer needs the additional specialized audio expertise required for composing audio for games.

Most game audio professionals agree that it may take four years just to understand the basics, then another several years to get acquainted with the specialized needs of the game industry. In the next section you'll read about how to be successful in game audio development.

> ## tip
>
> In 2008, the audio organization Interactive Audio Special Interest Group (IASIG) undertook a project called the *Game Audio Education Curriculum Guidelines*. Within the completed documents is a list of skills compiled by game audio professionals and educators that defines the skills required for game audio careers. This skills list is an excellent resource to help you with your game audio education.

Working In-House versus Out-of-House

In professional game audio, there are three different pathways when working with game developers: working in-house full time, working as a part-time contractor, or working freelance with your own company. In many cases, you may not have much choice about whether you fit into one category or another. For composers, most work is contracted. There are in-house composer positions in the marketplace, but it's much more common for sound designers to work in-house and composers to work on a freelance basis. Smaller game developers may employ in-house composers who are responsible for all audio, composing, and sound design. In this section you'll learn about the advantages and disadvantages of each route.

In-House Composer

In-house composer positions are some of the most sought after in the industry. In-house composer roles are also rarer than the opportunities in the other pathways. There are several successful examples of in-house composers working for developers, including Marty O'Donnell, formerly of Bungie, and Koji Kondo at Nintendo. In Japan, several game developers have kept a roster of composers on staff, including Capcom. Although working in-house for a game developer is rare, working in-house for a music production company is much more common.

The biggest advantage of working in-house is having a steady paycheck and securing company benefits. Companies may offer their employees benefits such as health insurance, disability insurance, and retirement plans. In addition, in-house composers do not need to worry about tax withholding, as the company automatically deducts taxes from their pay. Because they are working for a company, they may not have as much choice in the equipment, software, and studio choices that are made.

Another excellent advantage of working in-house with a developer is the ability to interact with the team on a daily basis. Most in-house composers believe a 100 percent in-house audio department will create a better product for that reason, compared to using external composers/audio people who aren't "living and breathing" the game along with the rest of the team.

One of the disadvantages of working in-house is that you have no choice in the type of projects that you're asked to work on, limiting the variety of music you might compose. In addition, there is not much flexibility in scheduling your own hours. Last, because you are working on a limited number of titles, the success or failure of those projects may have more impact on your career than if you were working on many different titles as a freelancer.

Once you secure a gig working in-house, rarely do you need to go out and sell your services to new clients. By comparison, sales and marketing are a large part of working as a freelance composer.

Audio directors are more likely to be hired as in-house employees than are composers. Many audio directors were composers in the past, but have chosen to lead entire teams of composers and sound designers for a game developer. In-house composers in the western United States often have a dual role as overall audio director and composer (e.g., Marty O'Donnell, formerly of Bungie; Russell Brower at Blizzard).

When working in-house for a music production company, composers often learn tricks and techniques from the composers around them. Because they are all audio experts, they share knowledge more readily than if they worked for a game developer with fewer audio experts. In a way, working for a music production company allows composers to continue their education.

Part-Time Contractor

An increasing number of companies are opting to hire people to work as part-time contractors. A composer or sound designer who is a contractor is hired for a nonpermanent position. For the company, this approach offers several advantages over hiring a permanent employee, including not offering benefits to the employee and being able to let the employee go when the project has finished or loses financing. These employees usually work on the payroll and receive a W2 tax form at the end of the year.

Contractors typically work full time on a project for a period of 6 to 8 months or more. This length varies tremendously, however, based on the size of the project and its complexity. After that time, the contractor will need to find another gig. Forging relationships and leveraging contacts is an important aspect of securing the next project. While working on the project, it's important to continue making progress on finding the next opportunity.

There are not many advantages to working as a part-time contractor except that these people tend to connect with lots of people while working on gigs, allowing them to leverage these contacts when looking for a new position. Another advantage can be the time off between jobs, which allows the composer to regroup if it's been an especially challenging project.

Contractors need to provide their own benefits and worry about retirement planning. From a practical point of view, these considerations can be very challenging to fund in the early part of your career. As your gigs start to become more lucrative over time, it's easier to invest in your own benefits.

Some composers have their own companies. If the developer pays you as a company, it won't withhold taxes, which means you'll need to put aside taxes for the government yourself. This route also confers some significant tax benefits, as you are able to write off equipment and software expenses as if you were working freelance. Many benefits are also tax deductible, so it's worth talking about this issue with an entertainment tax accountant.

Freelance and Your Own Music Production Company

Freelancers typically have their own small company that is hired by the game developer to work on a project. Freelancers have the most flexibility with their time and find many different kinds of work. Game developers typically pay them without taking out taxes, so composers need to be responsible about putting aside money for taxes. Health and retirement benefits are also the responsibility of the freelancer. Developers that hire companies or freelance composers to work on their projects issue 1099 tax documents to the composers at the end of the year.

Freelancers enjoy the benefit of being able to work on several projects at once, frequently with different developers. This allows more variety in the compositional material in terms of genre and style.

COMPOSER PERSPECTIVE

Duncan Watt

Successful contracting boils down to a few simple ideas—good communication, mutual trust, and a solid team vision. Bad communication makes bad games, and can be a creativity killer. Experienced teams keep good documentation, set up a good communication pipeline early on, and focus on keeping contractors aware of the inevitable changes during the development process.

Establishing trust is the key to creativity when collaborating. Trust goes both ways: some teams have had to deal with difficult contractors, so it may take some time to establish a good working relationship. Personal relationships and a positive attitude can help move this process along, as can hitting deadlines—and being willing to adapt and change direction as the project dictates.

In my experience, most issues revolve around personality-based decisions. There are always some people on the team who are more interested in themselves or their careers than the project or the player experience, and dealing with these people is part of the life of a contractor.

Great projects are the result of good team vision. All the cool ideas in the world don't matter if everyone's pulling the project in different directions. It's important to always take the team's vision into account when making creative decisions—making a game is a collaborative undertaking.

Contracting with a game team can be challenging. In the end, with open, accurate two-way communication, good vision, and a solid production pipeline in place, both the contractors and the team can focus on the one thing everyone wants: to make a great game.

Entrepreneurship is a key ingredient for a successful freelance composer. These composers must combine business savvy and sales and marketing expertise with the creative aspects of being a composer. Many composers choose to partner with others who complement their skills either in the creative side of things or on the business side.

Frequently composers end up being freelance by default because it may be difficult to secure an in-house position. Composers should be prepared to sell and market themselves to game developers in case a job doesn't materialize.

Table 25.1 shows the primary differences between the various pathways followed by composers.

Table 25.1   Comparison of Composer Paths

	In-House Composer	Part-Time Contractor	Freelance Composer
Benefits	Yes	No	No
Flexible schedule	No	No	Yes
Variety of work	Very little	Very little	Lots
Work environment	Team	Team	Solo
Taxes withheld	Yes	Yes	No
Sales required	None	Some	Frequent

Skill Sets

Many skills are required for working in game audio. The kinds of tangible skills you should develop to help you achieve success in your career composing for games are discussed here:

- **Aesthetics and Creative Vision.** First and foremost, composers need to be able to generate ideas. The game development team will look to their composer to lead creative decisions about the score. It's important to have plenty of music knowledge, both contemporary and historical, to help inform these decisions. In addition, if you want to be one of the top composers, you'll need to cultivate your creative vision to create innovative scores for games. This requires fearlessness in presenting new ideas and experimentation. The best creative ideas tend to be iterations of experiments from trying to create something new.

- **Audio and Digital Production Skills.** Audio production skills are necessary for composers. Many video game composers record instruments for their compositions themselves as well as mix their own tracks. In addition, composers need to deliver files to the developer in a certain file type and specification. These fundamental procedures require a whole host of aural knowledge, including acoustics, recording, signal flow, microphones, DAW expertise, editing, mixing, DSP, surround, mastering, audio formats, file conversions, batch converting, and archiving.

- **Compositional Skills.** It probably goes without saying that a successful composer knows quite a bit about music theory, melodic and harmonic construction, narrative development in a piece, arranging, and orchestration. In addition, composers today need to be able to perform extensive mockups of music regardless of whether live musicians are placed on tracks. Therefore, it is equally important that composition skills include sequencing expertise, synthesis techniques, virtual instrument construction, sampling fundamentals, and MIDI fundamentals.

- **Implementation Skills.** Although not essential to be successful in video game composition, implementation skills are incredibly useful for setting yourself apart from the pack and offering additional value and expertise to the game development team. As the market becomes more competitive, familiarization with audio middleware (Fmod,

Wwise), 3D middleware (UDK, Unity3d), version control systems (Perforce, SVN), asset management, and databases is becoming key to success in the crowded field of video game composers.

- **Teamwork.** The ability to work as part of a team is probably the most important skill to hone as a composer. As a composer, you'll need to manage the many different personality types on a project as well as be able to take feedback and criticism. Pulling a team together to make unified decisions about the audio can be challenging. Team-building skills can help realize the creative vision and audio goals through the game development process.

- **Entrepreneurial, Industry, and Business Skills.** Business skills are important for a composer. Working on your own demands that you take responsibility for your career without someone watching over you, reminding you what to do next. It's important for independent composers to be entrepreneurial and outgoing. Other business skills that an independent composer should be familiar with include organization, budgeting, scheduling, sales, and marketing, as well as creating contracts, proposals, and demo reels.

- **Sound Design.** Although sound design is not an essential skill to find success as a composer, developers of many small projects think of all the components of game audio as one thing. That is, they don't think of sound design as different from music, or even from dialog. Typically, these smaller projects hire a single composer to manage all of these disciplines at the same time. Knowing a little bit about how to create sound effects and record dialog can go a long way toward helping you win those jobs when you're first starting out. Sound design skills include Foley, field recording, sound manipulation techniques, DSP, and editing skills.

  Sound design is also increasingly being used by composers to augment their music palettes. Games like *Limbo* (2010) and *Amnesia: The Dark Descent* (2010) take advantage of sound design techniques to create extra-diegetic emotional contexts for much of the game's story.

- **Knowledge of Video Game Structure and Mechanics.** Knowing how games work is an essential skill for composers. Because composers will need to discuss game structure with the game development team to produce a good score, they'll need to be conversant with basic game mechanics, structure, production, game platforms, and team interaction.

note

Sales skills are important at almost every level of being a composer, whether you're just starting out working as a contractor selling to small game developers, or even working in-house selling budgets to executive producers and stakeholders. Most composers find sales tasks to be their least favorite activity, but sales skills are a necessity if you want to succeed as a composer.

Music Production Companies

A music production company is defined as a group of composers or sound designers who work together. Because the amount of work required for some of the biggest game titles is enormous, many game developers choose to work with a production company.

Music production companies offer game developers a wider array of musical talents. One of the most famous music production companies is Hans Zimmer's Remote Control in Los Angeles. It provides music for a wide range of media, including films and games. Because the group works collaboratively, its members are able to explore more directions simultaneously, offering game developers more options.

The advantage of working for a music production company early in your career is that you can continue your music education by observing the tricks and techniques of the other composers working around you.

Internships as Entry Points

Numerous successful composers today began their careers as interns working for composers, music production companies, developers, or publishers. Working as an intern can be a valuable experience in the industry that may lead to future employment. There are advantages and educational opportunities for people who want to enter into the game audio industry through internships.

Learning Experience

Many composers expect young interns to work just as hard as they did when they were interns, running errands, getting coffee, answering the phones, and so on. Successful interns need to have a good attitude about working hard for little or no pay. Some composers see it as a rite of passage to make it to the next level.

An internship involves a combination of hard work and education. Looking over the shoulder of a composer can be an incredible learning experience. Internships can vary tremendously in value, and sometimes the balance between learning and hard work is not optimal. Although higher education tries to educate students on what the real world is like, an internship provides insight into how the industry actually works. This experience can be crucial in helping the intern get a realistic portrait of the industry from best practices to collaboration.

Many states are tightening rules on internships, demanding that interns be paid unless the experience is overwhelmingly educational. Specifically, if the intern is doing tasks that would otherwise be performed by a paid employee (even "getting coffee"), then the intern must be paid.

Unfortunately, the music industry has a history of taking advantage of interns, and you may encounter such bad behavior from music employers. Even this book's author had the experience of being taken advantage of when an intern. If you are in this position, weigh your options carefully and know that it may be in your best interest to find other work or report the behavior.

Relationships

One of the biggest benefits of working at an internship is the ability to make contacts and create relationships that might lead to future work. Because our industry is based largely on recommending others' skills, having people in your corner is pivotal in ensuring your success. While working as an intern, you'll meet all kinds of people in the production chain, and it's important to remember that these are the same people you'll be seeing throughout your career. Make sure to have a positive, friendly disposition to connect with them.

Job Conversions

Occasionally, companies will hire interns to work for them full time after their internship ends. The key to securing such a position is to understand from the company's perspective why it would hire a new employee. A company needs to justify every expense. If you can save the company money in a quantifiable way, it will be more likely to hire you.

Companies will often have a set of duties that you need to complete each day. If you complete these duties quickly, managers will need to come up with other duties to keep you busy. If you make your own list of possible duties you could perform after you've accomplished your assigned tasks, you'll save these managers even more time. The best interns find tasks that will help the company in some way. Discover ways to improve the work environment. Create new time-saving ways of working. Interns who take this kind of initiative are the ones who get hired. Just be sure to bring your list to the manager for approval before implementing your suggestions.

Here's a list of ideas that might help companies save money:

- Create a library of instrument and drum loops from older sequences and demos.
- Find a better mechanism for sorting sounds on disk.
- Create instruments that the composer can use in his or her current projects.
- Record new sounds for the company's sound library.
- Label everything so it's easier for composers to work in the studio.

The best interns stay longer and work harder than anyone else, inventing and inspiring the people around them with new ideas. Make sure to fit into the culture, and recognize that there is a difference between helping make people's lives easier and being a nuisance by pushing your ideas on people. Find the right moment to speak up, but otherwise make yourself invisible to the process by doing your job really well.

Music Libraries

A music library is a collection of music that can be licensed for use in games and other media (e.g., commercials, films, industrial uses). Over the past several decades, the music library business has grown enormously.

In the past, music libraries were generally thought of as having low-quality music production or as mostly synthesizer music without live instruments. Many of today's modern music libraries (e.g., APM, Killer Tracks, Firstcom, Sonoton, 615 Music) have thousands of high-quality pieces with high-quality production and live musicians on their tracks. The gap between the quality of a custom composed score versus these libraries has become much smaller. In fact, some games in the marketplace have used music libraries for their entire scores, including the score for the widely successful title *Braid*.

The existence of high-quality, inexpensive music libraries has huge implications for composers, including replacing the independent composer entirely or providing revenues for the composer of the library.

Justifying Composer Fees

Game developers see costs as a primary reason to consider using a music library. Because of the inexpensive nature of music libraries, a game developer might not understand why a composer should command such high rates for a custom score.

As the quality of library music has increased, some games have begun to consider using music libraries because they are inexpensive compared to hiring a composer. Libraries can provide games with high-quality music for little cost.

If a composer is not able to write music that is better than a library track, why should the developer spend the extra money? It's important for composers to be able to explain why a custom score is better than one from a library. Here are some reasons why hiring a music composer may justify the added expense:

- **Score Unification.** Custom scores offer up musical themes, instrumentation, and genres that can be consistent throughout the game.

- **Better Synchronization.** The synchronization of licensed music in a game context is difficult because the music timing cannot be customized to a scene. A custom interactive score will allow the ability to hit specific moments in the gameplay.

- **Interactive Music.** Most music libraries contain only a single version of a track, so it's difficult to offer any kind of musical interactivity within a game if such libraries are used.

- **Exclusive.** A custom score is written exclusively for the game. The disadvantage of using a music library is that many music libraries offer nonexclusive licenses. Thus the music that you heard in a game may eventually end up in a television commercial, which takes away from the value of a game.

Additional Income Streams

As a positive for composers, because of the prevalence of music libraries in all media, composers can easily write music for music libraries as a secondary income source. The income from music libraries is much smaller than the pay for a gig working on an actual game or film. Usually the income from music libraries is derived from licensing or royalties for the use of your music.

Without the larger payout, composers who write for music libraries have to write a *lot* of music before doing so might become lucrative. Typically, when writing music for a music library, the composer signs over all of the publishing rights, making it difficult for him or her to use that music for something else in the future.

Review

Composers who choose to work in films and video games must keep in mind at all times that they are writing music for someone else, not themselves.

The video game industry earns $60 billion in annual revenues on a worldwide basis. Game budgets range from amateur games created from home for next to nothing, to small web games ($20,000–$30,000), to large casual games ($100,000–$500,000), to mega-console games that can have enormous budgets ($30 million or more).

In-house composers have access to company benefits, while freelance composers have more flexibility with the projects they're working on.

Many skills are required for a successful career in game audio, including creative vision, audio production skills, compositional skills, implementation skills, teamwork, entrepreneurship, sound design, and knowledge about game design.

A music production company is defined as a group of composers or sound designers who work together.

Numerous successful composers today began their careers as interns working for composers, music production companies, developers, or publishers. Successful interns need to have a good attitude about working hard for little or no pay. Some composers see this as a rite of passage to make it to the next level. The interns who get hired after their internships are over are the ones who were able to think about how to save the company money.

Custom scores have numerous advantages over library music, including score unification, better synchronization, interactivity, and exclusive licensing through work for hire agreements.

Exercises

1. Interview successful composers to get their perspectives about working freelance versus in-house. Ask them about the most important skills that you should learn to be successful as a composer for video games.

2. Audit a commercial music library for quality and the types of music offered. Is the library missing any particular genres? Does it offer variations on the same cue?

3. Speak to an internship manager at a company to find out which qualities determine whether the company would hire someone at the end of an internship.

CHAPTER 26

CONTRACTS, RIGHTS, AND WORK FOR HIRE

In this chapter, you'll explore the paperwork and agreements involved with composing music for a game. You'll learn about the concept of music for hire and discover how it applies to music copyrights. In addition, you'll explore the various kinds of documents you'll encounter as a composer, including music contracts, non-disclosure agreements, and various tax documents.

The Legal Side of Composing

The job of a video game composer involves more than just writing music. It also includes being a business person, a sales person, a computer technologist, a designer, an amateur programmer, and a music expert. This chapter explores the business side of composing for video games, including the various contracts and agreements that you'll encounter.

Composers encounter numerous legal documents when they first begin a job. For example, they may be asked to sign a non-disclosure agreement, and later they may sign a contract for employment. This chapter aims to get you acquainted with some of these legal documents but is not meant to replace the services of a lawyer who can offer good legal advice.

When first starting out as a composer in the industry, you might not have a lot of extra funds to spend on legal advice. You'll probably need that money for rent and electricity. All composers should know the basics of assessing agreements they'll receive when composing for games. Although lawyers are useful, their services can sometimes be prohibitively expensive when you're first starting out. A friend of the family who's an attorney and can give you free legal advice can be indispensable when your bank account is low.

I have signed many documents without legal support. Sometimes I have signed agreements that I have regretted because of provisions that I missed in the original agreement. It's likely that over the course of your career, you will also sign agreements that you will later regret. This is normal, and should be expected. Most successful composers can tell you about projects that they have done that had lousy contracts associated with them. You will gain new wisdom with every document and every project you complete.

The most important thing is to ask lots of questions about every agreement. If you don't understand a clause in a contract, ask the game developer about it and get answers to your questions so that when you see it again you'll know what it is. Of course, when you're asking the game developer to interpret contract language for you, you should note that the explanation is coming from the opposing party.

Online, you can find excellent generic contracts and agreements from Game Audio Network Guild (GANG; http://www.audiogang.org) that can be helpful when a game developer doesn't have a standard music contract. You can modify these documents for the specific project that you're working on to make sure you are compensated properly and to protect your music.

Non-disclosure Agreements

A non-disclosure agreement (NDA) is usually one of the first documents you'll sign before beginning a new project. An NDA is an agreement between two parties to keep all information and materials related to a game or project secret. This agreement is required by many game developers and publishers before they can reveal any information about a game or project.

Non-disclosure agreements are meant to protect the company's *intellectual property* or ideas from being stolen by another developer. If another company steals the game idea or mechanic, and is able to bring the game to market before the initial company, there is little recourse for the company with the original idea. There are lots of pieces of the game that can be copyrighted, including all the art, music, code, specifications, and design documents that go into the game. In contrast, the abstract "idea" of the game and methods of gameplay are not covered by U.S. copyright law:[1]

> Copyright does not protect the idea for a game, its name or title, or the method or methods for playing it. Nor does copyright protect any idea, system, method, device, or trademark material involved in developing, merchandising, or playing a game. Once a game has been made public, nothing in the copyright law prevents others from developing another game based on similar principles.

The non-disclosure agreement protects any materials, conversations, technologies, software, and ideas that the developer reveals to the composer candidate. It spells out the legal recourse and compensation of the development company if the materials are not kept secret. These provisions might include the composer being fired from a project or paying monetary compensation awarded by a court for the damages incurred.

Before beginning a project, the game developer or publisher sends a non-disclosure agreement to the composer to sign. There is typically no compensation involved when signing this agreement, as it is usually required during the initial contact stage, well before the composer or potential employee actually has the job. While the company is evaluating whether it will hire the candidate, it will likely reveal information about the project, which will need to be kept secret—hence the NDA.

As part of evaluating whether the composer is right for the project, the game developer may ask the composer to write demos that relate to the project. If the non-disclosure document is in place, then the game developer is free to reveal information about the project to the composer without the fear that the composer will steal the idea and bring it to another developer.

Legal protection of ideas is extremely important in software and hardware development. Leaks of ideas can have disastrous results, leading to complex court battles and monetary compensation. It's important to realize that when a composer signs a non-disclosure agreement, he or she must keep this information totally secret and not speak about it with anyone except for people directly related to the project.

In large companies that are working on multiple projects at a time, employees may sign NDAs that apply to only one of the projects. Thus they may be required to keep materials secret from other employees of the same company.

---

1. http://www.copyright.gov/fls/fl108.html

Materials that are distributed among a non-disclosed team are frequently watermarked on an individual basis. Then, if a copy of the file leaks to the public, the developer can trace the source of the leak and invoke legal measures if necessary.

For composers working on various games, it's important not to reveal any information or technology from one project to another. In addition, it's important for composers to remember to password-protect computers that are being used for a project in case they get stolen or hacked.

A standard NDA is a one-way agreement from the game developer to the composer or potential employee that is intended to protect the assets and intellectual property of the developer. What if you as the composer want to protect the ideas, methodology, and technology that you reveal to the game developer? This type of agreement, which is usually known as a *mutual non-disclosure agreement* (mutual NDA), legally protects both parties.

NDAs are a fairly standard practice throughout the game industry. In fact, you may be asked to sign an NDA if you walk into the entrance of a game developer's building. This measure is intended to protect the company if you see intellectual property on a whiteboard, or overhear a conversation about an unreleased game that could potentially damage the company if revealed to the public or another game developer.

In general, these agreements are standard and don't require a legal expert for their review before you sign them. Lawyers are extremely expensive, and you might go broke if you have one review every NDA that you receive. Look over the document carefully and if you have questions, first ask the game developer for clarification. If you are concerned that the company is taking advantage of you, check with a lawyer who has experience in the video game industry before signing.

Music Rights and Work for Hire

When you compose a new piece of music for yourself, you own all the rights to that music. The sound recording and the composition can both be copyrighted. If you used hired musicians to play your music, then they may have granted you the unlimited use of that performance in that recording in exchange for a monetary fee under a *work for hire* (WFH) agreement. Technically, the performance is considered a derivative work because you wrote the music and they recorded it.

There are two ways a game developer or game publisher can use that music in a video game:

- You can grant a license for the use of that music to the game developer or game publisher.
- You can reassign the ownership rights of that piece of music to the game developer or game publisher under a work for hire agreement.

A license agreement is typically used when a piece of music has already been finished and the developer wants to use that music in a game. In games such as *Grand Theft Auto V* (2013), for example, licensed music is used for the in-car radio. In exchange for monetary or promotional compensation, this music is licensed in perpetuity for use within the game.

Most music that is custom composed specifically for a video game is contracted under a work for hire agreement. Under a WFH agreement, the composer transfers the ownership rights to the game developer or game publisher. In addition, the composer warrants that the music is completely his or hers to sell and is free of any copyright infringement. The game developer or game publisher is then considered the legal owner of the music composition, not the contractor or employee.

When you as the composer assign all rights to a piece of music to a game developer or game publisher under a WFH agreement, you forfeit the rights to collect any additional revenue for that music. These agreements may also limit your ability to use your own music to promote yourself by including the music on demo reels or on your own website. If your agreement is on a WFH basis, you might want to consider asking for these additional rights.

Unlike much of the film industry, the video game industry doesn't have a common system in place for paying out royalties based on the success of the game. Game developers and publishers prefer to own all the content that is produced for the game so they don't have to worry about reusing any assets for marketing purposes, sequel titles, or expansions. In film or television, by comparison, a composer might receive another payment for a second use of the music. In games, almost all music is considered work for hire, for which the composer has assigned all rights to the music to the game developer or game publisher.

If you're working with a small developer, music that a game developer or game publisher owns from a WFH agreement is generally not registered with a performing rights organization (PRO) like Broadcast Music, Inc. (BMI) or American Society of Composers, Authors and Publishers (ASCAP). As a consequence, they will be missing out on a money-making opportunity if the music from the game is performed or broadcast. In addition, the game developer or game publisher cannot collect the author royalties related to these pieces of music. Performance royalties are paid 50 percent to the music publisher and 50 percent to the music composer. In many cases the music composer's royalties disappear back into the larger BMI and ASCAP money pool to distribute to other music if they haven't been registered to a composer.

If you're working with a large third-party publisher or platform holder like Microsoft, Electronic Arts, Activision, or Sony, it will register works appropriately with the PRO.

Unfortunately, when negotiating with a smaller game developer or game publisher, it may be difficult to retain publishing rights because the company is generally new to music publishing and might fear that this practice will cost it more money down the road. In actuality, registering music with a PRO could bring the game developer or game publisher royalties in the future from secondary use of the music in broadcast, film, or television.

When you grant a license for the use of your music instead of signing a WFH agreement, you might be able to keep possession of some music rights in the agreement. For example, you might be able to retain the music publishing and composer royalties that might be garnered from broadcast and performance.

When you hire musicians to play on your music, it's important that you obtain a separate signed contract or waiver from each musician stating that you own the performance. You will then own all the rights to the given sound recording, allowing you to sell it to the developer; the individual musicians also will not be able to contact the developer about getting paid. Game developers do not like being approached out of the blue by the musicians who played on a piece of music and demand additional payment or royalties. This is definitely bad for future business with that developer. Note that some game developers and game publishers will contract musicians to play on your compositions directly, in which case they'll get their own waivers signed.

The Project Contract

The project contract is an agreement between a game developer or game publisher and a composer who will provide the music for a project. Contracts are typically filled with legalese, which can make these documents difficult to read. The first contract that you encounter from a game developer can be a little intimidating. These contracts are not meant to confuse you, but rather to make sure that agreement is solid and specific about the work, the compensation, and the transfer of rights. Neither the composer nor the game developer wants any loopholes in the contract that allow one party or another to have the upper hand. A good contract should be fair and protect both the game developer and the composer.

If the game developer subcontracts the composer, the master agreement between the developer and the publisher will supersede any subcontract. Developer subcontracts most often reference the master agreement, or are in compliance with the master agreement. If the publisher hires the composer directly (which is quite often the case in AAA game development), then the composer usually signs a master vendor agreement and is issued a *statement of work* (SOW) and *purchase order* (PO) in a traditional supplier scenario—complete with payment terms, insurance requirements, NDA language, and so on.

When you receive a contract, it's important to ask questions about any language in the contract that you don't understand. If a game developer is trying to hurry you through the process by not explaining what a clause means, it could be a sign of bad things to come. A developer or publisher with honorable intentions will take the time to answer all of your questions and help you better understand the contract.

In this section you'll learn about contracts and the items that you may find in a contract. Note that contracts may be laid out in any order, and may not include some of the sections described here.

- **Project Information or Opening.** The first section of a contract typically identifies all the pertinent information about the two parties entering into the contract, including their names and addresses and the date of the agreement. This section also defines the name of the project or game that the composer will be working on, and the type of agreement between the two parties.

- **Schedule.** Contracts generally include a start date for the project and an estimated completion date. Additional exhibit documents are usually attached to the end of the contract that contain a more complete milestone schedule with payment dates.

- **Compensation.** The compensation section describes how the composer will be compensated for the work. This could be in the form of monetary compensation, royalties, bonuses for sales targets, or possibly a trade in services.

> **note**
>
> At the time of this book's writing, the average rate for video game music was $1,000 per finished minute worth of music. This number goes up and down based on an enormous number of factors, including the size of the game, the complexity of the score, the use (or not) of live musicians, and the skill of the composer. Compensation and these factors are discussed at length in Chapter 27, "Creating an Estimate."

- **Transfer of Rights.** This section describes the transfer of ownership rights from the composer to the game developer or game publisher. As noted earlier, most work in the game industry is classified as work for hire, and this section details exactly which authorship rights the composer will retain. The contract usually specifies how the compositions can be used and distributed in relationship to the game. In addition to the transfer of ownership, this section usually states that the developer can revise and alter the compositions without the permission of the composer, and even create derivative or alternative works. It may also include details about how royalties might be shared and whether the composer retains any of the rights to the music. This section outlines which compositions are included in the agreement. Frequently, the music rights of demo material that is not used in the game may revert back to the composer.

> **note**
>
> Provisions are sometimes included to compensate the composer for an audio-only distribution of the music as a separate product such as a soundtrack. Composers generally get paid a royalty for music-only distribution of the compositions from the game.

- **Confidentiality.** Similar to an NDA, the confidentiality section in a contract specifies that anything related to the project and intellectual property of the developer must remain secret during and sometimes after the product has been released.

- **Credit, Name, and Likeness.** This section of the contract spells out how the composer will be credited in the final game and promotional materials related to the game. Credits may take the form of a screen or box credit, beginning or end titles, or other means. The publisher can also secure the right to promote its product by using the composer's biography and background, and include the composer's information in promotional materials leading up to the game's release.

- **Expenses.** The expenses section details how various expenses related to the project will be paid and reimbursed. These project-related expenses could include materials, travel, and shipping.

- **Recording and Musicians.** The recording and musicians section of the contract outlines how any musician and recording expenses are to be paid and accounted for. Depending on the size of the project, the composer may be required to pay these expenses. Alternatively, on large projects, these expenses may be negotiated in a separate agreement along with other production fees (e.g., recording studios, orchestrators). This section may also detail the collection of musician release forms, which verify that any musicians who played on the project have been properly compensated and have released their performance rights to the project.

- **Awards.** The awards section of a contract details who receives the proceeds and any physical rewards from any music-related awards from the gaming community—that is, the game developer or the composer.

- **Warranties, Assurances, and Indemnification.** In this section, the composer warrants that the music is entirely original and that the composer is responsible for any lawsuits that may arise due to copyright infringement. In addition, the composer guarantees that he or she is the sole owner of the music recordings and compositions and can transfer the rights of these performances to the game developer.

- **Termination or Default.** The termination section of a contract outlines how the game developer or publisher can terminate the contract and how the compensation will be paid out under such circumstances.

- **No Obligation to Use.** This section allows the game developer or publisher to retain ownership to all the music without being required to use that music in the final release of the game.

- **Attorney Fees.** The attorney fees section outlines who pays for any attorney costs arising from a dispute about the contract after the contract is executed.

- **General Legal Items.** In most contracts, a section lists some of the general details of the contract, including the state under whose laws or jurisdiction the contract will be enforced, a statement that the contract cannot be assigned to another individual, and a statement that if a single part of the contract is unenforceable the rest of the contract will still be binding and intact. These clauses vary from contract to contract.

- **Exhibits and Addendums.** After the main part of the contract, the parties may attach exhibits that explore the details of the contract in depth. These may include a more detailed schedule with milestones and payment due information, an asset list, notes about scope, and the number of revisions.

The more detailed the contract is, the lower the risk for confusion when the project goes into development. It's important to nail down the scope of the project by listing in the contract the assets you'll create or the total number of minutes of music you'll provide for the game. If this is left open to interpretation, the client might have a different idea of how much music you need to create for the game.

The contract should state the number of revisions you'll make to a piece of music before incurring overages. The standard number of revisions composers typically specify in contracts before incurring overages is three. After that point, the composer would charge an agreed-upon overage fee that is spelled out in the contract. If these items are not agreed to in the initial contract, a lot of confusion may arise during the actual development, leading to either an unhappy composer or an unhappy developer.

Last, when the development of a project actually begins, it's important to keep the developer informed well in advance if you think that the project might go beyond the scope specified in the contract and you need to revisit an addendum to the contract. It's much harder to go back to a client and request additional money after you've already gone beyond the scope. Make sure to manage client expectations throughout the entire project, letting the developer know exactly how many minutes of music you've written and how many are left in the contract.

The Employment Contract

Another type of contract that you may see is an employment contract. Generally this type of contract is used when the game developer or music production company wants to hire a composer for a specific amount of time to create music for one or more projects. Employment contracts can be salaried full-time positions. They may also include benefit packages such as health insurance and retirement plans.

There are key differences between a project contract and an employment contract:

- Under an employment contract, the composer produces assets as long as he or she is employed at the company. There are no limits on the number of assets or the number of revisions on a project.

- Most employment contracts include an exclusivity or non-compete clause that allows the composer to work on only projects for that company.

Many of the items discussed in the previous section are likely to be included in an employment contract, including work for hire clauses and transfer of rights. Like any employment contract, such a contract should detail approximately how many hours per week the composer will work and whether the composer will receive any weekend, holiday, or overtime pay.

Non-compete clauses can be common in the video game industry. A non-compete or exclusivity clause in a contract specifies that the composer will work exclusively for the developer or music production company, and not for the competition. It should also state the type of work that falls under the non-compete clause. For instance, exceptions to the non-compete clause may include composing music that is not related to games or working on not-for-profit projects. It's important to think about how this will impact your work and to identify any exceptions that you need.

Demos

Game developers and publishers frequently seek out composers to hire when starting a new project. They may ask multiple composers to submit a portfolio of appropriate work for the project in development. In many of these cases, composers create new original music, known as demos, specifically for the upcoming project. This provides composers with an opportunity to show off their talents in hopes of getting the gig.

This demo process usually doesn't include a budget to pay the composers for this work. On larger-budget titles, however, the game developer may occasionally choose to pay for the development of these demos. This fee varies from company to company but generally ranges from $200 to $600 or more.

Game composers rarely make money composing demos for projects. Indeed, many composers spend much more than they get from a demo fee by hiring musicians and studios to make their projects really sound great. In general, if the composer who submits demos for a project is not hired, the rights of those demos revert back to the composer.

Large publishers have different expectations for demos: they usually pay a standard hourly rate for demos with the understanding that the work is wholly owned and work for hire. This agreement wouldn't allow the composer to use those demos for other projects if they weren't used in the game. In some instances, the composer has bought back the rights to a piece of music when the demo hasn't gone into the final product. In these cases, the composer usually refunds the publisher the full amount of the demo fee.

When Things Go Wrong

Most professional composers have, at one point or another, regretted a contract that they have signed, for one reason or another. They may have missed something in the original contract, or perhaps there was a misunderstanding about scope of a project.

Most commonly, the scope was not well defined in the contract at the beginning of the project. The composer in this scenario can feel as if he or she is being taken advantage of.

Once a contract has been signed and you start working on a job, it's very important to stay in close communication with the developer about the scope of the project. If the developer is made aware early in the project that the music work is a runaway train, it is much more likely to address your concerns. If you finish a job without letting the game developer know ahead of time that you're going to hit the company with a large overage bill, the developer will be less likely to pay it—and, in fact, might be quite angry about the situation.

Another reason to regret signing a contract may be how the compensation is calculated, especially under a royalty arrangement. It's important to spell out in the contract how royalties are calculated and how often you will receive a statement describing the latest sales.

As you enter into a contract, the most important thing to remember is that your career depends on your ability to maintain relationships over long periods of time. It's far better to keep a relationship than to get in a dispute about money. Contract disputes shouldn't get in the way of maintaining a long-term relationship with clients. It is far better to finish out a bad contract and fix the problem on the next one, because if there is an argument about the details of the current job, there may not be a next job at all.

Federal Forms

When you work for a game developer or game publisher in the United States, you'll be required to sign additional paperwork that defines how you want to be taxed on income and which type of entity the developer will be entering Into business with. The forms you'll fill out depend on whether you're working as an employee, as a sole proprietor, or as a corporation.

Employee

If you are paid as an employee in the United States, then you'll be required to sign a W-9 form that identifies you by your Social Security number. The employer will then withhold taxes from your paycheck to send to the Internal Revenue Service (IRS) and Social Security Administration. At the end of the year, you'll receive a W-2 form that states the amount you were paid as well as the amount that was withheld for taxes. If you're hired as an employee, you might also receive company benefits as part of the deal.

The advantage of being paid this way is that you don't need to worry about setting aside additional money to pay your taxes later. The disadvantage of filing as an employee is that it's harder to take tax deductions for equipment, software, and studio expenses.

Individual (Sole Proprietor)

If you are paid as an individual working as a sole proprietor in the United States, then you'll also be required to sign a W-9 form that identifies you by your Social Security number. At the end of the year, if you received payments totaling more than $600 from the company, you'll receive a 1099-MISC form that states the amount you were paid; you'll be responsible for paying tax on that total.

The advantage of being paid this way is that you can deduct business expenses such as equipment, software, and studio expenses from your overall income through Schedule C (an IRS document).

The disadvantage of being a sole proprietor is that there is no distinction between you and your business. In case of a lawsuit, a judgment against you might take not only your business assets but also your personal assets.

Another disadvantage is that you have to do your own withholding of taxes to the government. You must send quarterly estimated tax payments into the IRS accounting for any income that you received. Many musicians have gotten themselves into trouble by spending money that they should have sent to the IRS. Failure to pay estimated taxes can lead to large penalty fees along with interest on the payment due.

Corporation

One of the advantages of working as a company (i.e., a limited liability company [LLC] or a corporation) is that your business entity is separate from your person. This means that your personal assets cannot be involved in any legal proceedings. Other advantages include being able to more easily secure insurance and set up benefit plans.

If you are paid as a company in the United States, you'll also be required to sign a W-9 form by the game developer, but you'll list your company name and employer tax identification number (EIN) instead of your Social Security number. This allows you to collect checks without any taxes withheld, but you'll then be responsible for your own tax payments. At the end of the year, any company that has paid you more than $600 will report that income to the IRS. You, in turn, are responsible for paying taxes on that earned income.

Similar to the case with sole proprietors, you can easily deduct any legitimate business expenses from your earnings. Business expenses are removed from your total income, allowing you to pay taxes only on the money that remains.

Similar to working as a sole proprietor, you are responsible for withholding your own taxes from income you receive and sending estimated taxes quarterly to the government. There is also additional paperwork filing and fees associated with a corporation.

Review

Non-disclosure agreements are meant to protect a company's intellectual property or ideas from being stolen by another developer. Such an agreement protects any materials, conversations, technologies, software, and ideas that the developer reveals to the composer candidate.

Every composed piece of music has two different music rights that can be copyrighted: the sound recording and the composition.

A license agreement is typically used when a piece of music has already been finished and the developer wants to use that music in a game.

Music that is composed specifically for a video game is usually contracted under a work for hire agreement. Under such an agreement, the composer transfers the authorship rights to the game developer or game publisher.

When you hire musicians to play on your music, it's important to have them sign a separate contract or waiver form stating that you own the performance.

A project contract usually has the following sections: Project Information; Schedule; Compensation; Transfer of Rights; Confidentiality; Credit, Name, and Likeness; Expenses; Recording and Musicians; Awards; Warranties, Assurances, and Indemnification; Termination or Default; No Obligation to Use; Attorney Fees; General Legal Items; and Exhibits and Addendums.

An employment contract is used when the game developer or music production company wants to hire a composer for a specific amount of time to create music for one or more projects. Employment contracts can be salaried full-time positions. They may also include benefit packages such as health insurance and retirement plans.

Key differences between a project contract and an employment contract include the following:

- Under an employment contract, the composer produces assets as long as he or she is employed at the company. There are no limits to the number of assets or the number of revisions on a project.
- Most employment contracts include an exclusivity/non-compete clause, which states that the composer will work on only projects for that company.

When seeking out new composers, game developers may ask multiple composers to submit a portfolio or request new original music, known as demos, for the upcoming project. Demo fees vary from company to company but generally range from $200 to $600 or more.

When you enter into a contract, the most important thing to remember is that your career depends on your ability to maintain relationships over long periods of time. It's far better to keep a relationship than to get in a dispute about money.

When you work for a game developer or game publisher in the United States, you'll be required to sign additional paperwork that defines how you want to be taxed on income that you receive. Game developers that pay you as an employee will withhold taxes to send to the government; in contrast, if you are working as a sole proprietor or a company for a game developer, you'll need to withhold your own taxes and submit them on a quarterly basis to the government.

Exercises

1. Interview a successful composer about the types of project contracts he or she has signed.

2. Download several music employment contracts from the Internet and compare them. How are they alike? How are they different?

3. Ask a game developer if it has used a standard music contract in the past and whether it would be willing to show that contract to you.

CHAPTER 27

CREATING AN ESTIMATE

One of the first issues that a composer may have to tackle when attempting to get a gig is estimating how much to charge the client. Many different factors affect how much a composer should charge, including how large the project is, which rights the client is buying, and how many revisions might be necessary. This chapter walks through the process of creating an estimate and identifies things to watch out for.

Proposing Your Talents and Fees

One of the steps in the game development process is to hire a composer. Generally, this process begins with the developer putting out a call for composers to submit creative materials and an estimate of how much it would cost to hire that composer.

The creative materials may include demo music that is specifically written for the project, or a demo reel of music demonstrating the scope and quality of the composer's previous work. These materials help inform the game development team about the composer's writing style and creative abilities.

The document describing the various fees associated with hiring the composer is called an estimate, a bid, or a proposal. (This chapter uses the term "estimate" interchangeably with "proposal" and "bid.") The creation of an estimate is very similar to the process of assembling a résumé and cover sheet for a position at a company. The words, layout, presentation, and content are all taken into account during the developer's review of the candidates.

Composers at the very top of the industry have representation who will negotiate their fees and contracts with game developers. Unless you're in that top five percent, you'll probably be pitching and negotiating your own fees on projects. In this chapter you'll learn how to create an estimate for a game developer, including how to structure fees and costs, and explore the psychology of bidding for music jobs.

Questions for the Developer

To create an informed estimate for the developer, it's important to gather as much information about the game as possible. If you're unable to obtain the materials mentioned in the first part of this book (images, scripts, game design documents), you should obtain answers to some general questions to inform your proposal. In this section you'll learn about three types of questions you should be asking: game-related questions, audio-related questions, and budget-related questions.

The developer may not know the answers to some of these questions, and in some cases the developer may expect you to provide advice, especially in terms of the musical and other audio choices. In addition, the developer might want you to deliver an estimate without giving you too much information about the project because the company wants to keep most of the details secret. In this case, the developer may give you only very broad details about the project. Assemble as many answers to these questions as you can before you embark on your estimate construction so that you can create the most informed bid possible.

Game-Related Questions

When determining how much you should charge, there is an array of questions about the game that you'll need answered that will inform decisions about the music. The answers to these questions will help you determine which musical style and genre are appropriate, how many minutes of music you'll need to write, and how many original themes you'll need to write. Following are some example questions that will help you learn more about the game.

1. Which type of game is it (e.g., side-scroller, puzzle, FPS, RPG, tower defense)?
2. On which platform will the game player be able to play the game (e.g., Nintendo Wii U, Facebook, Xbox One, iOS)?
3. If you were going to play the game from beginning to end, how long would it take (if applicable—some casual games might not have an end)?
4. What's the overall story and setting of the game?
5. Are there prominent characters or locations in the game that I should know about?
6. How will the player interact with the game (e.g., keyboard, game controller, Kinect, LeapMotion, Rock Band instrument)?
7. Is there a core game mechanic or interface that I should be aware of?
8. How many levels are in the game, and how are they structured?

Audio-Related Questions

After you find out what the game is all about, you should get more specific about the audio elements of the game and ask about the developer's expectations. These questions will help you determine whether you'll be creating an estimate for just music or all the audio (music, SFX, and dialog), which genre or style of music is appropriate, how many musicians might be needed for live music performance, and so on. The developer may not know the answers to these questions, and may look to you for advice because you're the music expert.

Sometimes, the developer or publisher will have a predetermined "music list" of cues it needs delivered. In other cases, the composer may be required to create this list, which requires significant talent, creativity, and insight to do well. The composer would need to consider the extra time and effort to provide this asset list, and how those factors might impact the overall budget.

Many smaller development teams do not make a distinction between music, sound effects, and dialog. They consider all of the audio elements to be a single line item and may expect the composer to deliver all three elements.

Here are some questions to ask about audio-related issues:

1. Do you need an estimate for all the audio elements, or just the music elements?
2. Do you have a music direction in mind in terms of the music genre (e.g., orchestral, children's music, electronica)?
3. Is there a predefined list of music cues that need to be delivered, or do you need the composer to create that music list?

4. Do you have a direction for the instrumentation or the ensemble (e.g., quartet, orchestra, choir, rock band, gamelan)?

5. What are your expectations about live musicians playing on the project?

6. How many minutes of gameplay music do you need for the game?

7. Will you need music for cut-scenes or interstitial elements? If so, what are the estimated lengths of these elements?

8. Will there be menus, help screens, or tutorials that need music? If so, what are the estimated lengths of these elements?

9. Which production services and costs (e.g., musicians, studio time) will the composer be responsible for?

10. What are the expectations for the delivery format (e.g., stereo WAV, ProTools file, stems, Wwise, or FMOD banks)?

Budget-Related Questions

Budget-related questions are intended to inform the decisions that you make with regard to numbers on your estimate, including how many compositions the developer can afford. Some game developers will tell you what their budget is, but in many circumstances the developer might be unwilling to divulge budget information about a project—so don't be surprised if no answer about the budget is forthcoming.

1. Do you have an audio and music budget for the game already established?

2. If you (the game developer) cannot divulge the audio budget, can you (the developer) reveal the overall budget for the entire game to give an idea of the overall scope and size of the project?

Using an Estimate as a Sales Pitch

When a game developer asks you to submit an estimate for a game, it is generally in the process of determining which composer to hire for the game. This means that every interaction that you have with the developer can influence whether you ultimately get the gig. You should view the estimate as a sales pitch. It can help you get the gig—but it can also turn off the developer.

In many cases, the money is not the most important element in your estimate. Many companies are more reasonable than you might think in terms of working with you to find the best budget to suit the game.

The game developer will be taking note of every move you make, from how long it takes you to deliver your materials to how those materials are presented and organized. These factors could affect whether you get the job, so be timely with the delivery of your estimate and make sure that it is designed in a clear manner. This is an essential part of the sales process of trying to bring a client on board to work with you. You are pitching to the client.

It may help for you to put yourself in the shoes of the developer that is receiving estimates from composers. What would it take to make your estimate to stand out? How does it show that you would do a better job than your competition not only creatively, but also in terms of organization and reliability?

Many estimates that game developers receive are built from a standard template. Distinguish yourself from your competition by creating your own documents that express your vision for the project. Ultimately, the bid can either help improve your chances of getting the gig or hurt it. Make sure that you put careful thought into how you present yourself in this process.

The Psychology of Bidding

A couple different psychological aspects are important to consider when creating an estimate for a client. They include the overall price and the presentation of the estimate itself. In this section you'll learn about both of these aspects, including how they affect the client's perception of your music.

Price

When they are first starting out, composers tend to think if their estimate comes in with the lowest price, they'll automatically get the gig. The point that composers tend to overlook is that by giving a low price to a developer, they are saying that their music is cheap and possibly not of great quality. Most game developers want the best music for their game. By giving a low estimate, you may be suggesting that the quality of your music is not as good as that provided by the composer who is charging twice as much. In some cases game developers will pick composers who are more expensive because they believe they are getting better music, although this may have nothing to do with the level of the composer's creativity.

In the consumer marketplace, there are many different examples showing the psychology of pricing. Most consumers assume that if they spend more money, they get better value. For example, if you are buying steaks at the grocery store, the more you spend, the better the steaks you will get. This relationship seems very logical to consumers. When it comes to pricing services, many consumers think exactly the same way—that is, the more they spend on a service, the higher the quality they'll receive. If you're shipping an important package, for example, spending more on postage may translate into the package having a better chance of reaching its destination.

There are various strategies for bidding a job while taking this psychology into account. You could bid high, which might imply that you are really good at what you do, making the developer want to work with you. Of course, there is also the possibility that this ploy may back-fire. If you bid an outrageous amount for music, the client will think one of two things:

- Your music (and service) must be really awesome if you're changing that much.
- If you don't have a long résumé, you're totally inexperienced.

Creating an estimate is usually your best guess of what the client has in the actual budget. You have to balance this number with the psychology of pricing.

Presentation and Delivery

The presentation of your estimate can say a lot about who you are as a composer. Are you detail oriented? Are you organized? Are you a visionary? When preparing your estimate, it's crucial to think about these questions and to identify what your presentation is saying to the developer.

In general, make sure that your proposal looks professional, whether you're delivering it digitally or on paper. The layout should be clean and organized. Contact information should be easy to find even if the pages are misplaced.

Here is a list of some of the general guidelines to remember when creating a proposal:

- Developers may print your document, so number all the pages and include contact information on all the pages.
- Make sure the actual budgets are clear and organized.
- Itemize the deliverables. Developers may want to cut your deliverables list (e.g., 10 minutes of music instead of the 15 minutes listed in your estimate), so make it easy for them to recalculate the numbers without having to call you.
- Be concise and clear. Developers have limited amounts of time, so it's important to get your points across quickly.
- Include relevant pictures or icons to help capture the developer's attention. Developers are designers, so they enjoy good design when reading.

The Organization of an Estimate

The level of detail that you put into an estimate will vary, depending on the size of the game. On a AAA game, a publisher will want a lot of detail in the estimate; in contrast, on a smaller casual title, you might be able to provide broad strokes with less detail. An estimate should include the following elements:

- **Cover Letter.** A cover letter introduces the materials in the estimate. This page is usually more personal than the rest of the package. It could include a brief description of how the project came to you or who you spoke to, and a few bullet points about why the developer should consider you for the project. It could also give one or two details about the unique benefits of using you as opposed to another composer.

- **Creative Vision.** This section describes your overall creative vision for the project. Without your creative vision, the numbers on your bid won't mean much. It's important to describe the music you plan on creating. This may include how you might use specific themes, or a unique set of instruments, interactive design for the music, or the genre of the music. You may want to include references to your demos or other touch points to help the client understand your creative approach for the project.

> **note**
>
> The creative vision is the part that will most help you separate your estimate from the competition. To the developer, most estimates look pretty generic after a while. The creative section allows you to really show what you're worth by bringing your unique ideas into the project.

- **Breakdown of the Cost.** This "numbers" section breaks down and itemizes all the work you plan on putting into the project, concluding with how much it will actually cost. When working on smaller games, the composer is often asked to create all the audio for a project: music, SFX, and dialog. If this is the case, the cost section will need to be split between these different areas. Table 27.1 is a sample layout for the numbers section.

Table 27.1 Numbers Section Sample Layout

Music	SFX	Dialog
Original themes	Ambiences	Talent fees (with markup)
Rearrangements	SFX	Recording fees
Remixes	Sound design	Editing fees
Stingers and transitions	Field recording and rentals (if required)	
Live musicians	Surround mix (if required)	
Studio time to record live musicians	Implementation (if required)	
Surround mix (if required)		
Implementation (if required)		

> **note**
>
> Many publishers separate creative fees from production fees (e.g., live musicians, studio costs, orchestral preparation) and ask the composer to consider only creative fees. On large projects, production costs are often fenced in a different budget/line item and not up to the composer to decide. Check with the developer or publisher to see if these are separate line items.

- **Terms and Conditions.** Although what follows the bid is negotiation and signing of an actual contract between you and the developer, it's sometimes a good idea to discuss terms and conditions directly in your estimate. If there are no terms and conditions listed, it will be assumed by the developer that all the elements will be provided under a work for hire agreement. Terms and conditions that you might include in your estimate are the scope of the project, additional music, revisions, limits of use, limitations of work for hire, rights, licensing, and the ability to use music for self-promotion. These items are discussed in Chapters 26 and 28.

- **Demos or Mockups.** If you're delivering demos and mockups with your estimate, make sure to introduce those materials in your estimate by describing the music in terms of creative direction, vision, or background information.

- **Composer (or Company) Background.** Reiterating the point that this document is meant to help sell your services to a developer, you might also include a section that justifies why you should get the gig. This could include a list of previous games on which you've worked, a biography of the composer, and any other relevant background information that might help you get the gig.

Breaking Music Down into Components

Not all music costs the same. Music should be broken down into various categories reflecting the amount of work each category demands. A short transition, for example, should cost less than a 2-minute main theme. It's important to reflect such distinctions on your estimate so the client knows exactly what it is getting. In addition, this tactic enables you to negotiate the overall price with your client.

A remix or rearrangement of a main theme takes less time to produce than the creation of an original theme. Therefore, the remix or rearrangement should cost less, a difference reflected on the estimate. If the client can't afford to pay for five original themes, you can reduce the cost of your estimate by creating one theme and generating four additional variations of that theme. This is a common technique used to negotiate with a client and scale down an estimate that is beyond the developer's budget.

Following are several categories that you may want to include on your estimates to help the developer understand the types of music that you'll be composing and to give the developer the opportunity to choose cost-saving options:

- **Themes.** A theme takes the most time to write, and its development is the primary creative task of a composer in terms of creative vision for a project. Themes should be the most expensive music item and relate back to the story, character, or setting in some way.

- **Rearrangements and Variations.** Rearrangements and variations are good ways to keep the overall costs down by repurposing themes for alternative ensembles or adding variation to themes that have already been composed. Variations of themes are significantly easier to put together, as the composer is expanding and altering ideas instead of composing a new theme from scratch.

- **Remixes.** Another way to keep costs down in an estimate is to give the developer remixes of themes. A remix of a theme is usually an alteration of the overall instrument balances in a project. As an example, in an orchestral piece the composer might provide a remix for a theme by just including a brass and drums mix for one pass, or just the strings and woodwinds. Remixes are extremely inexpensive for the composer to create, yet give the developer more material to work from.

- **Stingers and Transitions.** Stingers and transitions are typically short pieces of music (3–12 seconds) that either connect two music events or provide a musical flourish during the level for the player. These events are usually more substantial than providing simple SFX and involve musical writing. Because they are short, they are difficult to link to a per-minute charge; instead, composers usually create a separate line item for these elements on an estimate.

Interactive Music versus Linear Music

The complexity of the music composition can dramatically increase the amount that you charge for music. Composing interactive scores takes more planning and labor for both the composer and the development team versus linear music. Creating interactive stems for all the music can take two to three times the work and effort of simply delivering a linear minute of music.

The following factors will help determine if you need to charge more:

- Delivery specifications
- Horizontal resequencing
- Vertical remixing
- Algorithmic composition
- Randomization
- MIDI with custom-created instrument banks

> **note**
>
> Implementation by the composer is not usually required, but if the music is particularly complex, the composer may need to become involved with the actual implementation at least in an advisory role. Some music production companies offer implementation as a service. It's definitely in a composer's best interests to be able to not only conceive the score but also make sure that the creative vision is carried all the way through implementation. Occasionally, composers see music cues misplaced in the game—they need to be on top of the developer to make sure their original intention is adhered to.

Determining How Much Music to Write

Games come in all shapes and sizes. There are too many variables to identify a standard amount of music for a game. For example, a music-centric game (like *Rock Band* or *Rez*) will include many more music assets than a social game (*Words with Friends* or *Farmville*).

To help you decide how much music you should produce for your game, Table 27.2 provides some very general guidelines.

Many games break these rules, of course, so look carefully at how the game might influence the duration of your music. For instance, if your game has lots of characters or locations (akin to *Final Fantasy*), you might choose to include many more minutes of music.

Another factor in determining how much music is necessary is the technology constraints. If your game will use mostly MIDI instruments on a handheld device, then you can deliver a lot of music because MIDI has such a small storage footprint. Many console games ship on Blu-Ray, so there are fewer limitations with the amount of audio for a project; even so, it's

Table 27.2 General Guidelines about the Amount of Music You'll Need to Compose

Game Type	Amount of Music	Examples
Internet game	10–20 minutes	*Diner Dash*, *Farmville*
Handheld or mobile game	30–60 minutes	*Scribblenauts*, *Sword and Sorcery*
Console game	2–3 hours	*Red Dead Redemption*, *Mass Effect*, *Halo*
MMO	5+ hours	*World of Warcraft*, *Guild Wars*

important to inquire how much space you might have based on the other resources in the game (art, dialog, SFX).

Knowing How Much to Charge

Unfortunately, there is no magic number when it comes to charging for music. In the previous section you learned that not all music costs the same. In addition, an incredible number of basic variables associated with music creation—including the style of music, music interactivity, and the number of live instruments—will affect pricing. This section outlines some more subjective elements that you'll need to take into account and offers guidance on how to calculate a specific number for your estimate. It's likely that your per-minute fee for music will change from job to job after taking these variables into account. The important thing to get across to the client is that you thought long and hard about the numbers you included and that you're able to justify them.

In the first part of this book, you read that audio typically represents 5 to 10 percent of the overall budget for the game. Start by estimating what this figure might be, and then work backward by developing an bid that best suits this figure. Many times you'll be guessing what this figure is because the developer has chosen not to share it with you. Use the rest of the information you collected in the question-and-answer phase to make an educated guess.

In the video game industry, it is frequently said that professional composers charge $1,000 per minute of finished music. This rule of thumb applies primarily to professionals who have been in the industry for a while, working on medium to large titles. Rather than blindly including this amount on your next bid, it's important to start by asking yourself how much it *actually* costs you to create one minute of music.

> ## note
> Revisions during a project are something that all composers face. Publishers and developers may request creative changes in the music, or they may change things in the game that require the composer to revise already-written music cues. For instance, it's quite common for developers to revise cut-scenes within a game, requiring the composer to go back and revise the music for timing. When creating an estimate for a project, composers frequently specific how many revisions are allowed before overages occur. A typical scenario would specify that the composer includes up to three revisions in the estimate, and any further revisions beyond that number would cost $X.

Calculating the Cost of One Minute of Music

The following steps aim to give you a more accurate picture of what it costs for you to create one minute of music:

1. Begin by looking at how long it takes you to write a finished piece of music. Some professional composers can write up to as much as 3 to 5 minutes of music per day. New composers can typically write about 2 minutes of music per day.

2. Calculate how many minutes of music you can write per month. Subtracting out weekends, a composer who can write 2 minutes per day can generally write 40 minutes of music per month.

3. Add up your monthly expenses, including rent, cell phone, Internet service, utilities, food, taking your significant other out to the movies, and so on. For this example, suppose you're a student just out of college who is living on less than $2,000 per month.

4. Divide your living expenses by the number of minutes per month and you'll get the lowest amount that you can charge for music *if* you were writing full time. In our example, $2,000 divided by 40 minutes equals $50 per minute of music.

    Unfortunately, composers rarely work every day writing music. So, for this example, let's say the composer spends half his workday pursuing leads and making new contacts to bring in work, and the other half actually writing. This would double the initial rate to $100 per minute of music.

5. It's important to factor in what the government will take away in taxes on any money that you earn. Taxes usually consume one-fourth of our earnings. Taking this into account, the example rate might go up to $150 per minute.

Now that you've calculated this target number, it is the absolute minimum you should be charging when estimating a job so you don't go into bankruptcy. There are still quite a few assumptions, including the biggest challenge: how long does it take you to sell one minute of music? Sales and marketing are discussed at length in Chapter 29, "How Composers Find Work." In addition, there are many other variables that we've omitted from the analysis here, including things like hardware and software purchases that you may need to work on a particular job.

Getting to Know the Client

You should charge the most that the client can afford. The best estimate matches the game developer's expectations in terms of both cost and creative vision. For you to provide accurate numbers in your estimate, you'll need to research the client that is asking for a bid. Working for Microsoft and Sony is very different than working for students operating out of their basement. Here are some questions whose answers will suggest whether you should bid higher or lower:

1.   What was the last game the developer produced? Was it successful?

2.   Who is publishing this title? Does it have successful backers?

3.   Does the developer have nice offices? Is the company spending lavishly?

4.   How many people are working for the developer?

Scale your numbers appropriately to match the company to which you're sending your estimate.

Review

Game developers ask composers to submit creative materials (demos) and an estimate of how much it would cost to hire them for a project.

To create an informed estimate for the developer, it's important to gather as much information about the game as possible (game images, scripts, game design documents). Ask the developer questions about the specifics of the game: type of game, platform, how long it takes to play, overall structure, and game mechanics. To clarify the audio direction, ask the developer about the genre and instrumentation. Finally, inquire about the overall budget.

An estimate can be used as a document to help sell you to the game developer.

The psychology of pricing says that attaching an inexpensive price tag to music may lead others to believe it is of lesser quality.

The finished estimate should include a cover letter, demo materials, creative vision statement, outline of the costs, terms and conditions, and background information about the composer.

Not all music costs the same. Themes demand the most work, whereas remixes and rearrangements are less expensive to produce.

The amount of music in a game depends on many variables, including the platform, the type of game, and the length of the gameplay.

Audio expenditures typically account for 5 to 10 percent of the overall budget for a game. The standard number quoted in the industry for a finished minute of video game music is $1,000.

When determining the costs for a project, make sure you research the company that is hiring you. This information will have a substantial impact on how much you choose to scale your costs up or down.

Exercises

1. Interview a successful composer to find out what he or she charges when working on a video game.

2. Create an estimate template that you can use when you pitch a new project.

3. Create an estimate for a game that is already in the marketplace. Count up the music assets in the game, assess their lengths and interactivity, and work through what you would charge for creating the score. Have a professional composer look at your estimate and provide you with feedback.

CHAPTER 28

CONTRACT NEGOTIATION TACTICS

As a composer, you'll want to price your music as high as possible for any given job. Unfortunately, on some jobs it may not be possible to receive what you're worth because of budget limitations for the client. Throughout your career, you'll need to negotiate with clients. In this chapter you'll learn how to conduct those negotiations, including some alternative ways to arrange deals if the client is not able to afford your services, such as exploring nonmonetary solutions.

Working for Less Than You're Worth

Frequently, the estimated cost you calculated to do a specific job is not equal to the budget that the game developer has for music. For instance, you may have calculated that the job will cost you $5,000 for your time but the developer has only $500 in the music budget. Should you take the job? When faced with this scenario, it's important not to devalue your time as a composer. Thankfully, there are many different ways to negotiate perks or benefits that might make up for the investment of time you put into creating the music for the project.

It's important to recognize that many developers understand that quality music costs money and they are not trying to underprice you for your work. But budget limitations are real for the developer, and a developer might not be able to pay everyone on the team what they're actually worth.

As we will discuss in Chapter 29, working for less money than you deserve is a way of showing a client how interested you are in the client's idea. It may be a great way to earn a client's respect and commitment for future projects. Investing in a project tells the developer that you want to work with the company and will help you build a long-lasting relationship with that client.

Of course, if you agree to do the entire job for less money, remember that you still need to deliver what you agreed to. If you "bid low" to get in the door, but then all the subsequent work is based on the low rate, you may not impress the client enough to be hired for future work. Moreover, if you set the expectation that your music is priced lower, then it may be difficult to increase your rates later. It's important to let the client know what the work really costs so it knows the investment that you're making in the project.

When a client calls and offers you $500 for a $5,000 project, you should ask if there's anything else that the developer can offer in return for your investment in the project. This type of negotiation requires the composer and the developer to think outside the box. Developers that find themselves in the position of not being able to pay people what they're worth may not know ways to incentivize their contractors with nonmonetary solutions. This chapter aims to suggest some solutions to help offset the monetary costs so that you can come to an agreement to work on a project.

COMPOSER PERSPECTIVE: ACNE—ATTITUDE CKEEPS NEGOTIATIONS EXCELLENT

George "The Fat Man" Sanger

- "Instead of getting right into a contract, how about if we start jotting down some deal points, or a memo of understanding? Here are a couple of things I like to see: I prefer a license deal to a work for hire. . . ."

- "I can see how you'd want to be protected against my [telling your secrets/using your Internet provider/making disparaging remarks about your company, whatever]. How about if we make this clause mutual?"

- "'Salesman wisdom' says that I shouldn't name my price first, and you're doing the same thing! OK, why don't you make me an offer that 'has dignity,' and if I can afford it, I'll take it."

- "I'm a bad negotiator, and I'll demonstrate that now by telling you that if you want, I'll agree to these deal points just as you've written them! But since this is a memo of understanding, do you really need this music to be exclusive to you in *all* media?"

Your attitude will remind them of The Truth: We're not after the bottom line—we want doing business to be sustainable and bearable, which means we're after The Relationship. Both parties are to be able to look each other in the eye and say, "Hey, I see what you're after, and it makes me happy to know I can give it to you. I think this is a pretty fair agreement." The negotiation process and the paperwork will reflect how well each party understands that. You can keep that spirit of fairness and mutual benefit alive in the language you use in negotiations.

And remember, you're safe if you bear "Halbreicht's Law" in mind: make sure there's something in the agreement that tells you how you can get *out* of this deal!

Collaborating with Developers

Working with a developer is all about collaboration. The composer and the developer both want the same thing—the best audio for their game. The problem is that not every project is given enough resources to support this goal. The word *compromise* is used when negotiating, and it can refer to both parties giving up something or making concessions. It's actually better to view the negotiating process as a *collaboration* to find the best solution for the project as opposed to a compromise.

The developer and the music team must work together to reach this goal by negotiating to find common ground on a project. Frequently, this involves going back and forth with numbers until a settlement is worked out.

The objective is to find a solution that works for both parties without either side being bitter about the final agreement. If the contract leans toward one side or the other, one party may become more resentful over time, leading to a bad relationship.

Later in the development cycle, after the project is already under way, the scope of the project may increase beyond the original contract. At that point, you'll need to negotiate a way to get through to the end of the project.

The best way to ensure that you have a good working experience is to have good communication between you and the client. If you start to realize that the scope of the project is starting to increase (a phenomenon known as *feature creep* in the industry), let the developer know right away.

If you wait until the end of the project to hit your client up with all kinds of overages because of feature creep, the developer will ask what happened and why you didn't provide any advance warning. This can lead to very difficult conversations at the end of a project, leaving a bitter taste in the developer's mouth.

The more open both you, as the composer, and the developer are with each other's needs, the better the job will go. Keeping close communication throughout the job is the key to having a successful relationship.

Composers at higher levels in the industry may have an agent, lawyer, or producer who might step in and negotiate business issues such as overages. This type of intermediary is valuable because the composer can then concentrate on the creative discussion without interrupting the conversation to talk about money. In this scenario, a composer might have a much more difficult time saying "no" to a change or revision, while an agent may have an easier time setting boundaries.

Renegotiating the Estimate

The first step is trying to figure out whether you can do a job for less money. Carefully go through the initial asset list to see whether you can save any money by removing nonessential assets or functionality in the music. Follow these steps to see if you can reduce the overall costs of the project:

1. Pare down the asset lists to the essential items.
2. Reduce the lengths of any compositions if possible.
3. Evaluate the number of original themes versus rearrangements and remixes.
4. Reduce the amount of interactivity in the music.

The first step when negotiating an agreement with the client is to revisit the asset list. The composer, together with the developer, examines each item on the asset list and pares the list down to only the essential ingredients. This process involves dividing the elements into groups, which may include these three categories:

- Essential (can't live without)
- Would like to have
- Can't afford right now (save for version 2.0)

Second, it's important to look at the lengths of the music pieces. Is it possible to reduce the overall number of minutes for the project without impacting the creative vision of the project? Of course, simply halving the amount of music may not mean you do half as much work. There's a certain amount of overhead associated with each cue, and then there's a certain amount of effort per minute. Rearrangements and remixes are less time intensive to create than a whole new theme, for example.

Third, it's important to evaluate what the music costs actually represent. Not all music is priced equally. For instance, music themes cost significantly more to produce in terms of time and money than a rearrangement or remix of a piece.

One solution for lowering the costs is to swap out individual themes with remixes or rearrangements. Thus, when reducing your asset list, determine whether there's a way to turn thematic material into remixes and rearrangements without affecting the overall creative objectives of the project.

In addition to dividing out themes and rearrangements, you can examine adaptive music. Adaptive music takes longer to create and is more expensive. Is it possible to pull out some of this interactivity and thereby lower the overall music costs without significantly damaging the end-user experience?

When paring down assets or interactivity for a game, it's important that you clearly communicate which assets the project should have versus what the game developer will end up with. If the end result is not enough music to adequately cover the game because of either too much repetition or no music in parts of the game that need it, the developer may still be unhappy with the final result.

Royalty Arrangements

Royalty arrangements are one way for a developer to reward a composer who has invested in a project based on the success of that game. If the developer didn't have enough initial money to adequately pay for the music, a back-end royalty arrangement might be a way to recoup the investment that the composer put into a project.

Royalty arrangements depend on the size and scope of the project and the amount of money the developer was able to pay for the project. When working with a small team of only three or four people, the amount of work that you put into the project may equal 10 to 15 percent of the total hours everyone spent on the project. In this case you might be entitled to significantly more of a royalty percentage than if the development team consisted of 10 or more people.

No industry standard exists for composer royalties in games because there is a tremendous amount of variability from project to project. Even though some historical data for royalties received by composers in film are available, there is no precedent in gaming because the industry is still relatively new and lacks any employee unions.

Generally speaking, on larger projects game developers and publishers are much less likely to enter into a royalty relationship because they have enough of a music budget to pay the composer an equitable rate for his or her work. In addition, publishers and developers generally dislike having to send checks to their composers on a quarterly or semiannual basis due to the administrative burden; they like to own all the assets free and clear in a work for hire arrangement. Therefore most royalty agreements are made between smaller independent developers that are not well funded or perhaps just getting off the ground.

Even though music and sound may represent 5 to 10 percent of the overall production budget for a game, many variables may affect the actual royalty percentage on a product. The biggest variable in a project is how much money is accumulated during the actual production phase of the project. If this number is closer to the number originally estimated on the project, the percentage will decrease.

A composer's royalty rate may range anywhere from 0.5 percent of net sales to 15 to 20 percent of net sales when the composer worked on a very small team and there was no upfront money. Because these numbers vary so widely based on so many variables, each deal should be negotiated individually using the parameters of that specific project.

Some indie game developers have profit-sharing plans for their employees and internal contractors. They believe that if you are sharing part of the risk, you should be rewarded if the game is successful.

If royalties are collected from net profits, then the developer can charge almost anything to the game's overall costs. Technically, if the developer wants to build DLC (downloadable content) for the game, the company could identify that effort as an expense from net profits—and you as the composer might not see any money. If possible, you should either take a smaller percentage of gross income or possibly define net profits in more detail. Following is an example of how you might clarify and define what net profits are:

- Net profits are calculated less all distribution and marketing expenses, including commissions payable to third parties for marketing; and less all expenses pertaining to the management and collection of grantees' revenue, including taxes, accounting fees, legal fees, and transfer fees.

- Production and development costs from the development of the title are not included when calculating net profits.
- Production and development expenses from additional DLC, software updates, ancillary products and expansions, and further development on the title are not included when calculating net profits.

Royalty options are generally something that a composer would explicitly trade in lieu of a larger upfront fee, or part of one. If an upfront fee is paid, it may be deemed recoupable from royalties by the developer. In this case, before the developer begins paying additional royalties to the composer, it will seek to recover the initial payout, essentially including the composer fee as an original cost before any profits are calculated.

Offering Discounts for Multiple Projects

Just like bulk retailers, you can offer discount pricing if the client decides to award you more than one job at a time. If a client doesn't have enough money to pay you what you're worth, you might ask if the company is working on any other projects on which your services might be needed. If a client can guarantee you two or more jobs, you can offer discount pricing because it saves you the trouble of searching for the next gig. The time you save in sales and marketing will make up for any discount that you offer.

This technique typically works only with clients that are working on a lot of smaller casual or educational games. A company that develops a lot of children's games, such as Lego, Cartoon Network, or Nickelodeon, may produce several games every other month. If you're able to tie into a steady stream of work, you might be able to offer the client discounts that you wouldn't normally be able to afford on a single job.

In turn, if the client gives you the opportunity to work on several jobs at the same time, the client saves money because it doesn't have to search for another composer. Asking for additional work is an excellent strategy to offset lower-priced projects.

Sometimes a client might have the power to guarantee that you'll work on a future project that it has coming up. This also may be an incentive to accept reduced pricing from the client. It should be said, though, that if the current job doesn't go well, you shouldn't hold the client's guarantee hostage if the company doesn't want to continue to work with you.

> **note**
> Not every project that you work on will go as well as you had anticipated. A relationship may turn sour for many reasons, including the client's unhappiness with the music you write, miscommunication, or adversarial relationships. When

this happens, it's important to remain respectful to the client and try to salvage any relationship that you can. If you continue down the path in a rocky relationship without making changes, the client may be less likely to work with you in the future. If the experience turns out be sufficiently unhappy for the client, it may even start spreading the word through the industry that you're difficult to work with. This can be disastrous for your career, so take every opportunity to reconcile with the client.

Being a composer requires both talent and professionalism. Composers should never assume that they will get by on their talent alone. The composers who are successful can both deliver the goods and be counted on as team players. Game development can be a dynamic environment, so adding a composer who is high maintenance and unreliable inserts an unnecessary variable in the equation.

Licensing

Another type of contract that is worth considering is a license arrangement. In this scenario, instead of a work for hire agreement, the composer grants an unlimited license to use the music exclusively for a certain amount of time. After the license has expired, all rights to the music revert back the composer. This type of deal is more frequently associated with projects that might have a temporary lifespan, like a web game or website.

At the end of a license, the client and the composer can negotiate a renewal of that license or decide to end the contract. In the latter case, the rights to the music would revert back to the composer. The composer could then sell the music to another client or a music library. This type of deal is an especially good idea when the circumstances of the project limit the amount of money that the composer can receive.

A license deal for the developer is especially enticing because of the lower upfront costs. When the date for the license renewal approaches, the client can determine the success of the project and choose either to invest in the renewal or to buy out the music. Note that the terms and conditions of future renewals or a buyout may be included in the initial license.

Additional Rights and Opportunities

Several ancillary rights can be requested when negotiating your contract for a project. These include publishing royalties and work on derivative products. This section explains both of these items and covers the essentials of what you need to know to negotiate for them.

Music Publishing and Performance Royalties

Work for hire agreements essentially take away all the composer's rights to use the music in any form other than the client's project. In addition, any rights to music publishing royalties and revenue may be forfeited in this agreement. Legally, this generally means that the composer can't even use works from the game on demo reels that he or she sends out. In this section we'll talk about the ancillary rights that you can request.

Many smaller or indie game developers may not understand how music publishing royalties work. The first step in requesting to keep music publishing royalties—whether it's the publisher's share or the composer's share—is to explain to the game developer what these royalties actually are.

Public performance royalties are generally accrued when a piece of music has been used in broadcasts such as radio and television, or in the performance of the work at a live venue such as Carnegie Hall. Networks and broadcast outlets, including performance spaces, pay blanket licenses to performance rights organizations (PROs) to broadcast or perform music. PROs in the United States include Broadcast Music, Inc. (BMI); American Society of Composers, Authors and Publishers (ASCAP); and SESAC (formerly the Society of European Stage Authors and Composers).

Composers affiliated with one of these agencies are able to get their share of the performance royalties as long as the pieces are registered with one of these agencies. Every piece of music has a publisher and a composer royalty. In some work for hire agreements, both the publisher and composer royalties may be forfeited to the game developer or game publisher. In your contract, you can request that you retain the publisher and/or composer portions of any royalties collected upon the performance of your music. Most larger game publishers will retain 100 percent of the music publishing royalties while letting the composer keep his or her share.

It's likely that when you start explaining all of these points to a small or indie game developer, the employees' heads will spin. Music publishing is fairly complicated and most game developers, especially new or independent game developers, have never dealt with the publishing rights of music before.

The reality for performance-based royalties obtained through music publishing is that the monies accrued for most video game music are very little. At the highest level of video game music, performance income may be worth fighting for because your music is being played at popular shows like *Video Games Live*. Requesting to keep performance-based royalties is not unusual, although the additional monies accrued in this fashion may be small or nonexistent. The game developer or game publisher may choose to grant you these rights because, in essence, it doesn't cost the company anything. If you're granted these rights, make sure that you register the cues with BMI, ASCAP, or some other PRO so you can collect any performance-based royalties.

Some game music that is registered with PROs may not have the composer's name attached; that money is put back into the general pool of money that is paid out to other composers and publishers. A PRO cannot pay out the composer's share of the royalty if the composer's name has never been registered. If the game publisher's contract retains all music publishing rights, the game publisher cannot receive the composer's share of the music publishing royalties. This is why it is easy for the game publisher to give you the composer's side of the music publishing royalty rights—because the company is not entitled to receive those monies under any circumstances.

Music rights are quite complex—whole books have been written on the topic. You may want to also consult a book or reference that specializes in these issues if you plan to include these rights in your contract negotiations. An excellent reference book on this topic is *Kohn on Music Licensing* by Al Kohn and Bob Kohn.

Guaranteed Work on Derivative Products

One of the additional things you can ask for in your contract is a guarantee to work on future versions of the same product. In legalese, such a guarantee is spelled out as "first right of refusal to compose music for future related ancillary and derivative products at an accepted market rate."

For example, if you are contracted to compose music for *Diner Dash* and have this clause written into your contract, then you're guaranteed to work on *Diner Dash 2* if that game is ever developed. The phrase "at market rate" means that if you are contracted to compose subsequent versions of the game, you cannot then overcharge the game developer because of its guarantee to work with you. *Market rate* refers to the general accepted industry rate, or going rate, for music services on the types of games that you're working on.

These types of clauses are often difficult to enforce, especially if you have a bad relationship with the developer from the first products. Nevertheless, such a clause does indicate good faith from the developer that it is willing to recognize your investment in the project, and it is definitely something that you should ask for if the amount that the company is paying you is less than the value you bring to the project. If the company won't work with you on derivative projects after it has agreed to this clause, it is probably better for you to let the project go than to pursue legal action against the company. Suing an employer is a good way to highlight yourself as *notorious to work with* and the rest of the industry may decide to keep their distance whether you win the court case or not.

Screen and Box Credits

Another perk you can request when negotiating a contract is that the developer provide a prominent screen or box credit. Having your name in the screen credits or on the box is essentially free advertising and marketing for your music services. Generally having your name in the credits is very inexpensive—almost free—for the developer, meaning that the company incurs almost no cost by adding your name to the game in the credits.

With smaller games, it may be possible to get your credit more prominently displayed in the game. For instance, the company might be able to add your name immediately after the names of the publisher and the game developer. This can be great advertising for your music services.

Review

Frequently, the estimated cost the composer has calculated to do a specific job is not equal to the budget that the game developer has for the music. A composer should not immediately say "yes" to a low budget, as it might define the composer's standard music rate moving forward.

The objective of a good contract is to find a solution that works for both parties. If the contract leans toward one side or the other, one party may become more resentful over time, leading to a bad relationship.

When the budget is insufficient for the music composition, work with the developer to pare down the overall budget and assets if possible; otherwise, look for other nonmonetary compensation. There are many solutions to help offset low budgets and come to an agreement to work on a project:

- Revising the initial estimate
- Royalty arrangements
- Bulk pricing
- Creating a license package instead of a buyout
- Ancillary rights, including music publishing and first right of refusal to work on derivative products
- Screen and box credits

Exercises

1. Role-play through a contracting scenario where one person plays the composer and the other plays the game developer who has a lower music budget.
2. Talk with local game composers about the types of agreements they have had with game developers regarding rights, work for hire, credit, and money.

CHAPTER 29

HOW COMPOSERS FIND WORK

No matter whether your plan is to work as an in-house composer with a game development team or as an independent composer, marketing and sales skills will be important keys to landing the next gig or advancing your career. In this chapter we'll explore how to network, build relationships, and use other tools to help a composer progress in this challenging career.

Building Relationships

Without sales and marketing skills, composers often find themselves without enough sustainable work. The ability to convince a client to pay you for your creative skills is essential. Many composers who are not working in-house spend a considerable amount of time looking for the next gig. At the beginning of a composer's career, sales and marketing talents are the most important skills to have. In this chapter you'll learn about various ways to sell your creative services.

When starting your career, the most important thing that you can do to ensure your success as a composer is to build relationships. If you successfully complete a job with the client, that client is more likely to return to you for future composing needs. Thus the relationships forged early in your career are critical to your long-term success as a composer.

If you look at certain Hollywood directors, you'll notice that they return to the composers with whom they established relationships over and over again. Examples of this type of relationship include Alfred Hitchcock and Bernard Herrmann, Tim Burton and Danny Elfman, Darren Aronofsky and Clint Mansell, and Peter Jackson and Howard Shore. The bonds between composers and game developers are very similar—for instance, Jack Wall working with Bioware on *Mass Effect 1* and *2*, Inon Zur working on the *Dragon Age* series, and Jesper Kyd working on the *Assassin's Creed* and *Hitman* series.

The best salespeople you have are the people with whom you've worked in the past and who continue to introduce and evangelize you to new contacts. When a composer gains the trust of a developer by doing a great job composing music for a game, that developer will continue to use that composer over and over again throughout the composer's career. In this instance, we use the term *game developer* to mean anyone who is working on the team for the game, including game designers, producers, art directors, programmers, and the owner of the company. As the careers of these people grow, they'll continue to recommend you from whatever company they end up at, creating a web of new interconnected contacts throughout the industry. The relationships with these people are key to having a successful career.

Establishing a relationship based on trust with a game designer means investing time and resources into a project that you believe in. At the beginning of a project, rarely does one know whether the project will be successful. Even for the game designer, there is no way to know whether the idea and all the hard work put into that idea will lead to a game that stands out from the herd. By working with the designer and believing in the developer's idea, a composer can solidify their relationship and strengthen the bond for future projects. The key is making the investment.

Now that we've stressed the importance of these relationships, it's essential to discuss how to build these relationships in the industry. There are many ways to meet potential clients, and throughout this chapter we'll explore the various means to connect with developers.

Networking

Networking is broad term used to describe the process of meeting and connecting with potential clients. The more people you know, the better your chances of selling your music to someone. There are many different ways to meet people, and we explore some of them in this section.

Introducing yourself to others can sometimes be terrifying if you're shy. (I am one of those people.) Three pieces of advice will help you take this first step:

- Introductions don't have to be complicated. They can be as simple as "Hi, my name is Michael and I'm a video game composer from Boston."

- The worst thing that can happen when meeting someone new is that the person won't respond in the way that you desired. The reward of connecting with someone new is far greater than the fear that the person may not respond in kind.

- Find your audience by looking for people with whom you enjoy talking.

Some people have a natural charisma that makes them "people magnets." Movie stars and some prominent composers (Hans Zimmer and Tommy Tallarico) are examples of this type of individual. To be a successful composer, you don't necessarily have to have this charisma, but lacking it means that you might have to work a little harder to find your audience.

I have been successful in game music over the course of my career in part because I really enjoy working with people who work on games. They become my audience because I enjoy relating to them personally and on a professional level. I find gamers easy to talk to because I also fit the stereotype of a gamer.

You have to find your audience and the people that you can relate to, whether these people are game developers, film directors, advertising executives, television producers, museum directors, fine artists, or someone else. It's likely that you will be most successful looking in the areas you find interesting.

If you want to be successful in gaming, you're likely to already be an expert in current and past video games, play games as a hobby, and be interested in talking about how games are made. Game developers will have an expectation that they can talk to you about what the best games are doing and how they want to reach that level someday. If you cannot relate to gamers, then you may want to look elsewhere for your audience.

COMPOSER PERSPECTIVE

Yoko Shimomura

Even if you are composing game music, I think it is not very good to just play games all the time or compose music all the time. Of course, it is very important to like games and to find joy in writing music all day long. However, many requests are made of you regarding game music, and I think the most important trait to have is the mental and emotional flexibility to meet any demands or opportunities. Therefore, I believe it is very valuable for you to experience as many things as you can on a day-to-day basis.

Experience everything! Listen to and write music that you are unfamiliar with, look at beautiful objects, read, eat delicious food, hang out and chat with your friends, or even sleep like you are dead! All of the joys and heartaches you experience from your everyday life will undoubtedly become a valuable asset for you when creating your compositions.

Meet as many people as you can and always wear a smile. You never know how your connections now will help you in the future, so it is important to keep yourself open to new opportunities and ideas.

At the beginning of your career, it's unlikely that you'll immediately start working for someone as accomplished as Koji Kondo, composer for the *Legend of Zelda* and *Mario* series. It's more likely that you'll work your way up through the ranks by first doing smaller jobs until you have a well-regarded reputation; you might find yourself working at that level after being in the industry for 10 or more years. Be sure to set small expectations when you're starting out, recognizing that jobs composing for money allow you to climb up through the ranks in an incremental fashion.

When you're first starting out in your career as a composer, start by networking with people you already know, including your family and friends. Let them know that you're interested in composing music—any kind of music. Start small and inch your way up the ladder. Be creative and invent composing jobs that can benefit others while you create a reel. For example, suppose you know a graphic designer: you might approach her about creating music for her website in exchange for her developing a logo for you or helping to design your website. Then ask her which other designers she knows for whom you might be able to create music.

Following is a list of some of the things you can do to meet game developers and start developing your audience through networking:

- Meet game development students at colleges or universities.
- Attend video game conferences like Game Developers Conference, Montreal Game Summit, Casual Connect, Indiecade, PAX, and many more.
- Participate in local game meet-ups or game jams.
- Join game organizations like the International Game Developers Association (IGDA) and participate in discussion boards.
- Contribute by doing service to our industry through the Game Audio Network Guild (GANG) or the Interactive Audio Special Interest Group (IASIG).

- Speak at game conferences, at colleges, or with local game developers about the importance of music and sound.
- Interview successful composers or audio professionals in your area and ask them about their career paths.

Throughout the rest of this chapter, you'll read about many of these ideas in more depth, as means to help you develop the skills needed to approach industry members.

Informational Interview

An informational interview is a technique often used by students and recent graduates, in which they interview an audio professional in the field they want to pursue. Such an interview allows you to learn about a professional's career path and how he or she got into the industry. In addition, you may be able to use this interview as a stepping stone to begin a longer relationship in which this composer can continue to give you advice.

Some of the questions that you might consider asking include the following:

- How did you get to the position that you're in today?
- What are the most valuable skills that I can learn before entering the industry?
- Which things do you look for in an assistant?
- Is there any software or hardware I should learn before entering the industry?
- What's the best way for me to find a job in the industry?

Some of the questions that you should ask relate to having a follow-up conversation. For instance, if in response to the software question the professional responds that you should learn Wwise, you could then send an email to that person several months later telling him or her it was good advice, and that you took the time to become an expert in that software. This will tell the person two things: (1) that you took the advice and (2) that you are responsible. This, in turn, keeps you in the forefront of the professional's mind in case he or she hears of any job opportunities.

Video Game Conferences

Worldwide, more than 50 different conferences take place every year that focus on video games. These conferences and summits spotlight many different areas of the game industry, including commercial games, casual games, serious games, and educational games.

Video game conferences are chock full of presentations and workshops in the various expertises of video game development, including game design, business, production, programming, art, and audio. These sessions are given by experts working in the field.

One of the primary reasons why people attend these conferences is to network with other game developers and look for work. In addition, audio professionals can learn about the latest techniques in audio for video games, including composition techniques, mixing, surround sound design, and implementation. Conference attendance fees vary widely. It may take several years of building relationships at these conferences to see a return on this investment.

Game conferences are crowded and full of potential competition. The more esoteric conferences will have less competition and might be a better starting point than jumping into something like the Game Developers Convention, which has 20,000 attendees. Setting realistic expectations is key to having a successful experience at a conference. The easiest contacts to make are lateral connections, meaning people who are currently at your same level in the industry.

Following is some advice for getting the most out of going to a conference:

- Meet people, make friends, swap stories, and build relationships.
- Speak and contribute.
- Learn by asking questions.
- Be brave and introduce yourself to your peers and potential clients.
- Have patience and be prepared to wait 3 to 5 years before seeing significant results.

Conferences are full of energy and vibrancy that can translate into excitement, encouragement, and motivation in the video game industry. Conferences happen worldwide, so you should first research local conferences in your area and attend those events. Here is a list of some video game conferences that game developers and publishers attend:

- **Game Developers Conference, San Francisco (Spring).** This is the largest of all the video game conferences, with approximately 20,000 attendees. Workshops and sessions are held in multiple tracks, including business, production, audio, game design, art, and programming.
- **Indiecade, Los Angeles (Fall).** This conference celebrates the independent game scene. The titles discussed at this conference typically are more leading edge and without large publisher involvement. Many of these titles go on to be very successful, and many game composers get their start working on these smaller independent games.
- **E3 Entertainment Expo, Los Angeles (Spring).** E3 is where game publishers introduce many of their new games.
- **Casual Connect, Seattle (Summer).** Casual Connect brings together developers of casual, social, mobile, and web-based games. The games developed by these attendees are typically played through mobile devices or on the web.
- **Games for Change Conference, New York (Summer).** This conference is dedicated to creating games for social change and education.

- **PAX-Dev (Penny Arcade Expo), Seattle (Summer).** This conference is primarily focused on independent games in the Northwest.

- **Audio-Only Conferences.** There are several audio-only conferences with a focus on games, including GameSoundCon, created by veteran Brian Schmidt (formerly of Microsoft), and AES Games in London, which is part of the Audio Engineering Society's offerings.

Working for Free

Working for free can be one of the most valuable tools for creating lasting connections with clients and getting your name out there. There are many nonprofit projects as well as indie games being created out of someone's garage that can potentially be great investments for composers.

Investing your time for free in a project can be an excellent way to show that you respect and believe in the project. In return, this will earn the respect and belief the client has in you, and the client might offer you paying gigs later on. In addition, the client will evangelize your services to other developers.

For many of the clients I've worked with over the last 20 years, I began working on projects that had little or no budgets. We've maintained long relationships because we work well together and believe in each other's talents. It's an incredible way to build loyalty.

Be aware that most mid-sized to large developers and publishers won't accept any work for free due to legal, ownership, and rights assignment issues. Working for free is generally an accepted practice only with student, small indie, or startup studios.

> ## warning
>
> **DON'T DEVALUE YOUR WORK**   You should work for free only if everyone on the project is making little or no revenue on the project. Otherwise, working for free can say to a client that your music is actually not worth anything, thus devaluing you as a composer. In addition, it's important to remember which projects are paying the bills: make sure that you divide your hours appropriately between projects that you're investing in and those that pay the rent.

Game Developer Organizations

Like most other industries, the games industry has several organizations with which you should be familiar. These organizations are similar to social networks in that they are communities of game developers helping each other grow and share information.

To use their contacts with these professional organizations as effective sales and networking tools, composers must actively participate in these groups. If you sit on the sidelines, you'll miss out on the opportunities spawned by these groups.

Contributing your knowledge and expertise to a group or organization is the best way to make new contacts and network. Just joining an organization is typically not enough to help you with networking opportunities. You can be an active participant by answering questions on forums, contributing to white papers, doing research, or writing articles.

Many of these organizations and groups also have local chapter meetings in many large cities, where you can physically meet together and discuss various opportunities. Some have scheduled speakers and various events that promote game development.

The following industry organizations are excellent places to begin to network and contribute:

- **IGDA.** The International Game Developers Association has many different special interest groups (SIGs) and local chapters around the world bringing together all of the various game development disciplines.

- **GANG.** The Game Audio Network Guild is an organization of game audio experts including composers, sound designers, audio producers, and audio implementers. It offers discussion forums, posts job opportunities, and hosts the game audio awards at the Game Developers Conference each year.

- **IASIG.** The Interactive Audio Special Interest Group works with audio professionals and manufacturers to develop standards and promote education in game and interactive audio.

Your Website and Blog

Your website is a valuable supporting sales tool that can help sell your services. Once you've met potential clients either in person or virtually, you can point them to your website, where they can listen to your previous work and read about your background.

On its own, a website promoting your music is unlikely to bring you work. A website that promotes your skills is much more important after the introduction has been made. Even if you are able to contract a job through just your website, it's unlikely that the gig will be exactly the type of work that you are seeking.

Here are some of the common elements that many composers include on their website:

- Music reels and videos that best represent the composer's work
- Biographical information including awards, repertoire, education, and previous work
- Contact information including social networks (Twitter, LinkedIn, Facebook)

- A newsfeed featuring what the composer has been working on, including recent articles and reviews of recently released games
- Links to games and/or articles that the composer has written
- A client area where clients can retrieve the latest materials for a job that is currently in progress
- A blog where you can convey working techniques, news, and other interesting facts to your audience

Many composers started out by making themselves experts in a specific area and sharing their knowledge of this area on blogs or websites. Composers who write interesting articles about music and sound attract followers, which in turn helps their chances of getting gigs. When a game developer subsequently inquires about that composer, he or she will have more name recognition.

When designing your website, make it unique, organized, and professional. Game developers are always interested in eye candy, so intriguing design is important in attracting their attention. In addition, your website should be easy for you to update. If you need something posted right away for a client, it's important that you be able to do this yourself. Various technologies allow for simple updating of websites including WordPress, WIX, and Squarespace.

Social Networking

Increasingly, social networks are being used by composers to network. It's important to use each network to evangelize to the world what you do. You should control the social network feeds to limit the amount of inappropriate information about you on the web. Many employers will Google you before hiring you, so it's important to build a solid reputation of excellent links and references about yourself.

Social networks can help you network with game developers. LinkedIn can be used to research how you are connected to a certain company or individual. If a job is available at Blizzard, for example, you can see if any of your current contacts know someone at Blizzard. If so, they might be willing to write a direct recommendation for you, thereby improving your chances of getting a gig.

Social networks can also be a good way to publicize recent projects that you've worked on, any awards or accolades you've won, and articles that you've written. They can help spread news about your successes, enhancing your reputation throughout the industry.

In many fields, employers have recently chosen to stop posting job openings, instead opting to let headhunters find the best employee for the job and bypassing the regular hiring process. This may matter more in the future, but you should make sure that your social networks advertise and evangelize your expertise; then, when a potential client is looking for someone with your talents, it will be easy to find you.

Cover Sheets and Résumés

Although résumés are not usually characterized specifically as sales and marketing tools, they share many of the same principles, including networking and the ability to sell your services to an employer.

Game employers looking for music and other audio professionals can receive literally hundreds of applications. If they already know you from meeting you at a conference or an informational interview, you'll move to the top of the list of potential candidates. When you're applying for a job, applying many of the networking principles will gain you a significant advantage if you are able to make direct contact with the decision makers. Networking before the job is available can be the difference between getting the job or failing to make the cut.

From firsthand experience in hiring employees, I can tell you that many résumés and cover sheets look so similar that they appear to have come from a factory. Almost every résumé lists the same set of skills and abilities. It's important to include something that makes you stand out somehow, by offering a personal anecdote or story to help connect the reader to you in some way. This could be a story about what inspired you to go into music or games, or it could be how a recent game changed the way you think about music. The reader should be able to connect on a personal level with you.

Additionally, it's important for a résumé to show skill expertise by example as opposed to a list. For example, don't just list Wwise as a skill that you know, but prove it by describing an example of how you used this audio middleware on a project.

The format of a résumé should be clean and organized, highlighting your career with bullet points and minimal text. If you have limited experience working on games or in music, it's still important to show that you can work with others or can show responsibility by having people rely on you. Composers sometimes offer other valuable skills besides composing to the job. Non-music related experience such as speaking an additional language, management experience, or production skills can make your résumé stand out.

Make sure to list all of the musical instruments you play, as well as any other specialized audio and game expertise you might have, whether it's doing voice-over for games or motion capture. If you haven't worked in games in the past, it can be very helpful to an employer if it knows you bring a wide range of expertise to the table.

Partnerships

Composers sometimes form business partnerships with individuals who have sales and marketing expertise. This allows the composer to focus on the creative aspects of their job as opposed to worrying about where the next job may come from. A composer can also form a partnership with another composer, orchestrator, or recording engineer, which can be a very effective way to get exposed to new clients.

Most partnerships that do not last fail because one party believes that he or she has taken on more responsibility than the other party. One way to resolve this conflict is to divide the profits based on the amount of work each individual is bringing to the table.

Another reason that partnerships sometimes fail is that the skill sets of the partners do not complement each other. In choosing a partner, look for someone who brings different skills to the table. The most important skill to have in a business is sales and marketing capabilities. Without this skill, it's very difficult to keep a partnership running successfully.

You can also form a partnership with a company that could offer you complementary services. For instance, if you have a close relationship with a visual effects company, it may help pitch your services on jobs that the company is working on. In exchange, you can recommend the company for jobs you're working on, or offer free music services like creating music for its website or logo. These partnerships and relationships can be extremely valuable in helping both partners grow. Trading services is common throughout the industry.

Representation and Salespeople

Successful composers at the very top of the industry are sometimes represented by agents who find work for them in exchange for a percentage of the monies earned. This percentage varies widely, depending on how much work the agent brings in and other factors such as the size of the job. In general, this percentage is somewhere between 10 and 20 percent of the gross revenue. In some cases, agents earn this percentage on all of a composer's jobs, even jobs that the agent didn't secure.

Because their salary depends on whether they can secure you work, there is definite incentive for agents to actively sell your services. Agents are highly connected industry professionals who have entrées into many different game developers. They are generally the first to hear about upcoming new projects and composer opportunities.

In addition to actively selling your services, agents typically will negotiate the contracts on the business side, leaving the composer to focus only on the creative side. This is an advantage because the business conversations won't happen at the same time that the creative direction is being discussed. The composer who has to discuss monetary overages or limits in the creative meeting can be very challenging because he or she sometimes has to play the bad guy. If the business aspects are handled by another person, then the creative discussions can be less adversarial.

General advice for a composer regarding representation is to be clear on what the expectations are (on both sides). Don't expect an agent to suddenly start getting you work; the composer still needs to own 100 percent of the responsibility, particularly if he or she is just starting out. Once you get the work, the agent should be able to step in and negotiate a better deal for you than you could on your own. Plus, it's beneficial for you to not "muddy the water" by being both the creative person and the person negotiating fees and following up on payments. You come across as much more professional if you have a good agent.

You might ask yourself why you can't just go out and get an agent now. Unfortunately, very few new composers have launched enough work into the marketplace to gain the attention and support of an agent.

> **note**
>
> Many agents and publishers do not accept unsolicited demos or bids—particularly from non-vendors. Thus, to work at this level, you need to attract their attention by composing for a successful indie or smaller game.

If you are thinking about working with an agent, examine the list of composers whom the agent currently represents to ensure that you fill a unique niche within this lineup. Otherwise, it may be difficult for you to stand out when an agent is pitching his or her composer lineup to a game developer.

In some instances, composers hire a salesperson to help create relationships with game developers. Frequently these salespeople work for a small salary plus a commission or percentage of any work that they bring in. In many industries, using salespeople can be an effective strategy for generating leads on upcoming projects. After the initial sales pitch, it's up to the composer to ultimately make the relationship work.

Advertising and Public Relations Agencies

Composers and music production companies can buy advertisements on prominent game websites (Gamasutra.com) or in print magazines (*Develop*). These ads do a good job of getting people to recognize your brand, but they aren't very effective at creating the one-on-one relationships typically needed to work with a game developer. Advertising may be able to create an initial introduction or buzz about your services, but ultimately it takes a lot of hard work to actually sell yourself to a client. Typically, music production companies are better suited for this type of investment than an individual composer.

Google Adwords is another investment that some composers use to get their name out into the industry, albeit with limited effectiveness. Its value depends on whether you can turn an initial inquiry into a one-on-one relationship with a game developer.

Public relations (PR) agencies can be a useful in getting your name out to the industry and advocating on your behalf. These agencies help spread information about you or your company within the industry in the following ways:

- Write press releases featuring you or projects that you've worked on, and get those press releases published online or in print magazines.

- Help create connections that allow you to write articles in your field, creating the perception that you are a leading expert in the industry.

- Help shape your public image through advertising, defining your target audience, tailoring your message, and building a web presence.

PR agencies are generally hired with a monthly retainer and paid by the number of hours worked, similar to legal services. Again, larger music production companies are probably better suited to using PR services. Many composers take it upon themselves to write their own press releases and articles. A PR agency will have easier access to media sources, such that its releases will be more likely to be placed in prominent publications.

Review

The ability to convince a client to pay you for your creative skills is essential to success as a video game composer. Without sales and marketing skills, composers often find themselves without enough sustainable work.

At the beginning of your career, the most important thing that you can do to ensure your success as a composer is to build relationships. If you successfully complete a job with the client, the client will be more likely to return to you for future composing needs. Thus relationships formed early in your career are critical to your long-term success as a composer.

The best salespeople you have are the people with whom you've worked in the past and who continue to introduce and evangelize you to new contacts.

It is critical to find your audience, whether these people are game developers, film directors, advertising executives, television producers, museum directors, fine artists, or someone else.

There are many places to meet game developers, including at colleges or universities, video game conferences, local game meetups or game jams, and game organizations like the IGDA.

An informational interview is a technique used by students and recent graduates in which they interview an audio professional in the field they want to pursue. Such an interview allows the student to learn about the professional's career path and how he or she got into the industry. In addition, you can sometimes use this interview to begin a longer relationship in which the professional can continue to give you advice.

Worldwide, more than 50 different conferences take place every year that focus on video games. At these conferences, game professionals can network and learn the latest techniques used in video games.

Investing your time for free in someone else's idea is an excellent way to show respect and belief in the project.

Contributing your knowledge and expertise to a group or organization is a great way to make new contacts and network.

On its own, a website promoting your music is unlikely to bring you work. Instead, websites function more by supporting sales materials that can help sell your services.

Many employers will Google you before hiring you, so it's important to build a solid reputation of excellent links and references about yourself on social networks.

On a résumé and cover sheet, it's important to include something that makes you stand out from the crowds—for example, offering a personal anecdote or story to help connect the reader to you in some way. In addition, it's important to show your expertise through examples as opposed to just listing those skills.

Successful composers at the top of the industry are sometimes represented by agents who sell their services in exchange for a percentage of the monies earned.

Advertising does a good job of getting people to recognize your brand, but it is less effective at creating the one-on-one relationships typically needed to work with a game developer.

Exercises

1. Attend a local game jam or IGDA meetup. Report on what you discovered.
2. Research the various game conferences in your area.
3. Conduct an informational interview with a local audio professional working in games.
4. Examine the websites of various game composers to see how they are marketing themselves and if there are ways to improve your own sales materials and website.
5. Create a cover sheet and résumé for a game audio job and get it reviewed by someone in the industry before sending it out.

CHAPTER 30

THE CHALLENGES OF WORKING AS A COMPOSER

Working in the video game industry as a composer can offer many rewards, but there are also many challenges and sacrifices you may encounter. This chapter aims to set realistic expectations and goals when pursuing a job as a composer, while also pointing out how composers deal with disappointment. Throughout this chapter you'll learn about some of the traits of successful composers, ways to deal with competition, strategies to move on from rejection and failure, and a few tips about how composers handle finances.

Setting Expectations and Goals

From my experience in the industry, and through speaking with composers and former students, the average length of time it will take you to find success as a video game composer is 3 to 5 years. That's as long as it takes many people to get a music degree! Unfortunately, being successful usually has nothing to do with how talented you are as a musician, but everything to do with finding sustainability among clients that want to pay for your music.

Between student loan debt (if you have any) and living expenses, 3 to 5 years may seem like an eternity. Many composers drop out of the industry because of how long it takes to establish themselves and how crowded the marketplace is. There are some things you can do to mitigate the length of this "getting yourself launched" time, including many of the options discussed in Chapter 29, "How Composers Find Work." Most important, you should focus on finding those clients that want to pay you for the music you write, and will return to you over and over again throughout your career.

When setting out on your career, set some goals for yourself—and write them down. Long-term goals may seem overwhelming when you're first starting out, so it important that you begin with yearly goals, then work your way back to monthly goals, then try to organize daily tasks to help you achieve your goals.

Some of your goals might include these achievements:

- Go to a local game meetup or conference.
- Meet local people who are working on games.
- Reach out via email to local game developers.
- Schedule an informational interview with a successful composer working in your area.
- Meet student developers at local colleges that have game design programs.
- Put up flyers at a local college promoting your music so that you can meet young developers.
- Secure your first title in which you compose music for the game.

When setting goals, it's important to have tangible outcomes that indicate growth in your career such as making a contact. You may notice that none of the example goals dealt with revising your website, updating your reel, or creating a new orchestral template for your DAW. These are more intangible goals, because they don't specifically push your career forward. Although these tasks seem like good things to work on, they can be serious time wasters that don't enable you to do the real work of meeting clients and performing work to further your career. Make sure you prioritize and focus on the tangible goals.

If you miss a goal, just know it's important to make at least a little progress every day. Don't be too concerned if you get off track of your goals. Revise your goal list as your priorities change and based on the progress that you're making. The first time you set goals, it will be hard to know how much is too much or too little. Do your best to make adjustments as needed, and get plenty of advice from your peers in the industry.

Traits for Success

One of the exercises that I created in my Video Game Scoring classes at Berklee College of Music is to ask the class, "Which traits do you need to have to be a successful composer?" We gather up a list of ideas and put them on the board, which in turn provokes a lot of discussion. Defining success is unique for each individual, but in this section I'll relate my own perspective of what makes a successful composer based on my experience in the industry as a composer, observing the successful people around me.

This chapter is a little different than the rest of the book. It's filled with my advice about the industry; it's as subjective as I can make it, but it is also personal. All composers have their own stories and their own advice. Invest the time to get as much advice as you can from local professionals. This investigation may actually lead to a gig someday, because it means that you are out in the industry meeting new people and talking about skills.

Passion

Probably the most important trait to have in this industry is to be passionate about what you want to do. People will notice your passion. You're embarking on a journey into a very crowded marketplace of composers, and one thing that will separate you from the rest of the pack is to be enthusiastic about your industry.

Passion emanates from your performance at work, allowing you to put in more hours because you want to, not because you have to. This will breed respect from your colleagues.

Most video game composers whom I've interviewed in the past share a single trait: they compose music for games because they love it and are passionate about it, not because they ever expected to make any money at it. They would compose music for games even if they weren't being paid for it. Indeed, they were often surprised the first time someone offered to pay them for their work. This kind of passion will help you through some of the disappointments that you might encounter along the way.

Speaking the Language

Video game developers love to talk about games. If you want to work in games, it's important that you can talk to your clients about games. What sparks your imagination? Which game did you play recently where the music did something really awesome? If you're passionate about video games, you'll learn to speak the lingua franca of this particular country.

This advice really applies to any industry. For example, if you're interested in being a film composer, become an expert on films, directors, and film composers.

COMPOSER PERSPECTIVE

Akari Kaida

It is important to always be aware of any opportunities and research information daily. If you are planning on working in the industry for a long time, always listen to the latest hits and popular media. Video games are fun products of people's exchange of ideas, and the music is an integral part of that exchange. Game soundtracks are similar because they are the product of the director and the sound team in constant communicant with each other. A new idea might lead to a new gig for you, so you always have to keep that in your mind. Of course, you must always compose what is asked. However, always keep in mind that there are opportunities for the sound team to come up with interesting ideas that you can incorporate to make the game better.

The game industry can be very unforgiving. You cannot keep up simply because you love games or music. You must also have a talent for music and technical skill, as well as the flexibility to try new things, good communication skills, good networking skills, and good finance skills. It is very rare to find someone with a solid grasp of all of these skills from the beginning. I myself have some deficiencies within these fields. However, in the end, I think the people who will succeed in this industry are those who love games and this music, and who continually find new and exciting things that push them to achieve higher and higher goals.

Also, the mentality among the general public seems to be that games are meant for men to play and the number of female gamers is still small. I believe that women can create games that other women will enjoy, and the limit to what amazing things games can accomplish Is still undetermined. I would love to see more women become active not only in the music industry, but also in the game industry.

Belief in Yourself

No matter how talented new composers are, if they don't believe in themselves, they will fail. Rejection is something every composer faces—many, many times. The best, most well-known composers in our industry have failed or received negative feedback not once but many times across their careers. Successful composers pick themselves up, and are so passionate about what they do that they strive to constantly get better after every rejection they may receive.

A lack of belief in oneself is the biggest barrier to entry and challenge in this industry. This career has many people knocking at the door to get in. You may be stuck in that line for a while, so while you wait, your belief in yourself will carry you through. You must be relentless in your pursuit to be successful.

Fear grips every composer at the beginning of a new gig or when working for a new client. It's not unusual, and you should get used to the fact that not every demo that you send out will turn into a job. You may send out more than 100 inquiries before you get a callback. This is not unusual, and should be expected.

As a teacher, I've observed extremely talented students who are never able to believe in themselves. This industry demands that you have some degree of self-esteem to overcome times when you experience rejection and failure. The question isn't whether you'll experience them, it's when.

COMPOSER PERSPECTIVE

Noriyuki Iwadare

To this day, I don't know what causes the good luck to land you one job versus another, but I believe that putting my absolute best into every job or opportunity that has presented itself in front of me has brought me to where I am today.

This industry is constantly changing and constantly trying to find the next new idea. From a composer's perspective, game music has no bounds regarding what genre or type of music it is required to be. It ranges from classical-inspired music to the latest pop songs, from traditional folk music to vast Hollywood-like orchestrations. You need to be able to say, "Yes, I can write it!" for any genre, or else you will not get the job. It may be a harsh world, but it is also a very rewarding one.

No matter what job you are presented with, you will probably experience many things for the first time. If you think, "I can't do It," and surround yourself with negative words, you will never be able to do it. Instead, think, "I can do it!" and "I will try my best!" Then give everything you have toward studying and learning that skill. Also, remember to always follow deadlines! This is very important.

I have been helped countless times by my many dear friends who have helped me develop the skills I needed to do many different jobs. Friends are very important, and you should always cherish and value the connections you make with another person.

Write Music for the Person Signing the Check

Creating music for games (or films) can be difficult. You have to get inside the game director's head and think about what music the director wants for the game. You are not writing music for yourself—you are writing music for someone else. The game developer must like the music you write before he or she will sign the check. If you aren't able to write music that the game director likes, no check, no next gig.

If you are very passionate about writing music but can't perceive someone else's vision, you might consider becoming a songwriter or classical composer, where you have a lot more liberty with the kinds of music that you'll write. Writing music for films and games is about making someone else happy, and sometimes the end result doesn't match your personal vision of what the music should sound like. Composers need to be able to overcome their own feelings sometimes when dealing with a client. The job is to align yourself with the creative vision of what the music should be.

Composers can be thought of as problem solvers. The video game needs music, and you need to step up and solve that problem by writing the best music for that game.

Reliability

Reliability is a trait that almost doesn't need to be mentioned. If you are unreliable, you probably need to quit now. Make sure that you can deliver the product by the deadline, and preferably earlier. Never over-promise, and always over-deliver. If a game developer can't rely on you to create music when you say you can, the company will never hire you again.

As you look at this list of skills, being unreliable is the single skill that is a *deal breaker*. You can have enormous talent at writing music, but a client will never hire you again if you can't deliver. Ninety percent of being successful in this industry is not about talent; it's about whether someone else can depend on you.

As a professional composer, you often set your own deadlines. Composers need to be able to have a lot of self-motivation to complete projects. Quite often they work by themselves. Some people enjoy lots of company and direction, in which case working on your own can be difficult and challenging. Make sure you find a work environment that works for you and allows you to be reliable and dependable.

Adaptability

When working with a client, you'll often receive feedback on your compositions. In many cases, clients may ask for revisions on those pieces. Rarely is a music cue perfect the first time a client hears it. Most clients are nonmusicians, so their feedback will also be nonmusical. You'll need to interpret this feedback and convert it into musical changes that you'll make to your composition.

When new composers receive feedback on their compositions, typically they are too afraid to make dramatic changes to their music. If a nonmusical client is asking for revisions, you need to account for the fact that the client probably won't be able to hear subtle musical changes that you make. In most cases, if the client asks for revisions, it generally means more than just adjusting the levels of your mix.

Composers must be adaptable. They must be willing to turn their compositions inside out, while maintaining a smile on their faces. Think of it as a challenge to raise your music to the level that your clients are hearing in their heads.

Entrepreneurship

Being a successful composer is only partly about the act of writing music. Most modern independent video game composers split their day between actual composition (50 percent), sales and marketing (30 percent), and meetings (20 percent). If you want to just compose music, either you'll fail in the video game industry or you'll need strong partners whose capabilities offset the other skills that you don't possess.

Sales, marketing, making contacts, tracking down leads, and business management are essential ingredients in being a video game composer. Without these skills, your chances of being successful diminish tremendously.

People Skills

If you're not anywhere near as charismatic as Hans Zimmer or Thomas Newman (and I'm in this group), you're going to have to work hard at meeting new people who want to work with you. The best advice that I can give you in this regard is to "find your people."

When I was just starting out, I thought that if I had a better pitch, or was friendlier, or had a better reel, that I could convince people to work with me. One thing I wish I had realized earlier in my career is that not everyone will like you no matter what's on your reel or how friendly you are. And that's okay. Find the people with whom you get along, whatever industry they are in. That industry might be gaming, but your niche might be in children's music, advertising, films, or wherever. You'll definitely know where you fit in as your career starts moving.

I was successful primarily in gaming because I enjoyed the people who worked in that industry and they liked my personality. Most companies and individuals would rather work with people they relate to than with someone who is super-talented. So, find your audience—and don't be disappointed when it takes some time, or you find that not everyone wants to work with you.

Talent

In my career I've met incredible composers who have been educated at the best music colleges in the world. I've also met astonishing composers who couldn't read a note but still could write a piece of music that was absolutely brilliant. Talent comes in all shapes and sizes. A key lesson that I've learned is that talent is only a small piece in the quest to be successful. As you look through the skills list presented in this chapter, you'll find that there are many skills involved in being a successful composer.

As noted earlier, clients often prefer to work with people with whom they can get along rather than someone with great talent. Game directors and producers use composers as their musical voice because they don't have one. Your ability to interpret that voice is more important than how much talent you have—which leads us to the next skill.

Humility

If you wait until the perfect gig comes along, you will fail. Take every gig that involves audio as long as you have space in your calendar and bills to pay. A successful gig means that you have a connection to the industry, and more important, that someone will want to hire you again in the future. I've been working with some of the same clients for more than 20 years. As they've risen in the game industry, they have brought me along for the ride, knowing that I'm dependable and can write the music that they're hearing in their heads.

Any job that you do successfully—even if there is no money involved—might mean a future gig from that client or person. Relationships are far more valuable in your early career than the money that you'll be bringing in. Your future success will be based on how many relationships you're able to maintain. Think of working for free as an investment that you're making in your future.

When you have a successful experience composing for a client, that client will evangelize your name to other clients. This is by far the best sales and marketing, and it's a kind of advertising that money can't ever buy. Your clients will begin to recommend you for gigs to other people in their network. This prospect again emphasizes the point that no job involving audio is beneath you; it's the importance of the long-term relationship that matters.

Many new composers who enter the industry have a singular vision of the composer they want to be (e.g., Marty O'Donnell, Jack Wall, Nobuo Uematsu). When their first gigs are not for the next *Halo* or *Final Fantasy*, they get super disappointed and eventually drop out of the industry. Make sure that you set a wide net in terms of the gigs that you are pursuing. Any gig is better than doing nothing.

Objectivity

Being able to listen to your own writing with objectivity will be the most difficult thing you do as a writer. If you've spent 60 hours composing a piece of music, it will be very difficult for you to analyze the music objectively with new ears.

When writing music for clients, try to deliver three to five tracks at the first meeting. As part of this set of music, generally it's not a good idea to send all incredible tracks. If you present five stellar pieces of music, a group of nonmusicians may find it difficult to decipher good music versus bad. So, include a piece of music whose sole purpose is to make the others sound better. That way, the clients can make a clear distinction between what's good and what's not.

This strategy has worked in 90 percent of the presentations that I've made. Sometimes, however, the client will choose the piece I included just to make the other pieces sound better. This experience has taught me several things. First, being objective about your own writing is the most difficult skill to master as a composer. Second, sometimes it can be very difficult to know why a client chooses one piece over another because music can carry such emotional weight.

Because it's challenging to be objective about your own writing after you've spent many hours on a composition, bring in an objective person who hasn't heard the music to get that individual's take on it before presenting to your client. This will give you some valuable insight into your own compositions.

Technical Skills

Another key to success for many composers in video games is the ability to learn new technology and software quickly. Because technology changes quickly, composers constantly face new software challenges. Many composers find themselves in the position of not only having to write a piece of music, but also writing it in a format or middleware engine that is totally new to them. Standards in the industry are clearly needed. As organizations like IASIG and GANG push companies to standardize their formats, the industry might eventually evolve into having a single set of standard formats (iXMF).

Several years ago at the Game Developers Conference, I heard a game industry veteran and former educator (Brenda Romero) rant that if you didn't know how to program (computers), you shouldn't consider going into the video game industry. People who know how to program do much better in the video game industry than those who don't.

With regard to direct application of music in video games, there is a serious need for music and audio programmers in the industry. In addition, many video game music implementers and editors must know some programming.

A handful of video game composers and sound designers know at least one basic scripting language like LUA, C#, or JavaScript. If you have experience in any of those areas, your résumé will leapfrog over those that don't have the same knowledge. Whether you choose to learn how to program or not, being fearless when it comes to learning new technology is essential for success in the video games industry.

Experience

One of the qualifications listed in many job postings for game audio positions is to have worked on three or more AAA titles. How can you expect to break into the industry if all the positions require that you've already worked in the industry? This is the game industry's way of telling you that it expects you to "pay your dues."

You can't ignore the requirement for experience, but employers don't just look at experience when hiring, they look at a whole person. What makes you a person that the client would want to work with? The best way to overcome the experience requirement is to showcase that you have a wide-ranging skill set with multiple areas of expertise. If you've had experience doing only one specific thing, you're going to be outgunned by the competition. Besides composition, perhaps you've done museum installations, done voice-over recording, worked on MOD files, know scripting languages, and so on. Demonstrating diversity can help you get a gig. Show the company that you are able to solve complex problems.

Most successful composers whom I've interviewed have told me that even if they had another gig serving coffee to pay the bills, they would continue composing on the side. Even when I considered myself successful as a game audio composer, I was still composing music for projects that I believed in for free. I would continue composing music for games because it's what I love to do, and would do it as a hobby even if I wasn't making money from it. Make sure to get experience on projects even if they do not make you any money. Such activities show that you have incredible passion for what you do.

Courage

It may help to be naive when it comes to this industry. If you don't think it's hard, it may not be. I've tried to be honest in this book about how challenging this industry can be. Russell Brower (composer, *World of Warcraft*) once said to a group of composition students, "You've picked the single most difficult career (video game composer), except for maybe professional acting." Know that you might fail a lot of the time, but with each failure you'll learn a lot and gradually succeed one step at a time.

It takes courage to succeed in the video game industry. Courage means letting go of the idea that you might fail. Composers in this industry may fail a lot before they become successful. With each failure, you'll also learn an incredible amount. Try to have the courage to try new things, to risk success.

Competition

When I first started bidding for composing jobs against competitors, I believed the other candidates were the enemy. I was angry and disappointed when I didn't get a gig. This thought was actually very misguided. Competitors are much better friends than enemies.

Competitors can actually help you get gigs. The truth is that when your competitors are super busy, they may need to recommend someone else for a gig. I've recommended many people whom I trust for gigs over the years to clients when I've been too busy. And I know that they would do the same for me. Competitors also may have overflow work, executing rearrangements or creating secondary cues. In such a case, they may call people they respect and are reliable to help out with the gig.

If you do become successful, when you get busy, you might find yourself in the position of recommending your competition for a gig.

Handling Rejection and Failure

Rejection is something that all composers must deal with, whether they fail to get a gig or are ignored when trying to meet new people. One of the exercises I do as part of the classes I teach is to have students fail on purpose, so as to try and release the fear of failing. There are many ways of dealing with rejection, so let's get some perspective by examining some typical scenarios:

- Rejection is common. The industry is crowded, and generally only one person gets the gig. If you weren't right for this gig, perhaps there is another gig waiting out there somewhere for which you are the right match.

- Rejection is not a reflection your self-worth. It's easy to become depressed when you don't get a gig that you looked forward to. Being rejected doesn't mean that you're not talented enough; rather, it means that the stars didn't align on this project. Successful video game composers pick themselves up, dust themselves off, and look for the next opportunity.

- Rejection is generally not about talent. Generally the person who gets the gig has an inside track that comes from knowing the client really well. So, get to know many clients really well; then, when a gig comes up, you'll be the first person in line.

- Projects are often heavily "gated," meaning they have to go through intense rounds of review by internal stakeholders before they are approved for full production. Changes at a gate review can cause changes in who is composing the music—a very common occurrence.

Failure is also something that you might face. Composers may get fired from gigs or face major revisions on a project. Here are some of the reasons why people fail on a project:

- Maybe you weren't the right fit. Writing music for a client requires a connection with the lead game designer or producer. It doesn't always work out.

- You made a huge mistake. Learn from it, and move on. Many composers have faced this issue at one point in their career. Rarely do these bumps in the road have huge impacts on your overall career trajectory.

- Life happens that interferes with your ability to work. A death in the family, a divorce, personal problems, and other issues can all take their toll when you're trying to work. Many composers face this at one point or another during their careers. Inform your client and be honest about the situation, and 9 times out of 10 the client will actually be supportive.

- Sometimes the factors leading to failure have nothing to do with you. I worked on a game once that was not working at all, so the cheapest option for the team was to redo the music. The game still sucked after it was released, but that failure didn't have anything to do with the music.

Finances

Most musicians and composers at some point in their career find that they have difficulty with finances. Managing income and taxes is very important for a working composer. Here are a few quick suggestions for balancing your finances.

Expenses and Budgeting

For video game composers, it's very important to keep detailed records of your income and expenses so that you can plan and budget. Create a list of income goals, along with planned expenses. Most composers and music production companies keep a large spreadsheet of outgoing expenses and projected revenues to plan their overall budgets. Use whatever works for you to keep track of all your expenses and how you'll make ends meet every year, month to month, day to day.

> **note**
>
> Many composers and sound designers lust after the latest gear and software. I've developed a rule of thumb with regard to using income to buy new equipment and software: I buy gear only if I can expense it on a real job. That means that I'm not spending money that I don't have just because I'm drooling over a newly released product. It's nice to have toys, but it's much better to pay next month's rent and be able to afford your taxes.
>
> There is, in fact, a minimum bar of production value needed to compete, and that does mean you have to make a minimum investment in equipment. Demos that, while compositionally interesting, were made by the default General MIDI sound

set will not be able to compete on the same level as demos created on more advanced equipment. Equipment investment is a balance between what you can afford and which level you want to compete at.

Taxes

If you are a freelance composer, find a good tax accountant who specializes in musicians to do your taxes. Accountants will definitely help save you money on your taxes. They will also help you with strategies for saving for retirement (which is generally a tax deduction), and help you with income and expense planning by determining what is tax deductible and what is not.

Most normal employees of companies have taxes sent to the government with each paycheck. In contrast, most freelance and contract composers do not have their taxes deducted when they receive their checks. Instead, they are responsible for sending in their tax money themselves. Usually this is done through quarterly payments to the state and federal governments (the IRS if you live in the United States). Many musicians get behind in their payments to the government and find themselves in huge debt.

Professional composers generally set aside 30 percent of their income into a separate banking account when they receive a check that doesn't have taxes taken out. This money is generally off-limits until the quarterly and yearly tax payments have been paid. It can be very difficult for new composers who are just getting by month to month to not spend this money, but that's precisely how many musicians find themselves in serious debt to the IRS. Back tax interest and penalties are extremely expensive, so try to keep on top of your requirement to submit estimated tax payments on time.

Legal Fees

When you're first starting out, having a lawyer who's charging $200 or more per hour review your contracts can be a daunting proposition if you're making less than $1,000 on the entire project. In those instances, you may choose to be your own lawyer instead of giving away the money you need for next month's cell phone and Internet bills. There are two pieces of advice that will help you.

First, the money that you spent on the lawyer will probably not equal the money that you'll earn or save because you actually used a lawyer. For example, if you spend $500 out of your budget to hire a lawyer to look at a contract, you want to make sure that the lawyer will save you at least $500 in the contract revision; otherwise, this service may not be worth the additional expense. As a suggestion, any contract that has a total music budget of less than $4,000 probably doesn't need a legal review on the contract documents. The money that you'll spend on legal fees is just not worth it.

Second, accept the fact that you may make some mistakes when reviewing documents yourself. There are plenty of great legal books and sample contracts that can help you make informed decisions when reviewing these documents. Invest some money and time in reading those resources. Also, there are many professional email and Internet forums where you can ask questions of experienced professional composers and get some free advice about a clause that might not look right. If you do realize that you made a mistake in a contract after you've already signed it, chalk it up to a learning experience that you won't repeat on the next job.

As I've discussed throughout this book, most composers encounter a bad deal or contract that they've regretted several times throughout their career. You will get better at revising contracts, and don't worry too much if you make a mistake—you're in good company.

Review

Have realistic expectations about how long it may take you to find initial success.

Successful composers share many of the same business and personal skills and traits: reliability, courage, perspective, humility, interpersonal skills, adaptability, belief in themselves, and a passion for video game music.

Set some goals, breaking them down into long-term and short-term goals. Then, create a list of daily tasks to help keep you on track to achieve those goals.

Competitors can actually be secret allies who can help promote you. Treat competitors with respect and friendliness.

Rejection is common, and it's not a reflection of your self-worth.

Failure is something that composers inevitably face. The best composers overcome failure by picking themselves up, believing in themselves, and looking for the next gig.

Try to budget and determine goals for your income and expenses. Keep a detailed record of your financial dealings. If you're working as a contract employee without taxes being taken out of your paychecks, make sure to put aside 30 percent of your income into a separate banking account for future tax payments. Tax accountants can help plan your expenses, deductions, and retirement savings.

Lawyers are expensive. Use them only when the amount that you'll earn or save equals or exceeds their fee. Otherwise, on small contract jobs (up to $4,000), look for free advice from professional composers and books and do your own legal review.

Exercises

1. List skills you think are important to being successful. Take this list to a composer in the industry to review how accurate your expectations are.

2. Write a terrible composition on purpose to see what it is like to fail.

3. Create a self-assessment that pertains to success as a composer in the video game industry. Then create an action plan to improve your skills that may need work.

PART VI

CONCLUSION AND APPENDIXES

- Conclusion
- Appendix A: Companion Website and Supporting Software Tools
- Appendix B: Glossary
- Appendix C: Game Music Canon
- Appendix D: Resources
- Appendix E: Composer Biographies

CONCLUSION

Where to Go from Here

Throughout this book I've tried to pass my knowledge of video game scoring to you. As you learn more and gather other perspectives from other game composers, you will begin to shape your future by developing new techniques of your own and innovating in other extraordinary ways.

I encourage you to break with convention with enthusiasm. Along this path you may experience many failures, but innovation does not happen without a lot of failed experiments. Be passionate about this industry, contribute to it, and find your place in it. Continue to learn and share so that we as a community can grow.

Throughout the appendixes and on the companion website, you'll find many additional resources to continue your learning, including information about popular game conferences, additional books, interviews, game footage, and scores. In addition, many higher education institutions, both online and in the classroom, are now teaching video game scoring, and I encourage you to find a program that works for you. See page 426 for information about accessing the site.

The Future of Game Scoring

Our industry has been changing rapidly over the past several decades. The ideas presented in this book are the culmination of using many of the fundamental tools available today. The future of game scoring will introduce many new techniques, and our ability to score games in better and more innovative ways will grow.

In the video game scoring industry, we've become fairly adept at creating adaptive music and implementing it into games. Unfortunately, we're not as good at developing adaptive systems to go along with our music. As players deconstruct these systems through gameplay, much of video game music becomes predictable. State changes are not subtle, and music scoring should be invisible. The next generation of video game composers will work to solve these problems.

For video game scores to become more innovative, it is likely that we will need to collect more data from our games and interpret those data to adapt the music in real time. The level of detail needs to be subtler and more interesting. Avoiding the obvious trappings of broad music state changes to maximize subtlety in the stories that we're trying to tell is what lies on the horizon in music innovation for video games.

Meeting this goal will require developers, publishers, and composers to experiment with new scoring methods and new music system designs. I encourage you to lead the effort to meet that challenge and innovate the next generation of music for video games. Above all, write great and inspiring music.

COMPANION WEBSITE AND SUPPORTING SOFTWARE TOOLS

Purchase of this book includes additional supporting materials that can be accessed via the companion website. There, you'll find links to articles and videos that support many of the ideas in the text. In addition, the companion website contains software tools and applications that reinforce the fundamental composition techniques introduced in this book.

Companion Website

This book has a website containing companion materials. To obtain the link to the site visit www.informit.com/title/9780321961587 and follow the directions for registering your product. Following is an overview of the supporting materials you'll find on the website:

- **Supporting Reference Materials.** The website includes many links that support the various topics in the book. You'll find related articles, video examples, and additional comments for each part of the book.
- **Discussion Forums.** The discussion forums are a place where you can ask questions about the text, suggest additions, and contribute your own ideas and informational articles.

Composer Tools

The software applications included with this book are meant to simulate various interactive and adaptive scenarios that composers frequently find in games. In turn, they help composers learn various fundamental composing techniques such as horizontal resequencing, vertical remixing, and writing effective transitions.

Detailed instructions are provided for each of the companion software tools that explain how to use that tool. You can use these tools to demonstrate how an interactive composition might work in a game so as to sell a client on the use of adaptive music in their game.

Each tool included with the book demonstrates a single, specific principle that can be used in adaptive music. Often when composers begin by using an advanced audio middleware engine like Wwise or Fmod, they don't know where to start. These middleware engines offer a vast array of features but don't inform the composer about the advantages and disadvantages of using one technique over another. The tools included with this book are meant to help composers understand these differences on a smaller scale before they move on to a more sophisticated audio middleware solution.

Here is a list of the core tools included as part of this book:

- Horizontal Resequencing Simulator Using Branching
- Horizontal Resequencing Simulator Using Advanced Branching
- Vertical Remixing Simulator
- Transition Simulator
- Sound Design Tool

GLOSSARY

Many of the terms used in this book may be
unfamiliar to readers. This appendix is designed
to help readers comprehend the advanced
terminology associated with composing music
for games.

2D Platformer A game type rendered in two dimensions (*x* and *y*) where the player controls a character that generally moves from left to right on the game screen. A good example of a 2D platformer is *Super Mario Bros.*

3D Game A game that is rendered in three dimensions (*x*, *y*, and *z*). In these games the player controls a character in a virtual world that can move front/back, left/right, and up/down.

3D Middleware A set of software libraries that allow game developers to build 3D game worlds quickly and easily.

5.1 Surround Generally referred to as "five point one." A surround speaker configuration that includes 5.1 channels, including left, center, right, left surround, right surround, and low-frequency effects (LFE). It is the most common home game surround setup. Alternative configurations of speakers include 6.1 and 7.1.

AAA Game Frequently referred to as "triple-A games." AAA games represent the highest budget level for game production and are usually released on at least one game console (e.g., PlayStation 4, Xbox One, Wii U, PC).

Adaptive Music Music that can change in real time based on a control input. These changes might include tempo variation, changes in the form, adding layers, or many other musical parameters.

Advergame Short for "advertising game." A game that is created in an effort to promote a product or service.

Aleatoric A compositional term that refers to randomness or variability in the performance or composition of a piece of music.

Anticipation In music, notes or chords that begin just before the downbeat of a measure; the chord anticipates the downbeat by playing on the eighth note before the downbeat.

Artificial Intelligence (AI) In video games, simulated character behaviors and how characters might act in various scenarios.

Audio Interchange File Format (AIFF) A type of uncompressed audio file format. This format has two parameters that determine the quality of the file: bit depth and sample rate. Higher values equal better-sounding files, while growing in size and disk space.

Avatar A visual representation of the player in the game world.

Baked-In See *prerendered audio file*.

Band Pass Filter (BPF) A type of audio equalizer that boosts only the frequencies around a specific center frequency. The frequency width of the filter is referred to as the Q.

BASS Audio Middleware Engine A commonly used software library and tool created by Un4Seen Systems that facilitates the use of MOD files in games across multiple game platforms.

Bleed See *microphone bleed*.

Bounce (Export) To render an audio file from audio tracks, DSP, and virtual instruments in a sequencer or digital audio workstation.

Branching A term used in adaptive music scoring for music that can transition to another piece of music, usually at the end of a musical phrase or musical demarcation like a downbeat. See *horizontal resequencing*.

Broadcast Wave File (BWF) A commonly used uncompressed audio file format based on the standard audio WAV format, but which includes additional data such as comments and timestamps.

Buyout A term used in contracts to describe the transaction that transfers the ownership of a performance, recording, or composition from one party to another for a specific fee.

Cadence A musical resolution from dissonance to consonance in a piece of music, which usually finishes a musical phrase or passage.

Casual Game A game that is meant to be played in short intervals over multiple sessions. Examples include *Candy Crush*, *Diner Dash*, and *Tetris*.

Central Processing Unit (CPU) The computer brain within a video game system, which does most of the calculations to play and visually render the game itself. In addition, it handles all audio processing from audio playback to DSP.

Chance Music Music that has been composed by random operations, or in which certain variables in the music are left up to the performance.

Cinematic An in-game, noninteractive, linear movie that can be typically scored like a film without the use of adaptive music.

Compression (1) File compression. (2) The reduction of the dynamic range of an audio file.

CPU Load How hard the central processing unit is working to render and play the video game. If the CPU load is too high, the system may not be able to play back audio or render a consistent frame rate to the screen.

Crossfading A technique by which the volume of one audio stream is faded out while the volume of another audio stream is faded in.

Cue A musical segment.

Cue Sheet   A list of musical cues. The cue sheet for a video game usually includes information about the cues' locations within the game, file names, and adaptive characteristics.

Cutoff Frequency   The frequency at which higher and lower frequencies are reduced; commonly used in synthesis filters like LPF and HPF.

Cut-Scene   See *cinematic*.

Decibel (dB)   A unit for measuring audio volume.

Demo(s)   Short for "demonstration material." Composers create musical demos to prove to a client that they are the best person for the job.

Diegetic Music   Music that is played on-screen by musicians or a music device, such as a phonograph, in the scene. Diegetic music is heard by characters or avatars that exist within the scene.

Digital Audio Workstation (DAW) Software that is used to record, edit, and play back audio and MIDI instruments. Examples include ProTools, Cubase, Digital Performer, Logic, Sonar, and Reaper.

DirectMusic   An important yet complicated adaptive music solution created for the advanced implementation of adaptive music systems within games. This system was deprecated by Microsoft with the release of Windows 7.

Dither   A mechanism by which noise is added to a digital sound file before reducing the bit depth so as to reduce the amount of distortion that normally would occur.

Downloadable Sample Bank (DLS)   A standardized file format developed by IASIG that contains a user-created bank of instruments, parameters, and their corresponding samples.

Extra-Diegetic Music   Music that only the viewer or player can hear and that emphasizes the emotional content in the story. The cast of characters in the scene do not hear the extra-diegetic music. Usually referred to as the underscore.

Filter   A type of audio equalizer frequently used in synthesis and sampling. Examples include LPF and HPF.

First-Person Shooter (FPS) A type of game that is displayed in three dimensions from a first-person perspective, usually involving lots of weapons. Examples include *Doom, Halo, Half-Life,* and *Portal*.

FLAC   A type of lossless audio file compression that will decompress a file so that it plays back identically to the precompressed version of the file.

Fmod Audio Middleware Engine   A commonly used software library and tool created by Firelight Technologies that facilitates the implementation of complex interactive music scores or sound design in games across multiple game platforms.

Foley   A type of sound effect that relates to human motion, footsteps, breathing, and so on.

Formant   In regard to an instrument, the overtone series above the pitch that the instrument produces, which determines the overall sound or quality of the instrument.

Frames per Second (FPS)   The number of frames per second that the video game is running at.

Full-Motion Video (FMV)   See *cinematic*.

Game Audio Network Guild (GANG)   A group of audio professionals that promotes and discusses music and audio for video games. The GANG Awards are among the most prominent music and audio awards distributed to video game audio artists and composers.

Game Design   The discipline in a game development team that creates the rules of a video game system and determines how the game will be played.

Game Developer   A team of experts from many disciplines (art, programming, audio, game design) that work together to build video games.

Game Developers Convention (GDC)   The largest annual congregation of game developers, which holds sessions in various game expertises including audio. It is usually held in March in San Francisco.

Game Mechanic   A rule or an action that defines the play in the game system.

Game Publisher   A company that provides funding and guidance to a game developer to produce a video game. The publisher also markets and sells the game after it's completed.

Gameplay   The time when a player is actively playing the game, directing a character, or solving a puzzle, as opposed to watching a cut-scene.

General MIDI Instrument Set   A set of 128 instruments divided into 16 categories, standardized by the MIDI Manufacturers Association. It is available on some game platforms.

Gig   A job, either short or long term.

Harmonic Framework   The combination of musical notes that make up a chord or chord progressions in a specific key and mode.

High Pass Filter (HPF)   A type of shelving audio equalizer that decreases frequencies below a specific frequency. The frequency at which the frequencies are decreased is usually called the cutoff frequency.

Horizontal Resequencing An adaptive music technique that composers use to change music in real time within video games. This technique cues up the individual music segments dynamically based on player decisions and outcomes.

iMuse One of the first adaptive music systems for games, created by LucasArts; it extended the MIDI file format. It defines the use of music markers that specify loop and branch points, allowing the music to adapt in real time to gameplay mechanics.

Indeterminate Music The capacity for composed music to be executed differently with each performance.

Intellectual Property The proprietary trade secrets, copyrights/trademarks, patents, and story ideas that a company develops and for which it wants to retain ownership.

Interactive Audio Special Interest Group (IASIG) A group of audio professionals that develops standards and white papers to promote interactive audio, including audio in video games. It is supervised by the MIDI Manufacturers Association.

Interactive Music See *adaptive music*.

International Game Developers Association (IGDA) A nonprofit organization composed of people who work in the video game industry. The IGDA works to connect game developers with one another in a community and solve industry problems.

Layered Score An adaptive score that has been separated into layers of instrument groups, which can be dynamically faded in and out based on the gameplay. See *vertical remixing*.

Lossless Compression A type of file compression that will decompress an exact copy of the files that were originally compressed. Examples of lossless compression include Zip archives and FLAC audio compression.

Lossy Compression A type of audio file compression that can save a large amount of space at the expense of removing some of the audio data from the file. Examples of lossy compression include Ogg Vorbis, MP3, and WMA.

Low-Frequency Effect (LFE). An audio effect in surround systems that is played out of the subwoofer at low frequencies. Examples include explosions and rumbles.

Low-Frequency Oscillator (LFO) A commonly used control in synthesis that can manage many different parameters, including the filter cutoff, volume envelope, and pitch of the oscillator.

Low Pass Filter (LPF) A type of shelving audio equalizer that decreases frequencies above a specific frequency. The frequency at which the frequencies are decreased is usually called the cutoff frequency.

Max (1) An open source, visual programming language distributed by Cycling74 for creating interactive music and audio. (2) A Mac audio converter tool developed by Sbooth.org.

Mickey Mousing A film scoring term describing music that is synchronized to every action in a scene. This technique is most often used in animation, and is considered cliché or humorous in dramatic settings.

Microphone Bleed When recording multiple instruments in a studio, the situation in which instruments are picked by microphones other than the ones specifically mic-ing the instrument.

Middleware A set of prewritten software libraries and tools to help with the development of games. Common examples of middleware in games include 3D middleware like UDK and Unity, and audio middleware like Fmod and Wwise.

MIDI File/MIDI Sequence See *Standard MIDI File*.

Miles Sound System Middleware Engine A software library and tool distributed by RAD Game Tools that facilitates the implementation of complex interactive music scores or sound design in games across multiple game platforms.

MMORG Massively multiplayer online role-playing game. Examples include *World of Warcraft* and *Guild Wars 2*.

MOD File A type of music file that has sequence, instrument, and sample data built into the file format. Common MOD file formats include XM, MOD, S3M, and IT.

MOD Tracker A computer-based sequencer, instrument editor, and sample editor that is used to create MOD files.

Mode A type of musical scale. Examples include major, minor, dorian, lydian, and aeolian.

MP3 A type of audio file compression licensed by Fraunhofer Institute. In certain circumstances, MP3 files do not loop properly, which is why many games prefer to use Ogg Vorbis compression. In certain instances, you may need to obtain a license to use MP3 compression in a game.

Multitracking When recording live instruments, the practice of recording the same part multiple times to simulate a larger section of instruments.

Musical Instrument Digital Interface (MIDI) A set of commands developed by the MIDI Manufacturers Association in the early 1980s that enable synthesizer and virtual instruments to communicate with one another and sequencers.

Non-diegetic See *extra-diegetic*.

Non-disclosure Agreement (NDA) An agreement between a game developer and a contractor that prohibits the contractor from disclosing any trade secrets of the developer or details about a specific project.

Obstruction and Occlusion The change in the sound equalization and reverberation when the listener is separated from the source of the sound by an object like a wall or stairs.

Ogg Vorbis A common type of audio file compression. Because it is an open source format, it can be used in game without a license.

Pd (PureData) An open source, visual programming language developed by Miller Puckette for creating interactive music.

Performance Rights Organization (PRO) An organization that collects performance royalties and distributes them to publishers and composers. Examples include Broadcast Music, Inc. (BMI) and the American Society of Composers, Authors and Publishers (ASCAP).

Playlist A list of musical cues that can be played in order or randomly.

Power-Up In video games, an in-game reward that sometimes gives the player a special ability or additional characteristics.

Prerendered Audio File (1) An audio file that has been recorded and exported to include any DSP effects (i.e., reverb, filters) in the file itself. (2) An exported audio file that has been created using virtual and/or real instrument tracks.

Programmable Sound Generator (PSG) A sound circuit used to generate sound that was commonly used in early arcade machines.

Public Relations (PR) Agency An agency that can help composers and musicians with press releases and advertising placements.

Resonance A term used in synthesis in conjunction with filters (LPF, HPF) that controls the amount of gain at the frequency cutoff.

Riff A short musical phrase.

Runtime The period during which the game is actually being played on the game system for which it is being developed.

Sequencer See *digital audio workstation*.

Serendipitous Sync Music that has not been written specifically to be synchronized with an event in the scene, but which synchronizes to what is happening in the scene accidentally.

SFX Sound effects.

Software Development Kit (SDK) A prewritten library of software that helps programmers build apps and games more quickly and effectively.

Sound Design (1) The use of sound effects as an extra-diegetic element. (2) The combination of sound effects, Foley effects, and ambience in a scene. (3) The customization of instruments or sounds through the use of synthesis or other techniques.

SoundFont A file format developed at Creative Labs that encapsulates a custom user-created bank of instruments with their corresponding samples.

Special Interest Group (SIG) A subset of a larger group that focuses on a specific topic.

Standard MIDI File (SMF) A list of MIDI commands ordered in time that can use up to 16 separate channels of data. These MIDI commands can be sent to either the General Midi Instrument Set or a custom user-created bank of instruments. MIDI files are very small in comparison to an audio file.

Stem A subgroup of instruments or audio tracks. It can be used in layering or for remixing the balance between instruments quickly.

Stinger A short musical phrase that signals a change in the game state or indicates a reward. Stingers are sometimes played on top of another musical cue.

Submix See *stem*.

Subwoofer A speaker, usually in a surround configuration, that outputs lower frequencies (usually less than 160 Hz).

Surround A speaker configuration that includes speakers in the front and rear of the player. See *5.1 surround*.

Synchronization The ability for music to emphasize a specific moment in the story, or for two audio files to play back using the same time frame.

Track A single channel onto which you can record audio, MIDI, or other data within a digital audio workstation.

Transition An audio segment that connects two pieces of music. Transitions usually help end one piece of music while introducing another.

Two-Beep (Two-Pop) An audible beep within an audio track that marks a specific time. This marker is usually placed exactly 2 seconds before the beginning of the cue.

Underscore The use of music in film or video games that supports the emotional component of the story and that cannot be seen on the screen (extra-diegetic).

User Interface (UI) An interface within a game that includes various types of non-gameplay screens, including menus, inventory, save, load, and help screens.

Vertical Remixing A method of composition also known as recombinations in which layers of music are added or taken away to create levels of intensity and emotion.

Voices The maximum number of sounds that can be played back at any one time within a video game.

WAV The most commonly used uncompressed audio file format. This format has two parameters that determine the quality of the file: bit depth and sample rate. Higher values equal better-sounding files, while growing in size and disk space.

Work for Hire (WFH) A type of contract that transfers the full ownership and rights of music to another party in exchange for compensation.

Wwise Audio Middleware Engine A software library and tool created by Audiokinetic that facilitates the implementation of complex interactive music scores or sound design in games across multiple game platforms.

Zero Crossing Point When editing an audio file, a point in a sound wave when the sound has no positive or negative energy.

GAME MUSIC CANON

This appendix contains a list of video games that have contributed significantly to the advancement of music in video games. Even more video game recommendations and resources can be found on the companion website. At the companion website, you can also contribute your picks for games that have played an instrumental role in paving the way for modern soundtracks for video games.

1970 to 1989

1978: *Space Invaders*, Tomohiro Nishikado

1980: *Pac-Man*, Toshio Kai

1981: *Frogger*, Japanese folk songs

1982: *Dig Dug*, Yuriko Keino

1984: *Marble Madness*, Brad Fuller, Hal Canon

1985: *Super Mario Bros.*, Koji Kondo

1986: *Castlevania*, Michiru Yamane

1986: *Metroid*, Hirokazu "Hip" Tanaka

1987: *Final Fantasy 1*, Nobuo Uematsu

1988: *Skate or Die*, Ron Hubbard

1989: *Populous*, Ron Hubbard

1989: *Shadow of the Beast 3*, Tim Wright

1990 to 1999

1990: *Wing Commander*, George "The Fat Man" Sanger

1991: *Street Fighter 2*, Yoko Shimomura

1991: *Toejam and Earl*, John Baker

1991: *Out of This World*, Jean-François Freitas

1991: *Monkey Island 2: LeChuck's Revenge*, Michael Land, Peter McConnell

1993: *7th Guest*, George "The Fat Man" Sanger

1993: *Doom*, Bobby Prince

1993: *Myst*, Robyn Miller

1994: *Earthworm Jim*, Mark Miller, Tommy Tallarico

1995: *Chrono Trigger*, Yasunori Mitsuda

1996: *Quake*, Trent Reznor

1996: *Resident Evil*, Makoto Tomozawa, Koichi Hiroki, Masami Ueda, Takashi Niigaki

1997: *PaRappa the Rapper*, Masaya Matsuura

1997: *Final Fantasy VII*, Nobuo Uematsu

1997: *Grandia*, Noriyuki Iwadare

1997: *GoldenEye 007*, Graeme Norgate, Grant Kirkhope, Robin Beanland

1998: *Banjo-Kazooie*, Grant Kirkhope

1998: *Diablo I*, Matt Uelmen

1998: *Metal Gear Solid*, Takanari Ishiyama, Gigi Meroni, Kazuki Muraoka, Lee Jeon Myung, Hiroyuki Togo

1998: *Legend of Zelda: Ocarina of Time*, Koji Kondo

1998: *Grim Fandango*, Peter McConnell

1999: *Final Fantasy VIII*, Nobuo Uematsu

1999: *Russian Squares*, Guy Whitmore

1999: *Vib Ribbon*, Masaya Matsuura

1999: *Space Channel 5*, Tetsuya Mizaguchi, Naofumi Hataya, Kenichi Tokoi

1999: *Silent Hill*, Akira Yamaoka

2000 to 2009

2000: *Deus Ex*, Alexander Brandon

2000: *No One Lives Forever*, Guy Whitmore, Nathan Grigg

2001: *Rez*, Tetsuya Mizaguchi, Keiichi Sugiyama, Tomonori Sawada, Koji Sakurai, Masafumi Ogata

2001: *Halo*, Marty O'Donnell, Michael Salvatori

2001: *Ico*, Michiru Oshima

2001: *Grand Theft Auto III*, various artists

2002: *The Elder Scrolls III: Morrowind*, Jeremy Soule

2002: *Hitman 2: Silent Assassin*, Jesper Kyd

2002: *Medal of Honor: Allied Assault*, Michael Giacchino

2002: *Kingdom Hearts*, Yoko Shimomura

2003: *The Hobbit*, Rod Abernathy

2004: *Katamari Damacy*, Yū Miyake

2004: *World of Warcraft*, Jason Hayes, Tracy W. Bush, Derek Duke, Glenn Stafford

2006: *Okami*, Masami Ueda, Hiroshi Yamaguchi, Hiroyuki Hamada, Rei Kondo, Akari Groves

2007: *Super Mario Galaxy*, Koji Kondo

2007: *Bioshock*, Garry Schyman

2007: *Lord of the Rings Online*, Chance Thomas, Stephen Digregorio, Geoff Scott, Brad Spears, Egan Budd

2008: *Spore*, Brian Eno, Kent Jolly, and others

2008: *Fallout 3*, Inon Zur

2008: *Dead Space*, Jason Graves

2009: *Uncharted 2*, Greg Edmonson

2009: *Plants vs. Zombies*, Laura Shigihara

2010 to 2013

2010: *Final Fantasy XIII*, Masashi Hamauzu

2010: *Mass Effect 2*, Jack Wall

2010: *Chime*, Ciaran Walsh (audio director)

2010: *Bit.Trip Runner*, Anamanaguchi

2010: *Amnesia: The Dark Descent*, Mikko Tarmia

2010: *Limbo Martin*, Stig Andersen

2011: *Portal 2*, Mike Morasky

2011: *Batman Arkham City*, Ron Fish, Nick Arundel

2011: *Fallout 3: New Vegas*, Inon Zur, Mark Morgan

2011: *Sword and Sworcery*, Jim Guthrie

2012: *Journey*, Austin Wintory

2012: *Vessel*, Leonard Paul

2012: *Red Dead Redemption*, Bill Elm, Woody Guthrie

2013: *Bioshock Infinite*, Garry Schyman

2013: *The Last of Us*, Gustavo Santaolalla

2013: *Rayman Legends*, Christophe Héral, Billy Martin

2013: *Peggle 2*, Guy Whitmore

RESOURCES

This section contains additional resources and links to continue your education in game audio.

Organizations

These organizations help promote game audio and are useful for making connections, asking questions, and helping to contribute to our industry:

- Game Audio Network Guild (GANG), http://audiogang.org
- Interactive Audio Special Interest Group (IASIG), http://iasig.org
- International Game Developers Association (IGDA), http://igda.org

Game Conferences

At the following game conferences, you can network with game developers and get educated in the latest techniques in game scoring and audio:

- AES Audio for Games Conference, http://www.audioforgames.net
- Casual Connect Conference, http://casualconnect.org
- Develop Conference, http://www.developconference.com
- Game Developers Conference, http://www.gdconf.com
- Game Sound Con, http://www.gamesoundcon.com
- E3, http://www.e3expo.com
- PAX (Penny Arcade Expo), http://paxsite.com
- Project BBQ, http://www.projectbarbq.com

Web Resources and Podcasts

The following web resources are excellent sources of information and interviews from some of the best composers in the industry:

- Game Audio Podcast, http://www.gameaudiopodcast.com
- TopScore with Emily Reese, http://minnesota.publicradio.org/radio/programs/top-score
- GameMusic.net, http://www.gamemusic.net
- Gamasutra.com Audio Articles, http://gamasutra.com/category/audio
- GDC Vault, http://www.gdcvault.com

There are also some hashtags you should follow: #gameaudio and #gamemusic.

Books

The following books offer more detailed information and are excellent references for many of the topics covered in this book.

Twentieth-Century Experimental Music

- *Experimental Music: Cage and Beyond (Music in the 20th Century), Second Edition,* by Michael Nyman, 1999 (ISBN-10: 0521653835)
- *Music 109: Notes on Experimental Music* by Alvin Lucier, 2012 (ISBN-10: 0819572977)
- *In Search of a Concrete Music* by Pierre Schæffer, 2012 (ISBN-10: 0520265742)

Film Scoring

- *Complete Guide to Film Scoring: The Art and Business of Writing Music for Movies and TV* by Richard Davis, 2010 (ISBN-10: 0876391099)
- *Music Composition for Film and Television* by Lalo Schifrin, 2011 (ISBN-10: 0876391226)
- *The Reel World: Scoring for Pictures* by Jeff Rona, 2009 (ISBN-10: 1423434838)
- *On the Track: A Guide to Contemporary Film Scoring* by Fred Karlin, 2004 (ISBN-10: 0415941369)

Game Scoring

- *A Composer's Guide to Game Music* by Winifred Philips, 2014 (ISBN-10: 0262026643)
- *DirectX 9 Audio Exposed: Interactive Audio Development* edited by Todd M. Fay with Scott Selfon and Todor J. Fay, 2004 (ISBN-10: 1556222882)
- *Music and Game: Perspectives on a Popular Alliance* edited by Peter Moormann, 2012 (ISBN-10: 3531174096)
- *Music in Video Games* edited by K. J. Donnelly, William Gibbons, and Neil Lerner, 2014 (ISBN-10: 041563444X)
- *The Oxford Handbook of Interactive Audio* (Oxford Handbooks) edited by Karen Collins, Bill Kapralos, and Holly Tessler, 2014 (ISBN-10: 0199797226)

Game Audio

- *The Essential Guide to Game Audio: The Theory and Practice of Sound for Games* by Scott Looney and Steve Horowitz, 2014 (ISBN-10: 041570670X)
- *The Game Audio Tutorial: A Practical Guide to Sound and Music for Interactive Games* by Richard Stevens and Dave Raybould, 2011 (ISBN-10: 0240817265)

- *The Complete Guide to Game Audio: For Composers, Musicians, Sound Designers, Game Developers* by Aaron Marks, 2008 (ISBN-10: 0240810740)
- *Game Development Essentials: Game Audio Development* by Aaron Marks and Jeannie Novak, 2008 (ISBN-10: 1428318062)

The Business of Game Scoring and Audio

- *Tasty Morsels of Sonic Goodness: The Fat Man on Game Audio* by George Sanger, 2003 (ISBN-10: 1592730094)
- *The Complete Guide to Game Audio: For Composers, Musicians, Sound Designers, Game Developers* by Aaron Marks, 2008 (ISBN-10: 0240810740)
- *Game Development Essentials: Game Audio Development* by Aaron Marks and Jeannie Novak, 2008 (ISBN-10: 1428318062)

History of Video Game Music

- *Game Sound: An Introduction to the History, Theory, and Practice of Video Game Music and Sound Design* by Karen Collins, 2008 (ISBN-10: 026203378X)
- *The Games Machines: A Complete History* by Wikipedians, 2012 (http://en.wikipedia.org/wiki/Book:The_Games_Machines)

Adaptive and Generative Music

- *Notes from the Metalevel: An Introduction to Computer Composition* by Henrich Taube, 2004 (ISBN-10: 9026519753)
- *Formalized Music: Thought and Mathematics in Composition* by Iannis Xenakis, 2001 (ISBN-10: 1576470792)

Audio Middleware

Here is a list of websites for many of today's most popular audio middleware solutions for games:

- Fmod by Firelight, http://fmod.org
- Wwise by Audiokinetic, http://audiokinetic.com
- Miles Sound System by RAD Tools, http://www.radgametools.com/miles.htm
- Fabric by Tazman Audio, http://www.tazman-audio.co.uk
- ADX2 by CRI Middleware, http://www.cri-mw.com/product/lineup/audio/criadx2/index.html

Game Engines and 3D Middleware

Here is a list of websites for many of today's most popular game-making tools:

- CryEngine by Crytek, http://www.crytek.com/cryengine
- GameMaker by Yoyo Games, https://www.yoyogames.com/studio
- The Source Engine by Valve, http://source.valvesoftware.com
- Unity, http://unity3d.com
- Unreal Engine by Epic, https://www.unrealengine.com

COMPOSER BIOGRAPHIES

Yoshino Aoki is a Japanese composer and singer. She is credited for the *Breath of Fire* series, *Shadow of Rome*, and the *Megaman NT Warrior* series. In 2006, Aoki left Capcom and started out on her own as an independent composer and singer. In 2009, she established Unique Note Co., Ltd., with Tetsuya Shibata, and she is working on many video games and musical titles as a composer and singer.

Vincent Diamante is the audio director at thatgamecompany, currently overseeing music and sound design for the studio's next project. Prior to collaborating on indie hits like *Skullgirls* and thatgamecompany's *Flower*, he worked on a variety of games in a variety of capacities: casual and hardcore, in-house and freelance, audio and game mechanics design. He continues teaching students at the University of Southern California board game and sound game design while trying to catch up to them in the latest competitive PvP games.

Ben Houge has been designing audio for video games since 1996. In seven years at Sierra, he composed the string quartet soundtrack for *Arcanum: Of Steamworks & Magick Obscura*, in addition to his work on *Leisure Suit Larry 7, King's Quest: Mask of Eternity, Half-Life: Opposing Force*, and other titles. In 2004, he moved from Seattle to Shanghai, where he spent four years at Ubisoft, most of which was dedicated to serving as audio director of *Tom Clancy's EndWar*. Since leaving Ubisoft in 2008, Houge has worked as a freelance audio consultant for companies including Hidden Path Entertainment, Red Rocket Games, and Harmonix Music Systems. In addition to maintaining an active practice in sound installation and digital art, he currently teaches in the Music Technology Innovation program at Berklee College of Music's campus in Valencia, Spain.

From Nagano, Japan, **Noriyuki Iwadare** started composing for video games after performing in many bands as a keyboardist. His music can be heard in the legendary franchise *Grandia*, which brought him numerous awards; in the *Lunar* and *Phoenix Wright* series; as well as at the Tokyo Disney Resort and on TV and radio. When not composing, he spends his time performing live shows with his band.

Akari Kaida, born and raised in Hyogo, Japan, is one of the most well-known female video game music composers in the Japanese game industry. In her career, she has composed for many games, especially for Capcom, where she used to work as a part of the sound team. Her major works include the *Mega Man* series, *Okami*, and *Breath of Fire*.

Four-time Emmy award–winning composer **Laura Karpman** maintains a vibrant career in film, television, video game, concert, and theater music. Her distinguished credits include Spielberg's miniseries *Taken; Odyssey 5* and *Masters of Science Fiction* (both Emmy-nominated); and numerous video games, including *Kinect Disneyland Adventures*, *EverQuest II*, *Guardians of Middle Earth*, *Kung Fu Panda 2*, *Field Commander*, and *Untold Legends*. A Juilliard-trained composer, Karpman was resident orchestral composer for Sony Online Entertainment and has received two GANG awards for her video game music, which has been performed by orchestras internationally.

Yuzo Koshiro is a prolific video game composer who is highly regarded as the master of FM synthesis and the greatest video game composer in the 16-bit era. Koshiro is also an incredible audio programmer and uses a DAW that he coded by himself. His works include *ActRaiser*, *Dragon Slayer*, *The Y's* series, and *Streets of Rage*, just to name a few.

Wired magazine calls **Bear McCreary** a "Secret Weapon." By the age of 24, he was launched into pop culture history with his groundbreaking score to Syfy's hit series *Battlestar Galactica*, for which he composed "the most innovative music on TV today" (*Variety*). His video game credits include Sony's successful *Socom 4: U.S. Navy Seals*, Capcom's *Dark Void*, and the innovative video game/television hybrid *Defiance*. A recent Emmy Award winner for *Da Vinci's Demons*, McCreary also composes music for *Marvel's Agents of S.H.I.E.L.D.*—the #1 series debut of the 2013 fall season, with 11.9 million viewers. He also scores *The Walking Dead*, which shattered records with 16.1 million viewers for its fourth season debut.

George "The Fat Man" Sanger scored *Thin Ice* for Intellivision in 1983 and has never stopped. Audio from "Team Fat" dominated the American PC scene with diverse games like *Loom*, *Wing Commander I and II*, *The 7th Guest I and II*, *NASCAR Racing*, *Putt-Putt Saves the Zoo*, and much of EA's *ATF* flight series. Sanger introduced General MIDI to games (in *The 7th Guest*) and helped establish standards for GM sound cards. He innovated with orchestral instruments in 1992, and introduced live instruments, lyrics, music videos, and digital recordings in games. Sanger has (co-)founded and hosted conferences and events to foster and inspire creativity and community (e.g., Project BBQ for music on computers, Project Horseshoe for game design, and the UT Videogame Archive). His book, *The Fat Man on Game Audio: Tasty Morsels of Sonic Goodness*, is a well-loved and much-quoted collector's item. "The secret of game audio is kindness."

Tetsuya Shibata is a Japanese video game music composer and sound director. He is credited with more than 20 musical scores produced for Capcom's video game releases, including the *Monster Hunter* and *Devil May Cry* series, as well as the scores in the *Darkstalkers*, *Power Stone*, and *Resident Evil: Outbreak* series. In 2009, the main theme music of *Devil May Cry 4*, "Out of Darkness," was nominated for the Original Best Vocal GANG Award at the Game Developers Convention. Shibata's later works with the company involved organizing orchestral recordings for the major releases *Resident Evil 5* and *Monster Hunter Tri*. In 2009, Shibata left Capcom and began his own sound studio, Unique Note Co., Ltd., with colleague Yoshino Aoki.

Yoko Shimomura is a veteran video game composer who resides in Japan. She has been recognized as the most famous female composer in both the Western and Eastern video game industries. While a part of the sound team at Capcom and Square-Enix before becoming a freelance composer, she worked on numerous popular games, such as *Final Fight*, *Street Fighter II*, *Mario RPG*, and most notably the *Kingdom Hearts* series.

Rich Vreeland makes music and sound for games and other multimedia, and has been doing so since 2006. He is best known for his work as "Disasterpeace," in the game *FEZ*, and in the generative music app "January." Rich lives in Berkeley, California, with his piano. He hopes that every consequent project he works on will be unique, and provide a new series of creative challenges. He hopes it will last forever.

Award-winning composer **Duncan Watt**'s career spans television, film, broadcasting, and digital games. His work appears in *Bioshock Infinite* (Irrational), *League of Legends* (Riot, also Audo Lead at launch), *Need for Speed Undercover* (EA), *Stargate Online TCG* (Sony), *Brothers in Arms: Hell's Highway* (Ubisoft), *Transformers: ConstructBots* (Hasbro), and many others. Watt spent two years as senior composer/audio designer at 38 Studios. He's also the voice of *League of Legends'* fan favorites Rammus and Blitzcrank.

Guy Whitmore's first game score, *Mixed Up Mother Goose Deluxe*, was nominated for Best Soundtrack by the AIAS. *Shogo*, *No One Lives Forever*, and *Tron 2.0*, built his reputation for highly adaptive music scores. At Microsoft Studios, he led the central audio team, contributing to the *Fable, Gears of War, Project Gotham Racing, Crackdown*, and *Halo* franchises. At PopCap Games/EA, Whitmore oversees franchises such as *Bejeweled, Plants vs. Zombies*, and *Peggle*. His work earned two GANG awards in 2014.

INDEX

Numbers

2D platformers, 25, 428
3D games
    defined, 428
    diegetic music in, 301
    middleware solutions for, 106
    software libraries for developing, 102
3D middleware
    defined, 428
    developing familiarization with, 345
    diegetic sounds, and dialog in, 306
    game engines and, 445
4'33 (Cage, 1952), 115–116
5.1 Surround, 318, 428
12-tone technique, Schoenberg, 113, 238
128-bit, and DVD-ROM-based game consoles,
    96–97

A

AAA games
    defined, 428
    estimates for, 370
    organization, revisions, and backups for,
        326–327
    play experience of, 17
    production process for, 54–55
AAC/MP4, iOS and Apple games, 303
Ableton Live
    choosing, 270
    export loop option in, 277
    seamless loops with, 128, 137
    time compression and expansion in, 214
    used by Cirque de Soleil, 40
Accelerando, tempo change, 212
Acoustic resonance, speakers for, 184
Active interaction, games vs. films, 16
Activision, 190
Adams, John, 119
Adaptability, as trait for success, 410–411
Adaptive music
    defined, 428
    interactive music vs., 36
    swapping out to renegotiate estimate, 383
Add, defined, 80, 314
Additive layers, vertical remixing, 159
Advergame, 428
Advertisements, on game sites, 402–403
AES Game Conference in London, 337
Aesthetics, skill of composer in, 344

AFM (American Federation of Musicians), 293–294
AfterBurner (1987) video game, 92
Agile software development methodology, 76–77,
    312–315
AI (artificial intelligence) states, 19, 428
AIFF (Audio Interchange File Format) files, 303, 428
Air pressure, and waveforms, 131–132
Aleatoric composition, 230–231, 428
Aleatoric performance techniques
    aleatoric composition, 230–231
    articulations, instrumentation, and
        dynamics, 234
    of György Ligeti, 117
    as interactive music, 40–41
    of Krzysztof Penderecki, 117–118
    overview of, 229
    pitch, 232–233
    review, 234–235
    rhythm, tempo and form, 233
    understanding, 231–232
Aleatory, defined, 230
Algorithmic and generative music systems
    applying algorithmic composition, 243–244
    generative music, 239–240
    mapping control inputs to music, 243
    MIDI and virtual instruments in, 205
    review, 244–245
    rules of game composition, 240–242
    utilizing, 238–239
Alpha stage, AAA game production, 55
Altered Beast (1988) video game, 94
Ambient (rubato), 170–171
American Federation of Musicians (AFM), 293–295
Amnesia: The Dark Descent (2010) video game, 176
Amplitude. *See* Volume (amplitude)
Amplitude (2003) video game, 25
Analog sound feedback, gambling and slot
    machines, 87–88
Analog tape loops, video games, 90–91
Anatomy, layer, 161
Android format, game audio, 305
Aoki, Yoshino
    biography of, 448
    perspectives of, 59, 275–276, 285–286, 338–339
Apocalypse Now (1979) movie, 176
Arcade machines
    circuits, 89–90
    golden age of, 91–92
    laserdisc games, 91
    programmable sound generator and rise
        of melody, 90–91

S

Sales pitch, estimate as, 368–369

Salespeople, relationships with game developers through, 401–402

Samba de Amigo (1999) video game
- as beat matching game, 190
- control inputs, 42
- as music game, 189
- player controller for, 190–191
- technology impact of, 79

Sample rate, 273, 303

Samplers, basic synthesis components, 177–181

Sampling sessions, 183, 295

Sand Buggy coin-operated racing game, 88

Sanger, George ("The Fat Man"), 18–19, 203, 450

Scene, establishing location with music, 26

Schaeffer, Pierre, 114–115

Schedule
- based on milestone dates, 326
- and milestone delivery in production, 313
- in project contract, 357
- project-tracking systems for, 313
- session preparation and planning, 286–287
- setting music production, 77–78

Schoenberg, Arnold, 113

Schyman, Garry, 22

Scope of project, 359–361

Scores
- analysis and critique of, 32–33
- branching, 149–150
- conceptualization phase, 28–31
- creating with middleware, 251–252
- crossfading, 145–147
- future of, 424
- for games, 4–5
- goals of, 58–62
- MID and virtual instruments. *See* Standard MIDI File (SMF)
- planning for interactive, 276–279
- transitional, 147–148
- video game techniques, 62–65

Screen credits, project contracts, 358, 388–389

Scripting languages, 310–311, 413

Scrum game development, 76–77, 312–315

SDK (software development kit), 435

Sea Wolf (1976) video game, 89

Second Cycle Bounce, Logic, 128

Secure File Transfer Protocol (SFTP), 79

Security
- backups, 327
- sharing documents, 79

Sega Genesis (1988), 94

Sega Rally Championship (1995) video game, 93

Self-esteem, as trait for success, 409

Self-motivation, as trait for success, 410

Self-worth, and rejection, 415

Sequencer
- building event-driven, 225–226
- choosing, 270–271
- defined, 434
- exporting sequence to another DAW, 290
- planning for interactive score, 276–279
- popular types, 270
- sequencing MOD files, 272
- sequencing Standard Midi Files, 272
- setup and track layout, 273–276

Sequences
- exporting to another DAW, 290
- in real time, 144–145
- session preparation and planning, 286–289

Serendipitous sync, 28–29, 434

Serialism principles, 113, 116

Sessions, recording
- flow and practices of, 291
- preparing for live recordings, 286–289
- preparing for what can go wrong, 289
- time management, 292

Settings, video game structure, 27

Seventh Guest (1993), 203

SFTP (Secure File Transfer Protocol), 79

SFX (sound effects)
- balancing with music when mixing, 300
- defined, 434
- in-game mixing of, 320–321

Shaker Loops (Adams, 1978), 119

Sharing documents, 79

Shark Attack video game, 91

Shibata, Tetsuya, 30, 450

Shimomura, Yoko
- biography of, 450
- perspectives of, 76, 92, 393–394

Shooting machines, 88

Shottstaedt, William, 240

Shyman, Gary, 73, 118

Signatory, contracting with AFM, 295

Silence
- enhancing music with, 163
- inserting between cues for tempo/meter changes, 279
- when fading layers in and out, 161

Silent film music, 39, 41

Silent Hill (1999) video game, 96

Simon (1978) toy game, 192–193

SimTunes (1996) video game, 193

Simulated performance, music as gameplay, 25

Sinbad pinball machine, 88

Size
- balancing compression with quality, 315–318
- downloadable games/on-board media storage, 317
- file formats and compression, 302
- of video game industry, 337–338

This page is a continuation of the copyright page, which begins on page vi.

7th Guest is a registered trademark of Virgin Games, Inc.

Advance Wars, Animal Crossing, Donkey Kong, Donkey Kong Country, Donkey Konga, Elektroplankton, GameBoy, GameCube, Fire Emblem, Legend of Zelda: A Link to the Past, Legend of Zelda: Ocarina of Time, The Legend of Zelda: The Wind Waker, Metroid, Metroid Prime, Nintendo DS, Super Mario Bros., Super Mario Galaxy, Super Mario Kart, Super Metroid, Wii, Wii U, SNES, WiiFit, WiiMote, and *Wii Music* are registered trademarks of Nintendo of America Inc.

After Burner, Call of Duty, and *Guitar Hero* are registered trademarks of Activision Publishing, Inc.

Angry Birds is a registered trademark of Rovio Entertainment Ltd.

Asheron's Call 2 is a registered trademark of Turbine Inc.

Assassin's Creed III, Child of Eden, Rayman Legends, and *Tom Clancy's End War* are registered trademarks of Ubisoft Entertainment Corp.

Asteroids, Lunar Lander, Marble Madness, Night Driver, and *Pong* are registered trademarks of Atari Games Corporation.

Audiosurf is a registered trademark of Audiosurf LLC.

Banjo-Kazooie and *GoldenEye 007* are registered trademarks of Rare Limited.

Batman Arkham City and *Mortal Kombat* are registered trademarks of Warner Bros. Interactive Entertainment.

Bejeweled, Dead Space, Deluxe Music Construction Set, Jade Empire, Mass Effect 2, Medal of Honor: Allied Assault, Plants Vs. Zombies, Peggle 2 Populous, Rock Band, The Sims, SimTunes, Spore, SSX, SSX Tricky, and *Wing Commander* are registered trademarks of Electronic Arts, Inc.

Berzerk is a registered trademark of Stern Electronics, Inc.

Bioshock, Bioshock Infinite, Grand Theft Auto III, L.A. Noire, and *Red Dead Redemption* are registered trademarks of Take-Two Interactive Software, Inc.

Bit.Trip Runner is a registered trademark of Gaijin Games Corp.

Braid is a registered trademark of Number None, Inc.

Castlevania, Dance Dance Revolution, Frogger, Gyruss, Metal Gear Solid, and *Silent Hill* are registered trademarks of Konami Digital Entertainment Co.

Choose Your Own Adventure is a registered trademark of Chooseco LLC.

Chrono Trigger, Deus Ex, Final Fantasy, Final Fantasy VII, Final Fantasy VIII, Final Fantasy X, Final Fantasy XIII, and *Hitman 2: Silent Assassin* are registered trademarks of Square Enix Holdings Co. Ltd.

CryEngine is a registered trademark of Crytek, LLC.

Cut the Rope is a registered trademark of ZeptoLab UK Limited.

Daytona USA, Dreamcast, GameGear, OutRun, Rez, Samba de Amigo, Space Channel 5, Sega Genesis, Sega Rally Championship, Sega Saturn, Sonic the Hedgehog, Space Harrier, Toejam and Earl, and *Virtua Cop* are registered trademarks of Sega Corporation.

Diner Dash is a registered trademark of PlayFirst, Inc.

DisneyLand Kinect, Adventures, and *Kingdom Hearts* are registered trademarks of Disney Enterprises Inc.

Dragon's Lair, Dragon's Lair II: Time Warp, and *Space Ace* are registered trademarks of Bluth Group, Ltd.

Defender, Gorgar, and *Marble Madness* are registered trademarks of WMS Gaming Industries.

Dig Dug, Galaxians, Katamari Damacy, Mappy, Pac-Man, Ms. Pac-Man, Rally-X, and *Tekken* are registered trademarks of Bandai Namco Games Inc.

Destiny and *Marathon* are registered trademarks of Bungie, Inc.

Diablo, Warcraft II: Tides of Darkness, and *World of Warcraft,* are registered trademarks of Blizzard Entertainment Inc.

Doom and *Quake* are registered trademarks of Id Software LLC.

Earthworm Jim is a registered trademark of Shiny Entertainment, Inc.

The Elder Scrolls III: Morrowind is a registered trademark of ZeniMax Media, Inc.

Fallout 3 and Fallout 3:New Vegas are registered trademarks of Bethesda Softworks LLC.

Fmod is a registered trademark of Firelight Technologies.

Grim Fandango, iMuse, and Monkey Island 2: LeChuck's Revenge are registered trademarks of LucasArts Entertainment Co. Ltd.

FreQuency, Amplitude, and Dance Central are registered trademarks of Harmonix Music Systems, Inc.

God of War, Everquest, Ico, The Last of Us, Little Big Planet, Mad Maestro! Parappa the Rapper, PlayStation, PSP, Uncharted 2: Among Theives, and Vita are registered trademarks of Sony Computer Entertainment Inc.

Grandia is a registered trademark of Game Arts Co., Ltd.

Half-Life, Portal, Source Engine, and Steam are registered trademarks of Valve Corporation.

The Hobbit and Lord of the Rings Online are registered trademarks of The Saul Zaentz Company Corp.

Jaws is a registered trademark of Universal City Studios, LLC.

Journey is a registered trademark of ThatGameCompany, LLC.

Kinect, Halo, XACT, DirectMusic, Windows, Xbox, Xbox 360, Xbox One, and Xbox Live are registered trademarks of Microsoft Corporation.

Lego and Lego Universe are registered trademarks of Lego Corporation.

Limbo is a registered trademark of Playdead Software.

The Lost World: Jurassic Park and Saving Private Ryan are registered trademarks of Amblin Entertainment, Inc.

Macintosh, iOS, iPad, iPhone, and OS X are registered trademarks of Apple Inc.

Mega Man X, Okami, Remember Me, Resident Evil, and Street Fighter 2 are registered trademarks of Capcom U.S.A., Inc.

Minecraft is a registered trademark of Notch Development Corporation.

Myst is a registered trademark of Cyan, Inc.

No One Lives Forever is a registered trademark of Night Dive Studios LLC.

Out of This World is a registered trademark of Eric Chahi.

Prince of Persia is a registered trademark of Waterwheel Licensing LLC.

Q*bert is a registered trademark of Columbia Pictures Industries, Inc.

Shadow of the Beast 3 is a registered trademark of Psygnosis Limited.

Sea Wolf is a registered trademark of Coastal Amusement Distributors, Inc.

Simon is a registered trademark of Milton Bradley Company Corp.

Skate or Die is a registered trademark of 3G Studios, Inc.

Space Invaders is a registered trademark of Taito Corporation.

Sword and Sworcery is a registered trademark of Superbrothers.

UDK, Unreal, and Unreal Development Kit are registered trademarks of Epic Games, Inc.

Unity and Unity3d are registered trademarks of Unity Technologies and Unity IPR ApS LLC.

Vessel is a registered trademark of Strange Loop Games.

Video Games Live is a registered trademark of Mystical Stone Entertainment, LLC.

Wwise is a registered trademark of Audiokinetic Inc.

informIT.com — THE TRUSTED TECHNOLOGY LEARNING SOURCE

PEARSON

InformIT is a brand of Pearson and the online presence for the world's leading technology publishers. It's your source for reliable and qualified content and knowledge, providing access to the leading brands, authors, and contributors from the tech community.

 Addison Wesley | **Cisco Press** | **IBM Press.** | **QUe** | **PEARSON** IT CERTIFICATION | **PRENTICE HALL** | **SAMS** | **vmware PRESS** | **Safari** Books Online

LearnIT at InformIT

Looking for a book, eBook, or training video on a new technology? Seeking timely and relevant information and tutorials. Looking for expert opinions, advice, and tips? **InformIT has a solution**.

- Learn about new releases and special promotions by subscribing to a wide variety of monthly newsletters. Visit **informit.com/newsletters**.

- FREE Podcasts from experts at **informit.com/podcasts**.

- Read the latest author articles and sample chapters at **informit.com/articles**.

- Access thousands of books and videos in the Safari Books Online digital library. **safari.informit.com**.

- Get Advice and tips from expert blogs at **informit.com/blogs**.

Visit **informit.com** to find out all the ways you can access the hottest technology content.

Are you part of the **IT** crowd?

Connect with Pearson authors and editors via RSS feeds, Facebook, Twitter, Youtube and more! Visit **informit.com/socialconnect**.

Addison Wesley

REGISTER

THIS PRODUCT

informit.com/register

Register the Addison-Wesley, Exam Cram, Prentice Hall, Que, and Sams products you own to unlock great benefits.

To begin the registration process, simply go to **informit.com/register** to sign in or create an account. You will then be prompted to enter the 10- or 13-digit ISBN that appears on the back cover of your product.

Registering your products can unlock the following benefits:

- Access to supplemental content, including bonus chapters, source code, or project files.
- A coupon to be used on your next purchase.

Registration benefits vary by product. Benefits will be listed on your Account page under Registered Products.

About InformIT — THE TRUSTED TECHNOLOGY LEARNING SOURCE

INFORMIT IS HOME TO THE LEADING TECHNOLOGY PUBLISHING IMPRINTS Addison-Wesley Professional, Cisco Press, Exam Cram, IBM Press, Prentice Hall Professional, Que, and Sams. Here you will gain access to quality and trusted content and resources from the authors, creators, innovators, and leaders of technology. Whether you're looking for a book on a new technology, a helpful article, timely newsletters, or access to the Safari Books Online digital library, InformIT has a solution for you.

informIT.com

THE TRUSTED TECHNOLOGY LEARNING SOURCE

Addison-Wesley | Cisco Press | Exam Cram
IBM Press | Que | Prentice Hall | Sams

SAFARI BOOKS ONLINE